THE PRAEGER HANDBOOK OF
RELIGION AND EDUCATION IN THE UNITED STATES

The Praeger Handbook of

RELIGION AND EDUCATION IN THE UNITED STATES

VOLUME 1: A–L

Edited by
James C. Carper and Thomas C. Hunt

Westport, Connecticut
London

Library of Congress Cataloging-in-Publication Data

The Praeger handbook of religion and education in the United States / edited by James C. Carper and
  Thomas C. Hunt.
      v. cm.
    Includes bibliographical references and index.
    ISBN 978–0–275–99227–9 ((set) : alk. paper) – ISBN 978–0–275–99228–6 ((vol 1) : alk. paper) –
    ISBN 978–0–275–99229–3 ((vol 2) : alk. paper)
  1. Church and education–United States–Handbooks, manuals, etc. 2. Religion in the public schools–United States–
  Handbooks, manuals, etc. 3. Church and state–United States–Handbooks, manuals, etc. I. Carper, James C. II.
  Hunt, Thomas C., 1930– III. Praeger (Westport, Conn.)
  LC111.P78 2009
  379.2'80973—dc22   2008041156

British Library Cataloguing in Publication Data is available.

Library of Congress Catalog Card Number: 2008041156
ISBN: Set: 978–0–275–99227–9
      Vol. 1: 978–0–275–99228–6
      Vol. 2: 978–0–275–99229–3

First published in 2009

Praeger Publishers, 88 Post Road West, Westport, CT 06881
An imprint of Greenwood Publishing Group, Inc.
www.praeger.com

Printed in the United States of America

The paper used in this book complies with the
Permanent Paper Standard issued by the National
Information Standards Organization (Z39.48-1984).

10 9 8 7 6 5 4 3 2 1

.

James C. Carper dedicates this work to the most important teachers in his life: His parents, Chris and Mary Jane Carper and Russ and Marj Wenger; sister and brother, Cherie and John; wife, Kathy; and children, Becky and Marci.

Thomas C. Hunt affectionately dedicates this work to his daughters, Staci and Eryn; and to Staci's husband, Derek, and their three sons, Nate, Zach, and AJ.

Contents

List of Entries

Preface

Contrary to earlier predictions, religion has not disappeared from American life. Politicians invoke it. Pundits debate its benefits. Scholars increasingly utilize it as a unit of analysis along with race, class, ethnicity, and sex. Journalists write about it. School administrators keep it at arm's length. Judges grapple with its place in the public square. A majority of Americans practice some form of it to a greater or lesser extent. And when it comes to religion's relation to education, most Americans have strong opinions about it. Indeed, the intersection of religion and education has seldom been a quiet one, especially since the genesis of modern public education in the middle decades of the nineteenth century. Since that time Americans have argued vigorously about the place of religion in the government-operated schools, the rights of religious students and their families, and the relationship of the state to religious schools. With some notable exceptions, those arguments have tended to generate more heat than light.

We developed *The Praeger Handbook of Religion and Education in the United States* as a resource for parents, journalists, policy makers, educators, religious leaders, and citizens as well as scholars interested in this area with the hope that current debates and discussions about the role of religion in American education will be more enlightened. Pursuant to this goal, the *Handbook* includes a chapter that introduces readers to the role of religion in American education from the 1600s to the present; 175 entries on themes, historical events, individuals, court cases, educational associations, religious schools, advocacy groups, projects, and movements that have shaped the relationship between elementary and secondary education and religion in the United States; and an appended table summarizing all U.S. Supreme Court decisions regarding religious liberty. All the entries are cross-referenced and provide suggestions for further reading.

The *Handbook* is our ninth joint effort as editors/authors of books in the field of religion and education. This ambitious project would not have been possible, however, without the efforts of others, especially the 39 contributors, who are either senior scholars whose work is widely recognized in their respective fields of expertise or up-and-coming young students of religion in American education. In addition to their superb contributions, Charles Haynes of the First Amendment Center and Warren Nord of the University of North Carolina at Chapel Hill offered sage advice regarding the content of the *Handbook*. We were also favored by John Witte of the Emory University Law School who graciously granted us permission to use his valuable summary of Supreme Court decisions dealing with religion.

We also recognize Marie Ellen Larcada, who, while a senior editor at the Greenwood Publishing Group, accepted the initial proposal of the project, and Elizabeth Potenza, an assistant editor at Praeger, who saw it through to completion. We are grateful for their backing of this work.

Finally, we thank a number of persons who provided us with much needed production and proofreading assistance, including Beth Barwick, Marci Carper, Janet Hawkins, Karen Hunt, and Andy Mull. They are a patient lot.

James C. Carper, University of South Carolina
Thomas C. Hunt, University of Dayton

Religion and Education in the United States

An Introduction

Religion and Education in Early America

During the Colonial and Early National Periods of American history, which spanned approximately 200 years, religion and education were inextricably intertwined. Throughout the 1600s and most of the 1700s, families and schools shared responsibility for the education of the young. Whether taught primarily at home or in the various kinds of schools that dotted the colonial educational landscape in increasing numbers, children were taught the rudiments of literacy, civil behavior, and the tenets of the Christian faith. Though the responsibility for education rested with families, colonial governments encouraged parents as well as schools to attend to the religious instruction of children. In 1642 and 1647, for example, the General Court of Massachusetts Bay Colony passed the first education laws in the New World. The 1642 law mandated that town officials see to it that parents and masters instructed children in reading, civil law, and Christian doctrines. Five years later, the Court's "Old Deluder Law" mandated the provision of petty and grammar schools, though not compulsory attendance, to ensure that children could read the Bible and thus discourage Satan's work. Other colonial governments passed similar laws encouraging religious instruction, especially for the poor. In 1650, for example, Connecticut required reading and weekly catechetical instruction for children and servants. Virginia, Pennsylvania, New York, and South Carolina, among others, also encouraged instruction in the principles of the Christian religion.[1]

Materials used by parents and schoolmasters during the 1600s and 1700s testify to the centrality of religion in the education of the young. In addition to the Holy Bible, parents often used devotional literature such as John Bunyan's *The Pilgrim's Progress* (1678) and John Foxe's *Actes and Monuments* (1563), better known as the *Book of Martyrs,* to teach their children reading skills as well as Christian doctrine and character. They also likely utilized the schoolmaster's tools of literacy and religious instruction such as the hornbook, a piece of paper attached to a thin board and covered with a sheet of horn, which usually presented the alphabet, the syllabarium, and often the Apostles' Creed or Lord's Prayer. Families and reading and writing teachers alike also used assorted local and imported texts and primers, originally devotional books, as well as catechisms to promote literacy and ensure orthodoxy. (Protestants emphasized reading so that the Bible could be known and interpreted individually and the catechism to ensure that it was interpreted properly.) One dimension of Protestant orthodoxy, anti-Catholicism, was part and parcel of many reading texts. Benjamin Harris's *The Protestant Tutor* is one example. Published in England in 1679 and circulated in the colonies, it warned young readers of the dire consequences (including "cruel Massacres") of a "Popish Successor" to the throne. Much less rabidly anti-Catholic than its predecessor, Harris's *The New England Primer* (ca.1690), often called "The Little Bible of New England," was the most widely used of the various primers, many of which were modified versions of the New England text, for example, *The New York Primer* and *The American Primer,* that circulated widely among the numerous Protestant schools and families scattered throughout the New World in the eighteenth century. As noted historian Lawrence Cremin points out, its popularity in the colonies (as many as three million were printed) was due to the fact that it "combined into a single volume the substance of the traditional hornbook...with the substance of the traditional primer (the Lord's Prayer, the Creed, and the Decalogue) and an authorized catechism."[2] Even after alterations in the "Alphabet of Lessons" (of the 24 stanzas only "In Adam's Fall We Sinned All" was not changed), the addition of literature more appropriate to children after 1750, and the inclusion of "worldly prints," e.g., animals and playthings, in the late 1700s, the religious doctrine of a Calvinistic bent remained a central feature of the *Primer* as well as its progeny.[3]

Schools that used hornbooks, spellers, catechisms, Psalters, and various primers to teach reading and Christian doctrines, such as original sin, the sovereignty of God, the authority of the Scriptures, and salvation through faith in Christ alone, were primarily extensions of families, individuals, churches, and local communities. While colonial governments passed laws that mandated or encouraged education of the young, schooling in the 1600s and 1700s was unsystematic, unregulated, discontinuous, generally uncontroversial, often financed from both public and private sources, and diverse. Furthermore, the term "public" was applied to schools that served a public purpose, regardless of how they were controlled or financed.[4]

By the mid-1700s, specialized institutions, such as schools, increasingly assumed traditional family responsibilities such as the education of children. Though not relinquishing the right to direct the education of their children, parents sent their children to school in growing numbers. The schools they patronized then as well as earlier were quite diverse. Reflecting the pluralism of the overwhelmingly Protestant population, schools in the colonial years embodied the religious preferences of the sponsoring community, society, or church. For example, New England town petty and grammar schools inculcated Puritan beliefs to a greater or lesser extent, while in the Middle Colonies, such as Pennsylvania, Baptists, Presbyterians, Anglicans, Moravians, Lutherans, and Quakers conducted schools for their faithful and occasionally the children of the unchurched. Roman Catholics, who were mostly English and by the Revolutionary Era numbered only between 25,000 and 30,000 out of a white population of about three million souls, founded few schools, mostly in Pennsylvania and Maryland. Though schooling was less accessible in the South, what was available provided significant religious instruction. For example, the Society for the Propagation of the Gospel in Foreign Parts, a missionary arm of the Church of England established in 1701, sponsored schools for African Americans and Native Americans in order to "Christianize" and "civilize" them, Princeton-trained ministers founded academies in North Carolina to foster piety and classical learning, and various societies supported free schools for the poor in Charles Town, South Carolina, that taught the Bible and the catechism.[5]

Unlike many revolutions, the American War for Independence did not lead to significant changes in extant educational arrangements. Despite sweeping proposals for more systematic, state-supported common schooling during and in the aftermath of the Revolution to undergird republican liberty, for example, those of Thomas Jefferson, Benjamin Rush, and Samuel Smith, colonial educational patterns remained largely unchanged through the early decades of the nineteenth century. The initiative for schooling still lay primarily in the hands of parents, churches, voluntary societies, and local communities. On the other hand, several states, New York and Connecticut for example, did provide significant funds to local schools and overall attendance increased markedly, in large measure due to the growing number of quasi-public district schools in rural areas and charity schools for the poor operated by voluntary societies in cities such as New York, Baltimore, and Philadelphia. As had been the case before the Revolution, these schools and others continued to provide religious instruction to the young as a necessary basis for maintaining Christian beliefs and encouraging moral behavior. District schools often used the Bible, Psalter, and catechisms as well as well as primers and spellers for reading texts and guides for pious living. Noah Webster's speller, grammar, and reader, for example, were widely used in district and other schools in the late 1700s and early 1800s. Less doctrinal and more patriotic and moral in content than the *New England Primer,* his volumes emphasized love of country, reverence for the founding fathers (especially Washington), proper pronunciation, and biblically based moral conduct. While the *Primer* concludes with the Westminster Shorter Catechism, Webster's speller/primer, popularly known as *The American Spelling Book* (1783) or "Blue-Backed Speller," ends with the "A Moral Catechism." Instead of communicating doctrinal orthodoxy per se, Webster focuses on the biblical basis for an appropriate understanding of, for example, mercy, humility, gratitude, justice, and charity. As he put it, "God's word...has furnished all necessary rules to direct our conduct." Likewise, charity schools, such as those sponsored by the New York Free School Society founded in 1805, provided ample amounts of moral and purportedly "nonsectarian" religious instruction for the well-being of their charges as well as social stability. Students were admonished to avoid lying, stealing, cursing, and disobedience. They were reminded that God could see, hear, and know all they said and did.[6]

Like their colonial ancestors, most Americans living in the decades following the War of Independence believed that moral education required the sanction of religion, specifically the Bible and, in the opinion of many, doctrines associated with a particular theological tradition. Indeed, the famous Northwest Ordinance of 1787 suggested that religion, morality, and education were inextricably intertwined: "Religion, morality, and knowledge, being necessary to good government and the happiness of mankind, schools and the means of education shall be forever encouraged." With the increasing diversity of the population and religious belief in the middle decades of the nineteenth century and the concomitant efforts to create universal, free, state-controlled common school systems, questions related to the role of religion in the education of the young became a matter of considerable public debate and disagreement.[7]

The Common School Period

The middle decades of the nineteenth century marked a period of intense debate about schooling that focused on issues of control, finance, and the role of religion in American education and led to major changes in educational beliefs and practices. Distressed by the social and cultural tensions wrought by urbanization, industrialization, religious revivalism, and immigration—which included many Roman Catholics—and energized by the values and beliefs of republicanism, Protestantism, and capitalism, educational reformers like Horace Mann, a Unitarian equally uncomfortable with orthodox Calvinism and Roman Catholicism, touted the messianic power of tax-supported, government-operated, universal common schooling. Common (public) schools, proponents claimed, would create a moral, disciplined, and unified citizenry prepared to participate in the political, economic, and social life of the country. Nonpublic schools, most of which were sponsored by religious bodies, were often cast as divisive, undemocratic, and inimical to the public interest.[8]

Most Americans at the time believed that religion, Protestant Christianity in particular, should play a central role in education of the young. But with the growing religious pluralism of the nation, the place of the Bible and religious doctrine in the common school often provoked controversy. With the exception of a few individuals and groups, such as Calvinists like Princeton theologian Charles Hodge and certain Lutheran denominations, that supported schools to preserve confessional purity, most Protestants supported the common school movement of the mid-1800s and accepted Bible reading without comment in the schools as a suitable nonsectarian practice. Many Roman Catholics, on the other hand, objected to the Protestant orientation of common schooling. They complained about Bible reading in the public schools, anti-Catholic material in the textbooks, and paying taxes for schools they could not in good conscience patronize as well as underwriting Catholic schools. Events in New York City, Massachusetts, and the movement to found and maintain Catholic parochial schools are illustrative of these issues involving the role of religion in American education during the middle decades of the nineteenth century as government became increasingly responsible for the provision of schooling.[9]

New York City

The burgeoning number of poor in New York City in the early 1800s apparently convinced Thomas Eddy, a wealthy Quaker, that something must be done to remedy their condition, for themselves and for the welfare of the community. His solution was the founding in 1805 of the New York Free School Society (FSS), a group of wealthy New Yorkers, who would provide a "virtuous education," and thence remedy the deplorable condition of the poor children that had been brought about by alleged parental neglect.[10] The Society's president, DeWitt Clinton, asserted that the Society would confront the problem of these wayward children by means of schools that would focus on the "morals of children" as well as the usual "elements of learning." The FSS claimed to be a nonsectarian, antipoverty group that would counter and overcome the evils of the children's upbringing.[11] Speaking a little more than a decade later in 1819, Clinton averred that the schools the Society had established were for the happiness of the parents and children "both here and hereafter." The parents were instructed that their children should observe the Sabbath because "public worship is a duty" humans owe their Creator. The most fundamental purpose of education was to "form habits of industry, and to inculcate the general principles of Christianity," grounding children in the "nurture and admonition of the Lord."[12] Following a conflict over use of public funds with the Bethel Baptist Church, the New York legislature changed the name of the Society to the Public School Society in 1826 and provided it with a new charter, which enabled it to act on behalf of the City in the education of children, with its property belonging to the City, making it a quasi-public agency.[13] The controversies of the 1820s were to pale before the strife that was to begin in the 1840s.

The governor of the State of New York in 1839 was William Seward, a Whig. A trip to Ireland earlier in that decade had apparently convinced him of Ireland's plight under the servitude of England and led him to believe that the thousands of Irish immigrants recently arrived in New York City deserved better treatment, including an education, which would allow them to go to a school "in which they may be instructed by teachers speaking the same language with them and professing the same faith."[14] These schools were to be supported by public funds.[15]

The Catholic Church, due to immigration, was growing in the new nation. One of the most serious concerns of the Catholic hierarchy at this time was the education of Catholic children. The bishops of the Church felt that it should be in institutions that protected and supported their faith.[16] The allegedly nonsectarian schools of the New York Public School Society did not meet this test.

The conflict began when some New York Catholics petitioned the city's Board of Aldermen for the Catholic "share" of public funds to educate Catholic children in Catholic schools. The Aldermen refused. John Hughes, the Catholic Bishop of New York, recently returned from Europe, then entered the controversy. He asserted that the Society's schools were biased against Catholicism, due to practices such as the devotional reading of the King James Version of the Bible and passages in textbooks used that referred to Catholicism as "Popery," and instances where Catholics were referred to as "inquisitional villains."[17] One of the Society's books, *An Irish Heart,* asserted that if Irish immigration continued on the same scale to the United States the nation would be "appropriately styled the common sewer of Ireland."[18]

Hughes vigorously advanced the Catholic claim for public funds for Catholic schools. He argued his case on the sacred rights of conscience for parents, which he said were being violated in this case. These rights, he averred, belonged to Protestants and Jews as well, not just Catholics. It was not fair, he argued, that Catholics were taxed for schools that they could not in conscience have their children frequent. The Society's representatives argued that their schools did not teach sectarian dogma but inculcated "common-core Christianity," to which Hughes replied that was in effect teaching Protestant sectarianism.[19]

Hughes was unsuccessful in his quest for public funds. While the Catholics did not win, the Public School Society lost and was absorbed into the public school system in 1853.[20] A ward system of public schools resulted. Hughes then led the movement to establish a separate Catholic school system, setting a trend that was to have national ramifications.[21]

Horace Mann and the Common School in Massachusetts

Known as the "Father of the Common School," Horace Mann was concerned with the growing social disorder in the United States, especially in his native Massachusetts. Accordingly, he abandoned a promising career in the Massachusetts legislature and in 1837 accepted the position of secretary of the State Board of Education in Massachusetts, announcing that "so long as I hold the office, I devote myself to the supremest welfare of mankind upon earth....I have faith in the improvability of the race."[22] Raised a Calvinist, Mann rejected orthodox doctrines such as original sin and became a Unitarian. In entering the area of education, Mann believed he was going into a "field of endeavor that promised universal salvation."[23] His concept of the common school was to present a new development in the relationship of religion to education in American culture.

The Massachusetts legislature in 1827 had enacted a law that forbade the use of any text in the state's public schools that was "calculated to favor any particular religious sect or tenet."[24] Yet that very law was to impress on pupils the "principles of piety, justice, and sacred regard to truth, love to their country, humanity, and universal benevolence, sobriety, industry, and frugality, chastity, moderation, and temperance and those other virtues, which are...the basis upon which the republican constitution is founded."[25]

Whigs and Unitarians dominated the State Board of Education at the beginning of Mann's term as secretary. For example, in 1837 Mann and nine of the ten members were Whigs, seven were Unitarians—all appointed by the governor.[26] Mann saw the common school and universal education "of the people as the only hope of Massachusetts."[27]

Not everyone agreed with Mann in this assessment, nor were they supporters of the very idea of the common school. Mann had conflicts with Catholics, with the Boston schoolmasters, and especially with some leading Congregationalist clergymen, who felt that the common school was bereft of religious influence. Mann tangled with the Reverend Frederick A. Packard, editor of the *American Sunday School Union,* over books that were used in the common schools, and with the Calvinist Reverend Matthew Hale Smith, who maintained that the State Board had "contributed substantially to the precipitous decline in the morals of youth and the rapidly accelerating incidence of juvenile delinquency."[28]

The common school was necessary, according to Mann, to combat the vices of poverty and crime that infested American cities. These cities, with the growth of industry and the masses of workers, posed a serious threat to the peace of American society. "Sectarian" schools, which were "particularly divisive" in his eyes, could not successfully combat these vices; thus the necessity of a common nonsectarian morality for the schools to espouse.[29] The common or public schools, according to Mann, were a "moral enterprise" in which "education, philanthropy and republicanism can combine to allay all of the wants and shortcomings which have traditionally beset human civilization."[30]

Mann held that in a religiously diverse society the only solution for schools was to embrace "common principles" from all creeds such as the "Fatherhood of God." Thus these schools could teach such "publicly accepted virtues" as "brotherly love, kindness, generosity, amiability" and leave to the home and church the "task of teaching the differing private sectarian creeds which sanction those virtues."[31] Social harmony, and thence social progress, would be the result. Poverty, which was a most debilitating vice, would be eliminated within "two or three generations by more and better public schools."[32] Sectarian schools, on the other hand, would only lead to "social interminable welfare," as they had in England.[33]

Mann repeated the God-given mandate of the morally beneficial common school and its personnel throughout his tenure in office, which lasted 12 years until 1848. It was that year, after he had been elected to Congress, that Mann penned his final report. In this document he addressed the charges that had been brought against the common school, viz., that it had excluded religion and its "common exponent," the Bible, or at the least had the tendency to "derogate from its authority and destroy its influence."[34] Mann averred that there had never been a thought to "exclude the Bible or religious instruction" from the schools. It was sectarianism that was to be kept out of the common schools. The advocates of religious schools, which were a "rival system" to free schools, the latter designed for the "whole people," had advanced the false charge that the common schools were "anti-Christian."[35] The Bible, he wrote, was in the schools by "common consent." It was present there because "Christianity has no other authoritative expounder." The common schools, while not sectarian, were indeed religious because of the presence of the Holy Scriptures:

> If the Bible, then, is the exponent of Christianity, if the Bible contains the communications, precepts, and doctrines, which make up the religious system, called and known as Christianity; if the Bible makes known these truths, which, according to the faith of Christians, are able to make men wise unto salvation; and if this Bible is in the schools, how can it be said that Christianity is excluded from the schools; wherever the Bible might go, there the system of Christianity must be.[36]

The moral, allegedly nonsectarian Christian education of the common school called on teachers to:

> Impress on the minds of children and youth committed to their care and instruction, the principles of piety, justice, and a sacred regard for truth, love to their country, humanity and universal benevolence, sobriety, industry and frugality, chastity, moderation, and temperance, and those other virtues which are the ornament of human society and the basis upon which a republican constitution is founded.[37]

Mann argued that the above "virtues and those duties towards God and man, are inculcated in our schools," and he called on "resident ministers of the Gospel" to assist in bringing children to their practice.[38]

Jonathan Messerli describes Mann's efforts on behalf of the common school as a "holy and patriotic crusade."[39] Likewise, Robert Michaelsen contends that Mann believed the common school was the sole institution that could bring about moral advancement in American society and that its primary purpose was moral. Mann's motto, he claims, might well have been "Common religion for the common school."[40] As William B. Kennedy points out, the common school was expected to teach common Protestant beliefs, which some scholars suggest mirrored Mann's Unitarian faith, while the denominational Sunday school inculcated doctrines particular to individual religious groups. This "parallel institutions strategy" satisfied most American Protestants.[41] As Oscar Handlin has pointed out, however, Americans clearly looked to the public schools as a "force for cohesion in a nation characterized by heterogeneity."[42]

Although Roman Catholics often objected to the common school and its purportedly "common religion" and began to lay the ground work for a separate school system during the middle decades of the nineteenth century, they and public school officials did attempt compromise arrangements in several locations beginning in the 1830s and extending to the 1890s. One such effort was the Lowell Plan, which operated in Lowell, Massachusetts, from 1831 until 1852. Under this arrangement public school officials approved Catholic teachers selected by parish pastors and the curriculum, which was to be devoid of anti-Catholicism. The parishes provided and maintained the school buildings, while the school board paid the teachers. After several years, a Catholic pastor, unable to find qualified lay teachers, brought in nuns to teach in the parish school. At that point the school board terminated the program.[43]

The Catholic Position on Schooling

The country's first bishop, John Carroll of Baltimore, concerned about the faith of Catholic children, made the first official statement of the American hierarchy about education in 1792. In his pastoral letter he referred to the "virtuous and Christian instruction of youth as a principal object of pastoral solicitude" and noted the "necessity of a pious and Catholic education of the young to insure their growing up in the faith."[44] Catholics made up about 1 percent of the population of the United States in 1800, but immigration was to change that as the nineteenth century progressed. Between 1821 and 1850 almost 2.5 million immigrants from Europe entered the nation with 1,713,251 coming in the 1840s. Over 1 million of the 2.5 million were Irish, with 780,719 of these arriving in the 1840s. As the years progressed, and the Catholic population increased, Catholic opposition to what they considered the pan-Protestant public schools increased. Conflicts with Nativists grew, some of which involved school issues. Catholic bishops, alone and in council, warned their Catholic flocks with the dangers inherent to the faith of Catholic children in these schools. Religious practices, such as the devotional reading of the King James Version of the Bible and textbooks, with portions offensive to the Catholic faith, were cited by the bishops as evidence of anti-Catholic bias in the common schools. Accordingly, the bishops urged Catholics to support and have their children attend Catholic schools for the preservation of their faith and their ultimate salvation.

By the middle of the nineteenth century the separate Catholic parochial (parish) school system was underway. Not all Catholics, including clerics as well as laypeople, joined in this crusade. Some felt that the Church's limited supply of money and personnel would better serve the cause of the Catholic faith in social programs, such as combating poverty, rather than be committed to primary education. German American Catholics, however, present in considerable numbers in the recently created ecclesiastical provinces of Cincinnati and St. Louis, with German American bishops and priests prevalent, were zealous in their support of Catholic schools. For instance, the bishops of the Cincinnati province in 1855, in a reference to public schools, admonished "pastors of souls again and again to strive by all the means in their power" to prevent children from attending those schools that present a "grave danger to their faith and morals."[45] The matter was so serious that three years later the Cincinnati hierarchy told pastors that a Catholic school was to be established in "every parish or congregation subject to them...under pain of mortal sin."[46]

Other Denominations

Catholics were the leading denomination in founding and maintaining faith-based schools in mid-nineteenth-century America. For the most part, Protestants were generally satisfied with the common school. There were, however, efforts by some denominations to have their own schools. Presbyterians, for example, embarked on such an endeavor. Lewis Sherrill has written of the attempts by Presbyterian Synods to establish and maintain parochial schools. Commenced in 1846, these attempts had effectively ceased by 1870.[47] Calvinist Day Schools, the result of the Secession of 1834, took root in Michigan and Iowa in the 1840s.[48] Quakers supported public schools and were involved in philanthropic efforts like the Public School Society in New York City. The Society of Friends did have a small number of primary schools and founded secondary boarding schools, one reason for which was to prepare teachers for their primary schools. They became enmeshed in an internal struggle over mixing Quaker youth with non-Quakers in their schools during these years.[49] The Episcopal Church was active in establishing secondary boarding schools in this era, most notably perhaps, Virginia Episcopal High School in 1839.[50] The "decidedly Protestant atmosphere which pervaded the public schools at the time" was the reason for the attempts by German Jewish immigrants to found schools. Few of these lasted more than several years.[51] While some Lutherans embraced the common school, others opted for their own schools. According to Jon Diefenthaler, as soon as they "began arriving on the North American continent from Germany in 1839" the forbearers of the Missouri Synod of the Lutheran church "saw the parochial day school as a means of insuring the faithfulness of future generations to their own firmly held beliefs," a position that was reflected in the Synod's first constitution in 1847 that called on every congregation to support a parochial school.[52] Indeed, from the end of the Colonial Period until the mid-nineteenth century Lutherans maintained the most extensive "system" of parochial schools in the country.[53]

Schoolbooks of the Common School Era

Books used in schools in the mid-nineteenth century reflected the Protestant nature of the country. Without a doubt foremost of these was the Bible, the King James Version. The Protestant Christian culture was evident in other popular books, especially the widely used *McGuffey Readers.*

The Bible

As noted above, the Bible was the most commonly used text in colonial households and schools, and the devotional reading of the Bible was a foundation of the allegedly nonsectarian Protestant Christian schools of the New York Public School Society and was termed by Horace Mann as the "authoritative expounder" of Christianity. Indeed, for most of the 1800s, nearly all Americans believed it was God's revealed word.

The Bible's proponents certainly included the American Bible Society, founded in part to advance its use in schools.[54] The Society aimed to have the Bible read in every classroom in the nation.[55] Civic agencies, such as the Baltimore City Council, while declaring that it never supported sectarianism in the City's schools, nonetheless proclaimed that the "Holy Scriptures" would be the source of diffusing a "salutary influence" among their students.[56] A Protestant leader of the period, the Reverend Horace Bushnell, declared that it was a "sacred duty" for all Christians to find a place for the Bible, which was not a sectarian book, in schools.[57] The request by Bishop Francis Kenrick of Philadelphia in 1843 to the Philadelphia School Board that Catholic children be allowed to read the Douay (Catholic) version of the Scriptures in public schools, a request that was granted, led to a riot in which two Catholic churches were burned and 13 people were killed.[58]

Protestant Christianity was viewed as the bulwark of the American Republic and the Bible was the linchpin of Protestantism in the view of many Americans. The goal seemed to be to "keep sectarianism out of the public schools" but to "keep religion in them," and keeping religion in the common schools usually meant, among other things, reading the King James Version of the Bible without comment.[59]

The experience of the State of Wisconsin may well serve as a case study to show the widespread presence of the Bible in American society at mid-century. The Wisconsin Constitution was approved in 1848. It upheld religious liberty and prohibited the use of public funds for religious purposes.[60] At the same time it prohibited any "sectarian instruction" in the common schools of the state.[61] The deletion of the words "no book of religious doctrine or belief" from the 1846 version of the Constitution that dealt with sectarian instruction is testimony that the Bible was not regarded as a sectarian book because those words would have "excluded the Bible" from use in the public schools.[62]

The place of the Bible in the social affairs of Wisconsin citizens also attests to its prominence. For example, masters were held responsible to give to their "apprentice, at the expiration of his or her service, a new Bible."[63] Prison keepers were required by law to "provide, at the expense of the county," a Bible for every prisoner who is "able and desirous to read it during confinement."[64] The "family Bible" was listed first among articles of personal property that were exempt from seizure by the public authorities on the occasion of a person's execution.[65]

Practices in schools and by school personnel also reflect the exalted standing of the King James Version of the Scriptures at this time as well as its being regarded as religious but not sectarian. The state superintendent of public education was held responsible to "discourage the use of sectarian books and sectarian instruction in schools."[66] It is clear both from the writings of the state superintendents and their decisions in appeals that the Bible was not considered a sectarian book and its devotional reading was not regarded as a sectarian practice in the decade following admission to the Union.

By the late 1850s superintendents were advising caution in its reading and discontinuation of its use if it led to controversy in the community. The Bible was held to be "pre-eminently first in importance among textbooks for teaching the noblest principles of virtue, morality, patriotism and good order—love and reverence for God—charity and good will to man," and advocated strongly for its use, at the same time "earnestly deprecating sectarian instruction in our public schools."[67]

That the Bible continued to be a major part of Wisconsin education in the 1860s is clear from a number of sources, one of them the *Wisconsin Journal of Education,* which in 1864 proclaimed that the Bible played a religious, but nonsectarian, role in the schools for there was "enough common ground" in it for "all sects to meet on and cultivate the spirit of Christian truth, love and brotherhood," without "diverging into sectarian bypaths."[68]

Several incidents in other areas during this period, however, suggest that the devotional use of the Bible in common schools was becoming a matter of controversy. Among them were several state court cases. (The First Amendment Religion Clauses of the U.S. Constitution were not applicable to actions of state and local governments until the 1940s.) The first of state courts to address the issue of the use of the Bible in public schools occurred in *Donahoe v. Richards,* 38 Me 376 (1854), in Maine. Here the court upheld the right of the school to select the Bible as a textbook and to expel a student who refused to read it, even though he claimed such reading would be a violation of his conscience.[69] In *Spiller v. Inhabitants of Woburn*, 94 Mass. 127 (1866), a Massachusetts court said the school was within its rights when it required every student to bow his/her head during the daily reading of the Bible and the saying of prayers.[70] Finally, in 1872 the Ohio Supreme Court reversed the ruling of a lower court in *Board of Education of Cincinnati v. Minor et al.*, 23 Ohio St. 211 (1872), and adjudged that religious instruction, including Bible reading, was not required by Ohio's constitution. It did not, however, rule the practice unconstitutional.[71]

Teachers' associations were of similar mind as to the Bible's role in the school and nation. An editorial in the *Wisconsin Journal of Education* in 1865 looked to the schools to contribute to the cause of religion "without usurping the office of preacher." The schools could accomplish this feat by "imparting the leading truths of the Bible and thus laying the foundations for parent and minister of the gospel to build upon."[72] In 1869 the National Teachers Association stated that the "Bible...shall be devotionally read," and its "precepts inculcated in all the common schools of the land." Then the organization voted against permitting any "partisan or sectarian principles in our public schools" because such would be a "violation of the fundamental principles of our American system of education."[73]

Samuel B. Fallows was an ordained Methodist minister, a Civil War veteran, and the Secretary of the Wisconsin Methodist Conference for several years prior to becoming state superintendent of schools in Wisconsin in 1870.[74] That same year the Methodists officially took note for the first time of the challenge to the Bible in the state's schools. Declaring that the common school system was a child of the Bible, they contended that popular education existed only among evangelical Protestants, with only Christianity being capable of providing the inspirational base for the system's existence. They identified Atheists and Catholics as assailants of the system, and defended the common school, which was based on the "religious principles of the Bible," which must continue to "inform and animate" the common schools for the good of the nation.[75]

The McGuffey Readers

Textbooks of the mid-nineteenth century embodied the widely held belief that the Bible was authoritative and should "animate" the common schools. Warren Nord, a professor at the University of North Carolina–Chapel Hill and long-time student of the treatment of religion in the public school curriculum, notes that Ruth Miller Elson "surveyed more than a thousand of the most popular nineteenth century texts used for the first eight years of schooling, and her study is fascinating in what it reveals about religion." Before the Civil War, "schoolbooks accepted without question the biblical account of the world, Adam and Eve included." In the second half of the century, when Darwinism appeared, it was not "purposeless Darwinian evolution, but was teleological—the working out of God's purposes."[76] God ordered nature, and he guided history. George Washington was "compared to Moses and Christ"; the deaths of John Adams and Thomas Jefferson on the fiftieth anniversary of the signing of the Declaration of Independence was a "sign of divine approval." Virtue was rewarded and vice punished in an "immediate and material sense." God did not wait for the afterlife, the schoolbooks made clear.[77]

Elson also points out that overwhelmingly the texts used in the common schools before 1870 rarely dealt favorably with Catholicism. She writes that the "school child in this period would associate Catholicism only with unpleasant behavior and subversive beliefs." The child would "imbibe not only the idea that its theology is false, but that it is inimical to industry, prosperity, knowledge, and freedom—concepts considered basic to all civilization." Texts would communicate that "Catholicism has no place in the American past or future, nor in the economic and political climate of the United States."[78]

Of all nineteenth-century schoolbooks, none are better known than the *McGuffey Eclectic Readers.* Authored by William Holmes McGuffey, a Presbyterian minister and college instructor, and first published between 1836 and 1838, the *Readers* are considered by some to be among the most influential books of the century. Indeed, historian of American education Edward Krug reports that the *Readers* had estimated sales of 122,000,000 by 1920.[79] Though distinctly Christian in outlook at the outset, by 1879, after McGuffey's death, their views had been "severely secularized." Nonetheless, they aimed to "unify the nation around a common worldview and value system."[80]

McGuffey's texts emphasized the moral virtues, such as industry, honesty, and temperance. Religion, as "a guide and necessity for life," was present in a "most wholesome and enlightened way."[81] McGuffey's virtues were intertwined with the temperance movement, and he condemned intemperance, gambling, and dishonesty. He warned of the "dangers of drunkenness, luxury, self-pride, and deception and proclaimed handsome earthly reward for courage, honesty, and respect for others."[82] The common school, bolstered by the *Readers,* was to serve, along with the church, as an "incubator of virtue."[83] Called "*the* schoolmaster of the nation" by some,[84] McGuffey was alleged to have done "more to mold American thinking than any other single influence except the Bible."[85]

Historian B. Edward McClellan asserts that the nineteenth-century textbooks, with the *McGuffey Readers* at the head, presented values as a "blend of traditional Protestant morality and nineteenth century conceptions of good citizenship" that taught the "love of country, love of God, love of parents, the necessity to develop habits of thrift, honesty, and hard work in order to accumulate property, the certainty of progress and the perfection of the United States."[86] Others agree. One author wrote that the *Readers* presented tastes that were "held in common, which constituted much of America's culture," especially "Its code of morals and conduct, its standards of propriety...its 'horse-sense' axioms." As such, they were to the average American the "storehouse of the fables, stories, mottoes, proverbs, adages, and aphorisms which constituted the largest body of ethical teaching he had, excepting the Bible, and the teaching of the Bible was overlapped by that of the readers."[87]

Failure to imbibe the biblically grounded moral precepts contained in the *Readers* and similar texts bore potentially grave consequences for the nation. For example, Harvey Minnich wrote in 1936 that "unless the youth of America is grounded in moral truths so cogently taught" in the *Readers,* unless "traits of character" they taught be firmly established in the students, unless the application of the moral virtues in society were stronger than the "organized forces of crime, immorality, and disrespect for law and order, America may not expect to be exempt from the decadence which befell the great dynasties of history."[88] As McGuffey once told a group of teachers from Ohio, the nation's privileged position among the nations of the world would be upheld only if Christianity remained the religion of the country and the foundation of its institutions.[89]

As exemplars of Protestant culture, the *Readers* shared in the anti-Catholicism, though of a mild variety, of the period. Catholics, however, were not the only group to receive less than fair treatment. Jews were occasionally the recipients of prejudicial treatment in the *Readers* as well.[90] This is not surprising. As Frederick Binder, a student of the common school movement, contends, the *Readers'* moral and social codes fit neatly into a school system that served as the "bastion of Protestant morality, patriotic nationalism, and social order."[91] Assessing the impact of that "bastion," Hugh Fullerton, a frequent contributor to popular magazines from the 1910s to the early 1940s, asserts: "For seventy-five years his [McGuffey's] system and his books guided the minds of four-fifths of the school children of the nation in their taste for literature, in their morality, in their social development and next to the Bible in their religion." Indeed, another scholar maintains that McGuffey's influence may have been "greater than that of any other writer or statesman in the west."[92]

Secular Trends in the Late Nineteenth Century

The world of William Holmes McGuffey began to crumble slowly during the latter part of the nineteenth century, and American education began to gradually take on the characteristics of what historian David Tyack called the "one best system."[93] Characterized by professionalization, specialization, differentiation, standardization, and other bureaucratic features, this "system" initially manifested itself in urban areas. Conflicts often arose between the advocates of this system and several ethnic and religious groups over who had primary rights in the schooling of the young. At the same time, Protestant influence in the public schools, as witnessed in devotional Bible reading with attendant religious exercises and prayers, and Protestant influence in personnel and textbooks, began to wane in many areas of the nation due in part to profound intellectual and cultural changes that were beginning to impact American society, for example, Darwinism, higher criticism of the Bible, and growing cultural and religious pluralism.[94]

Nevertheless, as Robert Michaelsen has observed, the "compound of evangelical Protestantism and enlightenment Deism" continued to be a "major component in the public school mix."[95] At the same time, however, "Americanism," with an emphasis on the use of the English language and patriotism, began to assume a greater role in elementary schooling. William Torrey Harris, at one time the Superintendent of Schools in St. Louis and later U.S. Commissioner of Education, argued that the "Will of Providence" had decreed the separation of religion and education in the nation, to be replaced by the moral agent of public schools.[96] These schools would advance humankind and the nation through the inculcation of the virtues of punctuality, regularity, perseverance, earnestness, justice, truthfulness, and industry.[97]

The nationalist spirit engendered by the Civil War extended to viewing the public school as the bulwark of democracy and the Union. As Warren Nord has observed, Americans, when faced with the growing number of immigrants, especially Catholics, looked to its public schools, which "became the cultural factories of Americanization, transforming raw material of foreign culture into good American citizens."[98] In this spirit President Ulysses S. Grant urged Civil War veterans to support the nation's free institutions, which included "free schools" and exhorted them not to allow "one dollar" to be appropriated for sectarian schools.[99] Grant's 1875 address was closely followed by a proposed amendment to the U.S. Constitution offered by Congressman James G. Blaine of Maine that would have prohibited any funds "raised by school taxation in any State" to be under the "control of any religious sect" or be "divided between religious sects or denominations." The so-called "Blaine amendment," which resembled constitutional prohibitions on public benefits once available for religious schools adopted by several states since the 1840s and fed upon secularist and anti-Catholic sentiments, passed the House of

Representatives in August 1876 by a margin of 180 to 7 with 98 not voting, but fell two votes short of the necessary two-thirds margin in the Senate where it passed 28 to 16 with 27 absent or not voting.[100]

The public school, an institution that evidenced the complete separation of church and state, was increasingly seen as competent to teach the lessons of common morality and good citizenship. As Edwin Mead, a critic of parochial schools, argued at the 1889 meeting of the National Education Association (NEA), the public school, as the "conserver of democracy brings the divergent elements of American Society together."[101] Private schools, the vast majority of which were religious, on the other hand, were often viewed as unpatriotic and divisive.

Distrust of religious, especially Catholic and Lutheran, schools led to proposals in several states in the late 1800s designed either to bring these schools into conformity with the public school model or to eventually eliminate them. Illinois and Wisconsin actually passed legislation to that effect. The short-lived Edwards Law of 1889 in Illinois mandated that all children between the ages of 7 and 14 attend a public school for 16 weeks a year, 8 of which were to be consecutive, and was clearly intended to force children into the "conserver of democracy" and limit the influence of religious schooling. Wisconsin's Bennett Law took a slightly different approach to regulating religious schools and pitted Christian groups against each other on questions of parental rights, the educational mission of the state, and the legitimacy of alternatives to the public school.

The Bennett Law

The Bennett Law, as it was popularly known, was enacted in 1889 by the Wisconsin legislature and signed into law by then-governor William Dempster Hoard. Its controversial features were the requirements that a child attend school in the public school district in which s/he resided and that certain subjects be taught in the English language.[102] Additionally, State Superintendent Jesse B. Thayer had campaigned for a compulsory attendance law that would require private schools to report their attendance to his office (something a number of them were not doing), on the grounds that such reporting would assist him to combat the evils of child labor.[103]

Heavily German, and with a substantial investment in parochial schools, Wisconsin's numerous Lutherans and Catholics objected to the residential and language provisions. Governor Hoard, a lay Methodist minister, strongly advocated the law on the grounds that it was necessary for citizenship. The use of the English language, he felt, was absolutely necessary for the country's traditions to be upheld and the young to become good Americans. The parochial school adherents, he maintained, were obstructing the right of the state to oversee the education for citizenship of the young.[104] The Bennett Law opponents, on the other hand, with Catholic and Lutheran leaders in the forefront, maintained that the state was interfering with the primary right of parents to educate their young. Some of them also believed that the state was trying to curtail, if not eliminate, their parochial schools. They argued that the state had no right to interfere with what was a parental function.[105]

Religious groups other than the Catholics and Lutherans entered the fray. Baptists, Congregationalists, Methodists, and Presbyterians generally favored the statute. These groups looked to the public schools as an "American" institution, and perceived the use of the English language by all of the state's children as necessary for forming good citizens. They opposed what they termed the entrance of the "Romish Church" into politics.

As one Methodist minister put it, the whole question came down to "American schools for American children."[106] Generally, the Protestant center saw the Catholic and Lutheran parochial schools as representing foreign interests, while the common school system was the "noblest product of American civilization."[107] Wisconsin's Methodists felt that the parochial schools advanced foreign ideas and were harmful to American life.[108] Presbyterians agreed, and felt that these "foreign ideas" were so dangerous to the common good that it was the task of the public schools to convert the children, lest Christianity be driven out of the state.[109]

The conflict spilled over into the political arena, with the result that George W. Peck, the recently elected Democratic mayor of Milwaukee defeated Governor Hoard in the fall 1890 gubernatorial election. The Bennett Law was the major bone of contention in that bitter contest. Humphrey J. Desmond, the editor of *The Catholic Citizen,* a lay Catholic newspaper in Milwaukee, prepared the bill that replaced the Bennett Law in the next session of the Wisconsin legislature. This bill eliminated the controversial district clause and the section that defined a school as one that taught specific subjects in the English language. Its enactment was the first of that legislative session.[110]

Bible Reading and the Edgerton Decision

In addition to the debates about the legitimacy of religiously affiliated schools in the latter part of the nineteenth century, many areas grappled with the issue of Bible reading and other religious exercises, e.g., hymns and prayers, in the public school. Roman Catholics, secularists, liberals, and believers of various stripes sometimes complained that the Bible was a "sectarian" book and should not be used in the secular common school. Often these disputes over religious exercises were settled at the local level through compromise, elimination, or acquiescence. In Wisconsin, however, the state's high court dealt with Bible reading in a manner that presaged the U.S. Supreme Court's 1963 decision that declared devotional Bible reading unconstitutional.

In 1886 several citizens of the town of Edgerton, Wisconsin, brought suit against the school board of that town over the devotional reading of the Bible in the local public school.[111] The petitioners claimed that the practice violated their rights of conscience as Roman Catholics and was thus in violation of Article X, Section 3 of Wisconsin's constitution.

John R. Bennett was presiding judge over the Circuit Court in Rock County, Wisconsin. In 1888 he sustained the practice and denied the petitioners' claim.[112] The *Catholic Citizen* then led a campaign among Catholics to support the petitioners in their appeal to the Wisconsin Supreme Court.[113] The case eventually reached the Supreme Court where, by a unanimous 5-0 decision, handed down on March 17, 1890, the justices upheld the Catholics' contention, and Wisconsin became the first state in the Union to adjudge devotional Bible reading in the public schools, even of a voluntary nature, to be illegal. Three justices wrote an opinion in the case. William Penn Lyon ruled that the practice constituted sectarian instruction and therefore was in violation of Article X, Section 3 of the state's constitution.[114] John B. Cassoday determined that Bible reading constituted worship in the proper sense of the term and hence was in violation of Article I, Section 18 of Wisconsin's constitution that forbade taking money from the public treasury for purposes of religious worship.[115] Finally, Justice Harlow S. Orton wrote a concurring opinion that proved to be the most offensive to Bible reading advocates. He penned that the state, and all of its institutions, was secular. Further, he averred that religion, including practices such as Bible reading, was a "cause of strife, quarrel, fights, malignant opposition, persecution and war and all evil in the state." The common schools, he contended, were "Godless."[116]

The Protestant response to the decision was a series of lamentations and predictions of gloom. Baptists, Congregationalists, Methodists, and Presbyterians denied the Bible was a sectarian book, bewailed the Court's interpretation of it as such, and forecast dire consequences to the state and nation as a result of banning the very book that had made the nation free.[117] Some Protestant clergy, such as the Methodist Reverend Mr. J. R. Creighton of the Summerfield Methodist Church in Milwaukee saw the "Romish hierarchy" responsible for the decision. Having won this round, Creighton wondered whether the "Church of Rome," which had been a longtime enemy of the Scriptures, would press on, hoping to bring about the "downfall of public schools and the establishment of sectarian schools on their ruins."[118]

Catholics generally rejoiced at the decision. The *Catholic Citizen,* which had spearheaded the fight against Bible reading, headlined its March 22, 1890, issue with the words: "Won the Case: Wisconsin Catholics Victorious in the Edgerton Bible Case."[119] An editorial in that issue proclaimed that "It is a great victory and it is everybody's victory, who believes in Justice, Equality, and Good-will among men."[120]

Catholic Internal Struggles and Other Schools

Controversy regarding the place of religion in American education in the latter part of the nineteenth century was not confined to debates about the relationship of government to denominational schools and the place of the Bible and other religious exercises in the public school. Several religious groups engaged in internal debates about the need for denominational schools. Between the 1840s and the 1870s, for example, Old School Presbyterians debated the wisdom of maintaining a system of schools, and Lutherans differed in their attitudes toward the public school. In the late 1800s, the Roman Catholic Church, claiming the largest membership of any denomination in the country, engaged in a lively debate regarding whether all Catholic children should be in parochial schools and whether compromise with the purportedly "Godless" public schools should be pursued.

As noted above, the Catholic hierarchy had expressed its concern over the presence of Catholic children in the pan-Protestant schools of the mid-nineteenth century. That concern continued when those schools took on a more secular character in the wake of the Civil War. The extant anti-Catholic prejudice in American society in that period lent gravity to the situation. As historian James Sanders has observed, many Catholics saw parochial schools as "a symbol of defiance against the established order that so despised their religion."[121]

In 1875, at the response of several members of the American hierarchy, the Congregation for the Propagation of the Faith, a Vatican agency that had charge over the missionary activities of the Catholic Church, issued its "Instruction" that addressed the school question. (In 1875 the Catholic population in the United States stood at 5,761,242 with 1,444 parish schools.[122]) Basically, the Congregation declared that the system of public education in the United States as it existed was opposed to Catholicism, constituted a threat to the faith of Catholic children, and called on the American bishops to prevent Catholics "from all contact with the public schools." The bishops were to establish Catholic schools, to which Catholics should send their children, and if they did not, and the danger of loss of their children's faith existed by attendance at public schools, those parents could not "be absolved."[123] The document was considered to be a victory for those bishops who supported the necessity of Catholic school attendance for Catholic children.

The controversy continued when in 1884 the American bishops met in Baltimore for a plenary council (Baltimore III) and took up the matter of Catholic schools. After expressing their concern that religion had been banished from American public schools, and an admonition to Catholic parents and pastors to "multiply our schools" and to "perfect them," the assembled prelates decreed that within two years every parish should have a school unless the bishop decided otherwise and that all Catholic parents were to send their children to these schools unless the bishop gave permission for them to do otherwise.[124]

The Catholic position on schooling had brought the Church into conflict with the civil state, both in Europe and in the United States. Pope Leo XIII had put forth the Catholic stance on that relationship several times during his pontificate, in which he stated that when conflict between church and state occurred in "mixed matters" such as education, Catholics had no choice but to "obey God rather than man." Turning to education, he repeated the Catholic position that parents have "exclusive authority in the education of their children." They were to exercise this authority by choosing schools that instilled the principles of Christian morality in their children and by opposing their children "frequenting schools where they [were] exposed to the fatal poison of impiety."[125]

John Ireland, the liberal Archbishop of St. Paul, Minnesota, had tried to develop friendly relations with the government and non-Catholic Americans. Invited to address the NEA convention in St. Paul in 1890, he took the opportunity to praise the free schools of the nation. In schooling affairs, Ireland first sought governmental reimbursement to all denominations for their schools and, failing that, proposed a compromise that would turn over those schools to the government for a minimal price; the local school boards would retain the religious teachers, and religion would be taught outside of regular school hours.[126]

Ireland's proposal met with disfavor by some Protestant groups and by conservative Catholic prelates, which led to a deep struggle between Ireland and his supporters and his "conservative" opponents in the hierarchy. Even the intervention of the pope's personal legate failed to stop the strife. It took a personal letter from the pope to Cardinal James Gibbons in 1893 in which he said that the decrees of Baltimore III were to be observed, that Catholic schools were to be "sedulously promoted," but it was up to the bishop of the diocese when attendance at public schools was to be allowed.[127]

Amidst the controversy, Catholic school attendance continued to grow. In 1880 there were 2,246 parochial schools with an enrollment of 405,234; ten years later, in 1890, schools numbered 3,194, and they enrolled 633,238 pupils.[128] At no time, however, was the motto of "Every Catholic child in a Catholic school" close to being fulfilled. The poverty of the Catholic population, abetted by clergy and laity who did not support the motto, made that goal an impossible one.

Other denominations also were involved in faith-based schooling, though nowhere near to the extent as Catholics. The Christian Reformed Church reported but four schools, two in Grand Rapids, Michigan, by 1880. Twenty years later, in 1900, there were 14 schools, seven in Grand Rapids. Several factors accounted for the slow growth, namely, the working class status of church members, which in the absence of effective compulsory attendance laws led to children working; the view that public schools were tolerable, especially in rural communities where "boards of education could employ Christian teachers and permit Bible reading and devotions"; and third, the view of parents that the Christian schools were "overtly narrow in aim," coupled with the untrained corps of young teachers who tended to marry after a few years of teaching.[129]

Seventh-day Adventist schools experienced slow growth as well throughout the 1880s, but the 1890s marked the formation of an "Adventist elementary system." Adventist schools multiplied in the United States and in other countries. The decade also witnessed the "beginning of Adventist educational work among American blacks in the South." George Knight, historian of Adventist education, contends that the "reform that began in the 1890s permanently changed the face of Adventist education." By 1900 Adventist elementary schools had increased from 18 (in 1895) to 220, some of which were outside the United States. And enrollment grew from 895 to 5,000 in that same period.[130]

Meanwhile Quakers continued their educational efforts on behalf of the freed slaves after the Civil War and into the 1870s, including founding normal schools to prepare teachers for this work.[131] During the latter years of the nineteenth century, the Episcopal Church exhibited a growing concern about the "quality and availability" of education among the urban and industrial poor, especially in the Northeast. The U.S. Census of 1890 reports there were 8,355 students attending "parochial" schools. Episcopal efforts in elementary and secondary schooling were concentrated in the East (86 schools), the South (170 schools), and Far West (51 schools), with "only 25 reported in the Near (mid) West."[132]

Jon Diefenthaler, a longtime student of Lutheran education, observes that between the end of the Civil War and the outbreak of World War I Missouri Synod Lutheran congregations grew at a faster rate than the denomination's schools. The newer German Lutheran immigrants, he maintains, emigrated due to political and economic concerns, not due to confessional loyalty. The combination of legal efforts of states, such as Wisconsin and Illinois, to curb Lutheran schools, with the view of the recent Lutheran immigrants that the Lutheran day school might obstruct their children's chances to realize the American dream through public schools, served to hold down Lutheran parochial school enrollment for a while.[133] By 1910, however, the Missouri Synod claimed more than 2,000 elementary schools with an enrollment of more than 100,000 students. One thousand schools were operated by other Lutheran Synods, and the German Evangelical Synod of North America maintained another 300.[134]

As noted above, the latter part of the 1800s witnessed a number of conflicts between the civil state and denominations, particularly the Catholics, over the issue of schooling of the young. It is well to realize, however, that compromise and cooperation, especially at the local (and sometimes at the state) level, did exist in this period. Benjamin Justice, for one, in his recent book calls attention to some of these relatively amicable relationships in New York State. Whether taking the form of drawing school attendance boundaries to arrange for "de facto" Catholic public schools, or displaying an open attitude to matters of faith and religious practice in dealing with citizens' concerns for their children in the public schools, some public school officials did what they could to avoid "wars over religion" in the public schools, which by 1900 enrolled about 92 percent of the nation's school-aged children and enjoyed a near monopoly on public funds for education.[135]

The Early Decades of the Twentieth Century

The arrival of millions of immigrants, the majority of them from southern and eastern Europe, between the years 1890 and 1920, had a profound impact on American society in general and on its schools in particular. Their presence led to an emphasis on citizenship education in the public schools, which were charged with the responsibility for inculcating religion and morality, based on natural moorings steeped in "American" virtues, in the youth.

The Role of the Public Schools

The "administrative progressives," as David Tyack has referred to them,[136] looked to the public schools to assimilate the young into American society. Other government leaders were of like mind. For instance, the director of Americanization in the U.S. Bureau of Education wrote that the schools should be the "hub upon which all the other forces of the State and community" rely in dealing with the immigrants.[137] An educational leader of the time, Ellwood P. Cubberley, penned that it was the role of the schools to implant in the immigrants' children "the Anglo-Saxon conception of righteousness, law and order, and popular government, and to awaken in them, a reverence for our democratic institutions and for those things in our national life which we as a people hold to be of abiding authority."[138] Cubberley was not finished. He called on the public school to address the "evils and shortcomings of democracy" that the immigrants had brought to the nation's shores. They would counteract those failings by inculcating "fundamental moral and economic principles" in the "masses." Public schools were necessary for the teaching of values and how to "utilize leisure time."[139] They were to instill the tenets of morality, a task heretofore carried out in the name of religion in education. Now, some believed, there were natural or secular underpinnings to the moral education of children, and these were located in the realm of public schooling.

The NEA joined in the program. In 1907 it created a Committee on Moral Instruction in the schools that frequently stressed the importance of its topic until it was replaced a few years later by the Committee on Training for Citizenship.[140] Four years later, in 1911 it published a 90-page document on a *Tentative Report of the Committee on a System of Teaching Morals in the Public Schools of the United States*.[141] The *Report* asserted that out of the technological developments of the nineteenth century there came "new moral problems of great importance" that required a "course of study for use in the public schools."[142] Following a lengthy list of virtues to be instilled in the students, the Committee argued that pupils "should not only have some idea of the meaning of these virtues but they should be trained in the practice of them until they become fixed habits." Moral training should never be "left to chance"; the school day should be organized so that the pupils have opportunities for "moral training daily."[143]

The NEA continued to address the issue of moral training as the second decade of the twentieth century progressed. Guidance was looked to as a field that provided ample chances to develop ethical character. It should enable students to become aware of what will lead the young to "appreciate one's duty and obligation" toward his fellow humans and society. Effective school guidance should lead the students to ask how they can "improve the moral conditions in my neighborhood."[144] Athletics and other extracurricular activities were singled out by NEA speakers as particularly apt opportunities to "liberate character—democratic character."[145]

The early decades of the twentieth century also witnessed the growth of the high school into a major educational institution. The "Seven Cardinal Principles" Report of an NEA committee in 1918 attests both to the high school's increasing importance and to the expanded social role it played in the nation. The goals for the secondary school curriculum now included such items as "ethical character," "worthy home membership," and "citizenship," goals that were absent in the 1893 report of the NEA's Committee of Ten on Secondary School Studies.[146] Under "Ethical Character," the Report's authors urged that in addition to the development of a "sense of personal responsibility and initiative, special consideration" should be given to the "moral values" to be amassed by the students, which included the possibility for a separate course on "moral instruction."[147] A related aim, "Citizenship," called on the public high school to permeate the organization, administration, curriculum, and student life of the school with citizenship-related activities.[148] Indeed, it was so important that the committee's members recommended that each school have a person who serves as "Citizenship Director."[149] The document also identified the public secondary school as the one agency that a democracy could control "definitely and consciously" for the purpose of "unifying" its people.[150]

Though education for citizenship, for being a "good American," received considerable attention as American society became more ethnically and religiously pluralistic, and by 1900 the formal curriculum had become largely secular due to, in addition to increasing religious pluralism, the influence of Darwinism, curricular diversification, and a growing emphasis on vocationalism, religion retained a place in American public education and was viewed as an important component of moral and civic education. Indeed, most school districts held homeroom religious exercises during the first part of the school day and Bible instruction remained common in the South and rural areas. Another approach to keeping religion in the public school was instituted by William Wirt, the progressive superintendent of the Gary, Indiana, public schools and founder of the so-called "Gary Plan," at the behest of local church leaders. In 1914 Wirt initiated weekday religious education, more commonly known as released-time religious instruction, whereby students were released from school to receive instruction at local churches during the special activities period. Over 600 students went to local churches—seven Protestant and two Jewish—for one hour each week. Released time spread rapidly, particularly after it gained Catholic support. By 1923, 48 states had districts sponsoring released-time religious instruction programs. And on the eve of the U.S. Supreme Court's *McCollum* decision in 1948, which declared released-time programs on school grounds unconstitutional, approximately 2 million students were enrolled.[151]

The Courts, Citizenship, and Religious Schools

The era of World War I and its immediate aftermath was one of emphasis on patriotism and "good citizenship," and laced with a spirit of xenophobia. The Ku Klux Klan (KKK) experienced a reinvigoration and was viewed in some quarters as a defender of patriotism and a white "Protestant America." The nation labored through the "Red Scare," propelled as it was by the birth of Soviet Communism and its stated goal to spread across the world. The schools, public and private, were vitally affected by the dominant climate of society. Given the suspicion of things "foreign," it was not long before clashes over the curriculum and the very existence of religious schools, especially Roman Catholic and Lutheran, reached the courts. Three of these cases reached the U.S. Supreme Court in the 1920s.

Meyer v. Nebraska (1923) was the first of the trilogy. In an act of anti-Germanism the State of Nebraska enacted legislation that made the teaching of a language other than English before the ninth grade illegal. Robert T. Meyer, a teacher in the South School of the Zion Lutheran Church near Hampton, Nebraska, taught in German as well as in English.[152] Meyer was arrested for violating the Nebraska law. The Nebraska Supreme

Court upheld the conviction, but the Supreme Court of the United States overturned that judgment, ruling that the Nebraska law violated the Fourteenth Amendment of the U.S. Constitution because it deprived language teachers and parents of liberty without due process of law. The state, it concluded, had not demonstrated any need for the prohibition of foreign language instruction.[153]

The *Meyer* decision served as the basis for the Court's decision in *Pierce v. Society of Sisters* in 1925. In a frontal attack on the very existence of private religious schools, the State of Oregon, following a KKK-inspired referendum that supported the subsequent action by the legislature, passed a bill that required nearly all children in the state between the ages of 8 and 16 to attend public schools while such schools were in session. The governor signed the bill and it became law. The Society of Sisters of the Holy Names of Jesus and Mary and Hill Military Academy contested the legislation. They contended that the intent of the statute was the destruction of private and parochial schools. Oregon argued that one of the purposes of public schools was to bring diverse elements of the population together for the benefit of the common good. Private schools of all types kept the people of the state apart and therefore were divisive. Basing its ruling on the Fourteenth Amendment, the high court ruled against the state of Oregon, stating that the enforcement of the law would result in the destruction of the appellants' primary schools. In additional comments, the Court said that parents have the right to send their children to private and church-related schools that provide religious, as well as secular, education. "The child," it declared, "is not the mere creature of the State."[154]

The third, and last, case of the wave of nationalism, nativism, and anti-foreign sentiment that swept the country in the 1920s was *Farrington v. Tokushige,* decided in 1927. This case, which emanated from the Territory of Hawaii, dealt with Japanese language schools and the attempt by the territorial government to regulate them. The Supreme Court found that the regulation of the schools far exceeded any legitimate governmental action. It held that the contested statute violated the Fifth Amendment to the Constitution, which imposes on the federal government the same due process requirements that the Fourteenth does on the states. The Court declared that "The Japanese parent has the right to direct the education of his own child without unreasonable restrictions," which it felt were present in this case.[155]

Religious Schools after the Great War

Despite the fits of anti-Catholicism and xenophobia in the 1920s that drove the aforementioned cases, the nation's largest nonpublic school system continued to grow. In 1917, Catholic school enrollment had reached 1,537,644 out of a total Catholic population of 17,022,879, and 5,687 parishes had schools.[156] Almost 20 years later, in 1935–1936, there were 1,945 Catholic secondary schools with an enrollment of 284,736 and 7,929 elementary schools with 2,102,889 students.[157] The Roman Catholic Church remained committed to a Catholic education for Catholic children. Indeed, in 1929 Pope Pius XI, in a world beset with totalitarianism, issued his famous encyclical, "The Christian Education of Youth," in which he reiterated Catholic teaching on the fundamental rights of parents as educators of their children and emphasized the "God-centered" nature of education.[158]

Catholics were not alone among the denominations in their involvement with schools. Calvinists labored with the question of preparing teachers for their elementary schools during these years.[159] Adventists were wrapped up with issues of educational standards, such as accreditation of schools and certification of teachers. The questions that arose led Adventists to establish their own graduate school in the 1930s and its own board of regents for purposes of accreditation.[160] Quakers, according to historian William Kashatus, experienced probably the "low point in the history of Friends education" in the 1930s when only 31 Quaker schools existed.[161] Greek Orthodox schools appeared, as that denomination grew as a result of immigration in the country.[162] Jewish schools witnessed an increase in institutions. In 1916 there were only four Jewish day schools in the United States, with an enrollment of nearly 1,000 students. All of these schools were in New York City. Between 1917 and 1930 a number of Jewish schools were founded across the country so that there were 35 in operation in 1940.[163] The Nazi Holocaust and the post–World War II immigrants contributed to the founding of additional Jewish day schools so that by 1948 their number had risen to 128 with an enrollment of 18,654.[164] The heavily German Lutheran schools went through some trying times as a result of the anti-German feelings due to World War I. The experience, as Jon Diefenthaler notes, "served to hasten the entrance of Lutheran schools into America's cultural mainstream." The Synod and its congregations remained "distrustful of the secular realm" but textbook policies were made "less restrictive," the "curricula of the Synod's teachers' colleges were upgraded," and by the late 1930s women were admitted to these institutions along with men.[165]

The World War II Era

Religion maintained an important place in the annals of American schooling in the period that began shortly before World War II until the 1960s. The NEA established a high-powered national group, the Educational Policies Commission (EPC), to deal with national policies for education in a democracy. Life adjustment education was born (and died), the nation and its schools were caught up in the post-Sputnik whirlwind, and the federal government declared a "crusade" of sorts in the War on Poverty. The courts, especially the U.S. Supreme Court, began to take a more active role in shaping policies and practices related to religion in the public schools and aid to students in religious schools, and private/religious schools experienced a phenomenal increase in enrollment.

The Educational Policies Commission

Established in 1935, the EPC was to span the Depression, World War II, the Cold War, and the early years of the War on Poverty until its demise in 1968. It witnessed the rise of movements such as the Civilian Conservation Corps, the National Youth Administration, and the National Defense Act, passed in the wake of Sputnik, and the Elementary and Secondary Education Act of 1965. Designated to be "representative of the full scope of public education in the country,"[166] it was also seen as an "amplification and interpretation of the seven aims" of the Cardinal Principles Report of 1918.[167] Dominated over the years by educational administrators, it counted leading citizens, such as Dwight Eisenhower and James Bryant Conant, as members. The EPC advocated democratic citizenship as a form of "natural" educational civic religion.

In its early years the EPC addressed questions that dealt with values and ethics, especially as they related to living in a democracy. As war approached, it shifted its aims somewhat to understanding the nature and goals of a democratic society. During the war, it stressed the importance of good citizenship in the moral defense of democracy, and the basic distinction between being a free citizen and a member of a totalitarian state. Its most famous publication, *Moral and Spiritual Values in the Public Schools,* came out in 1951. Here the Commission declared that the public schools were the appropriate agents to teach those values in a democratic society. Religious schools could not nourish common beliefs and posed a threat to national unity. Echoing common school reformers, the EPC asserted that if the United States were to "maintain a separate system of religious schools, the common public school system as we know it, with its indispensable contribution to unity and common loyalties, would disappear from the American scene." The Commission declared that the "vast majority of American youth should and will continue to attend the public schools," whence they derive "brotherhood, democracy, and equality."[168] In summary, the EPC proclaimed that "the public schools will continue to be indispensable in the total process of developing moral and spiritual values. They can and should increase their effectiveness in this respect. Their role is one that no other institution can play as well."[169]

The EPC closed its doors for good in 1968. Perhaps the best assessment of its legacy can be found in a position statement in its 1951 document: "there must be no question whatever as to the willingness of the school to subordinate all other considerations to those which concern moral and spiritual standards."[170]

The Courts, Education, and Religion

As groups such as the EPC espoused a moral, spiritual, and civic education in the public schools that was divorced from an explicit religious foundation, the U.S. Supreme Court's application of the Establishment and Free Exercise Clauses of the First Amendment to state and local policies and actions in the 1940s brought many controversies regarding the appropriate place of religion in public education and government aid to religious schools and students under the scrutiny of the Court. Textbooks, loans, the flag salute, transportation reimbursement, and released-time religious instruction were among the prominent early education issues decided by the high court. They presaged a veritable torrent of religion and education cases heard by the Court in the last 40 years of the twentieth century.

The State of Louisiana purchased textbooks and then lent them to all school children of the state, including those in private schools, most of which were Catholic. Cochran argued that this was using public funds for private purposes, and thus violated the law. In *Cochran v. Louisiana* (1930) the Supreme Court ruled in favor of the state, holding that the children, not the schools, were the primary beneficiaries of the practice. The case was decided on the Fourteenth Amendment, not the First Amendment grounds. This was the first case to employ what became known as the "Child Benefit Theory."[171]

The rights of religious students in the public schools captured the Supreme Court's attention next. In *Minersville v. Gobitis* (1940), children, members of the Jehovah's Witnesses, refused to salute the flag because for them it constituted a "graven image," and to salute it would violate their faith and deny them their constitutional right of religious liberty. The Minersville (PA) School District contended that the salute was intended to instill national loyalty and hence was a civil, not a religious, rite. The Court came down on the side of the school district. It reasoned that the public school was an agency of the state and had a right to make flag salute a condition of school attendance.[172]

Three years later, in 1943, the Court took up the flag salute issue again. The State of West Virginia required the Pledge of Allegiance of all students in public schools in the state for the purpose of fostering patriotism. The Jehovah's Witnesses, involved once again, offered to no avail a substitute "Pledge" in which they stated their respect for the flag and pledged allegiance to all laws that were in agreement with God's law in the Bible. The Supreme Court reversed the *Gobitis* decision, with the 6-3 majority voicing strong support of the basic freedoms contained in the First Amendment. It recognized that the state had a right to legislate for the general welfare, but that legislation must be a legally permissible means of achieving unity.[173]

In *Everson v. Board of Education* in 1947 the Supreme Court held by a 5-4 vote that a New Jersey statute that allowed local school divisions to cover the cost of transportation of students to nonpublic, religious schools was constitutional. In this case the Court expressly applied the no establishment clause to the states in the same manner as it had applied the Free Exercise Clause to the states in *Cantwell v. State of Connecticut*, 310 U.S. 296 (1940). Invoking the "child benefit theory," the Court held that the state had an obligation to the safety of its citizens. Though it upheld New Jersey's statute, the Court laid down what has become known as the "Everson Dicta," which defined prohibitions on state and federal government action in the area of religion, and adopted Jefferson's "wall of separation" metaphor as the defining principle of Establishment Clause interpretation.[174]

In 1948 the Court took up the place of religion in the public schools. In a case originating in Illinois, the high court held that the practice of releasing children from public school while the school was in session to attend religion courses taught by members of churches on the school grounds was unconstitutional because it used public funds and the success of the program was dependent on the police power of the state. As such, the Court ruled, it violated the Establishment Clause of the First Amendment.[175] A considerable amount of hostility was generated as a result of the *McCollum* decision, rendered as it had been, during the Cold War. The Court was accused of being "Godless" and the like. A released time case was brought to the Court in 1952, one which hailed from New York. This time though, the religion classes were held off the school grounds. Departing from its "separationist" position to a more "accommodationist" stance in *Zorach v. Clauson,* the Court upheld the practice by a 6-3 margin.[176]

The Status of Religion in the Public Schools

While there was overriding concern for citizenship or behavior-related issues and the prescriptive approach to religion in the public schools during this period, there was also interest in the descriptive, i.e., courses about religion. For instance, in 1947 the American Council on Education (ACE) raised questions as to who should teach these courses, and how those persons should be prepared. The ACE identified two dangers in this regard: (1) religiously committed people who would teach "along sectarian lines"; and (2) inadequately informed persons. These dangers could be avoided, the ACE committee declared, by "good teacher education."[177]

Following up on that recommendation, a few years later in 1954, the American Association of Colleges for Teacher Education (AACTE) began a five-year study of the relationship between religion and its sister disciplines in the curriculum. Part of the reason for that study, the AACTE stated, was that a "substantial portion" of teachers were "beginning their work incompletely informed in the field of religion and that this inadequacy would show itself in the teacher's own classroom." The AACTE final report on the matter relates that no evidence was uncovered during its study to challenge that assumption.[178]

The AACTE study dealt with the deficiencies in teacher education programs in religion as well as in other subjects in the curriculum. The recommendation of another ACE committee went right to the heart of the matter when it called for the "factual study of religion as the best solution confronting public education in dealing with religion."[179] This put the ACE squarely behind the position taken by the EPC in 1951 that advocated public schools could teach about religion, and that they could do this without "advocating or teaching any religious preference." Further, the failure to teach about religion was to neglect a portion of American life that was "essential for a full understanding of our culture, literature, art, history and current affairs." That "failure" was not seriously addressed until the late 1980s.[180]

Catholic and Other Religious Schools at Mid-Century

While the commissions were grappling with matters of religion and civic education in the public schools and the Supreme Court was addressing the first of dozens of cases dealing with religion and education, private schools, the majority of them Catholic, experienced phenomenal growth. Between 1941 and 1959, nonpublic school enrollment, the vast majority of which was Catholic, increased 118 percent compared with a 36 percent gain in public schools.[181] The burgeoning Catholic school population led to a revival of the question of governmental financial aid to the parents of Catholic school children or directly to the schools themselves. A new organization, composed overwhelmingly of laity, the Citizens for Educational Freedom, looked to political action to obtain what they felt was educational justice. They were led by a Jesuit political scientist, Virgil Blum, SJ, who wrote several books in which he argued that the child and his or her parents should not be penalized economically for exercising their basic right in choosing a school for their child. The right of school choice with public support, he maintained, was guaranteed to the parents under the Fourteenth Amendment.[182]

Smaller religious bodies also continued to operate schools. Some established nationwide organizations, while others were limited to several geographical locations. For example, the 1940s found the Seventh-day Adventists with a major commitment to all levels of Christian education. By 1940 the North American Division of the Adventists was divided into ten conferences with eight of those being in the United States. Each of these conferences had its own educational director.[183] Greek Orthodox schools, on the other hand, remained few and mostly confined to Chicago and New York City.[184]

The boys' schools in New England operated by the Episcopal Church had organized and had been meeting since 1904. In the early 1940s they were joined by an association of girls' schools. Episcopal parish day schools founded their own organization in 1949. Conscious of the accusation that they were "snobbish," Episcopal schools, partially due to the influence of the Social Gospel Movement, began in the 1940s to attempt to aid the poor. Parish day schools increased until they reached 60 in 1947. Additionally, the decision of the Supreme Court in the 1948 *McCollum* case led some Episcopalians to realize that the public schools had abandoned their initial commitment to the faith and morality of Christianity.[185]

Among Protestants, Lutherans remained the most committed to a separate school system and their schools continued to grow in number. As one scholar points out, the "baby boom" that followed World War II "triggered" a resurgence of interest in parochial schools among Missouri Synod Lutherans, who made up the majority of parochial school Lutherans. Their schools had increased to 1,323 with an enrollment of 150,440 by 1961.[186]

The Tumultuous 1960s and Their Aftermath

The turbulent 1960s left their mark on American society in many ways. The relationship of religion and education was no exception, especially regarding the place of religion in public schooling and permissibility of government aid to and regulation of faith-based schools. Often clashes over such matters that were once settled at the state or local level were increasingly resolved, at least to some extent, by the federal courts in general, and what one scholar has called the "Super School Board," namely the Supreme Court of the United States. Among the most controversial issues addressed by the Court were the long-standing remnants of the once Protestant-dominated public school system—prayer and devotional Bible reading.

Engel and Schempp

As part of their efforts on behalf of moral and spiritual education in the state's schools, the New York Board of Regents in 1951 composed a prayer, allegedly nondenominational, and recommended to be voluntary, to be said in New York's public schools. The prayer was as follows: "Almighty God, we acknowledge our dependence upon Thee, and we beg thy blessings upon us, our parents, our teachers, and our Country."[187] Some parents objected, charging that the government-sanctioned prayer violated the Establishment Clause of the First Amendment. In *Engel v. Vitale* (1962), the Supreme Court ruled 6-1 in favor of the plaintiffs, holding that the composition of a prayer to be said in the public schools, even if voluntary, violated the Establishment Clause. The decision led to considerable outcry from public figures, ranging from Billy Graham to Francis Cardinal Spellman of New York. Talk began, and continues to the present, of a constitutional amendment that would permit allegedly nondenominational prayer to be said in the nation's public schools. Such proposals have made little headway and the unconstitutionality of state-sponsored school prayer seems to be a settled matter.[188]

The devotional reading of the Bible, almost always the King James Version, along with attendant religious exercises, had been a common practice in most public schools since the mid-1800s. In 1962 eleven states, mostly in the South, required it by statute. Six states forbade it. The majority of the highest state courts in the nation had upheld the practice, holding that the Bible was not a sectarian book.[189] In *School District of Abington Township v. Schempp* and a companion case, *Murray v. Curlett,* the Supreme Court ruled that devotional Bible reading, followed by the Lord's Prayer, again voluntary, was unconstitutional because it violated the Establishment Clause of the First Amendment. The Court stated that government was to be "neutral" regarding religion, protecting all, disparaging none, and preferring none. Justice Tom Clark, writing for the 8-1 majority, set forth the famous test of religious neutrality: if the purpose or primary effect of a statute is either the advancement of or the inhibition of religion, then the measure violates the required government neutrality as to religion and is unconstitutional. This did not mean, Clark continued, that government should be hostile to religion; nor should religion's cultural role in the development of our society be ignored. He encouraged objective studies about religion, such as comparative religion and the literary or historical study of the Bible, to be included in the public schools' curriculum.[190]

The combined weight of the *Engel* and *Schempp* decisions had wide-reaching effects on education. The American Association of School Administrators recommended in 1964 that each public school division develop "constructive policy" that would "not only guarantee freedom from the establishment of religion but equally will foster freedom for religion."[191] Unfortunately, there is little evidence that local school districts heeded that advice. More potent, though, was the message that the decisions communicated to evangelical Christians, namely, that the public schools were no longer God-centered. Writing in 1993, James Carper and Jeffrey Daignault report that an estimated 8,000 to 12,000 Christian day schools opened after the mid-1960s, with their enrollment reaching approximately 1 million students by the early 1990s. Though some of these schools were short-lived, the "Christian day school movement" marked the first widespread secession from the public school system since the development of the Catholic schooling in the nineteenth century. Furthermore, conservative Protestants, who were once strong supporters of public education, became increasingly critical of what they perceived as establishment of "secularism" as the de facto religion of the public schools.[192]

The combination of the child benefit theory and the religious neutrality principle enunciated in *Schempp* was encouraging to those in the Catholic school movement who, unlike most evangelical Protestant school leaders, sought government aid for their financially endangered schools. They were further encouraged by the decision of the U.S. Supreme Court in the *Allen* textbook case in 1968. In that case, the State of New York required all local public school divisions to lend textbooks free of charge to all students, including those in private and parochial schools, from grades 7 through 12 in the interest of "public welfare and safety." The books were to be among those designated for use in the public schools. Central School District challenged the statute in court. Striking an "accommodationist" tone similar to that of *Everson* (1947), "separationist" dicta not withstanding, the Supreme Court upheld the practice, citing the child benefit and religious neutrality principles. It went further and stated that church-related schools have two functions: (1) sectarian or religious training and (2) secular instruction. Thus they served a public purpose.[193]

Catholic Schools Rise and Fall

On the heels of the highly controversial prayer and Bible reading decisions and proposed constitutional amendments, the largest alternative to the public school system reached its zenith and then began a period of decline that has continued virtually unabated until the present. In the mid-1960s Catholic schools fell on hard times. Their troubles had begun subsequent to the Second Vatican Council (Vatican II) that had been convened by Pope John XXIII in 1962. In 1965–1966 they reached their all-time enrollment high with 5.6 million pupils in elementary and secondary schools, constituting 87 percent of private school enrollment and 12 percent of all pupils in American schools.[194] Doubts about their mission existed, even in the face of studies like that authored by Andrew Greeley and Peter Rossi in 1966 that attested to their religious, social, and economic value.[195] The uncertainty about their effectiveness infected prelates, religious orders, and the laity. But it was the book by a lay Catholic, Mary Perkins Ryan, which perhaps best crystallized the internal doubts about Catholic schools. She asserted that the schools had well served a besieged, poor, immigrant population in the nineteenth century but they were now anachronistic. The Church's resources, personnel and fiscal, could best be used in religious education at all levels and by emphasis on the liturgy. Parents, she claimed, should take responsibility for the religious education of their children.[196]

Catholic school enrollment plummeted, a consequence of the loss of the sense of mission, the movement of Catholics to the suburbs, and the declining number of religious and clergy who taught in the schools, thereby increasing dramatically the cost of attendance. By 1971–1972 Catholic enrollment had declined to 4,034,785, and by 1981–1982 it had dropped to 3,094,000.[197]

Other Faith-Based Schools

Other religious schools, including homeschooling, grew modestly during this period and many attracted more diverse students. For example, Christian Reformed schools experienced a decrease in number between 1961 and 1965, but their enrollment increased from 39,969 to 42,275.[198] Dissatisfaction with public schools and the desire to have "their children educated in a small, caring environment" led many non-Quakers to "become attracted to Quaker education" during these years, especially at the preschool level.[199] In 1965–1966 the Society of Friends operated 32 elementary schools and 24 secondary schools with a combined enrollment of 42,275.[200] Episcopal day schools, on the increase, were challenged to accept students from different ethnic backgrounds. In fact, as David Forbes notes, the national organization of Episcopal schools "found it necessary to bar from membership any Episcopal school which did not expressly open its doors to persons of all ethnic backgrounds."[201] There were 209 Episcopal elementary schools in existence in 1965–1966 with 30,633 pupils and 111 secondary schools that enrolled 17,949 students.[202]

Jewish schools continued their rapid growth rate as they increased from 201 elementary and secondary schools in 1961–1962 with a pupil population of 39,830 to 272 with 52,589 students enrolled in 1965–1966.[203] Lutheran schools faced a similar situation to their Catholic brethren as to the necessity of their mission. The Johnstone Report of 1966 "intimated that the religious attitudes of public and parochial educated youth from solidly Lutheran families were exceedingly similar." More critical, according to Jon Diefenthaler, was the aging of the Lutheran population, which, combined with declining enrollment, forced the closing of some Lutheran parochial schools.[204] Lutheran Synods reported 1,377 elementary schools and 80 secondary schools in operation in 1965–1966 with a total enrollment of 188,521.[205] Additionally, the percentage of non-Lutheran students in Lutheran schools rose to 26 percent in 1972 and 5.4 percent of these were "unchurched." Both of those figures climbed gradually so that by 1982, 40.6 percent of students in Lutheran parochial schools were not Lutheran and 9.1 percent had no church membership whatever.[206] Seventh-day Adventists reported 865 elementary schools with 44,487 students in 1965–1966 and their secondary schools, numbering 284, enrolled 18,116 pupils.[207]

It was during this period that two other kinds of religious schooling appeared on the American educational landscape. The first of these were Islamic Community Schools, which first appeared in the New Jersey/New York area in the late 1970s (the origins of the Sister Clara Muhammed Schools can be traced back to the 1930s and the Nation of Islam).[208] The second was not an institution at all—rather, it was homeschooling. As Brian Ray, a nationally recognized homeschool researcher, points out, home-based education had existed throughout American educational history. It was during the late 1960s, though, that it experienced a revival. The homeschoolers of the 1970s made use of the educational jargon of the radical "reformers," such as John Holt, of the 1960s. Religion, however, motivated at least some of these homeschoolers. The estimated figure of K–12 students homeschooled in the mid-1970s was about 13,000; that number rose to 92,500 in the fall of 1982.[209]

One more denomination's efforts to provide a faith-based education for their children merits attention at this point. It is the story of the Amish. In 1930 there were only three Amish schools reported to be in operation in the United States. This number increased to five by 1940 and to 22 in 1950. By 1960 the number had risen to 89 and by 1970 to 242. Mark Dewalt, a long-time student of Amish education, contends that the consolidation of rural public schools coupled with the rise in the compulsory school attendance age combined to account for this meteoric rise of Amish private schooling.[210] Whether any of these religious schools or their students would be eligible to receive state aid provoked considerable public debate in the 1970s and 1980s and a significant amount of litigation.

Lemon and Beyond

As John Witte, the Jonas Robitscher Professor of Law at Emory University, has pointed out, "In more than 30 cases from 1947 to 1985, the (U.S. Supreme) Court purged public schools of their traditional religious teachings and cut religious schools from their traditional state patronage." The Court's "separationist logic" was especially evident between 1971 and the mid-1980s. During that time, the Court declared unconstitutional, among other benefits to religious schools/students, salary subsidies for private school teachers, state reimbursement for tuition charges to low-income parents, state reimbursement to religious schools for testing costs, state provision of certain supplies and counseling personnel to private schools, and provision of public school personnel to teach remedial courses in religious schools. There were, of course, accommodationist exceptions to the separationist rule regarding state aid to religious schools. For example, the high court upheld the provision of diagnostic services to students in religious schools and tax deductions for religious school expenses. The Court also applied separationist logic to religious activities in public schools in cases involving Ten Commandments plaques and state-mandated moments of silence for prayer or meditation. Guiding these decisions was the so-called "*Lemon* test."[211]

Lemon v. Kurtzman (1971) and a separationist reading the "test" it put forth influenced most of the Supreme Court's "no establishment" cases for the next 15 years. In this pivotal decision, which included cases from Pennsylvania and Rhode Island, the U.S. Supreme Court ruled that the "purchase of secular services," in this instance states paying part of the salaries of teachers of secular subjects in private schools, was unconstitutional. It was so, the Court reasoned, because it led to "excessive entanglement" between church and state because of the government surveillance of church schools required and hence a violation of the Establishment Clause of the First Amendment. The Court established far-reaching and controversial guidelines for dealing with subsequent church-state cases, much to the dismay of advocates of government aid to church-related schools. In the "Tripartite test" or *Lemon* test, the high court asserted that in order to survive an Establishment Clause challenge, a contested policy or practice had to satisfy the following requirements: (1) it must have a secular purpose; (2) its primary effect must neither advance nor inhibit religion; and (3) it must not create excessive entanglement between government and religion.[212]

While the Court was applying separationist logic in disestablishment cases, it was moving in the opposite direction in free exercise law. From the 1940s to the early 1980s, the high court interpreted the Free Exercise Clause in "expansive terms." For example, in the year following the *Lemon* decision, the Court granted the Amish, who believed that formal education should end at grade eight, an exemption from Wisconsin's compulsory education law that mandated school attendance through age 16. In *Wisconsin v. Yoder* (1972) the Court ruled that the Amish's First Amendment right superseded the right of the state to compel attendance. Writing for the Court, Chief Justice Warren Burger pointed to the "fundamental rights of parents" in guiding the "religious future of their children." Ironically, from the mid-1980s onward the Court narrowed free exercise protection as in *Yoder*, while disestablishment law moved away from separationist logic.[213]

In addition to the Supreme Court's decisions removing state-sponsored religious exercises from the public schools during the separationist era, several studies in the mid-1980s reported that religion had been downplayed or ignored in most textbooks. For example, Paul Vitz's analysis of elementary social studies books and readers and high school history texts, published under the title *Censorship: Evidence of Bias in Our Children's Textbooks* (1986), found that "Religion, traditional family values, and conservative political and economic positions have been reliably excluded from children's textbooks." He noted that early elementary social studies texts did not "contain one word referring to any religious activity in contemporary American life" and upper elementary books gave the impression that religion had virtually ceased to exist after the 1600s and 1700s. Vitz also discovered that basal readers were almost totally devoid of material and articles related to either Christianity or Judaism (though they did include articles about fossils, animals, and magic). High school history texts were not much better. Not one of the widely used textbooks, according to Vitz, "acknowledges, much less emphasizes, the great religious energy and creativity of the United States."[214]

People for the American Way (PFAW), the liberal special interest organization founded in 1981 to counter the growing clout of the so-called Religious Right, also studied the content of American history texts. Echoing the findings of Vitz's analysis, it concluded that: "These texts simply do not treat religion as a significant element in American life." Most of the texts, according to the PFAW study, also published in 1986, "give the impression that America suddenly turned into a secular state after the Civil War."[215]

Several years later, Warren Nord, author of the highly regarded *Religion & American Education: Rethinking a National Dilemma* (1995), reviewed textbooks in history, economics, home economics, and the sciences approved for use in North Carolina's public schools. In general, he found that little significance was attached to religion, if mentioned at all, in any of the texts. Though the American and world history books provided some coverage of religion, it gradually disappeared after 1800. Nord asserts that while publishers' fear of controversy may have contributed to the lack of serious attention to the influence of religion in texts, the secular mind-set of authors, publishers, and educational leadership and the marginal place of religion in our present, secular world played a much more important role.[216]

The lack of serious attention to the influence of religion, particularly Christianity, in the public school curriculum, the separationist logic of the Supreme Court in the 1970s and early 1980s, and the general loosening of custom and constraint in American culture, among other factors, prompted a variety of responses to the controversy over the place of religion in the public schools in the latter part of the twentieth century. Some conservative Protestants, already disturbed by the 1962 and 1963 decisions regarding prayer and Bible reading, simply exited the public schools for independent Christian day schools or homeschooling, both of which grew rapidly from the 1970s to the 1990s. Others looked to organizations such as the Eagle Forum (1972), Focus on the Family (1977), Moral Majority (1979), and Christian Coalition (1989) to assist them in combating "secular humanism" in the public schools and reintroducing Christian practices and perspectives. Their entry into the once-eschewed world of politics contributed to the formation of liberal organizations such as People for the American Way. With differing visions of the place of religion in American life in general and the public schools in particular, these organizations engaged each other in what became known as the "Culture War."[217]

Given the ever-increasing purview of the federal judiciary, it is not surprising that the courtroom became one of the major battlefields in this "war." In an effort to counter the well-established, "strict separationist" groups such as the despised American Civil Liberties Union (ACLU) and Americans United for the Separation of Church and State, conservative Christians founded a number of legal advocacy groups to challenge the widely perceived growing hostility to religious speech and practices in public institutions, especially the schools. Among them were the Rutherford Institute (1982), Liberty Counsel (1989), American Center for Law and Justice (1990), and the Alliance Defense Fund (1994). Their attorneys argued or filed briefs in the courts in support of free expression and assembly rights of religious students, equal access for religious groups to public school facilities, vouchers, and freedom to teach about alternatives to Darwinism.[218]

While conflict over religion in the public schools was certainly a major theme in the late 1900s, several initiatives to reach "common ground" on controversial issues during those turbulent years were successful and continue to the present. Much of the credit goes to Charles Haynes, who is currently a Senior Scholar at the Freedom Forum's First Amendment Center, which was founded in 1991. Indeed, between 1988 and 2006 he was the prime mover behind nine common ground statements regarding religion and public education that have been approved by a broad spectrum of religious groups, legal advocacy organizations, and educational associations. These statements address, among other issues, constitutionally appropriate ways of teaching about religion in the schools, religious holidays, equal access to school facilities, and student religious expression. Haynes has also been instrumental in resolving conflicts in school districts involving religion. His efforts to promote a "civil" public school, where religion is treated fairly, as opposed to a "sacred" public school, where a certain religion is privileged, or a "naked" public school, where religion is eliminated; and to encourage dialogue among groups that are often at odds with one another on issues of religion in the public schools have contributed to an emerging consensus on a number of previously contested issues.[219]

Despite efforts to create civil public schools where religion is treated respectfully and given due consideration in the curriculum, a significant number of Americans remain committed to schools that teach certain propositions of knowledge and especially dispositions of value, belief, and appreciation in a particular educational milieu that public schools cannot duplicate. Though the percentage of students attending nonpublic schools, the vast majority of which are religious, remained fairly constant in the latter part of the twentieth century, between 10 and 13 percent, the distribution changed significantly. Catholic schools experienced a steep decline in enrollment, while evangelical and fundamentalist schools experienced remarkable growth, particularly from the mid-1970s to the early 1990s, as did religiously motivated homeschooling from the late 1980s to the end of the century and beyond.

Catholic and Other Religious Schools in Late 1900s

Though still the largest segment of the nonpublic school universe, Catholic schools faced a myriad of challenges in the latter decades of the century. The diminished sense of mission, declining enrollments, the loss of religious personnel, and the exodus of Catholics from the central city to the suburbs combined to bring about a near-paralysis among Catholic educators. Sensing this, the American bishops in 1972 issued a pastoral, "To Teach as Jesus Did," in which they singled out the "unique setting" of the Catholic school as the only place where Catholic youth could "experience learning and living fully integrated in the light of faith." The bishops called on all Catholic educators to avoid, at all costs, a "defeatist attitude."[220]

The change to a predominantly lay professional staff brought with it more than financial difficulties. In 1968–1969 women religious made up 54.7 percent of the professional staff and lay faculty constituted 44.2 percent. By 1981–1982 the figures for the two groups were 24 and 75.4 percent, respectively, and by the late 1990s more than 90 percent were lay.[221] This change brought about a spiritual challenge to the Catholic school, which was supposed to be a "faith community." No longer was the majority of personnel trained in the spirituality of the religious order who staffed the school, and new means needed to be found to bring about the spiritual formation of the staff.[222]

The presence of so many lay professionals added to the financial burden of the schools. Pope Leo XIII, writing in 1891, had declared forthrightly that workers had the right to organize and to form associations to represent them, and that employers had the obligation to respect these rights.[223] His teaching had been reaffirmed by Pope Pius XI, who referred to Leo's encyclical as the "Magna Carta" of the social order.[224] Then, in Vatican II, the Church Fathers supported the rights of workers of "freely founding labor unions without risk of reprisal."[225] At this time, lay teachers in Catholic schools in cities such as Chicago, New York, and Philadelphia organized. Sometimes their efforts were resisted by Church officials. In Chicago, for instance, the strife led to a lawsuit that ended up in the Supreme Court.[226] The lay teachers, who had relied on the Church's own teaching from its official documents, bitterly resented the stance taken by some of the Church officials in some of these conflicts.[227] The dissension had a number of ramifications, one of them being the development of a new, different model dealing with labor-management disputes within the Church.[228]

Other activities, such as Catholic school boards at the local and diocesan level, were begun following the leadership of a leading Catholic school administrator, Monsignor O'Neill C. D'Amour, in the 1960s.[229] These boards took cognizance of the growing role of laypersons in the Catholic Church and its schools, in the wake of Vatican II. Writing in 1976, Andrew Greeley recommended the hierarchy get out of the business of schools, and turn them over to the laity. Greeley's unsolicited advice went unheeded.[230]

Some charged Catholic schools with being "racial escape valves" for segregationists at this time.[231] Other authors maintained that Catholic high schools, in particular, were now elitist institutions.[232] Meanwhile, the Supreme Court's decisions continued to go against proponents of government financial aid to Catholic schools, prompting Archbishop Joseph C. Bernardin, then president of the National Conference of the Catholic Bishops, that the Court "had distorted the restriction of the First Amendment to the point where it now requires hostility rather than neutrality toward religion."[233]

Catholic schools, then, faced major challenges as the 1990s began, the most serious being "money- or lack of it" and continuing enrollment decline and school closings.[234] In 1965–1966 Catholic schools numbered more than 13,000 with an enrollment of approximately 5.6 million. By 1988–1989, however, 8,719 Catholic schools were in operation with an enrollment of about 2.5 million. On the eve of the new millennium, enrollment had stabilized, but another 600 schools had closed. About 23 percent of their students were not Catholic, with 64 percent of African American youth not Catholic. The presence of so many non-Catholic youngsters in Catholic schools led to questions about the religious identity of Catholic schools, questions that had not been posed when the enrollment was nearly all Catholic.[235]

Other faith-based school groups faced challenges in the latter decades of the twentieth century as well. Some experienced declining or stable enrollments, while others witnessed rapid growth. Nearly all enrolled more religiously and racially diverse student bodies.

For example, the number of students in Seventh-day Adventist schools declined. In 1987–1988, enrollment was 80,184, in 1990–1991 the figure dropped to 69,716, and in 1999–2000 to 61,080. At the same time Adventist student bodies were becoming more diverse. Likewise, enrollment in Lutheran Church–Missouri Synod schools continued to decrease from approximately 188,000 in 1965–1966 to 166,000 in 1999–2000, while greater numbers of non-Lutheran families patronized the Synod's schools. Enrollments in Calvinist, Amish, Episcopal, Mennonite, and Friends schools fluctuated between expansion and contraction during the last decades of the century.[236]

On the other hand, Muslim, Jewish, and evangelical Protestant schools as well as faith-based homeschooling expanded rapidly in the late 1900s. By the late 1990s, for example, Christian day schools, whose leaders occasionally battled state officials over accreditation issues in the 1970s and 1980s, claimed more than 1 million students. Once conflated with "segregation academies," these schools enrolled a growing number of Americans of African descent, and in many urban areas black citizens started their own "fundamentalist academies." Jewish school enrollment also increased significantly during this period. Indeed, between 1980–1981 and 1999–2000 it grew from 96,173 to 169,751. Though Orthodox Jewish schools accounted for better than 75 percent of the enrollment by 1999–2000, schools affiliated with Conservative and Reform Judaism also experienced significant growth during this time. Muslim schools also grew in number and enrollment in the 1980s and 1990s. By 1992, as many as 82 schools were operating. Most were small and plagued by financial difficulties. By 1999–2000, their number had increased to 152 with an enrollment of 18,262.[237]

Though exact figures are difficult to determine, the number of children being homeschooled certainly ballooned during the last two decades of the twentieth century. Some scholars estimate that between the late 1970s and the late 1990s the number of children instructed by their parents jumped from approximately 15,000–20,000 to as many as 1.2 million. Religious convictions were usually the major force behind parents' choice of this kind of education for their children.[238]

Religion and Education in the Third Millennium

The role of religion in American education has been a matter of affirmation and dissention, conflict and consensus since the 1600s. This has certainly been the case since the advent of state-operated education in the middle decades of the nineteenth century. Citizens, religious leaders, educators, policy makers, jurists, parents, and occasionally students have grappled with, among other issues, the place of religion in the curriculum, the legitimacy of religious exercises, the relationship of the state to religious schools, state aid to religious schools, and, not surprisingly, the exact meaning of the First Amendment religion clauses as applied to education.

As pointed out above, during the last 60 years of the twentieth century many religion and education issues were addressed and more or less settled by the Supreme Court of the United States, for example, state-sponsored devotional exercises in public schools. On other issues, however, for example, government benefits for religious schools/students, the Court has been deeply divided and not followed a consistent pattern. Three decisions in the first years of the new century reveal these deep divisions and provide evidence of a Court grappling for a consensus understanding of the meaning of "no establishment" as applied to education.[239]

In 2000, the Court split three ways in a Louisiana case, *Mitchell v. Helms,* involving federal funding for the purchase of educational materials, including library books and computers, which were then loaned to private schools, most of which were Catholic. Four justices opined that the practice did not violate the Establishment Clause in that the government provided secular aid on a neutral basis to students in public and private schools. Two justices agreed, but expressed concern about direct monetary subsidies. Three justices dissented vigorously, and asserted that the Establishment Clause prohibits subsidy of religious education.[240]

The same year the high court grappled with the popular practice of prayers at public school athletic events. In a 6-3 decision the Court declared unconstitutional a school board authorized policy allowing students to decide whether there should be an invocation before the game and if so which student should offer it. Writing for the 6-3 majority in *Santa Fe Independent School District v. Doe,* Justice John Paul Stevens, who was among the dissenters in the *Mitchell* case, asserted that an authorized invocation was coercive and involved state endorsement of religion. In his dissent, Chief Justice William Rehnquist, a member of the *Mitchell* majority, charged that the Court "distorts existing precedent" and "bristles with hostility to all things religious in public life."[241]

In arguably one of the most controversial education and religion decisions in recent years, in 2002 a bitterly divided Supreme Court ruled 5-4 that Cleveland's scholarship or voucher program did not run afoul of the disestablishment clause. Writing for the majority in *Zelman v. Simmons-Harris,* Chief Justice Rehnquist echoed the rationale given by the four justice plurality in *Mitchell.* That foursome was joined by Justice Sandra Day O'Connor who shared Rehnquist's contention that the aid in question was neutral and indirect, since parents, not the government, chose where to use the voucher. Among the dissenters, Justice Stephen Breyer called the decision a "dramatic departure" from precedent and Justice David Souter raised the specter of "religiously based social conflict."[242]

Given the Court's current (and tenuous) position on government aid to religious schools, the new century has witnessed what may be a shift of the locus of litigation regarding aid to faith-based schools from the federal to the state courts. The Florida Supreme Court, for example, recently declared one of that state's voucher programs invalid on state constitutional grounds. If that is the case, proponents of state aid to religious schools/students will have to contend with "mini-Blaine amendments" found in a majority of state constitutions that restrict or prohibit any kind of aid to "sectarian" schools.[243]

While the Supreme Court has yet to reach "common ground" in the area of disestablishment law, consensus has been reached on some contested matters and conflict has been avoided through the efforts of numerous individuals and religious, educational, and legal advocacy groups. As noted earlier, the efforts of Charles Haynes and the First Amendment Center have led to a number of common ground agreements endorsed by a broad spectrum of parties with an interest in religion and education. These widely circulated agreements on matters such as religious holidays and religion in the public school curriculum have certainly reduced the number of "wars of religion" in the public schools.

Consensus building efforts have also been evident in the development of constitutionally appropriate materials for use in the public school. The Bible Literacy Project is a case in point. Founded in 2001 to "encourage and facilitate the academic study of the Bible in public schools," it has produced a beautifully illustrated text for use in public school English and social studies courses as well as Bible electives. *The Bible and Its Influence* (2005) is now used in 181 schools in 38 states. Though not without its detractors, the nearly 400 page textbook has been endorsed by a broad spectrum of religious leaders and by numerous religious, legal, and educational associations. This and similar efforts to give religion its due in the public school curriculum suggest a growing consensus on the importance and legitimacy of "teaching about" religion in public schools.[244]

For parents who want something more for their children than teaching about religion, religious schools of various kinds remain an option in the twenty-first century. As was the case in the latter part of the 1900s, enrollments in schools sponsored by or affiliated with some religious bodies are stable or declining in the early 2000s. Catholic school enrollment continues to fall as hundreds of schools, many of which provided an outstanding education to inner-city children, have closed since the turn of the century due to a lack of funds. Adventist and Lutheran enrollments have also declined. Jewish, Muslim, and homeschool enrollments, however, grew in the early 2000s as parents sought an education for their children that public schools could not provide.[245]

While the courts have settled some issues and educational, legal, and religious advocacy groups have cooperated to reach common ground on other controversial intersections of religion and education, conflicts over the place of religion in public education and the education of the public will likely continue. Debates will likely continue about, among other things, evolution and intelligent design, student religious expression regarding controversial issues, moments of silent meditation, the Pledge of Allegiance, Ten Commandments displays, viewpoint discrimination, vouchers and tuition tax credits, "gay/straight" clubs, religious garb in the public school, faith-based objections to class assignments, teacher participation in student-led religious activities, religious expression in school assignments and activities, and accommodating religious practices during the public school day. Though sometimes unnecessarily shrill and occasionally used by participants for crass purposes, such debates are a necessary part of a vital democratic process for learning how to live civilly with our deepest differences in an increasingly pluralistic culture. We hope the following entries help inform those debates.

NOTES

1. Lawrence A. Cremin, *American Education: The Colonial Experience, 1607–1783* (New York: Harper & Row, 1970), 124–125.

2. Ibid., 394.

3. Clifton Johnson, *Old-Time Schools and School-books,* Dover ed. (New York: Dover Publications, 1963), 69–99.

4. James C. Carper, "The Changing Landscape of U.S. Education," *Kappa Delta Pi Record* 37 (Spring 2001): 106–110.

5. Ibid.

6. Henry Steele Commager, ed., *Noah Webster's American Spelling Book* (New York: Teachers College Press, 1962), 169; and Carl F. Kaestle, *Pillars of the Republic: Common Schools and American Society, 1780–1860* (New York: Hill and Wang, 1983), 30–61.

7. Carper, "The Changing Landscape," 106–110.

8. Charles L. Glenn, Jr., *The Myth of the Common School* (Amherst: University of Massachusetts Press, 1988), 146–178; Kaestle, *Pillars of the Republic,* 75–103, 136–181.

9. James C. Carper and Thomas C. Hunt, *The Dissenting Tradition in American Education* (New York: Peter Lang, 2007), 159–176.

10. William O. Bourne, *History of the Public School Society of the City of New York* (New York: Arno Press and *The New York Times,* 1971), 3.

11. Diane Ravitch, *The Great School Wars, New York City, 1805–1973* (New York: Basic Books, 1974), 10.

12. Bourne, *History of the Public School Society,* 36–38.

13. Ravitch, *The Great School Wars,* 22–23.

14. Richard Shaw, *Dagger John: The Unquiet Life and Times of Archbishop John Hughes of New York* (New York: Paulist Press, 1977), 139.

15. Vincent P. Lannie, *Public Money and Parochial Education: Bishop Hughes, Governor Seward, and the New York School Controversy* (Cleveland: Case Western Reserve University, 1968), 21.

16. Neil G. McCluskey, ed., *Catholic Education in America: A Documentary History* (New York: Teachers College Press, 1964), 51–64.

17. Lannie, *Public Money,* 103–110.

18. Ravitch, *The Great School Wars,* 51.

19. There are a number of sources that treat this conflict. See, for example, Vincent P. Lannie, *Public Money and Parochial Education: Bishop Hughes, Governor Seward, and the New York School Controversy* (Cleveland: Case Western Reserve University, 1968).

20. Ravitch, *The Great School Wars,* 76–77.

21. Ibid., 80.

22. Joel Spring, *The American School, 1642–1996* (New York: McGraw-Hill, 1997), 101.

23. Ibid.

24. Robert S. Michaelsen, *Piety in the Public School* (New York: Macmillan, 1970), 72.

25. Neil G. McCluskey, *Public Schools and Moral Education* (Westport, CT: Greenwood, 1958), 21.

26. E. I. F. Williams, *Horace Mann: Educational Statesman* (New York: Macmillan, 1937), 118.

27. Ibid., 124.

28. Michaelsen, *Piety in the Public School,* 74.

29. Robert L. Church and Michael W. Sedlak, *Education in the United States: An Interpretive History* (New York: The Free Press, 1976), 90.

30. Lawrence A. Cremin, ed., *The Republic and the School* (New York: Teachers College Press, 1959), 5–7.

31. Ibid., 13–14.

32. Merle F. Curti, *The Social Ideas of American Educators* (Totowa, NJ: Littlefield, Adams and Co., 1959), 122.

33. Horace Mann, *First Annual Report Covering the Year 1837* (Boston: Dutton and Wentworth State Printers, 1838), 57.

34. Cremin, *The Republic and the School,* 101.

35. Ibid., 102.

36. Ibid., 105–106.

37. Ibid., 106.

38. Ibid., 107.

39. Jonathan Messerli, *Horace Mann: A Biography* (New York: Alfred A. Knopf, 1972), 249.

40. Michaelsen, *Piety in the Public School,* 76–79.

41. William B. Kennedy, *The Shaping of Protestant Education* (New York: Association Press, 1966).

42. Oscar Handlin, "Education and the European Immigrant, 1820–1920," in Bernard J. Weiss, ed., *American Education and the European Immigrant: 1840–1940* (Urbana: University of Illinois Press, 1982), 8.

43. Harold A. Buetow, *Of Singular Benefit: The Story of U.S. Catholic Education* (New York: Macmillan, 1970), 159.

44. Ibid., 45.

45. James A. Burns and Bernard J. Kohlbrenner, *A History of Catholic Education in the United States* (New York: Benziger Brothers, 1937), 138.

46. James A. Burns, *The Growth and Development of the Catholic School System in the United States* (New York: Benziger Brothers, 1912), 186.

47. Lewis J. Sherrill, *Presbyterian Parochial Schools, 1846–1870* (New York: Arno Press and *The New York Times*, 1969).

48. Peter B. DeBoer, "North American Calvinist Day Schools," in *Religious Schools in the United States K–12*, ed. Thomas C. Hunt and James C. Carper (New York: Garland, 1993), 70–71.

49. William C. Kashatus, "Seeking the Light and Nurturing the Intellect: A Brief History of Quaker Education in America," in ibid., 205–208.

50. David R. Forbes, "Episcopal Schools," in ibid., 370.

51. Harold S. Himmelfarb, "Jewish Day Schools: Growth in an Era of Religious and Educational Decline," in ibid., 383.

52. Jon Diefenthaler, "Lutheran Schools in Transition," in ibid., 420.

53. Walter H. Beck, *Lutheran Elementary Schools in the United States,* 2nd ed. (St. Louis: Concordia Publishing House, 1965), 10.

54. R. Freeman Butts and Lawrence A. Cremin, *A History of Education in American Culture* (New York: Holt, Rinehart and Winston, 1953), 172.

55. Ray Allen Billington, *The Protestant Crusade: 1800–1860: The Origins of American Nativism* (New York: Macmillan, 1938), 145.

56. W.K. Dunn, *What Happened to Religious Education? The Decline of Religious Teaching in the Public Elementary School, 1776–1861* (Baltimore, MD: The Johns Hopkins Press, 1958), 224.

57. Ibid., 260.

58. Warren A. Nord, *Religion & American Education: Rethinking a National Dilemma* (Chapel Hill: University of North Carolina Press, 1995), 73.

59. Elwyn A. Smith, ed., *The Religion of the Republic* (Philadelphia: Fortress Press, 1971), 23.

60. Milo M. Quaife, ed., *The Attainment of Statehood* (Madison: State Historical Society of Wisconsin, 1928), 714.

61. Herbert M. Kliebard, ed., *Religion and Education in America: A Documentary History* (Scranton, PA: International Textbook Company, 1969), 112.

62. H.C. Whitford, "Early History of Education in Wisconsin," *Reports and Collections of the State Historical Society of Wisconsin*, V, Part III (Madison: Atwood and Rublee, 1869), 343.

63. *The Revised Statutes of the State of Wisconsin, 1849* (Southport, WI: C. Latham Sholes, 1849), 404–405.

64. Ibid., 736.

65. Ibid., 541.

66. Ibid., 89.

67. Lyman C. Draper, "Moral and Religious Instruction in Public Schools," in the *Tenth Annual Report on the Condition and Improvement of the Common Schools and Educational Interests of the State of Wisconsin for the Year 1858* (Madison: Atwood and Rublee, 1858), 242–244.

68. "Religion in Schools," *Wisconsin Journal of Education* (NS), 1, 3 (September 1864): 80.

69. Alvin H. Johnson, *The Legal Status of Church-State Relationships in the United States* (Minneapolis: The University of Minnesota Press, 1934), 39–40.

70. Ibid., 41.

71. A.H. Wintersteen, "Commentary," 29 *American Law Register,* 324 (May 1890).

72. "Morals—Religion—The Bible," *Wisconsin Journal of Education* (NS), 1, 2 (May 1865): 289–290.

73. David B. Tyack and Elisabeth Hansot, *Managers of Virtue: Public School Leadership in America, 1820–1980* (New York: Basic Books, 1982), 74–75.

74. Dwight L. Agnew et al., eds., *Dictionary of Wisconsin Biography* (Madison: The State Historical Society, 1960), 126.

75. "The Relation of the Church to the Common School," in the *Minutes of the Twenty-Fourth Session of the Wisconsin Annual Conference of the Methodist Episcopal Church 1870* (Milwaukee: Index Printing Office, 1870), 29–31.

76. Nord, *Religion & American Education,* 67.

77. Ibid., 67–68.

78. Ruth Miller Elson, *Guardians of Tradition: American Schoolbooks of the Nineteenth Century* (Lincoln: University of Nebraska Press, 1964), 52–53.

79. Edward A. Krug, ed., *Salient Dates in American Education, 1635–1964* (New York: Harper and Row, 1966), 58–59.

80. John H. Westerhoff, *McGuffey and His Readers* (Nashville, TN: Abingdon, 1978), 19.

81. Benjamin F. Crawford, *The Life of William Holmes McGuffey* (Delaware, OH: Carnegie Church Press, 1974), 86.

82. Westerhoff, *McGuffey and His Readers,* 25.

83. Tyack and Hansot, *Managers of Virtue,* 21.

84. Westerhoff, *McGuffey and His Readers,* 13

85. Henry F. Pringle and Katherine Pringle, "He Scared the Devil out of Grandpa," *The Saturday Evening Post,* January 22, 1955, 30.

86. B. Edward McClellan, *Schools and the Shaping of Character: Moral Education in America, 1607–Present* (Bloomington, IN: ERIC Clearinghouse for Social Studies/Social Science Education and the Social Studies Development Center, Indiana University, 1999), 25.

87. Mark Sullivan, *Our Times: America Finding Herself* (New York: Charles Scribner's Sons, 1932), 22, 28.

88. Harvey C. Minnich, *William Holmes McGuffey and His Readers* (New York: American Book Company, 1936), 112.

89. Curti, *The Social Ideas of American Educators,* 19.

90. Elson, *Guardians of Tradition,* 83.

91. Frederick M. Binder, *The Age of the Common School, 1830–1865* (New York: John Wiley and Sons, 1974), 72.

92. Westerhoff, *McGuffey and His Readers,* 15–17.

93. David B. Tyack, *The One Best System: A History of Urban Education* (Cambridge, MA: Harvard University Press, 1974).

94. James Davison Hunter, *American Evangelicalism: Conservative Religion and the Quandary of Modernity* (New Brunswick, NJ: Rutgers University Press, 1983), 37.

95. Michaelsen, *Piety in the Public School,* 257.

96. William Torrey Harris, "Religious Instruction in the Public School," *The Andover Review* 11 (June 1889): 582.

97. Selwyn K. Troen, *Shaping the St. Louis System, 1838–1920* (Columbia: University of Missouri Press, 1975), 48.

98. Nord, *Religion & American Education,* 75.

99. "The President's Speech at Des Moines," *Catholic World,* 22, 130 (January 1876): 17.

100. Johnson, *The Legal Status of Church-State Relationships in the United States,* 21. For an informative discussion of the politics of the Blaine amendment and why "secularists" or "Liberals" in the 1870s and 1880s thought such an amendment was necessary, see Philip Hamburger, *Separation of Church and State* (Cambridge, MA: Harvard University Press, 2002), 287–334.

101. Edwin H. Mead, "Has the Parochial School Proper Place in America?" *National Education Association Journal of Proceedings and Addresses* (Topeka, KS: Clifford C. Baker, 1889), 145.

102. *The Laws of Wisconsin, except City Charters and Their Amendments Passed at the Biennial Session of the Legislature of 1889* (Madison: Democrat Printing Company, State Printers, 1889), 729–733.

103. *Biennial Report of the State Superintendent of the State of Wisconsin, for the Two Years Ending June 30, 1888* (Madison: Democrat Printing Co., 1888), 6–7, 42.

104. George W. Rankin, *William Dempster Hoard* (Fort Atkinson, WI: W.D. Hoard and Sons, 1924), 123–124.

105. See, for instance, the "Manifesto" of the three Catholic bishops of the state in Harry H. Heming, *The Catholic Church in Wisconsin* (Milwaukee: T.J. Sullivan, 1896), 283–286.

106. *The Bennett Law.* Newspaper clipping dated April 3, 1890. A scrapbook in the Library of the State Historical Society of Wisconsin, Madison.

107. *Milwaukee Sentinel,* July 7, 1890, 7.

108. *Minutes of the Wisconsin Annual Conference of the Methodist Episcopal Church, Forty-Fourth Session, 1890.* (n.p.: John Schneider Publisher, 1890), 56–57.

109. *Minutes of the Synod of Wisconsin of the Presbyterian Church 1890* (Madison: Tracy, Gibbs and Co., 1890), 8–14.

110. *The Laws of Wisconsin, Passed at the Biennial Session of the Legislature of 1891,* I (Madison: Democrat Printing Company, State Printer, 1891), Chapters 187, 217–218.

111. *The State of Wisconsin ex rel., Frederick W. Weiss, W.H. Morrissey, Thomas Mooney, James McBride, J.C. Burns and John Corbett, Appellants, vs. The District Board of School District No. Eight of the City of Edgerton, Respondent.*

112. Judge John R. Bennett, *Opinion in the Case of Weiss, et al,, vs. the School Board of Edgerton* (Edgerton, WI: F.W. Coon, 1889), 56–57.

113. See, for instance, *Catholic Citizen,* November 24, 1888, 1, 4.

114. Justice William Penn Lyon, *Opinion: Decision of the Supreme Court of the State of Wisconsin Relating to the Reading of the Bible in Public Schools* (Madison: Democrat Printing Co., 1890), 12–22.

115. Justice John B. Cassoday, *Opinion, Decision of the Supreme Court of the State of Wisconsin Relating to the Reading of the Bible in Public Schools* (Madison: Democrat Printing Co., 1890), 25–32.

116. Justice Harlow S. Orton, *Opinion, Decision of the Supreme Court of the State of Wisconsin Relating to the Reading of the Bible in Public Schools* (Madison: Democrat Printing Co., 1890), 32–35.

117. See, for instance, *Minutes of the Wisconsin Baptist Anniversaries 1890* (Janesville, WI: H.M. Antes, 1890); *Minutes of the Fiftieth Annual Meeting of the Congregational Convention of Wisconsin 1890* (Madison: Tracy, Gibbs and Co., 1890); *Minutes of the Wisconsin Annual Conference of the Methodist Episcopal Church, Forty-Fourth Session 1890* (n.p.: John Schneider Publisher, 1890); and *Minutes of the Synod of Wisconsin of the Presbyterian Church 1890* (Madison: Tracy, Gibbs and Co., 1890).

118. *Milwaukee Sentinel,* April 14, 1890, 12.

119. *Catholic Citizen,* March 22, 1890, 1.

120. Ibid., 4.

121. James W. Sanders, *The Education of an Urban Minority: Catholics in Chicago: 1833–1965* (New York: Oxford University Press, 1977), 37. The Lutheran and Presbyterian experiences are discussed in Carper and Hunt, *The Dissenting Tradition in American Education,* 160–186; and Kaestle, *Pillars of the Republic,* 164–166.

122. *Sadliers' Catholic Directory, Almanac, and Ordo for the Year of Our Lord 1875* (New York: D.J. Sadlier, 1875), 22.

123. "Instruction of the Congregation of the Propaganda de Fide," in McCluskey, *Catholic Education in America,* 122–126.

124. "Decrees of the Third Plenary Council of Baltimore 1884," in McCluskey, ibid., 93–94.

125. Leo XIII, "Sapientiae Christianae," in Joseph Husslein, ed., *Social Wellsprings,* I (Milwaukee: Bruce Publishing Co., 1940), 150–162.

126. John Ireland, "State Schools and Parish Schools—Is Union Between Them Impossible?" *National Education Association Journal of Proceedings and Addresses* (Topeka, KS: C.C. Baker, 1890),

179–184. Ireland's compromise plan became known as the Faribault-Stillwater Plan. It was similar to a previous plan started in Poughkeepsie, New York, in 1873.

127. Reilly, *The School Controversy, 1891–1893,* 228–229.

128. Buetow, *Of Singular Benefit: The Story of U.S. Catholic Education,* 179.

129. DeBoer, "North American Calvinist Day Schools," in *Religious Schools in America, K–12,* 74–75.

130. Knight, "Seventh-day Adventist Schooling in the United States," in ibid., 99–104.

131. Kashatus, "A Brief History of Quaker Education," in ibid., 208–209.

132. Forbes, "Episcopal Schools," in ibid., 370–371.

133. Diefenthaler, "Lutheran Schools in Transition," in ibid., 420–421.

134. William G. Ross, *Forging New Freedoms: Nativism, Education, and the Constitution, 1917–1927* (Lincoln: University of Nebraska Press, 1994), 48–49.

135. Benjamin Justice, *The War That Wasn't: Religious Conflict and Compromise in the Common Schools of New York State 1865–1900* (Albany: State University of New York Press, 2005).

136. Tyack, *The One Best System,* 126–129.

137. Fred Clayton Butler, "State Americanization: The Part of the State in the Education and Assimilation of the Immigrant," *United States Bureau of Education, Bulletin No. 7* (Washington, DC: Government Printing Office, 1920), 11.

138. Ellwood P. Cubberley, *Changing Conceptions of Education* (Boston: Houghton Mifflin Co., 1909), 15.

139. Ibid., 65.

140. Michaelsen, *Piety in the Public School,* 139.

141. National Education Association, *Tentative Report of the Committee on a System of Teaching Morals in the Public Schools* (Winona, MN: National Education Association, 1911), 342–433.

142. Ibid., 344–345.

143. Ibid., 345.

144. James B. Davis, "Vocational and Moral Guidance through English Composition in the High School," *Journal of Proceedings and Addresses of the National Education Association of the United States 1916* (Ann Arbor, MI: The Association, 1916), 715–716.

145. See, for instance, C.S. Hicks, "The Influence of Faculty Supervision on the Moral Effects of Athletes in High Schools and Colleges," *Journal of Proceedings and Addresses of the National Education Association of the United States 1912* (Ann Arbor, MI: The Association, 1912), 1147; and H. Neumann, "Moral Values in Pupil Self-Government," *Addresses and Proceedings of the National Education Association of the And United States 1913* (Ann Arbor, MI: The Association, 1913), 41–45.

146. National Education Association, *Cardinal Principles of Secondary Education* (Washington, DC: Government Printing Office, 1918), 10–11.

147. Ibid., 9–10.

148. Ibid., 8.

149. Ibid., 18.

150. Ibid., 22.

151. Ronald D. Cohen and Raymond A. Mohl, *The Paradox of Progressive Education: The Gary Plan and Urban Schooling* (Port Washington, NY: Kennikat Press, 1979), 18, 92–94; and Michaelsen, *Piety in the Public School,* 156–159.

152. William G. Ross, *Forging New Freedoms: Nativism, Education, and the Constitution, 1917–1927* (Lincoln: University of Nebraska Press, 1994), 3.

153. *Meyer v. Nebraska,* 262 U.S. 390 (1923); Ross, ibid., 5.

154. *Pierce v. Society of Sisters,* 268 U.S. 510 (1925).

155. *Farrington v. Tokushige,* 273 U.S. 283 (1927).

156. Buetow, *Of Singular Benefit,* 225.

157. Ibid., 226.

158. Pius XI, *The Christian Education of Youth (Divini Illius Magistrii)*, in *Five Great Encyclicals* (New York: Paulist Press, 1939).

159. DeBoer, "North American Calvinist Day Schools," in *Religious Schools in the United States K–12,* 77–78.

160. Knight, "Seventh-day Adventist Schooling in the United States," in ibid., 106.

161. Kashatus, "A Brief History of Quaker Education," in ibid., 210.

162. George C. Papademetrious, "Greek Orthodox Religious Schools," in ibid., 228.

163. Himmelfarb, "Jewish Day Schools," in ibid., 385.

164. Judah Pilch, ed., *Jewish Education Register and Directory 1951* (New York: American Association for Jewish Education, 1951), 39.

165. Diefenthaler, "Lutheran Schools in Transition," in *Religious Schools in the United States, K–12,* 421.

166. National Education Association, *A National Organization for Education: Educational Policies Commission* (Washington, DC: National Education Association, 1937), 3.

167. Edward A. Krug, *The Shaping of the American High School, 1920–1941* (Madison: The University of Wisconsin Press, 1972), 253.

168. Educational Policies Commission, *Moral and Spiritual Values in the Public Schools* (Washington, DC: National Education Association, 1951), 3–5.

169. Ibid., 100.

170. Ibid., 54.

171. *Cochran v. Louisiana,* 281 U.S. 370 (1930).

172. *Minersville v. Gobitis,* 310 U S. 586 (1940).

173. *West Virginia State Board of Education v. Barnette,* 319 U.S. 624 (1943).

174. *Everson v. Board of Education,* 330 U.S. 1 (1947).

175. *McCollum v. Board of Education,* 355 U.S. 203 (1948).

176. *Zorach v. Clauson,* 343 U.S. 306 (1952).

177. American Council on Education, Committee on Religion and Education, *The Relation of Religion to Public Education: The Basic Issues* (Washington, DC: American Council on Education, 1947), 27–29.

178. Evan R. Collins, "Summary and Problems," in A.L. Sehaly et al., eds., *Teacher Education and Religion* (Oneonta, NY: The American Association of Colleges for Teacher Education, 1959), 227–228.

179. American Council on Education, *The Function of the Public Schools in Dealing with Religion* (Washington, DC: American Council on Education, 1953), vii.

180. Educational Policies Commission, *Moral and Spiritual Values in the Public Schools,* 77–78.

181. Neil G. McCluskey, *Catholic Viewpoint on Education* (Garden City, NY: Hanover House, 1959), 107.

182. See, for instance, Virgil C. Blum, *Catholic Education: Survival or Demise* (Chicago: Argus Communications, 1969); and Virgil C. Blum, *Freedom of Choice in Education* (Glen Rock, NJ: Deus Books, 1958).

183. Knight, "Seventh-day Adventist Schooling in the United States," in *Religious Schools in the United States K–12,* 107–108.

184. George C. Papademetriou, "Greek Orthodox Religious Schools," in ibid., 230.

185. Forbes, "Episcopal Schools," in ibid., 372–374.

186. Diefenthaler, "Lutheran Schools in Transition," in ibid., 421–422.

187. Quoted in Thomas C. Hunt, "Religion and Education in the United States: A Legal Overview," in *Society, Culture, and Schools: The American Approach,* ed. Thomas C. Hunt et al. (Garrett Park, MD: Garrett Park Press, 1979), 47.

188. *Engel v. Vitale,* 370 U.S. 421 (1962).

189. Donald E. Boles, *The Bible, Religion, and the Public Schools* (Ames, IA: Iowa State University Press, 1965), 332–333.

190. *School District of Abington Township v. Schempp* and *Murray v. Curlett,* 374 U.S. 203 (1963).

191. American Association of School Administrators, *Religion in the Public Schools* (Washington, DC: American Association of School Administrators, 1964), 4, 28.

192. James C. Carper and Jeffrey A. Daignault, "Christian Day Schools: Past, Present, and Future," in *Religious Schools in the United States K–12*, 318.

193. *Central School District v. Allen*, 392 U.S. 296 (1968).

194. *U.S. News and World Report*, August 18, 1975, 55; *Education Week*, March 30, 1983, 14.

195. Andrew M. Greeley and Peter H. Rossi, *The Education of Catholic Americans* (Chicago: Aldine, 1966).

196. Mary Perkins Ryan, *Are Parochial Schools the Answer? Catholic Education in the Light of the Council* (New York: Guild Press, 1968).

197. Kenneth A. Simon and W. Vance Grant, eds., *Digest of Educational Statistics* (Washington, DC: U.S. Government Printing Office, 1987), 56.

198. National Center for Educational Statistics, *Statistics of Nonpublic Elementary and Secondary Schools, 1965–1966* (Washington, DC: U.S. Government Printing Office, 1968), 7.

199. Kashatus, "A Brief History of Quaker Education," in *Religious Schools in the United States, K–12*, 210–211.

200. National Center for Educational Statistics, *Statistics of Nonpublic Elementary and Secondary Schools 1965–1966*, 7.

201. Forbes, "Episcopal Schools," in *Religious Schools in the United States, K–12*, 375.

202. National Center for Educational Statistics, *Statistics of Nonpublic Elementary and Secondary Schools, 1965–66*, 7.

203. Ibid.

204. Diefenthaler, "Lutheran Schools in Transition," in *Religious Schools in the United States, K–12*, 423.

205. National Center for Educational Statistics, *Statistics of Nonpublic Elementary and Secondary Schools, 1965–66*, 7.

206. Diefenthaler, "Lutheran Schools in Transition," in *Religious Schools in the United States, K–12*, 423.

207. National Center for Educational Statistics, *Statistics of Nonpublic Elementary and Secondary Schools, 1965–66*, 7.

208. Jack Layman, "Islamic Full-Time Schools," in *Religious Schools in the United States, K–12*, 347–348.

209. Brian D. Ray, "Home Schooling Revitalized," in ibid., 244–245.

210. Mark W. Dewalt, "The Growth of Amish Schools in the United States," *Journal of Research in Rural Education* 17 (Fall 2001): 123–124.

211. John Witte, Jr., "The New Freedom of Public Religion," Center for the Study of Law and Religion, Emory University Atlanta, GA, n.d.; and John Witte, Jr., *Religion and the American Constitutional Experiment*, 2nd ed. (Boulder, CO: Westview Press, 2005), 185–191.

212. *Lemon v. Kurtzman*, 403 U.S. 602 (1971).

213. *Wisconsin v. Yoder*, 406 U.S. 205 (1972); Witte, *Religion and the American Constitutional Experiment*, 162–165, 185.

214. Paul C. Vitz, *Censorship: Evidence of Bias in Our Children's Textbooks* (Ann Arbor, MI: Servant Books, 1986), 14, 56–57.

215. People for the American Way, *Looking at History: A Review of Major U.S. History Textbooks* (Washington, DC: People for the American Way, 1986); and Anthony Podesta, "The Uphill Battle for Quality Textbooks," *Religion and Public Education* 13 (Summer 1986): 60–62.

216. Nord, *Religion & American Education*, 138–159.

217. See Stephen Bates, *Battleground: One Mother's Crusade, The Religious Right, and the Struggle for Control of Our Classrooms* (New York: Poseidon Press, 1993); Carper and Hunt, *The Dissenting Tradition in American Education*, 199–215, 240–245; James Davison Hunter, *Culture Wars: The Struggle to Define America* (New York: Basic Books, 1991); William Martin, *With God on Our Side: The Rise of the Religious Right in America* (New York: Broadway Books, 1996).

218. Ibid.

219. See Charles Haynes and Oliver Thomas, *Finding Common Ground: A First Amendment Guide to Religion and Public Schools* (Nashville, TN: First Amendment Center, 2007).

220. National Conference of Catholic Bishops, *To Teach as Jesus Did* (Washington, DC: United States Catholic Conference, 1973).

221. *Catholic Schools in America: Elementary/Secondary,* 1982 ed. (Englewood, CO: Fisher Publishing Co., 1982), xviii.

222. Alfred A. McBride, *The Christian Formation of Catholic Educators* (Washington, DC: Chief Administrators of Catholic Education. National Catholic Educational Association, 1981); Russell M. Bleich, ed., *The Pre-Service Formation of Teachers for Catholic Schools in Search of Patterns for the Future* (Washington, DC: Chief Administrators of Catholic Education, the Association of Catholic Colleges and Universities, National Catholic Educational Association, 1982).

223. Leo XIII, "Rerum Novarum" [On the Condition of Labor], in *Five Great Encyclicals,* 1–30.

224. Pius XI "Quadragesimo Anno" [Reconstructing the Social Order], in ibid., 125–167.

225. "Pastoral Constitution on the Church in the Modern World" ("Gaudium et Spes"), in Walter M. Abbott, ed., *The Documents of Vatican II* (New York: America Press, 1966), 277–278.

226. *National Labor Relations Board v. The Catholic Bishop of Chicago, et al.,* 99 S. Ct. 1313 (1979).

227. See, for instance, J. J. Reilly, "Teachers' Unions, Catholic," *The New Catholic Encyclopedia,* 17 (New York: McGraw-Hill, 1979), 648.

228. John J. Augenstein, *A Collaboration Approach to Personnel Relations* (Washington, DC: National Catholic Educational Association, 1980).

229. O'Neil C. D'Amour, "Parochial Schools without Parochialism," *Ave Maria,* April 24, 1965, 12–14.

230. Andrew M. Greeley, William C. McReady, and Kathleen McCourt, *Catholic Schools in a Declining Church* (Kansas City, KS: Sheed and Ward, 1976), 324–325.

231. See, for instance, John P. Sheerin, "Our Segregated Catholic Schools," *Catholic World* (March 1963): 333–334; "Are Parochial Schools Racial Escape Valves," *Christian Century,* October 26, 1968, 1298; and James C. Donohue, "Catholic Education in Contemporary Society," *National Catholic Educational Association Bulletin* 64 (August 1967): 13–17, for a discussion of this issue.

232. James L. Morrison and Benjamin J. Hudgkins, "Social Changes and Catholic Education," *Education* 98 (March–April 1978): 264.

233. *The National Catholic Reporter,* June 6, 1975, 1.

234. Walch, *Parish School,* 245.

235. F. H. Brigham, *United States Catholic Elementary and Secondary Schools 1990–1991: Annual Statistical Report on Schools, Enrollment, and Staffing* (Washington, DC: National Catholic Educational Association, 1991).

236. For information and data on these schools, see Hunt and Carper, *Religious Schools in the United States, K–12,* 69–82, 107–111, 211–214, 298–299, 373–378, 422–423; National Center for Education Statistics, *Private School Universe Survey, 1997–98* (Washington, DC: U.S. Department of Education, 1999), 9–10; and National Center for Education Statistics, *Private School Universe Survey: 1999–2000* (Washington, DC: U.S. Department of Education, 2001), 6.

237. For information and data on these schools, see Carper and Hunt, *The Dissenting Tradition in American Education,* 199–212, 218–233; Hunt and Carper, *Religious Schools in the United States, K–12,* 245–249, 347–352, 385–389; National Center for Education Statistics, *Private School Universe Survey, 1997–98,* 9–10; and National Center for Education Statistics, *Private School Universe Survey: 1999–2000,* 6.

238. Carper and Hunt, *The Dissenting Tradition in American Education,* 239–245.

239. Witte, *Religion and the American Constitutional Experiment,* 185, 203–227.

240. *Mitchell v. Helms,* 530 U.S. 793 (2000).

241. *Santa Fe Independent School District v. Doe,* 530 U.S. 290 (2000).

242. *Zelman v. Simmons-Harris,* 122 S. Ct. 2460 (2002).

243. Hamburger, *Separation of Church & State,* 335.

244. Bible Literacy Project at www.bibleliteracy.org. See also Haynes and Thomas, *Finding Common Ground.*

245. National Center for Educational Statistics, *Characteristics of Private School in the United States: Results from the 2003–2004 Private School Universe Survey* (Washington, DC: U.S. Department of Education, 2006), 15.

THE PRAEGER HANDBOOK OF
RELIGION AND EDUCATION
IN THE UNITED STATES

A

Abington School District v. Schempp and *Murray v. Curlett*

In 1963, the U.S. Supreme Court decided these two cases regarding the constitutionality of state-mandated prayer and devotional Bible reading in public schools. The District Court for the Eastern District of Pennsylvania found that the statute in question violated the Establishment Clause of the First Amendment as applicable to the states by the Due Process Clause of the Fourteenth Amendment and ordered appropriate injunctive relief. Abington Township School District appealed to the U.S. Supreme Court, which granted certiorari. In Maryland, a state court rejected a challenge to a law requiring the recitation of the Lord's Prayer at the beginning of the school day in public schools. The Supreme Court granted certiorari and consolidated the two cases.

Edward Schempp, a Unitarian, alleged that the required reading of ten verses of the Christian Bible over the public address system or in each classroom, followed by class recitation of the Lord's Prayer in the public school, was a violation of the First Amendment Establishment Clause, "Congress shall make no law respecting an establishment of religion." Schempp objected to the reading of certain New Testament passages with which he did not agree. Although the law permitted a student to abstain from participation and to leave the room if he or she submitted a written parental note to the school, Schempp found this alternative unacceptable, as he believed his children could be labeled as troublemakers and/or harassed by their classmates and/or teachers. Since the students who did not participate constituted a very small minority, Schempp believed his children were being singled out for their nonparticipation. He held that the reading of Christian Bible verses violated the First Amendment's guarantee of freedom of religion in that it respected "an establishment of religion," in this case, the Christian religion. Schempp, who professed no religion, stated that the Bible verses reading discriminated against Jews and Muslims who do not believe in Jesus Christ as Savior.

The trial court found that state law did compel the reading of the Bible verses and that such reading "even without comment, possesses a devotional and religious character and constitutes in effect a religious observance. . . ." Since the statute requires the reading of the

"Holy Bible," a Christian document, the practice "prefers the Christian religion." The First Amendment forbids any government preference or favor shown to one religion or no religion.

Briefs of *amici curiae* were filed by the American Jewish Committee, The Synagogue Council of America et al., and by the American Ethical Union. Experts on Jewish beliefs testified that the use of the New Testament, which presents Jesus Christ as the long awaited Messiah, was offensive to Jewish tradition and was "practically blasphemous."

The issue in *Schempp* then was the following: Did Pennsylvania law and the Township of Abington's policy, which, absent a written note from parents, required public school students to participate in religious exercises, violate the First and Fourteenth Amendment rights of the students to practice or not practice religion? In an 8-1 decision, delivered by Justice Tom Clark, the Supreme Court found that the required religious activities violated both the Free Exercise and the Establishment Clauses of the First Amendment.

In the second case, involving a situation much like the one in *Schempp,* Madalyn Murray and her son, William, appealed a judgment from the Maryland Court of Appeals, which held that a Baltimore statute requiring that the Bible be read or the Lord's prayer recited during opening exercises in the public schools did not violate the First and Fourteenth Amendments of the Constitution as the Murrays contended. The statute, first passed in 1905 in accordance with Article 77, 202 of the Annotated Code of Maryland, forbade any comment on the Bible chapter read and/or on the Lord's Prayer. The two petitioners stated that they were professed atheists who had tried unsuccessfully to have the school board rescind the rule and therefore were compelled to file suit for a writ of mandamus to rescind the act and cancel the practice.

Murray, a taxpayer, objected to the introduction of religion into the public schools financed by taxpayers. After her complaints, the rule was amended to allow students to be excused on the request of the parent, as was allowed in *Schempp.* Petitioners held that the rule, even with the allowance for students to be absent, violated their rights, "in that it threatens their religious liberty by placing a premium on belief as against non-belief and subjects their freedom of conscience to the rule of the majority; it pronounces belief in God as the source of all moral and spiritual values, equating these values with religious values," and thus, argued plaintiffs, the practice cast judgment on the "morality, good citizenship and good faith" of their beliefs and those of any other students who chose not to participate. Such could not be permitted as it would constitute a favoring of religion over no religion.

The justices acknowledged the history of religion and the part it has played in the life of the United States and its citizens. The Founding Fathers were not attempting to deny religion a place in the lives of citizens, but rather sought to guarantee that there would be no state religion and no preference for any religion over any others. The majority opinion quotes Judge Alphonso Taft in an Ohio court case, *Board of Education v. Minor* (1872), almost a century earlier in which he stated that the ideal of religious freedom is one of "absolute equality before the law, of all religious opinions and sects.... The government is neutral, and, while protecting all, it prefers none, and it disparages none."

Earlier cases such as *Cantwell v. Connecticut* (1940) had already determined that establishment of religion did not have to be of a particular religion but of religion in general or one religion over another. The First Amendment forbids the federal government to advance religion. Since the Fourteenth Amendment to the U.S. Constitution made the First Amendment applicable to the states, no state can pass a law favoring or inhibiting religion.

The wall separating church and state does not allow any government promotion of religion. Neither does it allow any prohibition of religion or the practice of religion. The majority opinion reiterated that there can be no

> fusion of governmental and religious functions or a concert or dependency of one upon the other to the end that official support of the State or Federal Government would be placed behind the tenets of one or of all orthodoxies....And a further reason for neutrality is found in the Free Exercise Clause, which recognizes the value of religious training, teaching and observance and, more particularly, the right of every person to freely choose his own course...free of any compulsion from the state.

The majority opinion also pointed out that the *Abington v. Schempp* and *Murray v. Curlett* cases represented the ninth time in 20 years that the First Amendment has been subjected to such scrutiny in terms of advancing religion. Absent a secular legislative purpose and a primary effect that does not advance nor inhibit religion, no government in the United States can pass a law that in any way favors religion over nonreligion or one religion over another. Justice William O. Douglas, in a concurring opinion, stated that the illegality of the activities in these two cases results not from the amount of funds expended in the practice, but rather the use to which the funds are put: "What may not be done directly may not be done indirectly lest the Establishment Clause become a mockery." The lone dissenter, Justice Potter Stewart, held that the records in the cases "are so fundamentally deficient" as to make it impossible to render an "informed determination of the constitutional issues presented" and he would have required additional evidence before rendering a final decision. *See also:* The Bible in the Public Schools; First Amendment Religion Clauses and the Supreme Court; Prayer in the Public Schools.

Further Reading: *Board of Education v. Minor,* 23 Ohio St. 211 (1872); *Cantwell v. State of Connecticut,* 310 U.S. 296 (1940); *Engel v. Vitale,* 370 U.S. 421 (1962); *School District of Abington Township v. Schempp and Murray v. Curlett,* 374 U.S. 203 (1963).

Mary Angela Shaughnessy

Academic Freedom

Academic freedom is a modern concept that derives from the nineteenth-century German research university. For college and university scholars it is a principle that protects their right to freely pursue intellectual inquiry and teaching within their area of expertise (guided by the standards established by their field) without fear of sanction if their research interests and/or findings are unpopular or controversial (*lehrfreiheit*). For college and university students, the concept represents their freedom to choose their own elective course of study (*lernfreiheit*). Neither has historically pertained to teachers or students in precollege settings, but recent controversies regarding the teaching of Intelligent Design in K–12 schools in the United States have led some parties to evoke the principle of academic freedom to support their positions. In order to understand this contemporary situation, it is necessary to explore the introduction of academic freedom in the United States in historical context.

Until the late nineteenth century, the Protestant Christian establishment nearly exclusively controlled education in the United States. Early primary and secondary schools were denominationally affiliated, and the "common school" movement spearheaded by

Horace Mann in the early nineteenth century promoted "common" Protestant Christian values in the form of daily Bible readings from the King James translation, moral lessons embedded in the ubiquitous *McGuffey Readers,* and a religiously defined nationalism that emphasized assimilation as an important function of education. The first colleges were formed to train Protestant Christian clergy and to promote a learned Protestant Christian citizenry. During the nineteenth century there was a boom of denominationally sponsored colleges that were established across the country to provide more opportunities for such training to a wider audience.

Several interrelated forces converged in the latter part of the nineteenth century to transform education in the United States from a system designed to promote ecumenical Protestant Christian values to one increasingly defined by secular standards of academic inquiry that included academic freedom. The influence of Enlightenment inspired European institutions of higher education, especially the German research universities; the prestige of the natural sciences and the epistemological change from revealed to discovered forms of knowledge as intellectually legitimate; the rising religious diversity engendered by immigration; and the economic shifts brought about by rapid industrialization were just a few of the forces that diminished the Protestant hegemony over education. This transformation was especially pronounced in colleges and universities, but primary and secondary schools followed (less uniformly and at a slower pace) culminating in the pivotal 1960s Supreme Court cases that banned school-sponsored prayer and Bible readings.

Though the loss of Protestant influence by the early years of the twentieth century was not as absolute as some theorists claim, the transformation from a Protestant Christian inspired understanding of higher education to a secular research university model as normative was evident by 1915 when the American Association of University Professors (AAUP) published their highly influential "General Report of the Committee on Academic Freedom and Academic Tenure." The 1915 report follows the German research university model in that it emphasizes the free inquiry of scholars and the central role they play in the promotion of "progress in scientific knowledge" that is portrayed as "essential to civilization" itself (American Association of University Professors, 1915, p. 24). Attention is given to the necessary conditions that will enable such free inquiry to flourish in ways unhindered by economic, political, or ecclesiastical forces. Specifically, it calls for scholars to be free to pursue research and teaching interests within their areas of expertise that should be guided and judged by their scholarly peers *rather than* those without sufficient understanding of the field (e.g., college and university trustees and prominent religious, business, and political benefactors). The 1915 report was widely embraced at the time of publication and served as the foundation for subsequent documents by the AAUP in 1940 and 1970, which further elaborated upon the fundamental tenets outlined above.

This background helps put in context the current use of academic freedom to both justify and challenge the teaching of Intelligent Design (ID) as an alternative scientific theory to evolution. Consistent with earlier articulations, central to the contemporary principle of academic freedom is the role that scholars play in (1) determining the criteria used to define the parameters of the field itself, (2) measuring scholarly competence, and (3) outlining acceptable research methods employed to advance knowledge and understanding. Academic freedom is compromised when those outside of the field successfully impose their views on any of these areas *or* when those within the field fail to follow established research guidelines. It is important to note here that academic freedom is not synonymous with freedom of expression more broadly defined. It is a unique concept that has been constructed to define the particular vocation of scholar in the same way that medicine and law have unique responsibilities affiliated with their professions. Minority views are thus not automatically given legitimacy, but should be protected if the criteria outlined above are met.

Contemporary proponents of ID evoke the principle of academic freedom in two primary ways: First, in support of the right of scholars to pursue this arena of research and teaching as a form of science, and second, in support of the right of students to be exposed to alternative views of evolutionary theory. Both rest on the premise that ID is a legitimate scientific enterprise, and this is precisely the premise that is contested by the scientific community itself.

Remember that academic freedom for scholars is based upon the assumption that those who evoke this right are intellectuals who have acted in compliance with the criteria established by the profession regarding what responsible scholarship entails. In spite of the assertions by proponents of ID to the contrary, the scientific community overwhelmingly rejects the portrayal of ID as meeting the requirements that constitute legitimate scientific inquiry. Though there are a handful of practicing scientists who continue to assert that ID is rooted in sound scientific methods, they have not been able to defend their assertions persuasively to their peers in the field. Given this fact, scholarly proponents of ID have not met a central requirement that is necessary to evoke the protections that the principle of academic freedom is intended to provide.

In relationship to students, some proponents of ID evoke academic freedom to defend the right of students to be exposed to alternative views of evolutionary theory in the spirit of free inquiry and the promotion of critical thinking skills. For example, in 2001 former Senator Rick Santorum of Pennsylvania introduced the following language that was attached to the education act titled *No Child Left Behind* (NCLB): "Where topics are taught that may generate controversy (such as biological evolution), the curriculum should help students to understand the full range of scientific views that exist, why such topics may generate controversy and how scientific discoveries can profoundly affect society" (Santorum, 2004; Forrest and Gross, 2007, p. 243). Though the "Santorum Amendment" only survives in modified form in the NCLB Conference Report and does not carry the weight of law, it has become a cornerstone in the ID movement's effective "Teach the Controversy" campaign. If the scientific community recognized ID as a legitimate scientific theory, such inclusion would be appropriate and sound. Given that this is not the case, defending its inclusion on the basis of academic freedom for students is a misrepresentation of the principle and in violation of one of its central tenants: the freedom for scholars to define the parameters of their field unfettered by interference by those outside of the profession who do not possess the knowledge to make informed judgments.

Given the definition of academic freedom itself, there is no legitimate basis for employing it to promote ID as a scientific theory. There is, however, ample basis to evoke academic freedom as a principled challenge to such representations as the following 2005 AAUP resolution entitled "Teaching Evolution" illustrates:

> The theory of evolution is all but universally accepted in the community of scholars and has contributed immeasurably to our understanding of the natural world. The Ninety-first Annual Meeting of the American Association of University Professors deplores efforts in local communities and by some state legislators to require teachers in public schools to treat evolution as merely a hypothesis or speculation, untested and unsubstantiated by the

methods of science, and to require them to make students aware of an "intelligent-design hypothesis" to account for the origins of life. These initiatives not only violate the academic freedom of public school teachers, but can deny students an understanding of the overwhelming scientific consensus regarding evolution.

This meeting calls on local communities and state officials to reject proposals that seek to suppress discussion of evolution in our public schools as inimical to principles of academic freedom. (AAUP, 2005, pp. 20–21)

See also: Creationism; Evolution; Intelligent Design; Science and Religion; Scopes Trial.

Further Reading: American Association of University Professors, "1940 Statement of Principles on Academic Freedom and Tenure with 1970 Interpretive Comments," at www.aaup.org; American Association of University Professors, "General Report of the Committee on Academic Freedom and Academic Tenure," *AAUP Bulletin* 1 (December 1915): 17–39; AAUP, "Resolutions," *Academe* 91 (July/August 2005): 19–21; Discovery Institute at www.discovery.org; Barbara Forrest and Paul R. Gross, *Creationism's Trojan Horse: The Wedge of Intelligent Design* (New York: Oxford, 2007); Richard Hofstadter and Walter P. Metzger, *The Development of Academic Freedom in the United States* (New York: Columbia University Press, 1955); *Kitzmiller et al. v. Dover Area School District,* M.D. Penn, 2005; George M. Marsden, *The Soul of the American University: From Protestant Establishment to Established Nonbelief* (New York: Oxford University Press, 1994); Walter P. Metzger, ed., *The American Concept of Academic Freedom in Formation: A Collection of Essays and Reports* (New York: Arno Press, 1977); Rick Santorum, "Academic Freedom at Stake," *Pittsburgh Post-Gazette,* December 25, 2004, www.post-gazette.com.

Diane L. Moore

Agostini v. Felton

This case, brought ten years after the 1985 *Aguilar v. Felton* decision, overturned *Aguilar,* which held that Title I remedial services for parochial students could not be provided in religious schools or on religious property. The decision involved application of the *Lemon* test, which consisted of three prongs. Any aid given to religious schools must (1) have a secular purpose; (2) neither promote nor inhibit religion; and (3) not foster excessive entanglement of the government with religion. Any government aid to, or activity in, a religious institution must pass all three prongs.

At issue in *Aguilar* was New York City's Title I program, which sent public school employees into religious schools in order to provide remedial education to disadvantaged children. Taxpayers brought suit and sought a ruling that this provision of services in religious schools constituted impermissible aid to religion and as such constituted a violation of the Establishment Clause of the First Amendment to the Constitution. Even though teachers and other professional employees were monitored and taught in classrooms from which all religious symbols had been removed, the U.S. Supreme Court in a 5-4 decision found that the New York City Title I program, as it was implemented in parochial schools while utilizing public school employees, required an excessive entanglement of church and state and thus violated the Establishment Clause. The district court, receiving the case on remand from the U.S. Supreme Court, issued a permanent injunction prohibiting the provision of Title I services on parochial school grounds.

Agostini and other parties bound by the injunction filed motions seeking relief from the injunction in the district court under Federal Rule of Civil Procedure 60 (b) (5), the relevant subsection of which states, "On motion and upon such terms as are just, the court may relieve a party...from a final judgment [or] order...[when] it is no longer equitable that the judgment should have prospective application." Their argument stressed the high costs of complying with *Aguilar* and statements by five justices in the case of *Kiryas Joel Village School District v. Grumet* that *Aguilar* should be reconsidered. Further, basing their argument on Supreme Court establishment clause cases subsequent to *Aguilar,* appellants alleged that *Aguilar* was no longer good law.

Justice Sandra Day O'Connor, writing for the majority in a 5-4 decision, stated that this federally funded Title I program providing supplemental, remedial instruction to disadvantaged children on a neutral basis was not invalid under the Establishment Clause, when government employees provide services on religious property with the safeguards present in the New York City program. O'Connor wrote, however, neither the exorbitant cost of compliance with *Aguilar* nor the justices stating an opinion that *Aguilar* should be reconsidered at a time when *Aguilar* was not part of the case at hand could be used as justification for the reversal of *Aguilar.* Nonetheless, decisions subsequent to *Aguilar* indicate that the Court no longer holds (1) that the mere presence of a public school employee engaged in instruction in a religious school constitutes a danger that religious proselytizing will occur or (2) the principle that all government aid that directly benefits the educational process in religious schools is unconstitutional. Further, O'Connor observed, there has never been any evidence presented that even one teacher attempted to teach or practice religion while providing government services in a religious school. The aid in dispute is not intended to aid religious schools or to foster religion but rather the aid is available to all students, those attending private as well as public schools, on a nondiscriminatory basis. The purpose of the aid is to benefit the student, not the school or religion.

The *Aguilar* decision relied on two premises that are now rejected: monitoring of instruction in religious schools by public school officials and the potential for political divisiveness constituted unlawful entanglement of the government with religion. Additionally, the doctrine of *stare decisis,* let the decision stand, does not keep the Court from acting on the change in law it has made in other cases and overruling *Aguilar.*

Earlier case law established the power of the Court to grant relief from an injunction if the individuals seeking relief provided evidence of significant changes in case or statutory law and/or factual conditions. Appellants provided evidence of significant changes in case law at the Supreme Court level. Thus, the Court ruled that relief from the injunction was appropriate. New York City can provide Title I services in parochial schools without violating the First Amendment. It should be noted, however, that because parties *can* do something does not mean they are required to do it. *See also: Aguilar v. Felton;* Government Aid to Religious Schools; *Lemon v. Kurtzman* and *Earley v. DiCenso.*

Further Reading: *Agostini v. Felton,* 521 U.S. 203 (1997); *Aguilar v. Felton,* 473 U.S. 203 (1985); *Kiryas Joel Village School District v. Grumet,* 512 U.S. 687.

Mary Angela Shaughnessy

Aguilar v. Felton

This 1985 decision ended the provision of Title I services in Catholic and other religious schools, until the U.S. Supreme Court reversed the decision in *Agostini v. Felton* in 1997. For 12 years, public school districts struggled to provide services to students in religious schools while not providing them on the property of, or in, the religious schools.

New York City expended federal monies granted it under the Title I program of the Elementary and Secondary Education Act of 1965 to pay the salaries of public school employees who taught in parochial schools under the program, which authorized federal financial assistance to local educational institutions to meet the learning needs of educationally deprived children whose families were low-income. Teachers were assigned by the city and public school field personnel charged with monitoring Title I classes supervised them. Taxpayers filed suit in a federal district court, alleged that the Title I program as implemented by New York City violated the Establishment Clause of the First Amendment, and sought an injunction to stop the provision of Title I services in religious schools. The district court granted summary judgment to the city based on its review of the record of another case involving an identical challenge and in which the program was ruled to be constitutional. The U.S. Court of Appeals for the Second Circuit, however, reversed, and the case came to the U.S. Supreme Court on appeal.

Briefs of *amici curiae* arguing for reversal of the decision of the appellate court were filed by the Council for American Private Education, the Catholic League for Religious and Civil Rights, Citizens for Educational Freedom, the National Jewish Commission on Law and Public Affairs, Parent Rights, Inc., and the U.S. Catholic Conference. Briefs of *amici curiae* supporting the Court of Appeals decision and asking for the Supreme Court's affirmation of that decision were filed by the American Civil Liberties Union, Americans United for Separation of Church and State, and the Anti-Defamation League of B'nai B'rith.

In a 5-4 decision, in which Justice Sandra Day O'Connor concurred in part and dissented in part, the U.S. Supreme Court found New York City's Title I program to be a violation of the Establishment Clause of the First Amendment. The Court also found unconstitutional the case of *School District of Grand Rapids v. Ball,* heard the same day, in which Catholic school teachers, paid by the public school district, taught classes in the Catholic schools that were not offered during the school day. The teachers posted a sign stating that the classroom was a public school classroom after school when the classes were in session. The Supreme Court found this practice to be a violation of the Establishment Clause as it fostered excessive entanglement of the government with religion.

The programs provided by Title I to parochial school students included remedial reading and reading skills, remedial mathematics, ESL, and guidance services. Regular public school employees who volunteered to teach in parochial schools provided the services. New York City's Bureau of Nonpublic School Reimbursement administered the program, made teacher assignments, and provided for field personnel observation of those employees providing services in Catholic schools.

The Title I employees were told to avoid involvement with religious activities and to not allow any religious materials in the classrooms. All material and equipment funded under Title I for the programs could be used only for those programs. Contact with other personnel in the school should be minimal. Administrators of parochial schools had to remove all religious symbols from the classrooms used for provision of Title I services.

In 1978, six taxpayers originally brought action to stop any further distribution of funds for services to private school students under the program. Quoting from both the 1971 *Lemon v. Kurtzman* and the 1975 *Meek v. Pittenger* decisions, the majority found that even though supervision might prevent teachers from fostering a primary effect of advancing religion, the system itself would "inevitably lead to an unconstitutional administrative entanglement between church and state."

In conclusion, the majority held that at least one, and possibly all, prongs of what has come to be known as the *Lemon* test were violated by the provision of Title I services in parochial schools: (1) aid must have a secular purpose; (2) aid can neither advance nor inhibit religion; and (3) aid cannot foster excessive government entanglement with religion. The violation of the third prong is definitely present and renders the aid unconstitutional.

Justices Warren Burger, William Rehnquist, and O'Connor filed dissenting opinions. Burger maintained that the decision would deny remedial services to innumerable students in desperate need of them. Rehnquist stated that the Court has created a theory in which aid must be supervised to make sure there is no entanglement, but that the supervision constitutes entanglement. O'Connor averred that there is not a single shred of evidence that in the 14 years of the program, any teacher in it attempted to advance religion in any way. Further, she believed the degree of supervision necessary has been exaggerated. *See also: Agostini v. Felton;* Government Aid to Religious Schools; *Lemon v. Kurtzman* and *Earley v. DiCenso.*

Further Reading: *Agostini v. Felton,* 521 U.S. 203 (1997); *Aguilar v. Felton,* 473 U.S. 402 (1985); *Lemon v. Kurtzman,* 403 U.S. 602 (1971).

Mary Angela Shaughnessy

Alliance Defense Fund

The Alliance Defense Fund (ADF) is a Christian legal organization whose purpose, according to its Web site, is to provide "the resources that will keep the door open for the spread of the Gospel through the legal defense and advocacy of religious freedom, the sanctity of human life, and traditional family values." It began in 1994 as a concerted effort by leaders of over three-dozen ministries who came together to found ADF. They believed that the sort of religion practiced, and political causes advanced, by evangelical Protestants and traditional Catholics were not being adequately advocated in the legal arena. Among the ministry leaders present at that meeting were Bill Bright (Campus Crusade for Christ), Larry Burkett (Crown Financial Ministries), James Dobson (Focus on the Family), D. James Kennedy (Coral Ridge Ministries), and Marlin Maddoux (*Point of View* Radio Program), a virtual who's who of leading religious conservatives.

ADF's founding President, CEO, and General Counsel is Alan Sears, a graduate of the University of Kentucky (B.A.) and the University of Louisville's Louis D. Brandeis School of Law (J.D.). A former Southern Baptist who converted to Catholicism, Sears has directed a multifaceted strategy that includes funding, litigation, a continuing education program for attorneys (National Litigation Academy), and a summer program for law students (The Blackstone Fellowship).

ADF has provided funding for over 2,000 cases and has litigated or assisted in scores of others including 33 victories before the U.S. Supreme Court as of 2007. Soon after its inception in 1994, ADF-funded parties won in the Supreme Court cases of *Rosenberger v. Rector and Visitors of the University of Virginia* (1995) and *Hurley v. Irish-American Gay, Lesbian, and Bisexual Group of Boston* (1995). Both are considered significant religious liberty cases, especially because of the role they played in subsequent landmark cases. The concept of "viewpoint discrimination" that played a pivotal role in the Court's opinion in *Rosenberger* was instrumental in the Court's opinion in *Good News Club v. Milford School District* (2001), in which the Court held that an after-school Christian group could not be prohibited from using public school facilities if they are being used as a limited public forum for the benefit of other after-school groups. The reasoning in *Hurley* was employed by the Court in its upholding of the right of the Boy Scouts of America to exclude homosexual scoutmasters on religious grounds in *Boy Scouts of America v. Dale* (2000).

In addition to *Rosenberger* and *Good News Club*, other public education U.S. Supreme Court cases in which ADF has been involved include *Zelman v. Simmons-Harris* (2002), in which the Court held that an Ohio voucher program may include religious schools without violating establishment clause; *Adler v. Duval County School Board* (2001), in which the Court declined to hear an appeal from the Eleventh Circuit Court of Appeals that upheld students' right to pray and discuss their faith at commencement exercises; and *Mitchell v. Helms* (2000), in which the Court ruled that direct government support of private schools including religious schools does not violate no-establishment clause of the First Amendment.

Through the National Litigation Academy (NLA), ADF trains attorneys in the areas of religious liberty, the sanctity of human life, and traditional family values. ADF offers the training free of charge and, according to its Web site, "each attorney makes a faith commitment to provide 450 hours of pro-bono time to the Body of Christ." Between 1997 and 2007, over 1,000 attorneys have graduated from the NLA, and they have provided over $70 million worth of legal work free of charge.

The Blackstone Fellowship (TBF) is a nine-week summer program for outstanding law students (mostly those who have just completed their first year of law school). The program consists of two parts: (1) a multiweek session consisting of lectures by a wide range of writers and thinkers, including university professors, attorneys, ministers, and policy analysts; and (2) several weeks of practical legal work in a variety of different venues, including law firms, think tanks, and ministries. It is a competitive program that accepted only 99 law students in 2007. Between 2000 and 2007, TBF has trained over 600 students. All are committed Christians from a variety of law schools and Christian traditions, including Baptist, Anglican, Presbyterian, Methodist, Catholic, Orthodox, Disciples of Christ, and Free Church. The purpose of TBF is to create a brain trust of exceptional Christian legal minds to become tomorrow's leaders in culture, business, the academy, politics, and law. *See also: Good News Club v. Milford Central School.*

Further Reading: Alliance Defense Fund, at alliancedefensefund.org; Hans J. Hacker, *The Culture of Conservative Christian Litigation* (Lanham, MD: Rowman & Littlefield, 2005); Jordan W. Lorence, Alan E. Sears, and Benjamin W. Bull, "No Official High or Petty: The Unnecessary, Unwise, and Unconstitutional Trend of Prescribing Viewpoint Orthodoxy in Mandatory Continuing Legal Education," *South Texas Law Review* 44 (Winter 2002): 263–295; Alan Sears and Craig Osten, *The Homosexual Agenda: Exposing the Principle Threat to Religious Freedom Today Values* (Nashville, TN: B & H Publishing Group, 2003); Alan Sears and Craig Osten, *The ACLU vs. America: Exposing the Agenda to Redefine Moral Values* (Nashville, TN: B & H Publishing Group, 2005); Jeffery J. Ventrella, "Square Circles?!! Restoring Rationality to the Same-Sex 'Marriage' Debate," *Hastings Constitutional Law Quarterly* 32 (Fall 2004/Winter 2005): 681–736.

Francis J. Beckwith

Alliance for the Separation of School & State

Founded in 1994 by Marshall Fritz, who served as Chairman of the Board until his death in 2008, the Alliance for the Separation of School & State is a nonprofit organization of a libertarian persuasion headquartered in Fresno, California, that advocates ending local, state, and federal government involvement of any kind in schooling. This would involve "repealing the compulsion of financing, attendance, content, and state regulation of teachers and institutions that are central to today's 'public schooling.'" The Alliance claims on its Web site a twofold mission: (1) "Show people how government wrested control of education from citizens and why it is so detrimental to freedom," and (2) "Show parents and others how they can take back their freedom and ensure a bright future for their children and our country" (Alliance for the Separation of School & State, at www.schoolandstate.org).

Best known for its pledge, "I proclaim publicly that I favor ending government involvement in education," the Alliance lists over 29,000 signers, including members of various religious groups, homeschool advocates, local talk show hosts, libertarian activists and writers, policy wonks, and a few academics. Better known signatories include D. James Kennedy, the late senior pastor of Coral Ridge Presbyterian Church; Marvin Olasky, a University of Texas professor and editor of *World* magazine; Mary Pride, homeschool advocate and author of *The Big Book of Home Learning;* Ed Crane, president of the Cato Institute; and John Taylor Gatto, New York State Teacher of the Year in 1991 and author of *The Underground History of American Education.* Those who take the pledge commit themselves to the proposition that parents, not the state, should be responsible for the education of their children.

The Alliance asserts that public schools are a "bundle of problems." Besides low academic achievement, it points to violence, cheating, bullying, immorality, drug use, and clashes of worldviews. The primary cause is government control, and the solution is for the government to get out of the schooling business and to return to something like the educational configuration that existed before the creation of state common school systems in the mid-1800s. Alliance members oppose charter schools and tax-funded vouchers on the view that, though these reforms are touted as ways to enhance competition and thus improve education, they in fact encourage family dependency on the government. If school and state were separated, the Alliance claims that the approximately $500 billion currently (2007) spent on public education could be used for a massive tax cut that would enable most Americans to purchase the kind of education they desire for their children from a variety of institutions, organizations, and individuals. Charitable giving would assist the minority of parents who could not cover tuition costs involved in what Fritz calls "Free Market Schooling." As the Alliance founder states:

> Free Market Schooling respects the rights of parents to choose the form, degree, and content of schooling they believe is best for their children. Children are not conceived by the state; they are not mere creatures of the state; they should not be fed, churched, clothed, entertained, or educated by the state. (Alliance for the Separation of School & State, at www.schoolandstate.org)

Though not a religious organization *per se,* the Alliance boasts a number of conservative Christian, Jewish, and Muslim supporters and includes on its Web site "A Special Word to

Parents of Faith." Here a collection of quotations drives home the point that education conveys a worldview and that parents of faith should realize that the state school inculcates a "man-centered" not a "God-centered" worldview. Fritz, who was once deeply involved in Christian education, believes that Christian parents should be just as concerned with what is taught in Monday through Friday school as they are with what is taught in Sunday school. Furthermore, he argues, the state has no more business determining the nature of weekday education than it does Sunday education because worldview formation is none of the government's business.

The organization provides resources to interested parties via its Web site and Alliance e-Notes. The Web site provides examples of problems in the public schools, arguments for separation (mostly of a market or moral nature), information about the pledge and a list of signers, stories of families who declared independence from the government school system, quotations, school statistics, and resources. Among the resources are books by libertarians, such as Murray Rothbard, and conservative Christians, such as E. Ray Moore, Jr., Director of the Exodus Mandate Project, and Bruce N. Shortt, an activist in the Southern Baptist Convention, who maintain that Christian parents should remove their children from the "godless" government schools. *See also:* Separation of Church and State/Wall of Separation between Church and State; Southern Baptists and Education.

Further Reading: Alliance for the Separation of School & State, at www.schoolandstate.org; James C. Carper and Thomas C. Hunt, *The Dissenting Tradition in American Education* (New York: Peter Lang, 2007); E. Ray Moore, Jr., *Let My Children Go* (Columbia, SC: Gilead Media, 2002); Sheldon Richman, *Separating School & State: How to Liberate America's Families* (Fairfax, VA: The Future of Freedom Foundation, 1994); Bruce N. Shortt, *The Harsh Truth About Public Schools* (Vallecito, CA: Chalcedon Foundation, 2004).

James C. Carper

American Academy of Religion

Founded in 1909, the American Academy of Religion (AAR) is the world's largest association of academics who research or teach topics related to religion. There are over 9,000 members composed largely of faculty at colleges, universities, and divinity schools in North America with a growing number from institutions of higher education in Asia, Africa, and Europe.

In addition to teaching about religion in higher educational contexts, the AAR has been involved in several initiatives related to promoting the study of religion in public schools in the United States. There are two discernible chronological phases to these efforts: 1974 to 1980 and 2000 to the present.

In 1973, religious studies scholar Nicholas Piediscalzi was approached by the AAR leadership to conduct a consultation on "Teaching about Religion in the Public Schools" to be held at the 1974 Annual Meeting. Participants heard reports about a variety of efforts to introduce the study of religion in the nation's schools. At the conclusion of the consultation, those in attendance voted to petition the AAR Board to authorize the formation of a working group to address these issues in an ongoing manner. The Board approved this request, and the "Working Group on Religion Studies in Public Education" was formed for a four-year term and conducted its first session at the 1975 Annual Meeting.

The working group constructed a four-year agenda to study the following dimensions of religious studies and public education: (1) the distinction between moral education and the study of religion; (2) religious studies as a separate discipline within public education; (3) professional programs in public education and religion studies (PERS); and (4) differing paradigms for PERS. The group published three volumes over a five-year period that were used by teachers, administrators, and scholars to educate public school teachers and the broader public about the resources available for teaching about religion in the schools from a nonsectarian perspective. AAR scholars on the working group also helped to create curricular materials at Pennsylvania State University, Florida State University, and the World Religions Curriculum Development Center in Minneapolis; establish graduate programs in PERS at Harvard Divinity School, Western Michigan University, the University of Kansas, and Wright State University; found state PERS committees to articulate policy guidelines and standards for school boards in Illinois, Iowa, Kansas, Michigan, Minnesota, North Carolina, Ohio, and Wisconsin; and establish or further support PERS centers such as the Public Education Religion Studies Center at Wright State University, the Kansas Center for Public Education Religion Studies, the Center for Public Education Religion Studies at San Diego State University, and the National Council on Religion and Public Education.

In spite of these early successes, most of the initiatives outlined above ended by the early 1980s. There are several reasons for this, but most can be captured under the twin umbrellas of unanticipated political controversies related to teaching about religion from a nonsectarian perspective and the failure of AAR religious studies scholars to work in coalition with other interested and affected parties such as teacher educators, public policy experts, and public school teachers themselves. As a result, many of these earlier efforts were politically and/or structurally unsustainable. This situation caused Nicholas Piediscalzi to lament in 1991 that, "All the activities of this [earlier] period and most of the materials produced are virtually unknown today" (Piediscalzi, 1991, p. 242).

Though members of the AAR continued to engage in the ongoing issues regarding religious studies and education throughout the 1980s and 1990s, the AAR itself did not play a leadership role in the way it did in the mid-1970s. The "Working Group on Religion Studies and Public Education" ended and issues related to religion and public education were taken up by the standing "Committee on Education and the Study of Religion" that also focused on higher educational contexts. Most of the efforts to promote teaching about religion in public schools between 1980 and 2000 were spearheaded by professional organizations such as the National Council for the Social Studies and think tanks such as the First Amendment Center.

In 2000, scholars helped to establish another dedicated group within the AAR aimed at focusing on religious studies in precollege contexts. They successfully proposed the creation of the "Religion in the Schools Task Force" charged with making "proposals to the Academy for initiatives...contributing to teaching about religion in the schools" (www.aarweb.org). In 2007 the Board approved a task force proposal for the creation of an AAR working group to construct a set of content and skill guidelines for teaching about religion in public schools across the K–12 spectrum. Learning from its past history, members of the task force are working with teachers and professional educational organizations to construct these guidelines in ways that will be most helpful for educators in the field. The guidelines are scheduled to be completed in 2010. *See also:* National Council for the Social Studies; National Council on Religion and Public Education.

Further Reading: American Academy of Religion, at www.aarweb.org; Anne Carr and Nicholas Piediscalzi, eds., *The Academic Study of Religion: 1975 Public Schools Religion Studies* (Missoula, MT: Scholars Press, 1975); Nicholas Piediscalzi, "Back to the Future? Public Education Religion Studies and the AAR in the 1970s and 1990s—Unique Opportunities for Development," *Religion and Public Education* 18 (Spring 1991): 237–251; Nicholas Piediscalzi and Barbara De Martino Swyhart, eds., *Distinguishing Moral Education, Values Clarification and Religion-Studies* (Missoula, MT: Scholars Press, 1976); "Religion in the Schools," at www.aarweb.org; "Religion in the Schools Task Force," at www.aarweb.org; Paul J. Will, ed., *Public Education Religion Studies: An Overview* (Chico, CA: Scholars Press, 1981).

Diane L. Moore

American Association of School Administrators

The American Association of School Administrators (AASA) was founded in 1865. It is a professional organization of more than 12,000 educational leaders. Most, but not all, members are superintendents of public schools, but others are other senior-level school administrators. The current executive director is Paul Houston.

The stated mission of the AASA is "to support and develop effective school system leaders who are dedicated to the highest quality public education for all children." AASA advances its mission by providing professional development for its members and engaging in public advocacy for public education. Both the state and the national offices engage in lobbying. Its current goals are the following:

To grow the organization by increasing membership and other revenue, using resources more effectively and "telling the AASA story" better to internal and external audiences;

To lead and shape the dialogue regarding the improvement of public education by advancing the Stand Up for Public Education™ campaign, taking a proactive lead on the reauthorization of the Elementary and Secondary Education Act, and advancing the primacy of the superintendent in school district leadership;

To enhance the competence of the superintendent and other school system leaders by developing and delivering high-quality professional development programs and developing new standards for school system leaders; and

To become the "go to" organization for superintendents by being a primary resource for hot topics related to school leadership and providing customized support to members. (American Association of School Administrators at www.aasa.org)

AASA has affiliate relationships with 49 state administrator associations, the Canadian Association of School Administrators, and the Association for the Advancement of International Education. Although not an affiliate, AASA has a long relationship with the New England Association of School Superintendents. State organizations are fairly autonomous. AASA is governed by an elected Governing Board and Executive Committee. AASA Bylaws, Beliefs and Position Statements are the primary documents that describe AASA's structure and reflect the organization's philosophy and approach to major issues in education. They are developed through the Beliefs and Positions Sub-Committee of the Executive Committee. Following review by the Executive Committee, these documents are voted on by the Governing Board. State organizations typically follow a similar procedure to develop policy positions for the state affiliates. The direction and focus of

AASA's advocacy is dictated by these policy documents. AASA's position statements regarding religion and schools include the following:

Position Statement 8: OPPOSITION TO VOUCHERS

AASA absolutely opposes undermining universal equal educational opportunity for all, supports the separation of church and state in public school funding, and opposes increasing the segregation of America's children by diverting public funds in support of vouchers and related initiatives.

AASA supports the application of public school academic accountability standards and regulatory requirements to all nonpublic schools receiving public funds.

AASA opposes local, state, and federal financial incentives that reward private corporations for supporting nonpublic school entities.

Position Statement 9: PUBLIC SCHOOL CHOICE AND CHARTER SCHOOLS

AASA supports public school choice and charter schools that operate under the auspices of local public school boards. AASA believes that there should be a level playing field, including nondiscriminatory and unconditional enrollment for all children. Therefore, the same regulations and accountability should apply to all schools receiving public funding. How charter schools are financed must be addressed so that their creation does not have an adverse effect on the quality of existing public schools.

Position Statement 11: VOUCHERS AND TUITION TAX CREDITS

AASA opposes vouchers and all forms of tuition tax credits for private or sectarian schools. We believe government-financed vouchers divert funds from public schools.

AASA primarily engages in advocacy on the issues within the position statements as adopted within the governance structure. As such, AASA is a leader in the debate on school vouchers and school choice. AASA joined in an *amicus* brief in the Supreme Court voucher case, *Zelman v. Simmons-Harris* (2002). AASA also led the effort to challenge the voucher program in the State of Florida. AASA was one of the eighteen cosigners of the document, *The Bible & Public Schools: A First Amendment Guide* (1999). This document represents accord on the general approach to religion in the schools.

On one end of the spectrum of opinion regarding the place of religion in public education are those who advocate what might be called the "sacred public school" where one religion (theirs) is preferred in school practices and policies. Characteristic of the early history of public education, this unconstitutional approach still survives in some school districts. In more recent decades, there are those on the other end of the spectrum who push for what looks to some like a "religion-free zone" where religion is largely ignored in public schools.

According to the *Guide:*

The sponsors of this guide reject both of these models and offer another approach—one in which public schools neither inculcate nor inhibit religion but become places where religion and religious conviction are treated with fairness and respect. In this third model, public schools protect the religious-liberty rights of students of all faiths or none. And schools ensure that the curriculum includes study *about* religion as an important part of a complete education. This is a vision of public education that is both consistent with First Amendment principles and broadly supported by many educational and religious organizations. (First Amendment Center, at www.firstamendmentcenter.org)

AASA is much more active in general advocacy for public education. Its most recent campaign, Stand Up for Education, states its goals as follows:

To increase awareness of the good news about public education among the public, the news media, and policy makers;

To empower school leaders to positively influence the dialogue about public education, respond to misinformation concerning public education, and maintain public support to continue improving education for each child; and

To advocate for three fundamental principles of public schooling: getting children ready for school; getting schools ready for children; and getting children ready for democracy. (www.aasa.org)

See also: Common Ground Documents; School Choice; Tuition Tax Credits; Vouchers.

Further Reading: Kate Beem, "Caught in the Middle," *The School Administrator* 23 (October 2006): 16–20; Melissa Deckman, "Governing with the Christian Right," *The School Administrator* 63 (October 2006): 26–30; Paul Houston, "Good News and Bad," *Phi Delta Kappan* 86 (October 2005): 496; Colby M. May, "Religion's Legal Place in the Schoolhouse," *The School Administrator* 63 (October 2006): 32–36.

Julie Underwood

American Center for Law and Justice

The American Center for Law and Justice (ACLJ) is a nonprofit public interest law firm and educational organization. It was founded in 1990 by evangelical leader Pat Robertson, who conceived and named it as a conservative counterweight to the American Civil Liberties Union (ACLU). The work of ACLJ is predicated upon the concept that "freedom and democracy are God-given, inalienable rights" and is dedicated to protecting religious and constitutional freedoms (American Center for Law and Justice, at www.aclj.org). It provides legal services for clients involved in an array of issues important to conservative Christians, including free speech for pro-life demonstrators, support for "traditional marriage," and the rights of religious people in the workplace and at school. The firm is led by Chief Counsel Jay Sekulow, who hosts a weekly television show and a daily radio show that reaches 1.5 million listeners on 550 stations nationwide, from which he often learns of potential test cases. He has presented oral arguments before the U.S. Supreme Court more than a dozen times. In 2006, the ACLJ received over $10 million in contributions.

The ACLJ Web site contends that "perhaps more than any other arenas, Christians find that their values and beliefs are under continual attack in the public schools." Sekulow and his legal team combat this perceived attack by arguing for, among other things, the teaching of Intelligent Design in science classrooms, "opt out rights" that excuse students from classes that interfere with their religious beliefs, school vouchers used to send students to religious schools, and an expansion of free speech rights that can allow for student-led prayer, evangelizing, and Bible clubs in the schools.

In ACLJ's first major Supreme Court case, the precedent-setting *Westside Board of Education v. Mergens* (1990), Sekulow argued that public schools must allow religiously affiliated clubs to meet after school hours if they extended that privilege to other noncurricular clubs. He also demonstrated what would become his trademark strategy, framing what would have previously been argued as a freedom of religion case as a freedom of speech case instead (Sekulow has been known to argue similar cases without even mentioning religion). This approach produced the result the evangelical movement desired: Justice Sandra Day O'Connor wrote for the majority that "There is a crucial difference between government speech endorsing religion, which the Establishment Clause prohibits, and private speech endorsing religion, which the Free Speech and Free Exercise Clauses protect." The ACLJ interpreted the Court's decision as a "chance for students to share the Gospel with their peers" (www.aclj.org).

Lamb's Chapel v. Center Moriches School District (1993), another of Sekulow's early successes in the Supreme Court, proceeded along similar lines. He secured the right of a church group to use public school facilities for the screening of a religiously based film after school hours by asserting that free speech guarantees religious speakers the same rights as nonreligious speakers. The Court was unanimous in its decision that religious groups could not be excluded from facilities that were open to nonreligious groups. The ACLJ published a letter after its victory in this case reminding Christians that the schools provide a precious opportunity to "[carry] Christianity into the fray where it can go head-to-head with other world views" and to "demonstrate its intellectual and practical superiority" (www.aclj.org).

The ACLJ has been an active contributor of *amicus curiae* briefs to the Supreme Court. In an instructive and unusual example, the ACLJ filed an *amicus* alongside the ACLU in *Morse v. Frederick* (2007) in support of the constitutional right of Frederick, a high school student, to raise a banner across the school grounds that reads "Bong Hits 4 Jesus." Sekulow explained that curtailment of Frederick's right to speech in this case could ultimately diminish the rights of religious students who desired to express a "pro-life or pro-family position." Thus the ACLJ's argument, though exceptional in its partnership with the ACLU and its opposition to the Bush administration, was consistent with its long-standing commitment to a robust freedom of speech.

While the ACLJ is best known for its litigious efforts on behalf of conservative Christians, it is important to note that it also bills itself as an educational organization and exerts broad influence in myriad other ways. In relation to the schools, it provides encouragement and resources for parents to advocate against sex education that sanctions homosexuality or other "amoralities," to support the teaching of Intelligent Design, and to prevent "New Age" practices or anything "related to the occult, such as visualizing conversations with dead historical figures, chanting a mantra-like slogan, practicing any form of meditation, and so on" (www.aclj.org). The ACLJ asserted political influence through Sekulow's high-level involvement in the second Bush administration, as demonstrated by his role as one of the men Bush tapped to oversee the nomination and confirmation processes for Supreme Court nominees John Roberts and Samuel Alito. The organization also enjoys close ties to Pat Robertson and his Regent Law School, where Sekulow has taught classes and from which the ACLJ draws broad legal support. *See also*: *Board of Education of the Westside Community Schools v. Mergens*; *Lamb's Chapel v. Center Moriches Union Free School District*.

Further Reading: American Center for Law and Justice, at www.aclj.org; *Lamb's Chapel v. Center Moriches School District,* 508 U.S. 384 (1993); Jeffrey Toobin, *The Nine: Inside the Secret World of the Supreme Court* (New York: Doubleday, 2007); *Westside Community Board Of Education v. Mergens,* 496 U.S. 226 (1990).

Shipley Robertson Salewski

American Civil Liberties Union

The American Civil Liberties Union (ACLU) was founded in 1920 as a small group of civil liberties activists, including Roger Baldwin, Crystal Eastman, and Albert DeSilver. Its membership has grown to over 500,000 members. The ACLU is supported by annual dues and contributions from its members, plus grants from private foundations. It receives no government funds.

The ACLU is a nonprofit and nonpartisan organization dedicated to protecting individuals' civil liberties. The work embodies the core belief that if the rights of society's most vulnerable members are denied, everybody's rights are imperiled. The ACLU is attuned to the rights of individuals who have traditionally been marginalized, including people of color; the lesbian, gay, bisexual, and transgender community; women; mental-health patients; prisoners; people with disabilities; and the poor. The mission of the ACLU is to preserve all of these protections and guarantees:

Your First Amendment rights—freedom of speech, association and assembly, freedom of the press, and freedom of religion supported by the strict separation of church and state;

Your right to equal protection under the law—equal treatment regardless of race, sex, religion, or national origin;

Your right to due process—fair treatment by the government whenever the loss of your liberty or property is at stake; and

Your right to privacy—freedom from unwarranted government intrusion into your personal and private affairs. (American Civil Liberties Union, at www.aclu.org)

The national headquarters of the ACLU is located in New York City. Currently, the leadership of the ACLU includes Executive Director Anthony D. Romero and President Nadine Strossen. The national board of directors consists of representatives elected by each state affiliate as well as at-large delegates elected by boards of each affiliate. Each state affiliate has an executive director and a board of directors.

The organization does most of its work through 53 locally based affiliates and associated chapters, each of which has a staff and a board of directors. The affiliates generally correspond to state (or equivalent) lines; Washington, D.C. and Puerto Rico each have an affiliate, California has three affiliates, Pennsylvania has two, Missouri has two (one combined with Kansas), and The Dakotas share one. These affiliates maintain a certain amount of governing autonomy from the national organization and are able to work independently from each other, if they choose to do so. Many of the ACLU's cases originate or are handled from the local level and are also handled by local lawyers from the individual affiliates.

The ACLU's most visible work is in litigation. At a national level ACLU handles over 6,000 cases a year in actual litigation, and thousands more situations are handled through less formal negotiations. This work is carried out primarily through the affiliates. For example, in a 20-month period beginning January 2004, the ACLU's New Jersey affiliate was involved in 51 cases according to its annual report—35 cases in state courts, and 16 in federal court. The New Jersey affiliate provided legal representation in 33 of those cases, and served as *amicus* in the remaining 18. They listed 44 volunteer attorneys who assisted them in those cases.

The work of the ACLU includes public information, local organizing, lobbying, and litigation. Some of the lobbying, federal and state, is organized by the "Action Network." Over 200,000 individuals are members of this network. The Network provides information and support, including "toolkits" for individuals to become involved in various civil liberties activities. The Network Web site includes success stories, including:

> Action Network members took action on the proposed Workplace Religious Freedom Act and helped stop it from passing. If it had made it into law, it would have strengthened the hand of police officers who want to pick and choose who they will protect, and emergency health care workers and mental health counselors who could abandon patients because their care conflicts with the worker's religious beliefs. The strong action taken by Action Network members helped stopped this proposed legislation cold. (www.aclu.org)

The ACLU is no stranger to taking controversial stances. It has defended organizations as diverse as the Ku Klux Klan and the pro-gun ownership group Second Amendment Foundation. Often, its clients are notoriously unpopular such as neo-Nazi organizations and the North American Man/Boy Love Association (NAMBLA), a group which supports lifting all age restrictions on pederasty. In the case of NAMBLA, the ACLU's Massachusetts affiliate defended the organization, on First Amendment grounds, against murder charges that were based solely on the fact that a man who raped and murdered a child had visited the NAMBLA Web site. Although the ACLU has clarified that it does not endorse NAMBLA's message, its defense of the group has been widely criticized. In particular, the ACLU's defense of NAMBLA came under intense criticism when the former president of the Virginia chapter of the ACLU was arrested on pedophilia charges.

The ACLU has long been a leader in the area of religious issues. The ACLU has been involved in many recent Supreme Court cases involving religious issues in the education context. For example, they have filed briefs in all of the following cases:

- *Elk Grove U.S.D. v. Newdow* (2004)—school district policy requiring teachers to lead classrooms in the Pledge of Allegiance;
- *Locke v. Davey* (2004)—state law prohibiting use of state college/university scholarship funds for students seeking pastoral degrees; and
- *Zelman v. Simmons-Harris* (2002)—state-funded vouchers for parents to send their children to religious schools.

The ACLU supports strict separation of church and state. It also advocates, however, for individuals' rights to religious freedom and free speech. In some situations this may appear as if they are arguing contrary positions. For example, in one case the ACLU filed suit alleging that the school district violated the First Amendment when it allowed a student to give a religious message during a high school graduation speech. On the other hand, the ACLU supported a student's right to sing "Awesome God" in a school talent show (www.aclu.org). *See also:* First Amendment Religious Clauses and the Supreme Court; Separation of Church and State/Wall of Separation between Church and State.

Further Reading: American Civil Liberties Union, at www.aclu.org; Rob Boston, "Invocation Confrontation," *Church & State* 60 (May 2007): 11–12; Samuel Francis, "ACLU Would Ban the Free Exercise of Religion in Alabama," *Human Events* 54 (May 1998): 10; LaTonya Taylor, "ACLU Fight Church Restrictions," *Christianity Today* 46 (June 2002): 15.

Julie Underwood

American Family Association

Originally the National Federation for Decency, The American Family Association (AFA) is a nonprofit organization founded in 1977 by United Methodist minister and evangelical leader Donald Wildmon. As the early "Decency" appellation suggests, the AFA was conceived of as an organization dedicated to fighting obscenity, especially focusing on the "normalization" of premarital and extramarital sex by the entertainment industry. Its stated mission now reflects a broader concern to "motivate and equip citizens to change the culture to reflect Biblical truth" (American Family Association, at www.afa.net). To this end, the group promotes activism among its members, organizing letter-writing campaigns, leading rallies and boycotts, and producing and disseminating materials in support of its positions. The AFA also sponsors American Family Radio, which owns 200 stations and is broadcast on 1,200 others; the AFA Foundation, which promotes "Biblical stewardship" and provides resources on charitable giving and estate planning for Christians; the *AFA Journal,* a monthly publication with a circulation of 180,000; and the Center for Law and Policy, a legal arm that represents and supports Christians in First Amendment cases and lobbies against pornography and obscenity. In 2006 it received more than $16 million in contributions, had assets of about $34 million, and claimed a half million members. The organization made headlines in 1998 when CyberPatrol, a popular Internet filtering software, blocked the AFA Web site on grounds of "intolerance" for its statements about gay and lesbian people.

The AFA's major concern in the public schools has been the right of parents to determine what students are taught about human sexuality. It refutes the value of sex education programs that address premarital sex and homosexuality, which it believes promote "pagan sexuality" (www.afa.net). In 2003, the AFA criticized a Pennsylvania high school Gay-Straight Alliance for its attempts to make the school a "safe" place for Gay, Lesbian, Bisexual, Transgender and Questioning (GLBTQ) youth. Steve Crampton, chief counsel, said that safe spaces for GLBTQ youth effectively constitute discrimination against youth with antigay religious convictions, arguing that such places could "violate free speech and stifle open discussions about homosexuality." The AFA usually contests the validity of strict church-state separation in the schools. In 2000, however, when the AFA filed suit in a federal court to impede a Massachusetts school district from supporting a series of tolerance-themed events entitled "Respecting Differences" (timed to coincide with "Coming Out Week"), it made the opposite claim: Crampton argued that because the event was cosponsored by several churches, the schools' involvement violated church-state separation. The motion was rejected by the court.

The AFA's concerns with sex education sometimes extend more broadly into the arena of multiculturalism, which it charges with rendering children incapable of moral decision making. It claims that multiple perspectives threaten to "produce moral confusion and cognitive dissonance" and "desensitize children to contrary values." In 1991, the AFA filed suit against a California school district for its use of the multicultural *Impressions* curriculum, which it accused of promoting witchcraft and humanism. Though the courts rejected these claims, the publisher (Holt) decided to discontinue the series, in spite of widespread praise from educators, in order to avert other legal battles. Other AFA activities related to education include the campaign to place "In God We Trust" posters in every public school classroom and similar efforts to link its theological claims with patriotism.

The AFA rose in political prominence during the second Bush administration when Wildmon was one of several evangelical leaders who participated in weekly calls with Tim Goeglein, top aide to Karl Rove. During this time he was also a leading member of the Arlington Group, a network of conservative activists working against gay marriage ("Christian Soldiers," *National Journal,* 2004). The AFA counts among its allies the Alliance Defense Fund and the American Center for Law and Justice, and Crampton sits on the Board of the National Council of Bible Curriculum in Public Schools. *See also:* Alliance Defense Fund; American Center for Law and Justice; Sex Education and Religion.

Further Reading: American Family Association, at www.afa.net; "Group: Gay Student Club Actions May Discriminate Against Others," *AP State and Local Wire,* July 29, 2003; Farah Stockman, "Schools Defend Tolerance Program," *Boston Globe,* October 13, 2000, sec. B, p. 3; Peter H. Stone and Bara Vaida, "Christian Soldiers," *National Journal,* 36 (December 2004): 3596–3603.

Shipley Robertson Salewski

American Federation of Teachers

The American Federation of Teachers (AFT) was founded in 1916 as a labor union advocating for the economic and professional interests of classroom teachers. It is an affiliate of the AFL-CIO and has over 3,000 local chapters, 43 state affiliates, and approximately 1.4 million members that are mainly concentrated in large urban areas. Membership includes K–12 classroom teachers, paraprofessionals and school-related personnel, higher education faculty and staff, nurses and other health care professionals, and government employees. The union is governed by elected officers and delegates and holds biennial conventions where leaders are elected, policy is formulated, and resolutions are passed on a variety of political and professional issues. The mission statement reads as follows:

> The mission of the American Federation of Teachers, AFL-CIO, is to improve the lives of our members and their families, to give voice to their legitimate professional, economic and social aspirations, to strengthen the institutions in which we work, to improve the quality of the services we provide, to bring together all members to assist and support one another and to promote democracy, human rights and freedom in our union, in our nation and throughout the world. (American Federation of Teachers, at www.aft.org)

In relationship to religion and education, the AFT supports teaching about religion in public schools and the free expression of religious beliefs of students within constitutional guidelines. These stances are represented by the AFT endorsement of "A Teacher's Guide to Religion in the Public Schools" published by the First Amendment Center in 1999. The only other issue related to religion and education that the AFT has substantively addressed is vouchers, which it has consistently opposed. Though it supports the right of parents to send their children to religious schools, it opposes the use of public funds to do so. According to the AFT:

> The main reason for this opposition is because public funding of private or religious education transfers precious tax dollars from public schools, which are free and open to all children, accountable to parents and taxpayers alike, and essential to our democracy, to private and religious schools that charge for their services, select their students on the basis of religious or academic or family or personal characteristics, and are accountable only to their boards and clients. (AFT, 2001)

See also: Common Ground Documents; National Education Association.

Further Reading: American Federation of Teachers, at www.aft.org; American Federation of Teachers, "The Many Names of School Vouchers" (2001), at www.aft.org; American Federation of Teachers, "School Vouchers: The Research Track Record" (2005), at www.aft.org; First Amendment Center, "A Teacher's Guide to Religion in the Public Schools" (Washington, DC: First Amendment Center, 1999).

Diane L. Moore

American Jewish Congress

The American Jewish Congress (AJC) is a voluntary, privately funded association founded in 1918 by Zionist and Jewish immigrant groups dedicated to defending the freedoms and rights of Jews and other minorities in the United States and to supporting the creation of the State of Israel. The AJC is a major spokesgroup on education issues, protecting students from discrimination, and anti-Israeli and anti-Jewish curricula and behaviors.

AJC has become, in its own words:

> a ferocious defender of religious liberty and the "separation of Church and State"—now becoming among the nation's foremost advocates in the Supreme Court of the United States for protecting religious rights and why we never are afraid to speak out against those (whether friend or foe) who attack those rights. (American Jewish Congress, at ajcongress.org)

Affiliated with the Council of World Jewry, the headquarters of the American Jewish Congress is located in New York City, and has five regional offices throughout the United States and an office in Jerusalem.

Illustrative of its position on church and state issues is AJC's response to cases involving teaching biblical versions of creation, often called "creationism," versus the Darwinian "scientific" approach. In a 1984 statement about curriculum in Texas, for example, the AJC's Nina Cortell explained:

> Our appearance at this hearing today arises from our concern that Proclamation 60 (both alone and together with Board Rule 5 abrogates the Establishment Clause in three fundamental

ways: (1) an omission of any reference to the Darwinian theory of evolution; (2) the Board Rule's requirement that evolution be singled out for a special negative treatment not required in connection with the teaching of any other scientific theory; and (3) the proposed textbook standards allow for the teaching of scientific creationism. (ajcongress.org)

Recently, the AJC objected to Georgia's inclusion of a sticker in public school science books advising readers to scrutinize evolution and treat it as a theory not a fact.

In addition to its concerns about place of religion in the public school curriculum, government aid to religious schools that the AJC believes blurs the line between religion and government has long occupied the organization. Voucher programs are a case in point. The AJC asserts:

> We believe that vouchers erode the principle of church/state separation, and that the funds which the use of vouchers would divert to religious and other private schools could be put to better advantage for all of our children by being used for enriching and revitalizing the public schools. (ajcongress.org)

The AJC embraces a "strict separationist" interpretation of the "no establishment" clause, which it advocates in legislative hearings and in briefs filed with the courts on major First Amendment cases. It also maintains a useful summary of court cases regarding religious practices in the public schools on its Web site. *See also:* Jewish Schools; Torah Umesorah (National Society for Hebrew Day Schools).

Further Reading: American Jewish Congress, at ajcongress.org.

Bruce S. Cooper

American Protective Association

The American Protective Association (APA) was founded on Sunday afternoon, March 3, 1887, in Clinton, Iowa. Henry F. Bowers was the lead organizer of this group that became known as the "new Know-Nothingism." Begun to a considerable extent as a reaction to the growing power of Roman Catholicism in the politics of the nation's large cities and in labor organizations, the APA experienced its largest success in Midwestern states and in eastern cities, such as Boston.

APA members took an oath in which they swore not to employ a Roman Catholic when a Protestant was available, swore never to go on strike with a Roman Catholic, pledged their opposition to a Roman Catholic who would run for political office, and vowed not to vote for a Roman Catholic candidate for office. The APA was fearful of the growing presence of Catholic schools in the nation, which they considered to be "un-American" and devoted primarily to the Vatican. Catholic schools had received considerable impetus from the Third Plenary Council of Baltimore in 1884. The APA viewed with alarm the visit of Archbishop Francis Satolli, the personal representative of Pope Leo XIII, to the American Archbishops on the school question, in 1892. Likewise they worried over the compromise with public education proposed by Archbishop John Ireland of St. Paul in his Faribault and Stillwater plans. School issues were credited with having a great deal of influence in building up of the organization in the last years of the nineteenth century. Statements by Catholic bishops and priests highly critical of public schools were cited as evidence of the overall Catholic opposition to public schools, revered as a true "American" institution by the APA.

The APA was critical of the role played by the Bureau of Catholic Indian Missions in the education of American Indians. The organization opposed the federal government entering into contracts with that Bureau to educate Indians. The APA was also involved in attempts in several places to discharge Catholic teachers from the public schools as well as being in opposition to Catholics serving as members of local public school boards.

By 1893 the APA had entered 20 states, with a membership that never exceeded 70,000. It was in 1893 that the APA was involved with a bogus letter, entitled "Instruction to True Catholics," allegedly signed by eight members of the American Catholic hierarchy, that urged Catholics to oppose public schools. Also in 1893 the APA had a part in publishing a letter that was falsely said to have been written by Pope Leo XIII, which called for American Catholics to massacre American Protestants on the feast of St. Ignatius of Loyola (which they mistakenly said was September 5). Additionally, the pope was said, in this bogus letter, to have absolved all American Catholics from any allegiance to the government of the United States.

The organization, which once had infiltrated elements of the Republican Party, waned by 1900. It ceased operation in 1911. *See also:* Anti-Catholicism in Education; Faribault-Stillwater Plan; Nativism.

Further Reading: Harold A. Buetow, *Of Singular Benefit: The Story of U.S. Catholic Education* (New York: Macmillan, 1970); Humphrey J. Desmond, *The A.P.A. Movement: A Sketch* (Washington, DC: The New Century Press, 1912); James Hennessey, *American Catholics: A History of the Roman Catholic Community in the United States* (New York: Oxford University Press, 1981); John Higham, *Strangers in the Land: Patterns of American Nativism 1860–1925* (New York: Athenaeum, 1970); Lloyd P. Jorgensen, *The State and the Non-Public School, 1825–1925* (Columbia: University of Missouri Press, 1987); Donald L. Kinzer, *An Episode of Anti-Catholicism: The American Protective Association* (Seattle: University of Washington Press, 1964).

Thomas C. Hunt

Americans United for Separation of Church and State

In a public message celebrating the sixtieth anniversary of Americans United for the Separation of Church and State (AU), the current executive director, Barry Lynn, notes: "2007 marks the 60th anniversary of the establishment of Americans United as one of the foremost defenders of the separation of church and state, the cornerstone of religious liberty in America." AU was founded in 1947 as a coalition dedicated to the principle of separation of church and state. As stated in Americans United history: "The decision was made to form a national organization to promote this point of view (that government support for religious education would violate church-state separation) and defend the separation principle" (Americans United for Separation of Church and State, at www.au.org).

Americans United was founded during the time that Congress was debating proposals for extending federal school aid to private religious schools. Originally, Americans United was founded under the title "Protestants and Other Americans United for the Separation of Church and State." In 1947 AU focused most of its attention on battling the Catholic Church and was seen as an anti-Catholic organization. AU's leaders envisioned a group with a nationwide focus that would be active on several fronts. The organization lobbied Congress, as well as state and local lawmakers, on the importance of maintaining church-state separation. At the same time, state and local chapters of Americans United were formed, and the organization began publishing *Church & State* magazine and other materials in support of church-state separation to spread their opinion to members of the general public.

As issues progressed, Americans United tackled new issues and other organizations as they emerged. In 1962 and 1963, the U.S. Supreme Court handed down landmark rulings striking down government-sponsored prayer and Bible reading in public schools. Congress considered amending the Constitution to protect the "right to pray in school." Americans United lobbied against any such amendment. The Americans United position was that no branch of government had the right to compel children to take part in religious worship and that voluntary student prayer remained legal. In the late 1970s, Americans United focused attention on responding to conservative religious organizations. The issues moved from school prayer to takeovers of public schools and religious control of school curriculum. At this time, education choice advocates began demanding tax subsidies for religious education through vouchers, tuition tax credits, and other avenues. Americans United was a leader among the opposition to these programs.

In the 1990s, Americans United directed attention to attacking conservative religious groups such as the Christian Coalition. The focus of much of this debate was on local politics, particularly local school boards. The rise of other organizations such as Focus on the Family, the Family Research Council, and the Alliance Defense Fund has kept Americans United busy in recent years. At the same time, the organization continues to oppose voucher initiatives in the states and seeks to block so-called faith-based initiatives in the federal government and in the states.

Today, the headquarters is located on Capitol Hill in Washington, D.C., and has a professional staff of 40 people. Americans United is an independent nonprofit organization with no ties to any larger group. It includes members from a broad religious, and nonreligious, spectrum, including Christians, Jews, Muslims, Buddhists, Hindus, and atheists. It is dedicated to the principle

> that all Americans have the constitutional right to practice the religion of their choice (or refrain from taking part in religion) as individual conscience dictates. The government must remain neutral on religious questions. This has been a guiding principle of Americans United since the organization was founded. (www.au.org)

The publicly stated mission of Americans United is to "preserve the constitutional principle of church-state separation as the only way to ensure religious freedom for all Americans." Americans United supports the following:

• The free exercise of religion
• The right of each religious group to define marriage on its own theological terms
• Judicial nominees that strongly support separation of church and state
• Groups that strongly support separation of church and state.

Americans United opposes the following:

• "Electioneering" by nonprofit churches and religious groups
• The faith-based initiatives of the Bush administration

- Religious education, mandatory prayer, and Bible reading in the public schools
- Educational vouchers that may be used to direct government funds to private religious schools
- The federal marriage amendment
- The presence of religious symbols on public property, for example, posting of the Ten Commandments in government buildings
- Teaching of creationism in public schools
- The agenda and activities of what it calls the "Religious Right."

Americans United carries out its work through community organizing, public information, lobbying, and litigation. Issues of its concern include:

- Faith-based initiatives
- Religion in public schools
- Church electioneering
- Free exercise of religion
- Evolution versus creationism
- Voucher and funding of religious schools
- Religious symbols of public property.

Americans United is often at the center of the debate regarding the role of religion in public schools. Its public statement on the issue states:

> Parents are the proper agents to determine what religion, if any, their children are exposed to. Public schools have no right to usurp parental authority by imposing religion on school-children. Mandatory prayer, Bible reading or other religious activities sponsored by public schools are fundamental violations of the right of conscience. Public school students have the right to pray on their own in a non-disruptive fashion, and schools may teach about religion as a part of objective instruction, but public schools must not sponsor religious worship. That job belongs to America's houses of worship. (www.au.org)

AU regularly files *amicus* briefs in courts across the nation, including the U.S. Supreme Court arguing on behalf of a clear separation of church and state. In recent years the organization has filed briefs in the following cases:

Hein v. Freedom from Religion Foundation
Good News Club v. Milford Central School
Zelman v. Simmons-Harris
Borden v. School District of the Township of East Brunswick (NJ)
Kitzmiller v. Dover Area School District (PA)
Selman v. Cobb County School District (GA)

See also: Anti-Catholicism in Education; Separation of Church and State/Wall of Separation between Church and State; Tuition Tax Credits; Vouchers.

Further Reading: Americans United for Separation of Church and State, at www.au.org; Rob Boston, "Slamming the Courthouse Door on Church-State Cases?" *Humanist* 67 (March 2007): 38–39; Rob Boston, "Victory in Iowa: Americans United Wins Sweeping Federal Court Ruling Against 'Faith-Based' Funding for InnerChange Prison Ministry," *Church & State* 59 (July 2006): 4–7; Hal Downs, "Michigan School District Rejects Fundamentalist Bible Course,"

Church & State 60 (February 2007): 3; Jeremy Leaming, "What's Wrong with This Picture?" *Church & State* 59 (September 2006): 13–15.

Julie Underwood

Amish/Mennonite Schools

The Old Order Amish and Old Order Mennonite share a common history in the radical Anabaptist movement of the sixteenth-century Swiss Reformation that condemned the power and gatekeeping function of clergy and cathedral in the life of the state church. Commonly known by their nineteenth-century dress and horse-drawn buggies, members still adhere to its principles of nonviolence and nonconformity by deliberately making decisions to reject modern society's technology and philosophy of personal success. Modern-day Mennonites have accommodated much of modern life while still adhering to the importance of peace and nonresistance.

The strands of Amish and Mennonite called "Old Order" affirm the *Alte Ordnung* (old order) of their nineteenth-century forebears rather than adopting and accommodating to modern inventions and ways of living. Some communities rarely interact with non-Amish and eschew electricity, telephones, and automobiles. Others have relatively normal relations with the rest of society and accommodate many modern inventions. But all Anabaptist communities, fearing assimilation or "worldliness" and seeking to reflect biblical teachings, stand apart from the world by their choices in dress, lifestyle, and use of technology.

Old Order Amish and Old Order Mennonite schools are one tool used by these communities to ensure the continuation of their Old Order way of life by preserving and passing on their deeply held beliefs and values and the "plain" lifestyle of farming and homemaking. Parents want their children to become useful, God-fearing, hard-working, self-supporting, and law-abiding members of the church community, without the modern emphasis on self-seeking ambition and self-serving competition. The schools only educate through the eighth grade and focus on affirming the social relationships, community norms, and language use of the community while equipping the children with the basic knowledge and skills to function economically in the community and, to varying extent, with the larger society. The schools reflect the family atmosphere of these church communities, providing an enormous sense of security. Members know they will be kept from loneliness and want from the day they were born until the day they die.

Until the 1940s and the Great Depression, the Old Order communities were content to have the public one-room schoolhouses in which one teacher taught eight grades. During World War II, Anabaptists found themselves unwelcome in the public schools because of their pacifist position. In addition, many states enacted compulsory attendance laws, requiring schooling through age 15 or 16, in order to delay entry of teenagers into the workforce and to secure the state monies that came only through student attendance. The school consolidation that followed meant bigger schools, more non-Amish children, more conflicts over what would be taught, and greater "worldly" influence. The public school ethos was taken to emphasize self-esteem development, recognition, and rewards, contrary to the Anabaptist emphasis on humility and others first. The public school was thus perceived as a prime Americanization agent that would immerse the Anabaptist children in mainstream culture, putting their spiritual well-being at risk. At first Anabaptist parents resisted these developments by refusing to send their children, an act that often resulted in the parents being fined or imprisoned. Other parents responded by holding their children back from first grade, by repeating eighth grade, or by securing a work permit allowing them to work at home. Eventually, the effect of all these cultural factors led the Amish and Mennonite parents to start their own private schools.

Mainstream resistance to Anabaptist schools continued, paving the way for a legal battle that would secure the rights of all faith-based schools. In the 1970s, the National Committee for Amish Religious Freedom became involved in *Wisconsin v. Yoder,* a legal confrontation in which Amish parents were arrested for refusing to send their 14- and 15-year-old children to public high school, and drove the case all the way to the Supreme Court. The Supreme Court acknowledged and affirmed the Amish way of life, its deeply rooted beliefs, its practice of caring for their own, and its self-supporting lifestyle, which needed no education beyond the eighth grade. The nonresistant Amish would never have pursued a case to the Supreme Court themselves, but they remain deeply grateful for the peace brought by the 1972 decision.

With the legal freedom to educate children as they wish and with the increased pressure from modernization and worldliness, Anabaptist schools are flourishing today. Old Order schools are usually one-room schoolhouses with one or two teachers. Teachers are usually young unmarried women with the same eighth grade education they will bestow on their pupils. Because further education for teachers is strongly discouraged by church leadership, Old Order teachers have formed an extensive network amongst themselves, meeting regularly to share ideas and encourage each other.

In these Old Order Amish schools reading in English is considered paramount. Legible handwriting is necessary in a world without telephones and computers, arithmetic for business transactions, history for understanding humanity, and health for thriftiness and cleanliness. Bible passages are read, songs are sung, prayers are offered, but instruction in religion is generally considered the responsibility of the church and the home. Subjects matter but the pedagogical emphasis is on discipline, the proper work ethic, and obedience to authority. Learning depends mostly on memorization, drill, copying questions, looking up the answers, and recitation at the front of the room, one grade or group at a time.

Because it is the parents' duty to "train up the child," Old Order schools are owned and operated by the families and the church members. Whether it is an Old Order Amish or Old Order Mennonite school depends on the group of parents and church members that started it. Parents choose a school board made up of three to five men to oversee one to three schools. The board collects money, hires and pays the teacher(s), selects textbooks, settles disputes, and sees to cleaning and repairs.

Though the Anabaptist strands from Old Order Amish to modern-day Mennonites share roots in the Anabaptist Reformation, they differ in their educational manifestations. Recently, those considered Old Mennonite and General Conference Mennonite joined to form the Mennonite Church USA. While these Mennonite schools, including high schools, retain specific Anabaptist emphases such as baptism, pacifism, radical social justice, and "being in the world but not of it," students and families from other denominations have influenced the schools to become more broadly evangelical. Although still oriented to peace and nonresistance, the schools increasingly resemble most evangelical Christian schools in America with respect to buildings, curricula, teacher training and pedagogy, and conditions of sponsorship.

Modern-day Mennonite schools are owned by one or more of 21 Mennonite Church USA conferences, which are generally divided by geographic regions, the largest located in eastern Pennsylvania. A few schools are owned by one or more congregations and a few are parent sponsored and controlled. The ownership body selects the board that oversees the operation of the school. Funding is usually a combination of tuition, church or conference donations, and individual donors. Partly to evangelize and partly to remain financially solvent, these schools are becoming much more "missional" in their orientation and are accepting many non-Mennonites.

The Mennonite pre-K–12 schools are organized as the Mennonite Schools Council (MSC), an arm of the Mennonite Education Agency in the Mennonite Church USA, and adhere to the "Confession of Faith in a Mennonite Perspective." The MSC plans various professional development activities "with sensitivity to the uniqueness of the supporting constituency of each member school." The MSC schools promote an education that is Christ-centered, educationally excellent, faith-infused, within a caring community, as well as emphasize peace and service. MSC schools teach students to respect and value all people as unique creations of God, to excel academically according to their God-given gifts, seek reconciliation and live peaceably with others, and own their Christian vocations within their local communities.

By 2005–2006, the National Center for Education Statistics reported that Amish and Mennonite schools and enrollment numbered 824 and 25,589 and 473 and 27,795, respectively. Their numbers appear to be increasing. *See also:* Council for American Private Education.

Further Reading: Mark W. Dewalt, *Amish Education in the United States and Canada* (Lanham, MD: Rowman & Littlefield Education, 2006); Karen M. Johnson-Weiner, *Train Up a Child: Old Order Amish and Mennonite Schools* (Baltimore: Johns Hopkins University Press, 2007); Donald B. Kraybill and Marc A Olshan, eds., *The Amish Struggle with Modernity* (Hanover, NH: University Press of New England, 1994); Mennonite Education Agency, at mennoniteeducation.org; National Center for Education Statistics, at nces.ed.gov; Frank L. Yoder, *Opening a Window to the World* (Kalona, IA: Iowa Mennonite School, 1994).

Steven C. Vryhof

Ansonia Board of Education v. Philbrook

This case involved a federal statute, Title VII of the Civil Rights Act of 1964, which prohibits discrimination on the basis of a number of categories, including religion. The statute requires an employer to make a reasonable accommodation to an employee's religious observance or practice, but only if that accommodation does not represent an undue hardship on the conduct of the employer's business.

The plaintiff, a teacher and employee of the board of education, challenged the school board's denial of his request to be absent for six school days during the school year to attend a religious conference. The teachers' collective bargaining agreement allowed teachers three days' annual leave for observance of mandatory religious holidays that would not be charged against the teacher's annual or accumulated leave. The agreement also permitted three personal days for necessary personal business without reduction in pay, but the board refused to allow these days to be used for religious purposes where an employee had already used the three religious days. The school board also had rejected plaintiff's request that he pay the cost of a substitute for the three days and not have the three days charged against his pay.

Plaintiff exhausted his Equal Employment Opportunity Commission administrative remedies and filed suit under Title VII against the school board in a federal district court in Connecticut. Following a two-day trial, the district court ruled that plaintiff had failed to prove a case of religious discrimination because he had not been placed by the school board in a position of violating his religion or losing his job. The Second Circuit Court of Appeals reversed and remanded for a determination of hardship with the test being that, once an employee has presented a reasonable accommodation, the employer is required to address hardship as to that particular accommodation. The U.S. Supreme Court granted certiorari and remanded for reconsideration of the appropriate test and the application of that test to the facts of the case.

In its 1986 decision, the Supreme Court redefined the appropriate test for interpreting compliance with Title VII. The Court determined that no basis existed in either the statute or its legislative history for requiring an employer to choose any particular reasonable accommodation. The terms of Title VII direct that any reasonable accommodation by the employer is sufficient to meet its accommodation obligation. Thus, once an employer has reasonably accommodated an employee's religious needs, the statutory inquiry is at an end. In effect, the Court rejected the Second Circuit Court of Appeal's interpretation of Title VII that an employer's accommodation obligation includes a duty to accept the employee's proposal unless that accommodation causes undue hardship on the conduct of the employer's business.

The interpretation of Title VII, however, had an as-applied component as well and, thus, the case had to be remanded to the federal district court to determine whether the school board's accommodation of plaintiff's religious beliefs was, in fact, reasonable. Although the Court declared that the school board policy in this case, requiring the teacher to take unpaid leave for holy day observance that exceeded the amount allowed by the collective-bargaining agreement, would generally be a reasonable one, the Court also cautioned that unpaid leave is not a reasonable accommodation when paid leave is provided for all purposes except religious ones.

The Court determined that the factual record was not complete as to how the school board had interpreted the personal leave provisions of the collective bargaining agreement in the past. While the school board contended that the necessary personal business category in the agreement, like other leave provisions, defined a limited purpose leave, the plaintiff asserted that the necessary personal leave category was not so limited, operating as an open-ended leave provision that may be used for a wide range of secular purposes in addition to those specifically provided for in the contract, but not for similar religious purposes.

On remand, the federal district court applied the Supreme Court's Title VII test and ruled that the collective bargaining agreement as administered, allowing three days' paid leave for religious observance and not allowing personal business leave days to be used for religious observance, was not discriminatory with respect to conditions of employment on account of religion. That decision was affirmed by the Second Circuit Court of Appeals under a clearly erroneous test, determining that plaintiff had furnished no evidence to support his claim that leave could be taken pursuant to necessary personal business provision of agreement for all purposes except religious ones. Plaintiff again sought appeal to the Supreme Court but with the Court's denial of certiorari, the case came to an end. *See also:* First Amendment Religion Clauses and the Supreme Court.

Further Reading: Ansonia Board of Education v. Philbrook, 479 U.S. 60 (1986); Civil Rights Act of 1964, 42 U.S.C. § 2000e(j); *Philbrook v. Ansonia Board of Education,* 925 F.2d 47 (2d Cir. 1991).

Ralph D. Mawdsley

Anti-Catholicism in Education

Between 1840 and 1960, Catholics and non-Catholics argued over who would control the education of Catholic children. Occasionally the arguments escalated into violence, and for most of those 120 years, there was a strong anti-Catholic bias against parochial schools.

During the nineteenth century, native-born Americans focused on the Catholic Church as the symbol of all that was wrong with the emigration of the foreign-born to the United States. There were attacks against Catholic churches, priests, nuns, and the laity in Boston, New York, Philadelphia, Baltimore, Cincinnati, Detroit, and St. Louis, among other cities.

The violence was the result of an anti-Catholicism deeply rooted in the American mind. Catholicism had been anathema since the establishment of the British colonies. The Catholic Church was mocked in both the popular and the religious presses, in novels, histories, children's books, and even almanacs. Using the pulpit and the press, some Protestant ministers and social reformers warned the nation to be on the watch for Catholic conspiracies to deprive America of its liberties. Exposing Catholicism as a national threat did nothing, however, about the millions of Catholic immigrants already in the country. Native-born Americans searched for ways to transform Catholic foreigners into productive, God-fearing citizens.

Among the social institutions that promised to "homogenize" Catholics was the common school. Even though they had no proof that this transformation process would work, common schoolmen spoke as if it were only a matter of time before immigrant children were acting and thinking like native-born children.

Catholic leaders accused common schoolmen of incorporating large doses of Protestant doctrine into the "nonsectarian" common school curriculum. Catholics further accused common schoolmen of a subtle campaign to win the allegiance of Catholic children and at the same time to denigrate the Catholic Church. The end result, noted Catholic leaders, was a generational conflict between these "Americanized" children and their immigrant Catholic parents. In response, local Catholic parishes opened their own schools.

Non-Catholics viewed the growth of parochial schools with alarm. Many public school advocates had hoped that Catholics would abandon their parish schools if public schools became nonsectarian, but it became increasingly clear in the decades after the Civil War that parish schools were not going to die out and would become a significant part of the American educational system.

Non-Catholics sought ways to end the Catholic campaigns to gain state funds for their schools. Throughout the 1870s and 1880s, many state legislatures amended their constitutions to prohibit the use of public funds for religious institutions. Between 1877 and 1917, some 29 states incorporated the amendment into their constitutions. Indeed, some state legislatures looked for ways to exert public control over portions of the parish school curricula.

In the late nineteenth century, non-Catholics were fixated on the persistence of foreign nationalism and culture in the United States, and parish schools were considered to be part of the problem. Some thought there ought to be a law that required parochial schools to conform to public school standards. The implication of these laws—state control over private schools—was unprecedented, but the vigor of the Catholic backlash came as a surprise to many Americans.

In the 1920s, Catholic educators became increasingly concerned about a growing antagonism toward parochial education on the part of many state legislatures. Legislation under consideration in several states threatened the very existence of parish schools, and when the citizens of Oregon passed a referendum requiring all children to attend public schools, the bishops swung into action.

Courts at all levels agreed that Oregon had no power to force Catholic children to attend public schools. Yet the U.S. Supreme Court, in a decision known as *Pierce v. Society of School Sisters,* was careful not to proscribe "the power of the state to reasonably regulate all schools." Following the Supreme Court decision, church leaders devoted their energies to encouraging Catholic schools to bring themselves up to the standards set by the state boards of education.

The contours of anti-Catholic attacks on parochial schools shifted in the years after the *Pierce* decision. At the root of the Catholic–Protestant conflict from 1930 to 1960 was the relationship between church, state, and school under the Constitution. In 1930, only five years after it had upheld the right of Catholic schools to exist, the Court upheld a Louisiana law that provided schoolbooks to all children in the state attending either private or public schools. The Court agreed that such a law was in the best interest of the state and did not breach the wall separating church and state. This decision (*Cochran v. Louisiana*) encouraged Catholics to think that other forms of state aid also might be ruled constitutional.

The devastation of the Great Depression followed by World War II temporarily ended the acrimony and argument between Catholics and Protestants over education, but a boom in parochial education after the war caused the tension to emerge once again. The opening round came in 1947, when the U.S. Supreme Court, in *Everson v. Board of Education,* permitted school districts to provide free bus transportation to parochial as well as public school students. In May 1949, Catholics protested a bill to provide federal aid to public schools because of a gratuitous provision of the bill prohibiting the states from using any portion of the funds to provide bus transportation for parochial school students as permitted in the *Everson* decision. Neither side was very happy in the struggle over aid to parochial schools.

The strain between Catholics and Protestants also was intensified by the establishment of Protestants and Other Americans United (POAU) for the Separation of Church and State, an organization opposed to any public aid to parochial schools. The POAU proclaimed that its goal was "to enlighten and mobilize public opinion in support of religious liberty." Legislative petitions and court action by the POAU were thinly veiled attacks on the Catholic Church.

The POAU did not represent mainstream Protestant opinion of Catholicism. In spite of serious disagreements with various Catholic positions, a number of Protestant groups sought a rapprochement with Catholicism during the latter 1950s. By the end

of the 1950s the POAU no longer was a force in interfaith relations. Catholics and Protestants had come to accept and tolerate their respective rights in a pluralistic American
society.

The anti-Catholic protests against Catholic education dissipated with the rapid decline
in the number and enrollment in Catholic schools starting in the 1960s. To be sure,
non-Catholics—led by the refurbished group now called Americans United for the Separation of Church and State—opposed both direct and indirect public aid for parochial
schools. But by the turn of the twenty-first century, virtually all Americans,
non-Catholic as well as Catholic, embrace the value of parochial education in American
society. *See also:* Americans United for Separation of Church and State; Blaine Amendment; Catholic Schools; Know-Nothing Party; Nativism; *Pierce v. Society of Sisters.*

Further Reading: Ray Allen Billington: *The Protestant Crusade* (New York: Macmillan, 1938);
Michael Feldberg, *The Philadelphia Bible Riots of 1844: A Study of Ethnic Conflict* (Westport, CT:
Greenwood Press, 1975); Mark Massa, *Anti-Catholicism in America: The Last Acceptable Prejudice*
(New York: Crossroad, 2003); Timothy Walch, *Parish School: American Catholic Parochial Educa-
tion from Colonial Times to the Present* (Washington, DC: National Catholic Educational Associa-
tion, 2003).

Timothy Walch

Anti-Defamation League

The Anti-Defamation League (ADL) is a special interest group founded in 1913 by
Chicago lawyer Sigmund Livingston in response to the pervasive and often vicious anti-
Semitism that he saw in his day. Livingston worked under the sponsorship of the Independent Order of B'nai B'rith, and his mission was "to stop, by appeals to reason and
conscience, and if necessary, by appeals to law, the defamation of the Jewish people...to
secure justice and fear treatment to all citizens alike...put an end forever to unjust and
unfair discrimination against and ridicule of any sect or body of citizens" (Anti-
Defamation League, at www.adl.org). Since its founding, the ADL has been involved in
many forms of antidiscrimination activism, including promoting a broader understanding of diversity through education, providing pressure to legislative bodies, and becoming
involved in the judicial process. Under the current guidance of Abraham Foxman and
Glen Lewy, the ADL has an annual budget of over $50 million, which is used to provide
educational resources and (where applicable) legal assistance regarding issues and topics as
diverse as terrorism, interfaith work, the Holocaust, civil rights, Israel, and hate crimes.

The ADL has been heavily involved in issues related to religion and the public schools
in both legal and educational contexts. It often cites Thomas Jefferson's "wall of separation" metaphor to represent its position that strict separation between church and state
is required to protect religious freedom. For example, the ADL has filed *amicus* briefs
supporting strict separation in several major Supreme Court cases dealing with religion
in public schools, including *Epperson v. Arkansas* (1968), where it was determined that
prohibiting teachers from teaching evolution in public schools was an unconstitutional
deviation from the Establishment Clause; *Stone v. Graham* (1980), where religious
displays (particularly the Ten Commandments) were banned from public school property; and *Zelman v. Simmons-Harris* (2002), where the Court ruled that a school voucher
program in Cleveland, Ohio, does *not* constitute the establishment of religion. The ADL

opposed that decision, arguing in their brief that the voucher program did violate the Establishment Clause. The ADL also filed a brief in *Hsu v. Roslyn* (1996) challenging the assertion that religious clubs protected by the Equal Access Act (EAA) should also be granted special privileges afforded to religious organizations. In this case, the special privileges sought related to the desire on the part of a Christian club to require that its officers be Christian. The Second Circuit Court of Appeals overturned the earlier ruling and supported the club's request.

The ADL has also been involved in many of the school prayer cases, including *Engel v. Vitale* (1962), which prohibited government sponsored prayer during the school day; *Abington v. Schempp* (1963), which disallowed Bible reading and recitation of the Lord's Prayer; and *Santa Fe School District v. Doe* (2000), a case that struck down a program that allowed for student-led prayer before football games. The ADL supported these and related strict separation rulings as a means to promote the free exercise of all forms of religious expression.

In addition to its legal advocacy, the ADL also provides comprehensive educational information about religion and the schools. Its Web site provides detailed attention to particular issues in a format aimed at educators, students, and parents. A particularly expansive section, entitled "December Dilemmas," addresses issues related to holiday music, holiday displays, religion in the classroom, and holiday assemblies. Here, again, the ADL supports strict separation through the articulation of a number of guidelines to "ensure that our public schools can best celebrate the religious freedom upon which our nation was founded" (www.adl.org). This stance is directly tied to its mission of eliminating bigotry and, more particularly, anti-Semitism in the schools through education. Other issues it addresses in its education section on the Web site include the EAA and how to interpret it, religion in the curriculum, student religious clubs, school facilities use, proselytizing on school grounds, dress codes, and the role of educators. The information the ADL provides is based on Supreme Court decisions, and its aim is to lessen conflict around these controversial topics in schools through education. By continually advocating for strict separation in legal and educational venues, the ADL claims to seek the most protection for all parties involved. *See also:* American Jewish Congress; Prayer in the Public Schools; Separation of Church and State/Wall of Separation between Church and State.

Further Reading: *Abington School District v. Schempp,* 374 U.S. 203 (1963); The Anti-Defamation League, at www.adl.org; *Engel v. Vitale,* 370 U.S. 421 (1962); Joan DelFattore, *The Fourth R* (New Haven, CT: Yale University Press, 2004); *Epperson v. Arkansas,* 393 U.S. 97 (1968); *Hsu v. Roslyn Union Free School District,* 85 F.3d 839 (2d Cir., 1996); *Santa Fe Independent School District v. Doe,* 530 U.S. 290 (2000); *Stone v. Graham,* 449 U.S. 39 (1980); James Traus, "Does Abe Foxman Have an Anti-Anti-Semite Problem?" *New York Times Magazine,* January 14, 2007, 30; *Zelman v. Simmons-Harris,* 536 U.S. 639 (2002).

Mary Ellen Giess and Diane L. Moore

Associates for Research on Private Education

Associates for Research on Private Education (ARPE), a special interest group of the American Educational Research Association (AERA), was founded in April 1977 in New York City by Donald A. Erickson, and other scholars, to support and promote research on nonpublic schools in the United States, the vast majority of which are faith-based. By the end of 1977, ARPE had 102 dues paying members, and by 1979 the number had more than doubled to 235. A survey showed that ARPE members felt isolated from mainstream educational research with its focus on public schools. What they wanted most from the fledgling organization was mutual support, and they hoped for an association in which to share their research ideas and findings with sympathetic colleagues. Early members also wanted to track studies of private education.

Thus, the feeling was that most research on K–12 education had focused on the public system, that those who studied private and religious schools were isolated and ignored, and that researchers interested in these nonpublic schools needed a support group and system for studying and publishing in this vital area. Like other special interest groups, ARPE is affiliated with AERA, the largest organization of researchers and teachers in the field of education, and posts the following purpose and description:

> To facilitate discussion and dissemination of information about developments in research, policy, and practice in private education, including religious, non-religious, and home schooling. ARPE publishes *the Private School Monitor* and holds occasional conferences that supplement AERA meetings.

Thus, ARPE meets yearly at the annual meeting of AERA, where it is scheduled for sessions as part of the national gathering. But ARPE also has functions on its own, such as publishing quarterly the *Private School Monitor,* a combination newsletter and scholarly outlet that started, under the guidance of Erickson, as an organ for tracking and summarizing relevant research in the field.

Since only a small minority of ARPE members ever attends the annual meetings and occasional conferences, the *Private School Monitor* has been a most consistent attraction. In its first issue, the *Monitor* described itself as "a regularly published source in which studies particularly pertinent to private schools are catalogued and abstracted for the benefit of scholars and practitioners." The *Monitor* then published, not reports of individual studies, but abstracts of individual studies and analytic reviews of *groups* of studies. It contained announcements and news items, but functioned primarily to apprise scholars and practitioners of publications elsewhere on private education research.

By the time the first issue of *Private School Monitor* appeared the spring of 1978, 36 "contributing editors" (the number rapidly rose to 75) were scanning journals and other sources for pertinent publications. The contributing editors, listed on the masthead, mailed photocopies of articles (or references to new books) to the ARPE headquarters, where abstracts and reviews were written for publication in the *Monitor.* At the time, the Education Resources Information Center (ERIC), a bibliographic data base, system badly neglected private school research, thus making the publication a valuable tool for scholars interested in the nongovernment sector of education.

The *Monitor* eventually stopped its abstracting service on private school research. And when Bruce Cooper took over the publication, he converted it into a newsletter and publisher of short articles on a range of topics related to private and religious schools. This emphasis has continued under other "first generation" ARPE leaders who have served as editors, including Patricia Bauch, James Carper, and Lyndon Furst.

At the present time, a new generation of leaders, including Larry Burton and Gary Railsbach, is providing strong leadership for ARPE, but what the organization needs in addition is an explicit shifted vision. The era of outright hostility by government agencies, universities, and many foundations toward private school research per se has ended. ARPE now needs to encourage an unending series of systematic efforts to do private school research through well conceived, skillfully executed studies and analyses. *See also:* Council for American Private Education

Further Reading: Associates for Research on Private Education, at arpe.org.

Bruce S. Cooper

Association for Supervision and Curriculum Development

The Association for Supervision and Curriculum Development (ASCD) can be considered the most proactive professional educational organization to support the teaching of religion in public schools in recent years. ASCD also has an organization's long-standing commitment to character education, which embraces moral standards that many religious organizations in the nation would support.

ASCD was founded in 1943. Its Web site identifies it as a nonprofit, nonpartisan organization representing 175,000 educators in more than 135 countries. Its membership includes superintendents, principals, curriculum and other supervisors, teachers, and professors of teacher education. Its mission is to advocate sound policies and to share best practices so that each learner benefits. To meet that mission, ASCD conducts workshops for professionals, publishes a journal, *Educational Leadership,* and produces a wide variety of resources for classroom use as well as resources appropriate for participants in public forums.

In 1962, the Association passed a resolution supporting teaching about religion in the curriculum, a year before the U.S. Supreme Court ruling in *Abington v. Schempp.* In 1981, ASCD members formulated another resolution opposing school vouchers. One of the arguments offered for this resolution is that vouchers lead to students in different school settings being isolated from each other.

In 1987 ASCD published its first resource in this area, *Religion in the Curriculum,* subtitled "A Report from the ASCD Panel on Religion in the Curriculum." It contained 13 recommendations relating to teaching historic religious facts and narratives. Two important outcomes of such teaching, it posited, were an increase of sensitivity and respect for religious diversity. Diane Berreth, director of Field Services for ASCD, chaired the panel, which included O. L. Davis, Jr., professor of Curriculum and Instruction, University of Texas, Edward Jenkinson, professor of English Education at Indiana University, Lee Smith, co-director of the World Religions Curriculum Development Center, Minneapolis, Minnesota, and Timothy Smith, professor of History, Johns Hopkins University.

That same year Charles Haynes contacted ASCD to see if the organization would support a pronouncement developed by a consortium of educational, religious, and civic groups. Diane Berreth became ASCD's representative at meetings. In 1988 the consortium released "Religion in the Public School Curriculum," a brochure/flyer that was widely disseminated. In 1989 another brochure by an expanding number of organizations on the topic of religious holidays was released.

As Ron Brandt noted in an overview in the December 1993/January 1994 issue of *Educational Leadership,* public education was on trial. Teachers, administrators, and school boards were under attack by religiously conservative persons and groups. They opposed whole language instruction, cooperative learning, and performance assessments, arguing that such innovations were contrary to their religious values. The theme of that issue was "Public Schools and the Christian Fundamentalists." It included ten articles, including case studies; representatives of conservative organizations, e.g., Robert Simonds of Citizens for Excellence in Education; and philosophical/historical pieces.

The April 1996 issue of *Educational Leadership* had as its theme, "Working Constructively with Families." It included an interview of Charles Haynes by Ron Brandt. Haynes acknowledged the reality of conflict and confusion by all sides on what can and cannot be taught regarding religion, but maintained an optimistic view that differences can be worked out civilly in a search for common ground. In the May 1998 issue, "Engaging Parents and the Community in Schools," there is a less overt treatment of the difference in values between some parents and public educators, but related concern that the schools need to be sensitive to criticisms.

The most significant project for the Association of Supervision and Curriculum Development regarding religion and education came in 1996. Editor Ron Brandt and Charles Haynes offered a vision statement on religion and education that could be endorsed by a broad coalition of religious organizations. ASCD actively participated in the production of "A Statement of Principles on Religious Liberty, Public Education, and the Future of American Democracy." Others included the Christian Coalition, American Center for Law and Justice, National Association of Evangelicals, and the Christian Legal Society, conservative groups heretofore absent from such statements. The American Association of School Administrators, National Education Association and American Federation of Teachers, National Associations of Elementary and Secondary Principals, and the National Congress of Parents and Teachers represented the "educational establishment." Other signers included the Carnegie Foundation for the Advancement of Teaching, the Anti-Defamation League, and People for the American Way. A total of some 20 organizations endorsed the statement, which was also endorsed by the U.S. Secretary of Education. The statement, which had six principles, was sent by the Department of Education to every school district in the country. The fourth principle offers the clearest expression of the boundaries of what public school teachers may and may not do: "Public schools may not inculcate nor inhibit religion. They must be places where religion and religious conviction are treated with fairness and respect."

In addition to the theme issue already described, the most focused treatment supporting the academic study of religion in public schools in the journal was Susan L. Douglas's article, "Teaching about Religion" in the October 2002 issue of *Educational Leadership*. She discussed in particular how the Islamic faith could be taught. A brief article by Joanne Rooney in the February 2007 issue, "Asking for Strength," conveyed the idea that public school teachers do pray for students privately, even though school-sponsored prayers are inappropriate.

The 1990s was a decade of major projects by ASCD in the field of public education religion studies. ASCD sponsored a book by Charles Haynes entitled *Religion in American History: What to Teach and How*. In 1998, Warren Nord and Charles Haynes coauthored *Taking Religion Seriously Across the Curriculum*, which ASCD published.

By the early to mid-1990s, advocates of teaching about religion found that reservations to teaching about religion, whether by reluctant teachers and administrators, liberal or conservative religious communities, responded to a plea to look for "common ground." Advocates for the term acknowledged that total agreement was unlikely, but rather respect for certain ground rules and subject content would allow instruction to occur. A teaching resource, *Finding Common Ground,* while produced by the Freedom Forum, was supported by ASCD.

Another approach adopted by ASCD during this decade was financial support and recognition of a special interest group on religion and education. Under the leadership mainly of Professor James Uphoff of Wright State University, a periodic newsletter appeared. From time to time, the newsletter was supplemented with descriptions of court cases, teacher accounts, and fact sheets regarding religion and history. The special interest group held meetings at the national convention of ASCD. As of this date, the special interest group is still in existence.

More recently (in 2000 and following), ASCD joined with the Freedom Forum and the First Amendment Center to become a supporter of the First Amendment School initiative. Elementary and secondary schools joining in that program agree to integrate curriculum units on the various freedoms described in the amendment. Of course, that includes the "establishment clause" and the "free exercise clause" related to freedom of religion. Two more recent books published by ASCD address this arena: *The Respectful School* (2003) and *The First Amendment in Schools* (2003).

As mentioned earlier, ASCD has also been involved with character education. In 1992, it became a charter member of the Character Education Partnership, a group promoting civic virtues and moral character development in youth. The November 1993 of *Educational Leadership* was devoted to character education.

In conclusion, ASCD deserves credit for being an active player in this field, devoting staff time and funding to a variety of projects and programs on topics related to religion and education. Its journal, *Educational Leadership,* remains an excellent resource. *See also:* Common Ground Documents; Religion and the Public School Curriculum.

Further Reading: Ron Brandt, "On Finding Common Ground with Religious Conservatives: A Conversation with Charles Haynes," *Educational Leadership* 53 (April 1996): 72–74; "Can Public Schools Accommodate the Christian Fundamentalists?" *Educational Leadership* 51 (December 1993–January 1994); "Character Education," *Educational Leadership* 51 (November 1993); "Engaging Parents and the Community in Schools," *Educational Leadership* 5 (May 1998); Charles Haynes, *Religion in American History: What to Teach and How* (Nashville: Association for Supervision and Curriculum Development, 1990); Charles Haynes and Oliver Thomas, eds., *Finding Common Ground* (Nashville: First Amendment Center, 2001); Charles Haynes, Sam Chaltain, and John Ferguson, *The First Amendment in Schools: A Guide from the First Amendment Center* (Nashville: Association for Supervision and Curriculum Development, 2003); Warren Nord and Charles Haynes, *Taking Religion Seriously Across the Curriculum* (Nashville: Association for Supervision and Curriculum Development, 1998); *Religious Liberty, Public Education, and the Future of American Democracy: A Statement of Principles* (Nashville: First Amendment Center, 1995); Banks Zakariya, *Religion in the Curriculum: A Report from the ASCD Panel on Religion in the Curriculum* (Alexandria, VA: Association for Supervision and Curriculum Development, August 1987).

Charles R. Kniker

B

Baptist Joint Committee for Religious Liberty

The Baptist Joint Committee on Religious Liberty (BJC), formerly the Baptist Joint Committee on Public Affairs, is a nonprofit education and advocacy organization that is dedicated to defending "God-given religious liberty for all" (Baptist Joint Committee, at www.bjcpa.org). The BJC was founded in 1936 by the Southern Baptists, Northern Baptists, and National Baptists in order to present a unified Baptist position in support of the separation of church and state. It maintains that its separationist stance is the quintessentially Baptist position, and it proudly refers to the fact that it was Roger Williams, Baptist theologian and founder of Rhode Island, who originated the phrase "a wall of separation between the garden of the church and the wilderness of the world." In the 1980s, as fundamentalists and evangelicals asserted increasing influence over the Southern Baptist Convention, this interpretation of religious liberty as linked to separation of church and state fell into disfavor, and by the mid-1990s the Southern Baptists had cut all ties to the BJC. In spite of this loss of support and funding, the BJC continues to represent 14 Baptist bodies, including the American Baptist Churches USA, Progressive National Baptist Convention Inc., Cooperative Baptist Fellowship, and the Baptist General Convention of Texas. In 2005, the BJC changed its name from the Baptist Joint Committee on Public Affairs to the Baptist Joint Committee for Religious Liberty to better reflect its singular focus on religious freedom issues. Its reported budget in 2006 was $1.1 million.

The BJC has been active in issues surrounding religion and the public schools since its inception, when it argued against school prayer, Bible reading, aid to parochial schools, and bills that might provide publicly funded transportation to religiously affiliated schools (a position that was perceived as anti-Catholic at the time). The BJC now utilizes a range of strategies in order to impact public discourse on these issues. It analyzes and reports on court developments and is an active contributor of *amicus curiae* briefs to the Supreme Court. Representatives of the BJC have testified before Congress and have influenced legislation through counsel as well as the drafting of policy statements. BJC lawyers are also active and prominent contributors to editorial pages at the *Washington Post* and the *New York Times*.

One of the chief concerns of the organization is the increased use of vouchers that fund attendance to religious schools, a practice that the BJC sees as an unforgivable entanglement of church and state. The argument is theological: religion should exist "unmolested, uncoerced and unassisted" and should be advanced only by "the persuasive power of the truth it proclaims" rather than by "the coercive power of the state" ("BJC Resolution on Aid to Religious Schools" at Baptist Joint Committee, at www.bjcpa.org). The organization is also a prominent voice in teacher training and curricular matters. It provides teachers resources such as analyses of popular Bible curriculums in use in public schools. (It has tentatively endorsed the Bible Literacy Project as an example of responsible and constitutional use of the Bible.) It has also waded into the evolution debates, supporting the teaching of evolution in science classrooms and ardently contesting the widespread characterization of evolution and religion as inherently opposed. Evolution and Christian beliefs are not incompatible, according to the BJC, and Intelligent Design can be taught in social studies or comparative religion classrooms.

The BJC is committed to what it sees as the theological interdependence of free exercise and no establishment clauses, and has confronted the second Bush administration publicly and repeatedly over what it sees as the prioritization of the exercise over the establishment. Of particular relevance here, it has argued that the Department of Education's guidelines on prayer in the No Child Left Behind Act is a demonstration of an "uneven approach" that punishes schools for curtailing free exercise (the right to pray) but not for defying no establishment (as when a teacher demands students pray).

The BJC has a proven record of coalition building. In 1995, it helped to produce "Religion in the Public Schools: A Joint Statement of Current Law," which was signed by 30 religious, educational, and civil liberties organizations spanning the ideological spectrum. Brent Walker, the executive director, has cosigned Letters to the Editor with Rabbi David Saperstein of the Religious Action Center of Reform Judaism. As a religious organization that argues against religious intrusion into the public square and the public schools, the BJC continues to challenge the prevailing polemic of the culture wars. *See also:* J.M. Dawson Institute for Church-State Studies; Separation of Church and State/ Wall of Separation between Church and State; Southern Baptists and Education.

Further Reading: Baptist Joint Committee, at www.bjcpa.org; Laurie Goodstein, "Bitter Over Ruling, Groups See Trouble for Minority Faiths," *Washington Post,* June 26, 1997, sec. A, p. 1; K. Hollyn Hollman, "New Guidelines Offer Unbalanced View of Religion in Public Schools," *Report from the Capital,* February 19, 2003, p. 3.

Shipley Robertson Salewski

Becket Fund for Religious Liberty

The Becket Fund for Religious Liberty is a nonprofit public interest law firm focusing on the defense of the free expression of religious faith in the public arena. Founded by attorney Kevin Hasson in 1994, the Becket Fund is both nonpartisan and broadly interfaith in scope, defending the rights of individual believers and institutions representing a wide range of religious traditions. The Becket Fund is expressly committed to a vision of religious freedom that sees such freedom as a fundamental human right that government cannot deny to the people. This vision sees the source of religious liberty is in the dignity of the human person, not in a grant of privilege from the government.

Because of the nature and source of religious freedom, the fund is committed to defending the rights of religious believers and religious institutions to be active in the public square without having to bracket their faith.

The fund is named after St. Thomas à Becket (A.D. 1118–1170), a cleric who held important posts during the reign of King Henry II of England. Starting as Henry's chancellor, Becket eventually became Archbishop of Canterbury, and in that role opposed moves by Henry to subordinate the Catholic Church to the English crown. Eventually, Becket's opposition proved frustrating to the king, causing Henry to complain openly about Becket to a group of his knights. Inspired by the king's complaints, these knights killed Becket while he said mass in Canterbury Cathedral. From the time of his death, Becket has been seen as a martyr for the principle of religious freedom from government control.

The fund is headquartered in Washington, D.C., and operates with a full-time staff and a board of advisors. Kevin Hanson is the current chairman of the board and president of the fund. The composition of the board of advisors reflects a diversity of political, professional, and religious affiliations, all by individuals who are well-known for their defense of a robust role by religion in public life. The board's current membership consists of former U.S. Attorney General William Barr; Senator Orrin Hatch; law professors Stephen Carter, Douglas Laycock, and Douglas Kmiec; clergymen Rabbi Ronald B. Sobel, Father Richard John Neuhaus, and Cardinal Francis George of Chicago; John M. Templeton, Jr.; and Sargent Shriver and his wife, Eunice Kennedy Shriver.

The Becket Fund has three main venues in which it carries out its work: the media; academic scholarship; and the courts via litigation. In addition, it sponsors conferences on various topics related to the intersection of religion and public life. The fund actively pursues seven primary areas of interest in carrying out its mission to promote and defend religious liberty. Those areas of interest are religious liberty on the international stage, in education, in employment law, in prisons, and religious liberty and its impact on education, the right of free association, and in the public square. In addition to work in these specific areas, the Becket Fund also sponsors lectures by noted figures in the religious liberty landscape, and continuing legal education programs for attorneys.

The public interest legal work undertaken by the fund is extensive, and it includes representation on behalf of a wide range of religious individuals and institutions across the faith spectrum: Christians, Jews, Muslims, Hindus, Buddhists, followers of Native American religions, Santeria, and others. It has participated in a large number of appellate cases as an *amicus curiae* ("friend of the court"). The fund has taken a leading role in a variety of cases dealing with school vouchers, and has worked to challenge state Blaine Amendments. The fund has also been active in recent litigation regarding the constitutionality of the Pledge of Allegiance, as well as prisoners' rights litigation and religious land use. In addition to its work on behalf of individuals, the fund has also taken cases defending the religious liberty rights of institutions, including, e.g., the right of religiously affiliated educational institutions to hire faith-specific religion teachers. In addition to its work in domestic courts, the fund has also begun to expand its efforts beyond the United States, appearing on behalf of clients before various international tribunals.

The Becket Fund has a strong presence on the Internet, and provides detailed summaries of its legal cases, the scholarship supported by the fund, media releases, and other work and events the fund sponsors. In addition to its primary Web site, the Becket Fund also operates several topic-specific sites that provide additional in-depth information on specific issues of concern. Those additional Web sites currently address the Religious Land Use and Institutionalized Persons Act of 2000, state Blaine Amendments, the rights of religious leaders to address moral and political issues in their congregations, and religious liberty in Sri Lanka. *See also:* Blaine Amendment; The Pledge of Allegiance.

Further Reading: Becket Fund for Religious Liberty, at www.becketfund.org; Blaine Amendments, at www.blaineamendments.org; Lanka Liberty, at www.lankaliberty.com; Free Preach.org, at www.freepreach.org; RLUPIA.com, at www.rluipa.com.

Mark DeForrest

Bender v. Williamsport Area School District

This case involved a challenge to the school district's refusal to permit a religious club, Petros, to meet on school premises during a school-day activity period for purposes of Bible reading and prayer. Because a wide range of groups were permitted to meet, student plaintiffs filed suit against the school district, alleging violations of the First Amendment's Free Speech, Free Exercise, and Establishment Clauses. A Pennsylvania federal district court resolved the case on its merits, dismissing the students' free exercise claim because not allowing plaintiffs to meet during the activity period did not force them to forego their religious belief in group worship since they were still free to worship together as they pleased before and after the school day and on weekends in a church or any other suitable place. The district court, however, found a free speech violation because the school had created a limited public forum during its activity period and the exclusion of Petros did not represent a narrowly drawn content-based restriction that furthered a compelling state interest. In rejecting the school district's claim that it had a compelling interest in preventing a no establishment clause violation, the court applied the tripartite *Lemon v. Kurtzman* (1971) test, finding a secular purpose in permitting a wide range of student groups to meet, no advancement of religion, and no excessive entanglement between the school district and religion.

The Williamsport school district took no appeal from the district court's decision permitting Petros to meet on school property and complied with the district court's judgment. School board member John Youngman, Jr., who was still a member of the school board and was the only member to vote against permitting Petros to meet during the activity period, appealed the decision to the Third Circuit Court of Appeals. The Third Circuit reversed the district court and determined that, notwithstanding plaintiff's protectable free speech rights in the religious club, permitting Petros to meet would advance religion and create an excessive entanglement in violation of the *Lemon v. Kurtzman* standard. In balancing the students' free speech rights against no establishment problems the court endorsed a per se rule that "group prayer activity, held on school premises, conducted as part of an organized high school activity program, at which a school monitor must be present, and which takes place during the hours of compulsory school attendance, violates the Establishment Clause."

With conflicting decisions on the merits by the federal district court and the Third Circuit, the U.S. Supreme Court granted certiorari and the stage was set for the Supreme Court to determine which of the conflicting views should prevail. Instead, the Court vacated the order of the appellate court and remanded the case to the district court, limiting its decision to only a procedural determination that, since no member of the school board had been sued in his individual capacity and since the board had voted to comply with the district court's order, school board member Youngman had no standing to appeal in his individual capacity. In the absence of any evidence that Youngman was a parent or that he or his children had suffered injury as a result of permitting the Bible Club to meet, the Supreme Court followed the long-standing interpretative principle that the Court will not address the merits of a case if the case can be disposed of on procedural grounds.

The Supreme Court's decision in *Bender v. Williamsport Area School District* has largely passed into oblivion. The failure of the Court to address substantive rights of students has meant that the case has little precedent value. The challenge involving the religious rights of students in public schools, however, has not gone unresolved. One year after the federal district court's decision in *Bender*, Congress in 1984 enacted the Equal Access Act (EAA), which served to provide a resolution to the kind of facts represented in that case. The EAA prohibits school districts receiving federal financial assistance with limited open forums from denying equal access to, or discriminating against, any students who wish to conduct a meeting within that limited open forum on the basis of the religious, political, philosophical, or other content of the speech at those meetings. In effect, Congress through the EAA reached the substantive solution that the Supreme Court had failed to achieve in *Bender v. Williamsport Area School District*. *See also:* Equal Access Act.

Further Reading: *Bender v. Williamsport Area School District,* 563 F.Supp. 697 (M.D. Pa. 1983); *Bender v. Williamsport Area School District,* 741 F.2d 538 (3d Cir. 1984); *Bender v. Williamsport Area School District,* 475 U.S. 534 (1986); Equal Access Act, 20 U.S.C. § 4071; *Lemon v. Kurtzman,* 403 U.S. 602 (1971).

Ralph D. Mawdsley

Bennett Law

The Civil War led to a heightened sense of nationalism in the northern states. States turned to their schools to foster this sense of nationalism. Accordingly, they intensified compulsory attendance legislation and their supervision of practices that they deemed indispensable to forming good citizenship in the nation's youthful citizens. Teaching certain subjects in the English language was one such tool. The efforts of states on behalf of preparing "good Americans" was especially critical in those states with a high population of immigrants, particularly those who maintained parochial schools that held on to old world customs, including language.

Wisconsin was one such state. In 1890 there were, according to the U.S. Census, 249,164 Catholics and 160,919 Lutherans in the state, making up about 75 percent of the membership of churches in the state. There were also 66,065 students in parochial schools that year, putting Wisconsin first among north-central states in parochial school enrollment; 37,854 of these were in Catholic schools and 26,359 in Lutheran schools.

State superintendents of public instruction had complained about the fact that often these schools did not report their attendance, nor other factors, such as the language of instruction used, to the superintendent. Thus, in 1889 Governor William Dempster Hoard, a Republican and a former lay Methodist minister who had served in the Union army as a chaplain, called for legislation that would require these schools to report their attendance to the local superintendent and authorize local superintendents to inspect all the schools in their districts to determine if the students were being taught to read and write English, enabling them to become full citizens of the state and nation.

The Wisconsin legislature enacted the Bennett Law in 1889, and it was signed into law by Governor Hoard. Its key features were defining a school as a place where English was the language of instruction and requiring a student to attend school in the local district in which he or she resided. Lutherans, followed by Catholics, objected. The Catholic bishops of the state termed the law unnecessary, offensive, and unjust. Catholics and Lutherans claimed that the civil state was interfering with the educational mission of their churches, which held that parents, not the state, were the primary educators of their children. Governor Hoard and his followers replied that it was the right of the state to require that all schools within its borders develop good citizenship in the students and to inspect all schools to ensure that such education was taking place.

The first site of conflict was the mayoral election in the city of Milwaukee, heavily German and equally heavily Catholic and Lutheran. Estimates were that about one-half of Milwaukee's population in 1890 were either born in Germany or had one parent born there. Catholics and Lutherans stood together, and the candidate they supported, George W. Peck, won the election. Governor Hoard, meanwhile, had complained that the two religious groups were interested only in their churches and not in the welfare of civil society. He urged these two bodies to follow the example of the other Protestant groups in the state who were in general support of the law. (Unitarians, who regarded the public school as the chief bulwark of American liberty, were the most supportive religious body of the Bennett Law. They argued that the state's schools, and all of its institutions, should be secular.) Catholics and Lutherans, however, the only churches with a significant parochial school population, perceived the law as an attack on their schools, to eliminate them, or at least curtail them.

The law played a significant part in the 1890 gubernatorial election in which Peck soundly defeated Governor Hoard in his bid for reelection. Commentators generally acknowledged that religious and ethnic forces had contributed to the result. The Bennett Law was repealed and the law that replaced it—the first one passed by the legislature in 1891—did not include the residence clause or require that certain subjects be taught in English. German Lutherans and Catholics, the latter not limited to those with German backgrounds, were convinced that the Bennett Law was an attack on their schools and, in the case of German Americans, on their language and culture as well. Some felt that the overriding issue of the struggle was who should control the education of children. Governor Hoard and his supporters looked to the civil state; Catholics and Lutherans looked to their parents and their church. Hoard held that one purpose of schools was to free the young from ecclesiastical control, that the goal of the two churches was their growth with scant care for American citizenship. In Hoard's view, churches had perpetuated religious bias and did not have a clear view of or commitment to building citizenship in the young. Catholics and Lutherans rejected Hoard's position, and in a long and bitter struggle protected their schools in Wisconsin from what they considered to be the heavy-handedness of state control. *See also:* Catholic Schools; Lutheran Schools; State Regulation of Religious Schools.

Further Reading: Colman J. Barry, *The Catholic Church and German Americans* (Milwaukee: Bruce Publishing, 1953); Harry H. Heming, *The Catholic Church in Wisconsin* (Milwaukee:

T.J. Sullivan, 1896); Thomas C. Hunt, "The Bennett Law: Focus of Conflict between Church and State," *Journal of Church and State* 23 (Winter 1981): 69–93; John P. Koehler, *The History of the Wisconsin Synod,* ed. Leigh D. Jordahl (St. Cloud, MN: Sentinel Publishing Company, 1970); Christian Koerner, *The Bennett Law and the German Protestant Parochial Schools of Wisconsin* (Milwaukee: Germania Publishing Co., 1890); George W. Rankin, *William Dempster Hoard* (Fort Atkinson, WI: W.D. Hoard and Sons, 1923); Roger E. Wyman, "Wisconsin Ethnic Groups and the Election of 1890," *Wisconsin Magazine of History* 4 (Summer 1968): 269–293.

Thomas C. Hunt

The Bible in the Public Schools

Colonial Times

Throughout a large portion of American educational history the Bible has played a prominent role. Not only did academic scholars and teachers view the Bible as the central textbook, but also as Gilpin observes, "The English Bible played a major role in establishing the methods and goals of colonial education" (Gilpin, 1982, p. 5). Kent Greenawalt notes, "Education in the early American colonies was almost entirely private and substantially religious" (Greenawalt, 2005, p. 13). To New England and Mid-Atlantic settlers in particular, the Bible and education were inextricably connected. The New England colonies had perhaps the highest literacy rate in the world. The reason why New England's leaders placed such an emphasis on literacy is because the ability to read enabled one to study the Scriptures and this diligence in examining the Bible facilitated salvation. The passion that the Puritans and Pilgrims, in particular, possessed about the Bible and literacy helps explain why myriad individuals kept record of the titles and number of books that they owned and why the overwhelming number of these books were Bibles, commentaries, and other religious works.

In the minds of American settlers not only was the Bible to serve as the central book throughout a student's schooling, but also the curriculum and textbooks used were to have a definite religious orientation. They maintained that moral education was even more indispensable than academic education. They believed the earlier assertions of Cicero, later echoed by Martin Luther King, Jr., that the most dangerous people in the world were those who were intelligent but lacked virtue.

Teachers of the colonial era in dame schools, in which women taught young children, in more formal charity schools (private schools that enabled most students to attend free of charge), and in town school settings regularly instructed children in the study of the Bible, particularly highlighting the gospels, the epistles, Old Testament history, Psalms, Proverbs, and the prophets. The most popular extra-biblical text was the *New England Primer,* which sewed biblical truths into nearly every subject matter, including grammar and spelling.

Revolutionary War Period

The prominence of the Bible as the school's primary textbook continued into the years just prior to the Revolutionary War, the Revolutionary War period, and into the decades following the Revolutionary War. The overwhelming majority of the nation's school leaders believed that the Bible should remain the central textbook in American education.

These individuals included Noah Webster, who earned the nickname "the nation's school master," Benjamin Rush, who signed the Declaration of Independence and was also regarded as the nation's foremost physician, and Thomas Dilworth, who was a prolific writer of school textbooks at the time. Webster probably did more to contribute to and guide the development of the American education system than any individual during the Revolutionary War era. He wrote the most prominent textbooks of the era that together were entitled, *A Grammatical Institute of the English Language*. Among these textbooks it was his speller that became the most popular of his books, selling 75 million copies by 1875 in a nation whose population during the 1800–1875 period was only a fraction of that number. Like many of the textbooks of the era, "Webster's speller was chock-full of Bible quotations and religious fare" (Prothero, 2007, p. 75).

Dilworth's books "were even more religious than those of Noah Webster" (Prothero, 2007, p. 75). In fact, Dilworth's books relied so heavily on the Bible that Webster criticized his books as inadvertently discouraging religious commitment because of the teeming references to God. Webster stated, "Nothing has a greater tendency to lessen the reverence which mankind ought to have for the Supreme Being than a careless repetition of His name upon every trifling occasion" (Prothero, 2007, p. 75). Dilworth's books, however, were generally less doctrinal than the *Primer*. Nevertheless, his books were some of the most popular in America during the mid-to-late 1700s. Dilworth's speller, *A New Guide to the English Language* (1740), was especially well received.

Sunday schools also became popular in the post–Revolutionary War period, in which the Bible served as the central text. Robert Raikes founded the first Sunday school in England by 1780 and it was established in the United States in 1785 in Virginia by William Elliot. In many respects, the Sunday school was a forerunner of the common schools. It focused on biblical instruction, the memorization of Scripture verses, and the importance of early literacy.

During the first half of the nineteenth century in particular, the advance of the charity school movement accelerated, and this further contributed to the widespread use of the Bible throughout the nation's schools. As scholars have pointed out, the Christians of the first few centuries A.D. were the first group to call for the widespread education of all people. The continuance of this attitude plus the effects of the Great Awakening of the mid-to-late eighteenth century, and an intense emphasis on publishing gospel tracts and literature contributed to maintaining the Bible's central place in the curriculum. During this period there was a phenomenal emphasis on Bible literacy in every facet of American society, and particularly in the schools. Americans of the era believed that Bible literacy facilitated salvation. Coupled with this emphasis on Bible literacy was the practice of the memorization of Scripture verses. Between 1829 and 1831 alone, the American Bible Society printed and distributed more than 1 million copies of the Scriptures although the total population of the United States was only 13 million. Charity schools represented the perfect means to spread Bible literacy among America's youth. Charity schools were quasi-private schools that enabled families to pay for tuition on a sliding scale, depending on their income. Various charity schools did receive some public money. Nevertheless, for about 80 percent of American children, this meant that they attended school free of charge. These charity schools were the precursors of the common school movement and most of them eventually became public schools.

African Americans were among the primary beneficiaries of charity schools. Many of them attended charity schools, which in most cases were integrated in the North in cities like Philadelphia, New York, and Baltimore, and a vast number of other cities and towns in which nearly all of them went free of charge (Woodson, 1915). Biblical truths not only saturated the moral education curriculum of these schools but also frequently manifested themselves in instruction of other subjects as well. Leaders of the charity school movement were quick to ascribe their city's low crime rates to the presence of Bible-based character education in their schools. For example, DeWitt Clinton, president of the largest charity school society in the United States in New York City, had special praise for the efficacy of this instruction. In a celebration of numerous years of existence, he declared, "Of the many thousands who have been instructed in our free schools in the City of New York, there is not a single instance known of anyone being convicted of a crime" (Fitzpatrick, 1969, p. 54).

Mid-1800s

The charity school system remained largely intact until the mid-1800s, largely due to the generosity of wealthy Americans who contributed to the charity schools so that hundreds of thousands of children could go to school free of charge. Over time, public tax dollars also were used to support charity schools. The United States was not, however, a wealthy country in the first half of the 1800s. Only a small segment of the population was wealthy. With the arrival of a wave of poor immigrants in the mid-1800s the ratio of wealthy to poor people changed considerably. Consequently, there was no longer a sufficient percentage of wealthy people to completely financially subsidize the educational needs of most Americans. A confluence of other factors also contributed to the demise of the charity school system, including rapid urbanization and other demographic and cultural factors.

The demographic changes just described plus the vision and determination of Horace Mann, Henry Barnard, and others led to the rise of the public (common) school movement. Mann had a background in law and politics and emerged as the first secretary of the Massachusetts Board of Education in 1837. He contended that given the demographic changes that had taken place in the country, taxation was now necessary to support the education of America's children.

In spite of the shift toward a state-financed and regulated common school system, Mann averred that Bible teaching, though not specific doctrines, remain a vital part of the curriculum. In fact, Mann adamantly asserted that American society would pay a sobering price if religious education were ever removed from the curriculum. He stated:

> But, it will be said that this great result, in practical morals, is a consummation of blessedness that can never be attained without religion; and that no community will ever be religious without a Religious Education. Both of these propositions I regard as eternal and immutable truths. Devoid of religious principles and religious affections the race can never fall so low that it may not sink still lower. (Kliebard, 1969, p. 73)

In Mann's view, moral education was the centerpiece of the public school curriculum. Mann agreed with George Washington and nearly all of the nation's founders that moral training and Bible education were inseparable. Mann believed that the pivotal moral truths that school children were to learn and apply were found in the Bible. Mann asserted in his ninth annual report that "No community can long subsist unless it has religious principle as the foundation of moral action, nor unless it has moral action as the superstructure of religious principle" (Mann, 1846, p. 86). Some religious leaders of the time, however, believed that Mann, a Unitarian who was equally skeptical of Catholicism and Calvinism, did not emphasize the Bible as an inspired document to the degree that they would have liked. And indeed, a great deal of this unease probably has much to do with the presentation of the Bible in a state-sponsored sphere rather than a private one. Although some religious leaders were critical of Mann for propounding a nonsectarian approach to biblical study, Mann's personal letters and his annual reports suggest that he believed he was on a mission from God and that he viewed Scripture more highly than his critics contended.

Many of Mann's contemporaries in leadership positions echoed his convictions and affirmed that it was essential for the nation's children to learn biblical truths in order to live moral lives. Henry Barnard, the first secretary of the Connecticut Board of Education, was the second most influential leader in the establishment of the public schools and, like Mann, was a Whig. He was from a devoutly religious family and believed, like Mann, that he was responding to a call from God to disseminate both moral and scholastic truths through the public schools. Other key educational leaders also reflected the prevailing view at the time, that the public schools were a moral enterprise even more than they were an academic enterprise.

As much as most contemporary Americans support the notion of the public schools, Horace Mann and his colleagues initially faced tremendous opposition in their efforts. Originally, the public school movement was a conservative movement supported by Whigs, whose stronghold was largely in the North and opposed by Democrats, whose base was largely in the South. In addition, many parents had reservations about public schools. Two of the main concerns they had were that they believed that the state was usurping the role of parents by making the schooling experience far less personalized. Second, when parents utilized private schools, these schools were generally church-based neighborhood schools in which the parents nearly always already knew the teacher personally. In the case of public schools, however, the teachers were often previously unknown to the parents even in cases in which the schools were small. If one cogitates over the matter, it is an act of trust for parents to send their children to schools to be instructed by teachers that they have never met. Consequently, when public schools first became a nationwide movement, parents were skeptical about sending their children, whom they generally regarded as pearls, off to perfect strangers.

A man emerged who sought to address these concerns. Johann Pestalozzi asserted that the teacher should function like a mother away from home. Previously hesitant parents found this approach reassuring and it allayed their fears. Pestalozzi also believed that children should gradually be weaned off their dependence on their mother and teacher so that their reliance would be on God. In order to accomplish this goal, Pestalozzi believed that the Bible and other Christian literature and perspectives should represent the very core of the curriculum. He affirmed the salience of a Christ-centered education. Pestalozzi stated:

> Thus it is evident that the truth of fundamental and organic education and the totality of its means issues forth from the divine spark which is planted into human nature and harmonizes with the spirit of Christianity. On the other hand, it is equally evident that our present education with all its artificiality, corruption, and routine does not spring forth from the divine spark in the depth of man, but from his brutal and sensuous desires. Consequently,

it contradicts the spirit and evidence of Christianity and can have no other effect but to undermine it. (Pestalozzi, 1801, p. 423)

Pestalozzi, like his predecessor Johann Amos Comenius, could not conceive of a fruitful curriculum without the presence of the rich Christian flavor. Robert Ulich notes,

> Both Pestalozzi and Comenius were so intrinsically religious that their piety shines through every one of their works. They could not speak of nature without thinking of God as its creator; they could not speak of the human being without sensing the divine in even the poorest soul. For both parental love and the good family were the reflection of the fatherly love of God on the level of human relations. . . . Finally, for both, education was not merely a way of teaching and learning, but the human attempt to participate in the divine plan to unfold the best in individual man and in humanity as a whole. (Ulich, 1968, p. 30)

Pestalozzi's views, along with the perspectives of Mann and his contemporaries, contributed to the continuance of an important place for the Bible in public school curriculum as a means of moral education.

Given that the common schools naturally needed a common curriculum, leaders of the movement looked to utilize a writer of school textbooks who could capture the most essential qualities and truths that the leaders of the common schools wanted portrayed in their books. In other words, these leaders wanted a writer who could promote a civil religion. The author who best fulfilled this commission was William Holmes McGuffey (1800–1873). McGuffey was a minister from western Pennsylvania who penned what was collectively generally referred to as the *McGuffey Readers*. The *Readers* became the preeminent textbooks used in America's schools from the 1830s to the 1890s and during their tenure sold about 120 million copies, making the books one of the three top selling in American history (Jeynes, 2003, 2007).

The *McGuffey Readers* included numerous Bible accounts and verses designed for application to one's life. Beyond this, the readers contained Christian and biblical principles such as the golden rule, responsibility, the work ethic, forgiveness, and honesty. Because of their widespread use for so many years and the nature of their content, some have called the *Readers* the most influential books in American history. They helped ensure that the Bible would not only maintain a key position in the curriculum in a general sense but also that it would possess widespread influence across the country. The *McGuffey Readers* were less biblical than the *Primer* and after 1878, following McGuffey's death, they gradually started to become less Bible-centered.

The Bible also had an exceptionally important place in the kindergarten. Friedrich Froebel (1782–1852) founded the first kindergarten in Germany in 1839, but the kindergarten did not arrive on America's shores until 1855 in Watertown, Wisconsin. By 1898, however, the number of kindergartens in the United States soared to nearly 4,500.

The rapid increase in the number of kindergartens was key for biblical instruction in the schools because in Froebel's original rubric he highlighted the spiritual and biblical purpose of the kindergarten. Froebel was both a minister and the son of a minister. In his view, the primary purposes of the kindergarten were totally distinct from the elementary school. Specifically, he affirmed that the kindergarten should be a garden of children growing up to experience unity with God and with each other. He stated, "Education consists in leading man as a thinking intelligent being growing into a self-conscious and free representation of the inner law of Divine Unity, and teaching him the ways and means thereto" (Cohen, 1977, p. 5). To Froebel, kindergarten was the place where children developed the moral and social foundation to function as productive adults in a civic and social sense as well as in an academic and moral sense. In the *Education of Man,* Froebel stated, "And God-likeness is and ought to be man's highest aim in thought and deed" (Froebel, 1898, p. 59).

The kindergarten, as it was practiced in Europe and the United States, was a highly religious enterprise. About half of each kindergarten session involved reading Bible stories, singing hymns, praying, and other religious exercises. In Froebel's view, in order for children to grow and experience unity with God they needed to be exposed to Christian truths and principles through the Bible and other means.

In the mid-1800s as the common school movement grew, it was clear that these schools represented the perspectives of the vast majority of Americans who were Protestant. In these schools, teachers used a version of the Bible generally used by Protestants, usually the King James Version of the Bible. Largely in response to this, Catholic parochial schools began to multiply during the mid-nineteenth century. Catholics wanted to use their own translation of the Bible called the Douay Version and to freely encourage their own religious practices.

The inclusion or exclusion of the Bible from the schools in the nineteenth century generally did not involve conflict between the religious and the secularists, but rather usually involved friction between Protestants and Catholics. In 1800, Catholics generally made up only 2–3 percent of the population of major cities like New York, Chicago, and Philadelphia. By 1850, however, Catholicism had become the largest denomination in many major cities across the United States. As one might expect, membership in all Protestant denominations combined far outnumbered Catholic membership. Nevertheless, many Protestants were wary of increased Catholic power. There were a number of reasons for Protestants feeling ill at ease. First, myriad Protestants were well aware of the many historical injustices committed by European Catholics against Protestants and some Protestants were concerned that history could repeat itself if Catholics became too numerous or potent. (Catholics, of course, could cite their own litany of injustices at the hands of Protestants.) Second, on some issues Catholics maintained somewhat different beliefs than Protestants, e.g., interpretation of the Bible. Third, some Protestants believed that the Catholic Church was corrupt and did not honor the Bible in the same way that Protestants did, but instead esteemed papal edicts. These beliefs caused the rise of some anti-Catholic groups who often misunderstood the Catholic perspective. In addition, Catholics were accustomed to having their own schools in Europe, and they viewed their increasing numbers as an opportunity to exercise their new political power.

The Philadelphia Bible riots in May and July 1844 resulted from this tension. The riots involved conflicts between Irish immigrants and nativist residents who believed the assertion by some that Catholics wanted to remove the Bible and religious education from the schools.

Before this time the school day in Philadelphia began with the reading of the King James Version of the Bible, a practice favored by most Protestants. In November 1842, Bishop Francis Kenrick wrote a letter to the board of controllers of public schools, asking that Catholic children be allowed to use the Douay Version of the Bible and be excused from other religious teaching while at school. From the Catholic perspective, the requests were accommodating in nature. From the Protestant viewpoint, the two requests combined were separatist and uncompromising. Approximately 5,000 militiamen quelled the violence that broke out in the summer of 1844, but not before 15 people were killed, 50 were injured, and several Catholic churches were torched by Protestant mobs. Such conflicts hastened the development of Roman Catholic schools.

In late 1869, a similar controversy erupted between Protestants and Catholics in Cincinnati, Ohio. Previous to this time, Cincinnati schools had practiced the daily reading of the King James Version of the Bible and the singing of hymns. Catholic Archbishop John Purcell objected to this practice. Later, Rabbis Isaac Mayer and Max Lilienthal concurred. Although Cincinnati congregations at the time were largely conservative Protestant ones, the irony of the situation is that the only two ministers on the Board of Education were two Unitarian ministers whose congregations constituted less than two-tenths of a percent of the city's population (Michaelsen, 1969). The Board initially voted to suspend Bible reading and the singing of hymns. Although an Ohio Superior Court initially overturned the decision, the Ohio Supreme Court eventually upheld the decision in 1873 (Michaelsen, 1969).

The case commonly known as the "Edgerton Bible Case" of 1890, also involved a difference of opinion between Catholics and Protestants regarding the role of the Bible in the public schools. The Edgerton case was one brought before the Wisconsin Supreme Court on the reading of the King James Version of the Bible without comment. Catholics objected because they viewed the Douay Version as superior and believed that the Catholic Church was the only infallible interpreter of the Scriptures. The school board, on the other hand, argued that people should be free to interpret the Bible as individuals and that one could always withdraw from such readings. The Wisconsin Supreme Court ruled that the reading of the Bible was unconstitutional. It is important to note that the incidents in these states were isolated cases and that until 1962 and 1963, the reading of the Bible was widespread. Nevertheless, some historians note that the uncompromising stands of both the Catholics and Protestants may have hastened the removal of Bible reading from the schools (Ravitch, 2000; Sekulow, 2006).

The 1900s

With the rise of Deweyian pragmatism in the early twentieth century, educators in colleges and universities began to ponder using the Bible less in elementary and secondary schools. Nevertheless, John Dewey and his colleagues, for example, William H. Kilpatrick, believed in the value of moral education. In addition, although Dewey, Kilpatrick, and other "liberal" professors enjoyed influence at the higher education level, the actual practices in many schools remained focused on Bible and moral instruction (Jeynes, 2003, 2007). Most school districts across the country held homeroom devotional times during the first part of the school day. This usually included readings from Scripture and prayer (Dierenfield, 1962).

By the 1920s, the nation's Bible belt had moved from New England and other northern cities to the South and rural areas. Nevertheless, most of the nation remained highly religious. These facts caused something of a bifurcation in terms of how educators handled matters of Bible instruction. In the South and rural areas, Bible and religious instruction generally remained an integral part of the existing curriculum (Dierenfield, 1962).

One of the most common ways of providing Bible instruction in eastern and northern public schools was via what was called Weekday Religious Education (WRE), a program sponsored by the International Council of Religious Education, a multifaith religious group. The WRE was a released-time program in which once a week public school students would leave their classrooms to receive religious instruction from their churches. Most major cities in the North participated in this program, and the numbers of participants steadily increased in the decades that followed. By the end of World War II, 1.5 million students in 2,000–3,000 communities left their classes for released time, including 170,000 in New York City alone. The students taking these Bible and religious classes studied Noah's ark, the Creation, George Washington Carver, the nation's religious heritage, and "issues of racial equality and justice" (Zimmerman, 2002, p. 141). Parents who chose to enroll their children in WRE programs liked the programs because they offered more biblical instruction than typically found in the public schools.

In *McCollum v. Board of Education* (1948), the U.S. Supreme Court struck down the practice of these religious education classes on public school grounds. Erwin Shaver, America's leading religious educator and the chief organizer of the WRE, was quite surprised by the decision because it overturned an earlier Illinois court decision upholding the constitutionality of the program. The *McCollum* decision, however, proved to be only a temporary setback for the WRE programs because the weekday classes simply moved off public school grounds. In *Zorach v. Clauson* (1952), the U.S. Supreme Court upheld New York's off-campus WRE system. This instilled new life in released-time efforts, after an initial 10 percent drop in nationwide WRE enrollment following the *McCollum* decision. By 1959, the number of students participating in WRE surged to 4 million. In recent years, however, the number of students participating in released-time programs has dropped to around 300,000 (Zimmerman, 2002).

Prior to the U.S. Supreme Court decisions of 1962 and 1963, public school devotional times and Bible reading were common. According to a nationwide study by Richard Dierenfield, who likely conducted the most extensive study of religion in the public schools just prior to 1962, Bible reading was widespread at that time. For example, among communities with a population of over 100,000, Dierenfield found that 63 percent of school districts had "homeroom devotional services" in their schools. These devotional services included Bible readings and prayer, but also sometimes included "devotional teachings" and the singing of hymns. Bible reading occurred in 54 percent of these school districts. In addition, 79 percent of American school districts included the "teaching of spiritual values" (e.g., reverence for God, faith, and love). His study also indicated that 99.44 percent of school systems included "teaching of moral values" and 76 percent of school districts provided materials to help instructors teach about religion. Research also indicates that 42 percent of school districts had Gideon Bibles distributed among them and 22 percent held chapel services (Dierenfield, 1962; Fenwick, 1989).

Some regional differences were evident in Dierenfield's findings. Generally, the Northeast and the South were most likely to hold devotional services and Bible readings. Before 1962 over 80 percent of northeastern school systems and 79 percent of southern school systems had homeroom devotional services. These results are fairly predictable given that the Northeast was the nation's Bible belt until the early 1900s, when the South earned that title. Bible reading was practiced in 77 percent of the South's school systems and in 68 percent of the Northeast's systems. Midwestern school systems (81 percent), however, were the most likely to provide materials to teachers for instruction in religion. Midwestern schools were also slightly more likely than northeastern school systems (77 percent to

75 percent) to teach about spiritual values, although they trailed southern schools in this area (94 percent).

The U.S. Supreme Court Decisions of 1962–1963 and Their Aftermath

In many respects, if one had examined the general religious situation in 1960, one would probably not have anticipated the 1962 and 1963 U.S. Supreme Court decisions. In 1960 the United States was squarely in the midst of what many called the "Eisenhower revival." Polls indicated that 69 percent of Americans attended church each week and the number of students benefiting from WRE instruction was at an all time high. Children could purchase praying dolls in the stores, and the struggle against religiously oppressive communism spawned a realization of the salience of religion (Zimmerman, 2002).

Not surprisingly, in this kind of an atmosphere, Bible reading without comment and/or devotional readings was present in a majority of American school districts. As Edwin Gaustad and Leigh Schmidt note, "Public schools grew up in the midst of a Protestant ethos that not only allowed Bible reading, but also praying and hymn singing as a routine part of the school day" (Gaustad and Schmidt, 2002, p. 358). Concurrently, however, a small number of Americans led by the American Civil Liberties Union (ACLU) sought to eliminate the devotional reading of the Bible in the public schools.

Three U.S. Supreme Court Decisions in 1962 and 1963 radically changed the practice of Bible reading and moral instruction in the public schools. As Andryszewski (2002) notes, "Most people approved of these practices in their public schools" (p. 21). The first of these three U.S. Supreme Court decisions, *Engel v. Vitale,* was handed down on June 25, 1962. Technically, the case addressed school prayer rather than specifically addressing the reading of the Bible. Speaking for the Court, Justice Hugo Black declared that state officials could not compose an official state prayer for recitation. A year later, in June 1963, the U.S. Supreme Court handed down two additional decisions: *School District of Abington Township v. Schempp* and *Murray v. Curlett.* The *Abington Township v. Schempp* decision stated that Bible passages and the Lord's Prayer could not be recited, "even if individual students may be excused from attending or participating in such activities at the request of their parents."

Justice Potter Stewart filed dissents in each of these cases, using words that proponents of Bible reading and freedom of religious expression often use to bolster their cases. In the *Schempp* dissent Stewart asserted:

> As a matter of history, the First Amendment was adopted solely as a limitation upon the newly created National Government. The events leading to its adoption strongly suggest that the Establishment Clause was primarily an attempt to insure that Congress not only would be powerless to establish a national church, but would also be unable to interfere with existing state establishments.

Furthermore, Stewart averred:

> If religious exercises are held to be an impermissible activity in schools, religion is placed in an artificial and state-created disadvantage...And a refusal to permit religious exercises thus is seen, not as the realization of state neutrality, but rather as the establishment of a religion of secularism, or at least, as governmental support of the beliefs of those who think that

religious exercises should be conducted only in private. (*Abington Township v. Schempp*, 374 U.S. 203 [1963])

Some legal experts objected to the Supreme Court's decisions on the basis of not only the decisions themselves but also the unusual dearth of judicial experience of the justices (Michaelsen, 1970). In nearly every case, the justices were appointed to the Supreme Court following a long history of political rather than judicial experience (Michaelsen, 1970). Chief Justice Earl Warren had served as governor of California for ten years before his appointment; Justice Hugo Black had been a U.S. Senator for ten years; Justice Arthur Goldberg served as Secretary of Labor; Justice William Douglas was Chairman of the Security and Exchange Commission; and Justice Felix Frankfurter was an assistant to the Secretary of Labor and served as a founding member of the American Civil Liberties Union (ACLU). Ironically, the only justice with extended federal constitutional experience before he began his service on the Supreme Court, Justice Potter Stewart, was also the only justice to object to the removal of prayer and Bible reading.

Following the 1962 and 1963 Supreme Court decisions, many political leaders and most of the general public openly criticized the Court. In the *Congressional Record* for the day after the *Engel v. Vitale* decision, not one member of Congress defended the Court's decision. Some congressional leaders initiated a movement to impeach the Supreme Court Chief Justice Earl Warren. Senator Eugene Talmadge asserted that, "the Supreme Court has set up atheism as a new religion." Many of the nation's leaders voiced firm opinions in the hours and days following the Supreme Court's *Engel* decision in June 1962 and similar decisions in 1963. Congressman Frank Becker, a Catholic, called the *Engel* decision, "the most tragic in the history of the United States." A 1963 Gallup Poll indicated that Americans were opposed to the *Engel, Murray,* and *Schempp* decisions by a three to one margin. In spite of the unpopularity of the decisions, one should note that the Court actually encouraged teaching *about* the Bible, as long as it was done objectively.

After the failure of an initial attempt to pass a constitutional amendment that would have allowed students the liberty of having Bible reading and prayer in the schools, politicians did not aggressively address the issue again until the election of Ronald Reagan. He made it a major priority of his administration to restore religious liberty in the public schools.

Although Reagan's attempt to get a constitutional amendment passed failed, the effort made it clear that most Americans and their political leaders favored increased religious liberty in the schools, though not necessarily state-sponsored devotional exercises. This momentum yielded a new venture to reduce discrimination against people of faith called the Equal Access Act. Eventually enacted by Congress in 1984, it embodied the principle of a U.S. Supreme Court case from 1981, *Widmar v. Vincent* (Andryszewski, 1997). In the *Widmar* case the U.S. Supreme Court ruled that a *university* could not explicitly deny the equal use of its facilities to religious groups and that to do so discriminated against people of faith. The congressional Equal Access Act extended the *Widmar* principle to include public secondary schools (Andryszewski, 1997). The act made it possible for student-led Bible study clubs and other religious groups to meet at the same time and with the same rights as nonreligious groups and clubs. The Supreme Court affirmed the provisions of the Equal Access Act in *Board of Education of Westside Community Schools v. Mergens* in 1992.

One year later, in *Lamb's Chapel v. Center Moriches Union Free School District* (1993), the Court ruled that if a public school opens its facilities to various community groups during nonschool hours, it may not exclude groups with a religious viewpoint. In *Good News Club v. Milford Central School* (2001), the Supreme Court ruled that a New York school district could not refuse an adult-led Christian ministry to children after hours access to its school facilities. These "equal access" decisions were important Bible reading cases because the majority of the applicable religious groups studied the Bible.

Recent Developments

In the early part of the twenty-first century, scholars and educators revisited the specific wording of the 1962 and 1963 U.S. Supreme Court decisions and noted that the justices actually encouraged the academic study of the Bible as long as it was done in an objective way. For example, in the *Schempp* (1963) case, the Court stated, "Nothing we have said here indicates that such study of the Bible or of religion, when presented objectively as part of a secular program of education, may not be affected consistently with the First Amendment."

The reanalysis of these decisions sparked an effort to reintroduce the Bible into the schools both for its historical value and as a tome of great literary import. For many centuries the authors of books from most of the world's continents, Europe, North America, South America, and Australia, wrote with the assumption that the reader would have a working knowledge of the Bible. As a result, many of the great books of the world have themes, titles, and references to the Bible. William Shakespeare alone cites the Bible about 1,300 times. Moreover, such books as *Grapes of Wrath, East of Eden, War and Peace,* and a host of others cannot be fully comprehended unless one has a solid knowledge of the Bible. Authors such as Charles Dickens, Fyodor Dostoevsky, Leo Tolstoy, and Ernest Hemingway are also difficult to fathom without a thorough knowledge of the Bible. Perhaps the most convincing reality of all is that the Bible is not only easily the best-selling book in the history of humanity, but it has been the world's best-selling book each and every year in recorded history and has remained so to this day.

Both American and world history have also been profoundly influenced by the Bible in particular and religion in general. Whether one reads about George Washington's miraculous eschewing of certain death during the French and Indian War that had such a dramatic impact on his Christian commitment, or the Puritans and Quakers teaching slaves the truths of the Bible, or the role of the Bible in the women's suffrage and civil rights movements, knowing the Bible is essential to comprehending American history. With all these facts in mind, it is easy to understand why many academics believe that an adequate knowledge of the Bible is part and parcel of a complete education. Recent research confirms that Bible literacy is strongly associated with higher academic outcomes and better social behavior among students. These results help justify offering courses in the Bible as literature in hundreds of school districts across the country. Some states have even passed legislation so that these courses are offered as electives across their state, and a myriad of school districts offer the Bible as literature as an elective course. The *Bible Literacy Project* and other efforts are underway to encourage the instruction of the Bible as literature in public schools. Given that these efforts do not entail a devotional use of the Bible, which the Court struck down in 1962 and 1963, and instead emphasize the teaching of the historical and literary significance of the Bible, which those Court decisions actually encouraged, the expansion of the Bible as literature course offerings in the public schools is likely to continue. *See also:* Academic Freedom; Bible Literacy Project; The Common School; Mann, Horace; Moral Education; National Council on Bible Curriculum in Public Schools; Religion and the Public School Curriculum.

Further Reading: *Abington Township v. Schempp,* 374 U.S. 203 (1963); Tricia Andryszewski, *School Prayer: A History of the Debate* (Springfield, NJ: Enslo, 1997); Paul Blanshard, *Religion and the School* (Boston: Beacon Press, 1963); *Board of Education of the Westside Community Schools v. Mergens,* 496 U.S. 226 (1990); Dorothy H. Cohen, *Kindergarten and Early Schooling* (Englewood Cliffs, NJ: Prentice-Hall, 1977); Richard B. Dierenfield, *Religion in American Public Schools* (Washington, DC: Public Affairs Press, 1962); *Engel v. Vitale,* 370 U.S. 421 (1962); Lynda B. Fenwick, *Should the Children Pray?* (Waco, TX: Baylor University Press, 1989); Edward. A. Fitzpatrick, *The Educational Views and Influence of DeWitt Clinton* (New York: Arno Press, 1969); Friedrich Froebel, *Education of Man* (New York: Appleton and Company, 1898); Edwin S. Gaustad and Leigh E. Schmidt, *The Religious History of America* (New York: Harper San Francisco, 2002); W. Clark Gilpin, "The Creation of a New Order: Colonial Education and the Bible," in *The Bible in American Education,* ed. D.L. Barr and Nicholas Piediscalzi (Philadelphia: Fortress Press, 1982); *Good News Club v. Milford Central School,* 533 U.S. 98 (2001); Kent Greenawalt, *Does God Belong in the Public Schools?* (Princeton, NJ: Princeton University Press, 2005); William Jeynes, *American Educational History: School, Society, and the Common Good* (Thousand Oaks, CA: Sage Publications, 2007); William Jeynes, *Religion, Education and Academic Success* (Greenwich: Information Age Publishing, 2003); Herbert M. Kliebard, *Religion and Education in America* (Scranton, PA: International Textbook Company, 1969); *Lamb's Chapel v. Center Moriches Union Free School District,* 508 U.S. 384 (1993); Horace Mann, *Ninth Annual Report* (Boston: Dutton & Wentworth, 1846); *McCollum v. Board of Education,* 333 U.S. 203 (1948); Robert Michaelsen, "Common School, Common Religion? A Case Study in Church-State Relations, Cincinnati 1869–1870," *Church History* 38 (June 1969): 201–217; Robert Michaelsen, *Piety in the Public School* (London: Macmillan, 1970); *Murray v. Curlett,* 374 U.S. 203 (1963); Johann Pestalozzi, *Leonard and Gertrude* (Philadelphia: Groff, 1801); Leo Pfeffer, *Church, State and Freedom* (Boston: Beacon, 1953); Stephen R. Prothero, *Religious Literacy* (San Francisco: Harper San Francisco, 2007); Diane Ravitch, *The Great School Wars: A History of New York City Public Schools* (Baltimore: Johns Hopkins University Press, 2000); Jay Sekulow, *Witnessing Their Faith: Religious Influence on Supreme Court Justices and Their Opinions* (Lanham, MD: Rowman & Littlefield, 2006); Robert Ulich, *A History of Religious Education* (New York: New York University Press, 1968); Carter G. Woodson, *The Education of the Negro Prior to 1861* (New York: Putnam's, 1915); Jonathan Zimmerman, *Whose America? Culture Wars in the Public Schools* (Cambridge: Harvard University Press, 2002); *Zorach v. Clauson,* 343 U.S. 306 (1952).

William Jeynes

Bible Literacy Project

The Bible Literacy Project (BLP) is a nonprofit organization established by Chuck Stetson, a former vice chairman of the National Bible Association, and Richard Scurry to promote the academic study of the Bible in American high schools. According to its Web site, the organization offers the "first and only student textbook for public high school and non-devotional electives about the Bible." In cooperation with Concordia University in Portland, Oregon, it also provides the "only university-based online teacher training program for how to teach the Bible in public school" (Bible Literacy Project, at www.bibleliteracy.org). The organization is funded by grants (including a sizable award from the John Templeton Foundation), donations, and sales.

Central to the BLP's efforts is the conviction that "an educated person is familiar with the Bible," a slogan found in its promotional materials. In 2005–2006, the organization released two reports arguing that most teenagers lack biblical literacy and that such literacy is essential for success in college (Wachlin, Johnson, and the Bible Literacy Project, 2005 and 2006). These publications helped generate visibility of the organization, which published its textbook, *The Bible and its Influence,* in September 2005 (Schippe and Stetson, 2005).

The nearly 400-page textbook is divided into 40 chapters, split approximately evenly between the Hebrew Bible and the New Testament. Chapters typically focus on pivotal stories of the Bible (i.e., the creation narratives, Abraham and Sarah, the Exodus experience), particular biblical books, or groups of related biblical books. Each chapter provides a summary of the pertinent biblical materials as well as related examples of biblical themes and allusions in music, art, literature, and political thought. The book is extensively illustrated with images of classic paintings and statues of biblical characters and scenes. It was written with the legal guidelines described in *The Bible and Public Schools: A First Amendment Guide* (The Bible Literacy Project and the First Amendment Center, 1999) in mind. According to the BLP, drafts of the textbook were reviewed by over 40 consultants from diverse religious perspectives (Jewish, Roman Catholic, mainline and evangelical Protestant) and professional backgrounds (high school teachers, academics of various fields, lawyers, and religious leaders). Endorsements ranged from Chuck Colson, founder of Prison Fellowship, to Marc Stern of the American Jewish Congress to Richard Sklba of the Catholic Biblical Association. A teacher's guide with additional background materials and suggested discussion questions and projects appeared in 2006.

The reception of the BLP's textbook in religious, academic, and civil libertarian circles has been mixed (Chancey, 2007). Although many magazines reviewed it very favorably, some groups and individuals alleged that it was too liberal for public school usage. The textbook drew particularly heavy criticism from Christian Right organizations when lawmakers in Alabama and Georgia introduced legislation to promote its usage in 2006. The charge of liberalism led the BLP to make slight revisions when it re-released the textbook that same year. Some Jewish organizations, such as the American Jewish Congress and the Anti-Defamation League, have expressed cautious support for the BLP, in part because they see its textbook as less problematic than an alternative curriculum produced by the National Council on Bible Curriculum in Public Schools. Americans United for the Separation of Church and State has greeted the organization with skepticism, noting Stetson's involvement with evangelical Christian groups such as Promise Keepers and with Republican politics, suggesting that the textbook downplays negative examples of the Bible's cultural influence and criticizing as misleading its discussion of the Bible's impact on America's Founding Fathers (Conn, 2006). Some biblical scholars have argued that the textbook underutilizes biblical scholarship, contains factual errors, and reflects a Protestant bias, while others have hailed it as a major accomplishment that takes seriously the Bible, the diverse religious sensibilities of students, and the legal limitations established by the courts (Chancey, 2007, and www.bibleliteracy.org). *See also:* The Bible in the Public Schools; National Council on Bible Curriculum in Public Schools.

Further Reading: The Bible Literacy Project, at www.bibleliteracy.org; The Bible Literacy Project and the First Amendment Center, *The Bible and Public Schools: A First Amendment Guide* (New York: Bible Literacy Project; Nashville: First Amendment Center, 1999); Mark A. Chancey, "Bible Bills, Bible Curricula, and Controversies of Biblical Proportions: Legislative Efforts to

Promote Bible Courses," *Religion & Education* 34 (Winter 2007): 28–47; Joseph L. Conn, "The Bible Literacy Project: Chuck Stetson's Trojan Horse?" *Church & State* 59 (January 2006): 19–21; Marjorie Haney Schafer, Cullen Schippe, and Chuck Stetson, eds., *The Bible and Its Influence: Teachers Edition* (New York and Front Royal, VA: BLP Publishing, 2006); Cullen Schippe and Chuck Stetson, eds., *The Bible and its Influence* (New York and Fairfax, VA: BLP Publishing, 2005 and 2006); Marie Wachlin, Byron R. Johnson, and the Bible Literacy Project, *Bible Literacy Report: What Do American Teens Need to Know and What Do They Know?* (Front Royal, VA: BLP Publishing, 2005); Marie Wachlin, Byron R. Johnson, and the Bible Literacy Project, *Bible Literacy Report II: What University Professors Say Students Need to Know* (Front Royal, VA: 2006).

Mark A. Chancey

Blaine Amendment

Introduced in the U.S. House of Representatives in 1876 by James G. Blaine of Maine, the Blaine Amendment was a heavy-handed and ultimately unsuccessful effort to outlaw the distribution of public funds for the support of parochial education. Although the Blaine Amendment never passed into federal law, the term came to be applied to similar laws that were passed in 29 states across the country in the years from 1877 to 1917.

In the years after the Civil War, non-Catholics were particularly concerned about the ethnic cast of many parish schools, and public schoolmen and legislators sought ways of influencing the content of parochial education. Non-Catholics also sought ways to end the Catholic campaigns to gain public funds for their schools. Throughout the 1870s and 1880s, Catholics and non-Catholics conducted separate campaigns to increase their influence over the growth and content of parochial schools.

Fearful of the growing power of the Catholic Church in the United States, non-Catholics launched two separate legislative efforts, one to prohibit the use of public money for parochial schools and a second campaign to monitor and control the content of parochial school curricula.

In an effort to stop the endless Catholic efforts to obtain public funds for their schools, many state legislatures considered amending their constitutions to prohibit the use of public funds for religious institutions. Such amendments were approved by voters in Illinois, Pennsylvania, and Colorado, but defeated in New York, Michigan, Ohio, and New Jersey.

The campaign escalated in September 1875 when President U.S. Grant condemned the use of public funds for religious schools. "Encourage free schools," Grant proclaimed, "and resolve that not one dollar of money appropriated to their support, no matter how raised, shall be appropriated to the support of any sectarian school." His speech made a national issue out of the various Catholic campaigns in the states.

Grant followed his speech with a December message to Congress calling for a constitutional amendment to prohibit any state from giving funds to religious schools. Soon after Grant's speech, Congressman James G. Blaine of Maine introduced a bill in Congress to accomplish the president's proposal.

Not surprisingly, Catholics throughout the nation were very vocal in their opposition. In fact, the *Catholic World* suggested rather caustically that Congress should prohibit the use of public funds for "sectarian" and "atheistic" public schools as well. Catholic protests may have had an effect on Congress. Even though the amendment passed the House of Representatives in August 1876, it failed in the Senate.

The national campaign to prohibit public money for parochial schools ended as quickly as it began, and many Catholics dismissed the matter as little more than politics. But this was wishful thinking. The Blaine Amendment, as it came to be called, had a significant effect on the states. Over the next four decades nearly 30 states incorporated the amendment into their constitutions. Indeed, some state legislatures looked for ways to exert public control over portions of the parish school curricula.

In the late 1880s, as the Blaine legislation became increasingly popular, state legislatures also began efforts to control the content of parish schools. Some legislators thought that there ought to be a law that required parochial schools to conform to public school standards. This idea materialized in law in Illinois and Wisconsin in 1889 and the resulting controversy reverberated around the nation. These laws were logical extensions of the climate established by the Blaine Amendment.

The implication of these new laws—state control over private schools—was unprecedented, but the vigor of the Catholic backlash came as a surprise to many Americans. To most Americans, it was just another law; but to Catholics, it was a threat to the very purpose and independence of their schools.

The battleground for this controversy was the Midwest, principally the states of Illinois and Wisconsin. Legislatures in these states attempted to control the content of parish schools by law. Coalitions of Catholics and Lutherans stopped their attempts.

The defeat of the private school laws in Illinois and Wisconsin constituted a turning point in the campaign for control over parochial education. For the next 35 years, Catholics shifted their attention to controlling the growth and development of Catholic education from *within* the denomination. The disagreements with the state over who would control the parochial schools were set aside for a generation.

Both Catholic and public schoolmen learned important lessons in their efforts to control parochial education during the last half of the nineteenth century. Both sides learned that control of parochial education was elusive. Successful campaigns must be based on patience, persistence, and persuasion, not fiat or legislation.

The spirit of the Blaine Amendment and subsequent efforts to control parochial education came to a hiatus in the middle of the 1920s when the U.S. Supreme Court issued the landmark decision in *Pierce v. the Society of School Sisters*. In this decision the Court noted that the state had the power to "reasonably regulate" parochial schools but had no authority to abolish or control these institutions. From that point on, state legislatures made only marginal efforts to influence parochial schools.

But the concept of prohibiting state funds for the support of parochial education has not completely passed into history. The ongoing debates in state legislatures and in state courts over the legality of tuition tax credits and school vouchers are reminiscent of the Blaine debates more that 125 years ago. In 1999 the Arizona Supreme Court made reference to the Blaine Amendment in *Kotterman v. Killian,* which upheld the constitutionality of tax credits for individual donations to scholarship programs sponsored by nonprofit organizations, and the U.S. Supreme Court noted Blaine in *Zelman v. Simmons-Harris,* a 2002 decision that upheld the constitutionality of the Cleveland school voucher program. *See also:* Anti-Catholicism in Education; Government Aid to Religious Schools; Tuition Tax Credits; Vouchers.

Further Reading: Harold A. Buetow, *Of Singular Benefit: The Story of U.S. Catholic Education* (New York: Macmillan, 1970); Marie C. Klinkhammer, "The Blaine Amendment of 1875: Private Motives for Political Action," *Catholic Historical Review* 42 (1956): 15–49; Timothy Walch, *Parish*

School: American Catholic Parochial Education from Colonial Times to the Present (Washington, DC: National Catholic Educational Association, 2003).

Timothy Walch

Board of Education of Kiryas Joel Village School District v. Grumet

A New York statute, Chapter 748 of New York Laws, enacted in 1989 created a school district, the boundaries of which intentionally coincided with the boundaries of the Village of Kiryas Joel, in which virtually only practitioners of Satmar Hasidim, a strict form of Judaism, lived. These individuals live almost outside the modern world and have no wish to be assimilated into it. Sexes are segregated outside homes; Yiddish is the primary language; television, radio, and English-language materials are prohibited; girls wear modest dresses while boys wear head coverings and special garments. The Torah is interpreted strictly.

Children belonging to the sect attended religious schools and received special education (services for the deaf, mentally handicapped, and other disorders) in an annex of one of the religious schools. The 1985 Supreme Court decision of *Aguilar v. Felton,* however, ended the offering of Title I and other governmentally provided special education services in religious settings.

The statute gave locally elected school boards authority over elementary and secondary education in the village. In an effort to provide the needed special education services and to comply with *Aguilar,* the separate public school district, which would provide only special education, was established. If a non-Hasidic child not in need of special services were to move into the village, the district would pay tuition for attendance at another public school. Before the new district could begin operations, taxpayers and the association of the state boards of education brought suit alleging that Chapter 748 and the creation of a new school district based on religious affiliation violated the Establishment Clause of the First Amendment, which states, "Congress shall make no law respecting an establishment of religion. . ." by creating a district to which only residents of Kiryas Joel had access. The state trial court granted summary judgment for the petitioners. The intermediate appellate court and the New York Court of Appeals affirmed the judgment and ruled that the primary effect of Chapter 748 was the advancement of religion prohibited by the Establishment Clause.

The U.S. Supreme Court granted certiorari (review) of the decision. The Archdiocese of New York, the American Center for Law and Justice, the Christian Legal Society, and the Knights of Columbus filed briefs of *amici curiae* urging reversal. The American Jewish Congress and Americans United filed briefs of *amici curiae* supporting the upholding of the lower court decisions for separation of church and state.

In a 6-3 decision, the U.S. Supreme Court ruled that the New York statute did violate the Establishment Clause of the First Amendment because it definitely created a school zone excluding the nonreligious and persons who practiced a religion other than Hasidic Judaism. Justice David Souter delivered the opinion of the Court. Since the Kiryas Joel Village School District was not created simply as one of many school districts eligible for, and receiving, equal treatment under the law, there is no guarantee that any other religious group wanting its own school district will receive one, and the Court was faced with a case-specific creation of a school district for a specific religious community. Thus, there would be no way for the Court to review such action by the state so that the principle of governmental neutrality with regard to religion was safeguarded.

The Court could find no historical context to support this seemingly special treatment of the villagers of Kiryas Joel; in fact, the majority opinion states that the historical trend is at odds with the act in question. The Court acknowledged that the Constitution allows the government to accommodate religious needs by alleviating specific burdens, yet held that Chapter 748 crossed the line from accommodation of religion that can be permitted to respect for an establishment of religion that cannot be allowed. Other religiously neutral alternatives for providing special education to Satmar children exist that did not violate the Establishment Clause. The Court observed that an appropriate program could be housed in one of the existing public schools or at a neutral site near one of Kiryas Joel's parochial schools. If the education provided by the alternatives proved educationally unsatisfactory, the state could enact legislation making additional demands on all school districts in terms of special education or bilingual and bicultural education. Souter wrote, "Because this unusual Act is tantamount to an allocation of political power on a religious criterion and neither presupposes nor requires governmental impartiality toward religion, we hold that it violates the prohibition against establishment." *See also: Aguilar v. Felton.*

Further Reading: *Aguilar v. Felton,* 473 U.S. 402 (1985); *Board of Education of Kiryas Joel Village School District v. Grumet,* 512 U.S. 687 (1994).

Mary Angela Shaughnessy

Board of Education of the Westside Community Schools v. Mergens

Board of Education of the Westside Community Schools v. Mergens (1990) involved a facial challenge to the constitutionality of the Equal Access Act (EAA) enacted by Congress in 1984. In the EAA, Congress prohibited public secondary schools receiving federal financial assistance and with limited open forums from denying equal access to, or discriminating against, students who wished to conduct a meeting within that limited open forum on the basis of the religious, political, philosophical, or other content of the speech at such meetings. This prohibition, however, was limited only to noncurriculum-related, student-initiated, and student-led clubs that met during noninstructional time.

The public high school in *Mergens* had denied students' request to form a Christian club that would meet after school on school premises. While the school permitted the Christian club to meet informally after school, the high school refused to officially recognize it as part of the school activities program, which carried with it access to the school newspaper, bulletin boards, the public address system, and the annual Club Fair. When the students filed a lawsuit alleging an EAA violation, the school district raised two defenses. First, while the school did permit other student clubs to meet, school officials claimed that they were all curriculum-related. Second, the school alleged that the EAA violated the Establishment Clause by requiring religion on public school premises.

The federal district court dismissed the students' claim, finding that permitting the club to meet would violate the Establishment Clause. On appeal, the Eighth Circuit Court of Appeals reversed, holding that the school had violated the EAA and that permitting the club to meet would not violate the Establishment Clause.

The U.S. Supreme Court granted certiorari and, in affirming the decision of the Eighth Circuit, held that the school fell within the requirements of the EAA. Regarding the school's first defense, the Supreme Court found that the school permitted a wide range of noncurriculum-related clubs. The Court rejected the school's effort to identify some noncurriculum-related student clubs as curriculum-related ones, for example, arguing that the chess club was part of the math curriculum or that the scuba diving club was part of the physical education curriculum. The Supreme Court rejected such efforts and determined that a student group had to be "directly related" to subject matter courses before it could be considered to be curriculum-related. Thus, a group of math teachers encouraging students to play chess to improve math skills was not sufficient to make chess curriculum-related if chess itself was not offered as a separate course. In addition, the Court interpreted the EAA quite literally to find that a public secondary school's permitting even one noncurriculum-related student group to meet triggered obligations under EAA. Thus, this meant in *Mergens* that the school was required to provide access to the same benefits available to other student clubs, such as the school newspaper, bulletin boards, the public address system, and the annual Club Fair.

The Court also upheld the constitutionality of the EAA against an establishment clause claim, finding that allowing a wide range of student clubs to meet, including the Christian club, had a secular purpose and that high school students were not likely to perceive that a religious club meeting on the same basis as other clubs constituted government sponsorship of religion. In rejecting the establishment clause challenge, the Supreme Court distinguished between "*government* speech endorsing religion, which the Establishment Clause forbids, and *private* speech endorsing religion, which the Free Speech and Free Exercise Clauses protect." Considering the large number of student clubs at the school and that the EAA protects only clubs meeting during noninstructional time, the Court was satisfied that "secondary school students are mature enough and are likely to understand that a school does not endorse or support student speech that it merely permits on a nondiscriminatory basis."

Mergens is a key Supreme Court decision reflecting a change in the treatment of religion in public schools. Three years after *Mergens,* the Supreme Court delivered its unanimous landmark decision in *Lamb's Chapel v. Center Moriches Union Free School District* (1993) that religious speech was a fully protected subset of expression under the Free Speech Clause. The EAA has continued to undergo interpretive challenges, particularly as to whether "noninstructional time" can include activity periods that occur during the school day where other secular clubs have been permitted to meet. *See also: Everson v. Board of Education of the Township of Ewing; Lamb's Chapel v. Center Moriches Union Free School District.*

Further Reading: Board of Education of the Westside Community Schools v. Mergens, 496 U.S. 226 (1990); Equal Access Act, 20 U.S.C. §§ 4071-4074; *Lamb's Chapel v. Center Moriches Union Free School District,* 508 U.S. 384 (1993); Ralph D. Mawdsley, "The Equal Access Act and Public Schools: What Are the Legal Issues Related to Recognizing Gay Student Groups?" *Brigham Young University Education and Law Journal* (2001): 1–33.

Ralph D. Mawdsley

Board of Education v. Allen

The U.S. Supreme Court heard this school textbook case on an appeal from the Court of Appeals of New York. New York's education law required that all children in grades 7 through 12, including those in the private schools, be loaned textbooks free of charge by the local public school authorities. Until 1965, the law, 701 of the Education Law of the State of New York, authorized public school boards to use public funds to purchase textbooks to be rented or sold to public school students. In 1965, the state legislature amended 701 and required, beginning in 1966–1967, that local school boards purchase textbooks and lend them without charge "to all children residing in such district who are enrolled in grades seven to twelve of a public or private school which complies with the compulsory education law."

Appellee Allen, the state commissioner of education, could remove board members if boards failed to lend books to parochial school students within their counties. The appellant school boards asked the court to rule that the statute was invalid and violated both the state and federal constitutions, as it allowed the use of state funds for the purchase of textbooks to be lent to parochial students. Further, appellants sought an order forbidding the state commissioner of education to remove board members from office for failing to comply with the law. To prevent their removal, the board members had approved and submitted a budget that included funds for the purchase of textbooks to be lent to parochial school students; to remedy this inclusion of funds that appellants viewed as unconstitutional, they also sought an order preventing the use of government monies for the purpose of purchasing textbooks to be lent to students in parochial schools.

The trial court ruled that the statute was unconstitutional under the First and Fourteenth Amendments since, as appellants argued, loaning textbooks to students in religious schools constituted aid to religion. Summary judgment was granted to the appellants on the pleadings. On appeal, the Appellate Division reversed the trial court and ordered the case dismissed since it ruled that the appellant school boards had no standing to attack the statute (they were neither recipients of the aid nor taxpayers, but rather boards that had no stake in the outcome). The New York Court of Appeals held that the appellants did have standing, but that the law did not violate the provisions of the state or federal constitution since the law was to benefit all school-age children, regardless of the school attended, and the textbooks loaned had to be approved by school authorities prior to the loan. Therefore, reasoned the court, loaning textbooks to students in religious schools was neutral and violated neither the Establishment nor the Free Exercise Clause of the First Amendment.

Justice Byron White referenced the 1930 *Cochran v. Louisiana State Board of Education* case, in which appellants argued that a Louisiana statute requiring the provision of schoolbooks to all students without charge did not serve a public purpose and thus violated the Fourteenth Amendment. Chief Justice Charles Evans Hughes, delivering the majority opinion, concluded that Louisiana's interest in the secular education provided to private school students was a public concern. Therefore, the provision of textbooks was proper.

Citing *Everson v. Board of Education* (1947) as the case most "nearly in point" to this one, the U.S. Supreme Court discussed its reasoning in *Everson* as support for its decision in *Allen*. In *Everson,* the Supreme Court held that the Establishment Clause forbids the government from adopting laws, the enactment of which would aid one religion, aid all religions, or constitute a preference of one religion over another. Nonetheless, it found that New Jersey's practice of reimbursing parents for the expenses of busing their children to parochial schools was constitutional. In its reasoning, the Court stated that the Establishment Clause does not keep a state from giving benefits of state law to all citizens without regard to religious affiliation. The Court acknowledged that government reimbursement of transportation monies for parochial school students did help children attend church schools and even that, without the transportation aid, some children would not attend church schools because the parents would not be able to, or would choose not to, pay both tuition and transportation costs. In *Everson,* the court compared the reimbursement of transportation costs to the public provision of fire and police services, sewage facilities, and other services, the provision of which did not constitute aid to religion even if religious institutions profited from them. Therefore, the indirect benefit accruing to a religious school from the reimbursement of transportation monies to parents did not constitute a violation of the First Amendment, as the purpose of the law was to get all students to schools, both public and private, and not to aid religious schools in particular.

Justice White also wrote that the *Schempp* case stated a test to be applied in any cases in which aid to religion was alleged: if the statute has a secular purpose and a primary effect that does not advance nor inhibit religion, it is permissible. Thus, the Supreme Court found that the "express purpose" of the 701 law compelling the loan of secular textbooks to all students was to support education of the young and to allow all children the benefits of a textbook loan free of charge. Thus, any direct benefit is to parents and children, who do not have to buy the books, not to the schools. The Court could find no evidence presented that religious books of any kind had been loaned under the program. Further, the court stated that school authorities should be able to distinguish between allowed secular texts and forbidden religious books, and no evidence was presented indicating that they could not make the distinction or that they approved any religious books.

Parochial schools serve two functions: the provision of secular education and education in a specific religion; however, there is no evidence that teaching in a sectarian school is a religious activity or that the "intertwining" of the two functions results in secular text-books being used in the teaching of religion. Appellants argued that since textbooks are the primary medium of instruction, it is only logical to assume that teachers in religious schools use all textbooks, even secular ones, to provide instruction in religious principles or at least to comment on textbook contents from a religious standpoint; appellants maintained, therefore, that loaned textbooks could and probably were used as an aid to religious instruction; since the textbooks were the property of the government, the government was involved in the promotion of religion. Additionally, appellants maintained that providing textbooks at no cost to students in religious schools enabled their parents to have more money available to pay tuition and other religious school expenses; thus, the religious school as well as the children, benefited from the textbook loan.

The majority opinion found that appellants had presented no specific evidence that the statute caused unconstitutional state involvement with religion and/or religious instruction. Therefore, the Court found no violation of the Establishment Clause of the First Amendment. Appellants were also unable to demonstrate that the law coerced them in the practice or nonpractice of religion.

The Supreme Court recognized that private, including parochial, schools do at least an acceptable job of delivering secular education. Since no evidence was offered supporting appellants' contention that any or all textbooks are used by parochial schools and their teachers to teach religion and/or that anyone is being coerced into a religious practice, no constitutional violation can be found.

It should be noted, however, that the decision that a state *may* provide textbooks does not mean that the state *must* provide textbooks. The decision to provide or not to provide textbooks to parochial school students rests with the state legislatures. There is no constitutional bar to the provision of textbooks to students in schools affiliated with a religion, but there is no constitutional mandate to provide them. In 2007, very few states offer text-books or transportation reimbursement to students attending private schools. *See also: Cochran v. Louisiana State Board of Education.*

Further Reading: *Board of Education v. Allen,* 392 U.S. 236 (1968); *Cochran v. Louisiana Board of Education,* 330 U.S. 1 (1947); *Everson v. Board of Education,* 333 U.S. 203 (1947); *Lemon v. Kurtzman,* 403 U.S. 602 (1971).

Mary Angela Shaughnessy

C

California 3 Rs Project: Rights, Responsibilities, Respect

The California 3 Rs Project is a nonprofit, nonpartisan teacher and community education program of the California County Superintendents Educational Services Association (CCSESA) in cooperation with the Freedom Forum First Amendment Center at Vanderbilt University. The Project is built on the conviction that the guiding principles of the First Amendment to the U.S. Constitution stand at the heart of democracy and at the foundation of citizenship in a diverse society. Foremost among these shared civic principles are the "3 Rs" of religious liberty as defined in the *Williamsburg Charter,* a reaffirmation of religious liberty signed by nearly 200 leaders from every sector of American life in 1988:

> *Rights*—religious liberty, or freedom of conscience for people of all faiths and none, is an inalienable right founded on the inviolable dignity of the human person. A society is only as just and free as it is respectful of this right for its smallest minorities and least popular communities.
>
> *Responsibilities*—citizens have an obligation to guard for others those same rights they wish guarded from themselves. The survival of the American experiment in religious liberty depends upon the acceptance and exercise of this civic duty.
>
> *Respect*—debate and disagreement are vital in a democracy. Yet if we are to live with our differences, *how* we debate, and not only *what* we debate, is critical. At the heart of good citizenship and strong schools is a commitment to the civic values that enable people from differing ethnic backgrounds and religious convictions to treat one another with civility.

The California 3 Rs Project originated in large part as a response to debates that arose when the California State Board of Education adopted a new History-Social Science Curriculum Framework in 1988. This framework acknowledged the importance of religion in human history and stressed that "students must become familiar with the basic ideas of the major religions and the ethical traditions of each time and place" (California Department of Education, 1988/1997, p. 7). It went on to specify where and how the topic of religion in American and world history should be addressed in the elementary and secondary school curriculum.

The response to this new framework was mixed. Some citizens, educators, and scholars applauded the fact that the academic study of religion, which had long been neglected in America's public schools, was now being acknowledged for its important contributions to basic historical and cultural literacy as well as to education for citizenship in a religiously diverse society. But others were more ambivalent or critical. Many teachers and school administrators felt unprepared to deal with the new curricular content and with the range of pedagogical challenges and potential or perceived legal issues that might be associated with the study of religion in public schools. Some parents and community members were concerned about bias and inconsistency in the implementation of the new curriculum, and several religious and secular advocacy groups sought to politicize the discussion as a means of mobilizing their own constituencies. In some local school districts, these concerns erupted into open conflicts over school board policies, textbooks, curricula, and student religious expression, thereby opening up yet another front in America's ongoing "culture wars" during the 1990s.

It was against this background of confusion and controversy that representatives of the CCSESA met with Charles C. Haynes of the First Liberty Institute at George Mason University in 1991. Their purpose was to develop a teacher and community education program designed to promote the civic principles that would enable local communities and schools to "learn to live with their deepest differences" by "finding common ground" on issues of religion and values in public schools. With initial funding from private foundations, the 3 Rs Project opened an office in 1993 with Nicholas Piediscalzi serving as project director. When Haynes accepted a position at the Freedom Forum First Amendment Center in 1994, the 3 Rs Project became a joint program of the CCSESA and the First Amendment Center.

The 3 Rs Project builds upon a "consensus approach" to religion and religious liberty in public schools that has been set forth in several "statements of principles" endorsed by a remarkably broad range of educational, religious, and civic organizations. According to this approach:

Public schools may not inculcate nor inhibit religion. They must be places where religion and religious conviction are treated with fairness and respect.

Public schools uphold the First Amendment when they protect the religious liberty rights of students of all faiths or none. Schools demonstrate fairness when they ensure that the curriculum includes study *about* religion, where appropriate, as an important part of a complete education. (Haynes and Thomas, 2007, p. 6)

The 3 Rs Project has a statewide organization and partners with county offices of education and universities to offer professional development programs for teachers on First Amendment principles and teaching about world religions and their influence in history. It also publishes a quarterly bulletin with articles directed at school and district administrators on current religious liberty topics and issues. The Project's Steering Committee and Advisory Board consist of representatives from educational, civic, and religious organizations throughout California. Margaret Hill has served as Project Director since 2002. *See also:* First Amendment Center; Utah 3 Rs Project: Rights, Responsibilities, Respect.

Further Reading: California 3 Rs Project, at http://score.rims.k12.ca.us/score_lessons/3rs/ index.html; California Department of Education, *History-Social Science Framework for California Public Schools* (Sacramento: California Department of Education, 1988/1997); Charles C. Haynes and Oliver Thomas, *Finding Common Ground: A First Amendment Guide to Religion and Public Schools* (Nashville: First Amendment Center, 2007).

Bruce Grelle

Calvinist Schools

Christian schools in the Calvinist or Reformed tradition are somewhat unique in that they have a long history (more than 150 years) and they are generally operated by parent-controlled societies rather than by a diocese, a denomination, or an independent church. Dutch in ethnic heritage, Calvinist in theology, Christian Reformed by denomination, these schools were established by immigrants from the Netherlands in 1857 in order to preserve their ethnic and religious traditions and to live out their understandings of *covenant,* the obligations of people in relationship to God, and *kingdom,* the mandate to seek and do God's will on earth. Similar to other ethnic and denominational groups in the United States, they exemplify the struggle of many cultural groups trying to protect and pass on their deeply held values and practices amidst the pressures of an increasingly diverse and sometimes antagonistic world.

The Calvinist approach to Christian schooling can be traced back to the Reformation and Dutch independence from Spain. Calvinism dominated religious thought and colored the new national church with its well-defined theology, Presbyterian Church order, and strong moral sense. The Calvinist tradition exercises a high conception of the role of education, not simply as a means of maintaining doctrinal purity but as training for the larger Calvinistic program in politics, economics, and social relations. Calvinists hold a high view of Scripture as the "inspired Word of God." The noted themes of Scripture—trinity, creation, the fall, covenant, redemption, kingdom, Christ's lordship, new heaven, and new earth—form the background to all scholarly inquiry and all human activity.

Perceived secularization in the Dutch national church and in the government schools during the first half of the nineteenth century and the potato famine of the 1840s resulted in secession and emigration to North America. At first the early settlers affiliated with the Dutch Reformed Church, but in 1857 four tiny Western Michigan congregations split (over weak doctrinal standards, lodge membership, and hymn singing) and formed the Christian Reformed Church (CRC), the denominational foundation for the American expression of Calvinist day schools. Because these immigrants felt that public schools reflected the bland American Protestantism of the day, that America constituted a spiritually dangerous environment, and that the young people especially would lose their faith and take on the superficialities of American religious life, the first schools were established to preserve among the young the Dutch language and heritage and Calvinist faith and piety.

Most schools were affiliated with a CRC church until 1872, when the Synod of the CRC officially turned over control of the schools to parent societies. The churches continued in supervisory roles, but this marked an important shift in sponsorship: from a parochial to a parental school system.

While the first schools were designed to isolate and protect the youth, resulting in modest academic achievement, another wave of immigration at the beginning of the twentieth century brought the intellectual influence of Abraham Kuyper from the Nether-lands and the genuinely Reformed idea of active Christian engagement with society and culture. The central thrust of Kuyper's thought was that Christ was King over *all* of life, that He redirects and regenerates a culture marred by personal and social sin, and that Christians must work to put all of life, including politics, business, science, the arts, and education, under His rule. They would "transform" culture by analyzing societal issues and responding to them in a distinctly Christian way.

Between the two World Wars, in the local and nationwide push to Americanize, the schools dropped the Dutch language and raised academic expectations and teacher train-ing standards, but continued to focus more on piety than cultural engagement. The schools continued to struggle with three cross-purposes: to isolate from American culture and preserve the heritage, to accommodate the wider culture and adopt its values, or to transform the culture based on biblical principles. The key motivator for starting the schools—the anxiety about how to be Dutch in America—was now replaced by the anxi-ety of how to be Christian in a secular world.

In 1920 an umbrella organization was formed, Christian Schools International (CSI), located in Grand Rapids, Michigan, which now claims almost 500 American and Cana-dian schools as members. The schools employ nearly 10,000 full-time and part-time faculty members who teach nearly 100,000 students. CSI assists member schools with curriculum and teacher guides, textbooks and magazines, accreditation services, insurance and pension plans, leadership development, online courses, and consulting services.

During the latter half of the twentieth century, the schools became increasingly diverse. Parents from various denominations sent their children for the schools' academic excellence and religious environment. CSI sought to assist its members in maintaining their essential Calvinist nature and purpose, to declare an identity in an age when being Dutch and Christian Reformed was no longer the defining set of characteristics, and to open doors to a population more ethnically and denominationally diverse. One CSI publication, *From Vision to Action: The Basis and Purpose of Christian Schools,* suggested that Reformed Christian schools seek to embody the triple dimensions of *conserver, inquirer,* and *reformer* in itself and in the lives of its students.

As conserver, the Reformed Christian school community preserves and passes on the story—the meaning, the purpose, the roots, the cultural anchor points, the accumulated wisdom, the world-life view—of its tradition. As inquirer, the Reformed Christian School hopes to instill in students a love of learning and inquiry, for cultivating the life of the mind, for thinking critically and fruitfully about the world and human experience. Finally, as reformer, the Reformed Christian School is guided by the vision of a new and better world: the Kingdom of God. Reformed Christian educators seek to model and teach a life of constant *re-forming*: questioning, evaluating, changing, growing, a life of discipleship that is responsive to God, the creation, the structures of society, and the host of humanity. These three goals—*conservation* of the Christian worldview, *inquiry* into all aspects of life and the world, and *reforming* the world by living a life of discipleship responsive to God and his Word—form a thread of continuity in Reformed educational thought.

Curriculum in Calvinist day schools generally resembles the subject matter divisions of the government schools. Textbooks, from both secular commercial and Christian publish-ers, are common. A Christian perspective on subject matter is frequently addressed and under constant assessment. Evangelism is not a priority. The schools prefer to focus on academics and Christian living and service, leaving explicit evangelism to the churches. In the words of a CSI publication, students are led to "know God and to respond to him in every dimension of the creation and in every aspect of their lives," to "apply the transforming power of the gospel to contemporary society and culture," and to "bring the healing power of Jesus Christ to a fallen world."

Two emphases for Reformed Christian schooling are worth noting: community support and the culture-affirming curriculum. First, because Reformed Christian schooling is an enterprise of the entire community for the good of the world, the financial responsibility for the school's operation is not simply the task of a tuition-paying parent, but all churches and all members of the Christian community. Second, the Reformed Christians assume a culture-affirming stance. Because God created and redeems the entire world, culture and society are seen by Reformed Christians as good and God-given, and therefore must be affirmed, celebrated, and enhanced. While rife with problems, culture is still seen as the arena for God's goodness to people. *See also:* Common Ground Documents.

Further Reading: James D. Bratt, *Dutch Calvinism in America: A History of a Conservative Subculture* (Grand Rapids, MI: Eerdmans Publishing Company, 1984); Christian Schools International, at csionline.org; George Stob, "The Christian Reformed Church and Her Schools" (Ph.D. diss., University of Michigan, 1955); Steven C. Vryhof, *Between Memory and Vision: the Case for Faith-Based Schooling* (Grand Rapids, MI: Eerdmans Publishing Company, 2004).

Steven C. Vryhof

Cantwell v. Connecticut

Jesse Cantwell and his two sons, members of the Jehovah's Witnesses, a religious sect, who claimed to be ordained ministers were arrested and charged with statutory and common law offenses. Each was ultimately convicted of inciting a breach of the peace and violation of a Connecticut statute. The sons had their conviction for inciting a breach of peace overturned. All three were convicted, and the convictions were sustained of violation of statute 294 of the General Statutes of Connecticut, which required anyone who wished to solicit donations for a religious cause to apply for a certificate from the secretary for the Public Welfare Council of the State who was required to determine if the cause was a legitimate religious one. The secretary alone had the discretion to make that decision and to give or refuse to give a certificate:

> [the secretary] shall determine whether the cause is a religious one or is a bona fide object of charity or philanthropy and conforms to reasonable standards of efficiency and integrity, and if he shall so find, shall approve the same and issue to the authority in charge a certificate to that effect. Such certificate may be revoked at any time.

A government official, then, was charged with determining what constituted a religious cause and licensing those who were, in his opinion, religious. No matter how religious a cause may in fact have been, without the secretary's approval, no one could seek donations on its behalf, except from other members of the religious institution claiming the cause. Violation of the statute could result in a fine of not more than $100 or imprisonment for not more than 30 days or both.

The Cantwells appealed the conviction under the statute as they maintained it was offensive to the Due Process Clause of the Fourteenth Amendment because it denied them their First Amendment rights of freedom of speech and free exercise of religion. (Although the statute had been upheld in the lower courts, its validity was being questioned under the federal Constitution and the conviction on the count of inciting disturbance of the peace raised a federal question under the U.S. Constitution.) The U.S. Supreme Court accepted jurisdiction over the claims and appeal.

Cantwell and his sons, as members of the Jehovah's Witnesses, would travel to cities and towns and knock on people's doors or stop them on the streets and ask them if they would agree to listen to a phonograph recording of one of their books. After the playing of the record, the Jehovah's Witnesses would ask the listener to buy the book. If the listener declined, he or she was asked for a donation toward the cost of publication and a pamphlet was left. Appellants argued that their activities did not constitute seeking donations for a religious cause but rather the sale of books and distribution of pamphlets.

On the day of the contested incident, Cantwell stopped two gentlemen in the street and asked their permission, which was given, to play the recording on the phonograph. The recording, entitled "Enemies," was highly critical of religion in general and of the Catholic religion in particular. The two gentlemen, both members of the Catholic Church, were insulted. One said he felt like "hitting" Cantwell and the other asked him to leave. Cantwell left with no incident and no violence or threatened violence.

Justice Owen Roberts wrote the majority opinion, which held that the Connecticut statute, as applied to the appellants, constituted a deprivation of freedom without due process of law and therefore violated the Fourteenth Amendment as it made the First Amendment applicable to the states. States, like the federal government, have no power to create a law that either respects an establishment of religion or contradicts the free exercise of religion. States have the right to regulate the time, place, and manner of religious expression, meetings, street solicitations, and the like so as to protect the peace and rights of the community.

Requiring persons who wish to solicit for a religious cause to apply for a license, the granting of which can be made only by a state official upon his determination that the religious cause is valid, however, is an impermissible involvement in the free exercise of religion. Thus, the Connecticut statute was unconstitutional.

The conviction on the count of inciting a disturbance of the peace was also set aside. The facts of the case show no invasion of anyone's rights or of any incitement of anyone to disturb the peace. The state has no right to punish someone for the expression of an unpopular religious view in the absence of any conduct posing a danger to the public. *See also:* First Amendment Religious Clauses and the Supreme Court.

Further Reading: *Cantwell v. State of Connecticut,* 310 U.S. 296 (1940).

Mary Angela Shaughnessy

Catholic League for Religious and Civil Rights

The Catholic League for Religious and Civil Rights is a social action organization that purports to be the largest Catholic civil rights group in the United States. Established in Milwaukee in 1973 by the Reverend Virgil Blum, S.J., the stated purpose of the Catholic League is to defend the right of Catholics against discrimination and to encourage

Catholic participation in American public life without defamation. The Catholic League takes the First Amendment as the source of its inspiration and works to safeguard both the religious freedom rights and the free speech rights of Catholics whenever and wherever they are threatened.

Although discrimination against Catholics has declined markedly in the United States since the election of John F. Kennedy to the presidency in 1960, the League quickly responds to criticism of the Catholic Church by social critics and the "liberal" establishment. Among other comments on its Web site, the League quotes Yale professor Peter Viereck, stating that "Catholic baiting is the anti-Semitism of the liberals." The literature and information published by the League about anti-Catholicism has a sense of urgency. In fact, the League's Web site claims that "today's brand of anti-Catholicism is more virulent and more pervasive than ever before in American history....Quite simply, Catholic bashing has become a staple of American society."

In addition to soliciting financial donations and member support from among a growing number of conservative Catholics, the League devotes most of its time to responding to what it refers to as "slanderous assaults" made against the Catholic Church. League representatives, most often longtime president William Donohue, conduct press conferences and appear on television and radio talk shows to defend the Church.

Of particular concern to the League are "bigoted" portrayals of Catholic clergy and women religious in the popular media. A common response from the League to an unflattering portrayal of the clergy is to organize a boycott of the program and the program's sponsors. The League also defends students or employees who claim religious discrimination in their schools or places of employment.

The League is also involved in a number of other related activities. For example, when Catholics are slighted by public officials or Catholic public officials take positions contrary to Church teachings, the League responds through the media. When Catholic interests are "threatened" by public policy initiatives, the Catholic League offers testimony before legislative bodies to try to change those policies. League activities are reported in a monthly journal entitled *The Catalyst* that is distributed to members and friends.

Among the Catholic causes defended by the League are the rights and benefits of parochial education. Available on the League's Web site is an assortment of brief position papers on a variety of educational topics including anti-Catholicism and the history of Catholic school funding, religious liberty in public schools, school choice, and Catholic studies programs at public colleges and universities. Even though education is important, the League devotes far more attention to other issues. For example, the League has issued annual reports on anti-Catholicism since 1994 and the League's Web site provides a vigorous defense of the actions of Pope Pius XII during World War II.

The League is supported through donations from its membership. The League Web site is very clear in stating that the organization receives no support from formal Catholic organizations such as the United States Conference of Catholic Bishops. There are many clergy among the membership, but all funding comes from individuals, not the Church. The League Web site notes that there are no political candidates or elected officials on its board of directors. It is true, however, that the board is made up of conservative Catholics, several of them former officials of recent Republican administrations.

The driving force behind the League and its spokesman for the past two decades has been William A. Donohue, a former Catholic schoolteacher and college professor.

As director of the League, Donohue has written three books and numerous articles, many of them on religious freedom and civil liberty. His first book, *The Politics of the American Civil Liberties Union,* was published in 1985. His second book, *The New Freedom: Individualism and Collectivism in the Social Lives of Americans,* appeared in 1990. His third book, *Twilight of Liberty: The Legacy of the ACLU,* was published in 1994.

Donohue is an articulate, some might say combative, advocate in defense of conservative Catholicism. Although the League claims to be nonpartisan, it seems clear from Donohue's ties to the Heritage Foundation, the National Association of Scholars, Catholics United for the Faith, and the Ave Maria Institute that the organization is deeply rooted in a traditional, conservative view of the Catholic Church and its place in the American democratic experience. *See also:* Anti-Catholicism in Education; Catholic Schools.

Further Reading: Catholic League for Religious and Civil Rights, at www.catholicleague.org; Philip Jenkins, *The New Anti-Catholicism: The Last Acceptable Prejudice* (New York: Oxford University Press, 2004); Mark Massa, S.J., *Anti-Catholicism in America: The Last Acceptable Prejudice,* revised ed. (New York: Crossroad Publishing, 2005).

Timothy Walch

Catholic Schools

Catholic schools constitute the largest sector of private schools in the United States. With a rich history that reaches back into the 1700s and a tradition that continues into the twenty-first century, Catholic schools have made significant contributions to the American cultural landscape, helping to educate millions of students, often recent immigrants, ethnic minorities, and the urban poor. The success of Catholic schools provides evidence of the value of religious freedom, the importance of faith-based institutions in constitutional democracies, and the richness of cultural diversity when equality of opportunity is supported in a national context (Walch, 1996).

2006–2007 Descriptive Statistics

Enrollment in K–12 Catholic schools in 2006–2007 was 2,320,651. Of this total, 1,662,412 were in Catholic elementary and middle schools, and 638,239 in Catholic high schools. Minority student enrollment stood at 596,149, representing 25.7 percent of the total enrollment. Non-Catholic enrollment was 329,615, or nearly 14 percent of the total enrollment (McDonald, 2007).

The total number of Catholic schools in the United States was 7,498. Of this total, 6,288 are elementary schools and 1,210 are high schools. Catholic schools employed 159,135 full-time equivalent professional staff, creating a student/teacher ratio of approximately 15:1. The professional staff was composed of 95.6 percent of laymen and laywomen and 4.4 percent of vowed religious men and women, including clergy. Of the laity, 74.5 percent were women, 21.1 percent men. Of the clergy, 3.2 percent were religious sisters, 0.6 percent religious brothers, and 0.6 percent priests (McDonald, 2007).

Although Catholic schools can be found in all parts of the United States, approximately half of all the schools (49.3 percent) are located in the Great Lakes and Mideast regions. Moreover, Catholic education is also a heavily urban phenomenon, with 43.6 percent of schools located in the inner city. With the general population patterns seen in U.S. culture involving growth in the South, West, and Southwest, Catholic education is also experiencing some growth in these areas.

The diversity of Catholic schools is apparent in the composition of the national student population. The percentage of minorities in Catholic schools has more than doubled in the past 30 years. Minority students currently account for 25.7 percent of all enrollment, a significant increase from 19.4 percent in 1980, and only 10.8 percent in 1970. Although most students in Catholic schools are of the Catholic faith, non-Catholic enrollment has also experienced significant gains, rising from 2.7 percent in 1970 to 11.2 percent in 1980 to 13.6 percent in 2006 (McDonald, 2007).

Catholic schools are funded in large part by tuition, typically charged to parents for their children to enroll and attend. In most Catholic schools, however, tuition and other fees usually constitute only a portion of the actual per pupil expense for educating the child. The gap, or difference between charged tuition and actual per pupil cost, often takes the form of scholarship aid, parish subsidy, or some other form of tuition assistance in order to meet the full and true cost of the education provided. The average tuition in Catholic elementary schools for 2006–2007 was $2,607, representing only 61.7 percent of the actual cost per pupil of $4,268. Approximately 87 percent of elementary schools offer some type of scholarship or financial assistance. The high school situation is even more pronounced as high schools are more expensive to operate and tuition costs are therefore always higher. Average Catholic high school tuition was $6,906, while per pupil costs at the high school level were $8,743.

The National Catholic Educational Association, a membership organization for all Catholic schools in the United States, estimates that Catholic schools are providing nearly $20 billion of educational services to the youth of America by operating these schools and educating its students. With the average per pupil cost to educate one student in U.S. public schools approaching $9,000 in 2007, Catholic schools are saving U.S. taxpayers the dollars that would be required to educate these students if the nearly 2.5 million students in Catholic schools were to attend their assigned public school. While it is unlikely that this would occur, these savings are real and animate the desire of Catholic educators and other professional educators in the private sector to seek some form of constitutionally acceptable support for their schools.

History

Catholic schools have been an important part of U.S. history since the colonial era, when Catholic schools were established in Louisiana and Florida (Hunt, Joseph, and Nuzzi, 2004). Missionaries from Europe were the most zealous in working to spread their faith and to teach the young to do the same. This early period was fraught with great challenges, as French and Spanish missionaries suffered many setbacks in attempting to educate Native Americans. Other missionaries from England encountered difficulties of a religious nature in the form of discrimination from the dominant Protestant culture of that era. Catholicism itself was faced with the question of its very survival, and this included the schools. Walch (1996) stated that it was not until the 1820s that it became clear that Catholicism would survive in the New World.

Immigration was the driving force behind the growth of Catholic schools in the mid-nineteenth century. As millions of Europeans flocked to the shores of America in quest of a better life for themselves and their families, they found solace and support in the ethnic enclaves of Catholic parishes and schools. These institutions supported both their national and religious identities, and provided for a system of mutual collaboration and participation. The parishes offered a place where families could gather and seek comfort from like-minded adults. The religious traditions of ethnic groups could be preserved, even given prominence in the new parish, and schools created an opportunity for advancement and for educating the young in the customs, culture, and ethos of the group. The wave of immigration began in 1820, and by 1875 there were 1,444 Catholic schools operating in the United States (Hunt, Joseph, and Nuzzi, 2004).

At least two other groups of Catholics played a significant role in the quick establishment and growth of Catholic schools. The first was the bishops, who provided some of the institutional support; and the second was the nuns, the religious sisters, who provided the necessary human resources in the form of teachers, administrators, and staff to establish schools without the need for exorbitant start-up funds for salaries.

In general, U.S. bishops supported the building of Catholic schools. As public education became more Protestant, Catholic bishops worried that such schools might pose a danger to the faith of Catholic children. This was especially the case with the public recitation of the King James Version of the Bible in public schools, as well as frequently required devotional exercises. By 1884, Catholic bishops had had enough. They decreed, during a meeting in Baltimore, that every Catholic parish was to have a parish school and that all Catholic parents were to send their Catholic children to that school. While this vision was never realized, it provided the impetus for the erection of Catholic schools and a sustained building program that lasted for nearly 80 years.

The religious orders of sisters supplied a free and steady stream of personnel to staff schools during this period. Living in community at or near the parish and working for little more than basic sustenance, the religious sisters were the teachers and principals in Catholic schools, and contributed an invaluable service to Catholic education in this period of rapid growth. Without the presence and commitment of these women, the vision of the bishops might never have been addressed in a productive way, for the funds to staff schools were not readily available. Moreover, by their lifestyle and religious vocation, the sisters provided a living example of faith in action that became a part of what was taught and experienced in the school. Religious orders of men also provided services in staffing Catholic schools, in the form of ordained priests and vowed religious brothers.

Catholic schools enjoyed a broad popularity in the period after World War II and this was in many ways a period of continued growth. By academic year 1965–1966, Catholic school enrollment had reached its historical, all-time peak of 5.6 million students, an astonishing 87 percent of the country's nonpublic school enrollment. But the success was not to last. In the wake of the Second Vatican Council and cultural shifts both in the United States and in the Church, enrollments fell and schools began to close. A significant struggle facing schools in this period was the declining numbers of available vowed religious and the concomitant fiscal demands of hiring an increasingly lay faculty. Because the sisters had worked for decades for little or nothing, the costs of operating a school were limited to supplies, utilities, and small stipends. As fewer vowed religious were available in the period following Vatican II, laymen and laywomen had to be hired to fill the teaching positions once held by sisters. Tuition became more common, and as the price of Catholic education rose, an enrollment spiral was created. Although Catholic schools experienced a slight increase in enrollment in the 1990s, the general enrollment pattern has been downward since 1966 (McDonald, 2007).

There is a resurging interest in professional preparation programs at the university level for those who desire to work as teachers and principals in Catholic schools. Many Catholic colleges and universities offer teacher preparation programs, typically conceived as postgraduate service, for those who wish to teach in Catholic schools. The oldest and largest of these programs is the University of Notre Dame's Alliance for Catholic Education (ACE) Teacher Formation Program, although over a dozen other universities have followed ACE with similar programs (Alliance for Catholic Education, at ace.nd.edu). A similar effort can be seen in professional preparation programs for Catholic school principals. The University of San Francisco was an early leader in this area with its Institute for Catholic Educational Leadership programs, dedicated exclusively to preparing leaders for Catholic schools. The largest program in the United States for Catholic school principal preparation is currently the University of Notre Dame's ACE Leadership Program, though many other Catholic colleges and universities house similar programs. The presence of so many university-based preparation programs for teachers and administrators for Catholic schools helps to ensure that the human resource needs of the Catholic educational system can be met by highly qualified laymen and laywomen.

Philosophy

Catholic educational philosophy is rooted in a Christian anthropology that affirms that every person is made in the image and likeness of the creator God. This divine origin of every person is the basis of human dignity and requires that every person be treated in such a way as to honor, manifest, and celebrate this inherent, God-given dignity. Before God, there is a radical equality among all people, for each person shares equally in this participation in the divine image. Catholics see this worldview affirmed in the Bible, beginning in the creation accounts of the Book of Genesis, and following through the Christian Gospels of the New Testament. In the Catholic school, this vision is an overriding concern and is taught to all students, in age-appropriate ways, in a formal religion class. Catholic schools also espouse a theory of permeation or infusion, where teachers and administrators are challenged to see to the inculcation of these values throughout the curriculum and extracurricular activities in ways that are congruent with the goals and objectives of the various classes and activities (Hunt, Joseph, and Nuzzi, 2001).

Catholic schools are also animated by the steady and long-standing involvement of the Catholic Church in educational efforts in places such as seminaries, universities, and religious houses of formation. Although there is not a single, overarching Catholic viewpoint on education that could be called a Catholic philosophy of education, the philosophical tradition of Thomism certainly occupies a pride of place in Catholic educational institutions (Hunt, Joseph, and Nuzzi, 2001). Many scholars believe that the Thomistic system has found its best educational articulation in the works of the French philosopher Jacques Maritain. Along with Thomas Aquinas, Maritain embraced a decidedly theological worldview that continues to inform Catholic educational practice. Theology, therefore, is at the heart of Catholic educational practice, and it is the constitutive elements of Catholic theology that give Catholic education in general, and Catholic schools in particular, their unique Catholic identity and curricular content. Thus, unlike other educational systems, especially those in the public sector, Catholic schools do not take their cue from educational philosophy, but from Catholic theology.

From the practical side of operating a Catholic school, Catholic theology focuses the attention of the educational community on the person of Jesus Christ, as revealed in the Christian Gospels and as handed down in the Christian tradition over the centuries. There is a certain Christocentricity to the Catholic school. "From the first moment that a student steps foot in a Catholic school, he or she ought to have the impression of entering a new environment, one illumined by the light of faith, and having its own unique characteristics" (Congregation for Catholic Education, 1988). The purpose of the Catholic school is not simply to teach religious truths or to inform students about what the Bible teaches about Jesus; the school is to provide an encounter with the person of Jesus through the entire experience of educational processes. "Christ is the foundation of the whole educational enterprise in a Catholic school" (Sacred Congregation for Catholic Education, 1977), for "the Catholic school loses its purpose without constant reference to the Gospel and a frequent encounter with Christ" (Sacred Congregation for Catholic Education, 1977).

With Catholic theology at the core of the educational enterprise of the Catholic school, theological concepts and beliefs are easily operationalized in the daily conduct of the school. Catholic theology espouses, as does all of Christian theology, a belief in the death and resurrection of Jesus as recounted in the Gospels. This passing of Jesus through death to new life forms an essential core belief in the Catholic system and has major implications for the administration of a school or parish. Because of the centrality of Jesus's suffering and death, and the significance accorded that salvific act in the Bible and throughout the Christian tradition, Catholics believe that all suffering has meaning and purpose and that the particular vicissitudes of an individual's life are but a participation in what Jesus has already suffered and redeemed. Catholic schools teach that all of life's struggles—in the classroom, at home, on the athletic field, in relationships, through sickness, and even by death—are but examples of the ways that Jesus's example of dying and rising are made manifest in today's world. In this way, the theological components of the Catholic belief system inform Catholic educational practice and provide a context in which to understand and appreciate all the dynamics and struggles of modern-day life. Similar existential, practical applications can be made for other theological convictions, including the incarnation, the Trinity, and the Eucharist.

Since Catholic schools have been historically at the service of the poor and continue to be located in predominantly urban areas where recent immigrants and ethnic and religious minorities can be readily found, the Catholic educational system perhaps represents the Catholic Church's best work for social justice on behalf of the poor. The Catholic school can be understood, therefore, not only as a place where religious values are taught, but also where they are lived in a tangible way. While many Catholic schools are located in suburban areas and serve a population best described as economically elite, the history and philosophy of Catholic education show that Catholic schools have often done their best work in underresourced environments with the marginalized and the poor.

Catholic Education Research Today

Scholarly research on Catholic education is experiencing a period of dynamic growth. The past decade has seen the publication of several major works contributing to the growing status of the field of Catholic education, as well as the establishment of a refereed journal dedicated exclusively to Catholic schools. *Catholic Education: A Journal of Inquiry & Practice* was initially founded by four Catholic universities—Saint Louis, Fordham, Dayton, and San Francisco—but its sponsorship has now grown to include all the major Catholic universities in the United States. The journal serves as a venue for the scholarly productivity of professors with interests and specializations in Catholic schooling, and it provides an opportunity for professional networking for the various preparation programs run by the sponsoring universities. The journal's editorial offices resided initially at the University of Dayton, before transferring to the University of Notre Dame. Boston College is slated to be the next home for the journal, and the editorial offices will continue to rotate, every five years, among the sponsoring universities.

Significant scholarly contributions in recent years have included: *Catholic Schools in the United States: An Encyclopedia* (Hunt, Joseph, and Nuzzi, 2004); *Handbook of Research on Catholic Education* (Hunt, Joseph, and Nuzzi, 2001); *Catholic Schools at the Crossroads* (Youniss and Convey, 2000); *Catholic Schools* Still *Make A Difference* (Hunt, Joseph, and Nuzzi, 2002); and *Parish School* (Walch, 1996). In 2006, the University of Notre Dame issued a report from a university-based task force, *Making God Known, Loved, and Served: The Future of Catholic Primary and Secondary Schools in the United States.* This report called for national efforts to help strengthen the field of Catholic education more broadly by inviting researchers to include the Catholic sector in their educational research efforts. The report also called for more research within the Catholic sector in order to better understand the challenges facing Catholic schools and to make certain that efforts at renewal are data-driven and research-based.

Other recent scholarship involving Catholic schools has been in the area of sector effects and of trying to understand the differences between schools across a variety of disciplines. One area of great interest to policy makers has been the field of civic engagement. Legislators and educators alike have a keen interest in understanding what educational processes result in graduates who are highly engaged civically. A good citizenry is arguably at the core of democracy, so schools work diligently at social studies education and civics education in order to advance the future of the republic and to ensure an engaged and thoughtful voting public. In recent studies (Campbell, 2006), Catholic schools have consistently been among the highest producers of civic engagement, and more so than public schools. Such a finding has important public policy consequences in the age of school choice, vouchers, and tuition tax credits, and such research merits careful consideration. Catholic schools, even given their sectarian theological focus, contribute to the common good of American society in ways that are civically measurable and demonstrable. Additional sector effect studies analyzing other variables have also been a major area of study, especially in the sociology of education (Hallinan, 2006).

Catholic identity has also been a common theme in recent Catholic school research (Hunt, Joseph, and Nuzzi, 2002). The identity question attempts to address the unique or constitutive elements of Catholic schools, asking the question, "what makes a Catholic school Catholic?" In other words, apart from the regular menu of classes, sports, extracurricular activities, student groups, and social events, what are those components of a Catholic school that are unique to it, and not found in other schools, public or private? Researchers and practitioners maintain that this is a crucial question, the answer to which should dictate whether or not the Catholic school has a sufficient reason to exist. Recent scholarship has suggested that relationships are at the heart of Catholic identity, and that any Catholic institution—school, hospital, or social service agency—will work at establishing, maintaining, and strengthening three dynamic, interrelated relationships within the institution. Those relationships are with the local bishop, with Jesus Christ, and with the universal church (Hunt, Joseph, and Nuzzi, 2002). Catholic identity can be understood, therefore, as being constituted by and through a relationship with Jesus Christ, the church he founded, and the official representatives of that church in our historical situation.

Future Directions

Catholic schools will undoubtedly remain the largest private provider of education in the United States, though the structure of the Catholic school system is undergoing some changes. Whereas in previous decades, the parish school was the dominant model for organizational design, this is no longer always the most feasible scenario. Recent developments involving shifting demographics, the decline in available vowed religious, and financial constraints have caused Catholic schools to create new governance models that depart from the parish school model as a way to fund Catholic schools more broadly. Among these models are consolidated schools, where several parishes cooperate in supporting a single Catholic school; regional schools, where the school serves a variety of parishes and is incorporated as a separate legal entity; and private Catholic schools, where highly motivated individuals form and fund their own Catholic school, independent of any parish resources.

At the high school level, the most innovative approach in recent years has been the emergence of the Cristo Rey network of Catholic schools. Established exclusively in urban centers, Cristo Rey high schools form strong alliances with the business community and seek salaried employment for high school students in nearby businesses. Four students typically share one, full-time job, with each student spending one day per week on the job. The income earned from the gainful employment helps to offset the tuition, while parents pay the balance of the cost.

Governance is emerging as a central theme in the renewal of Catholic schools (University of Notre Dame Task Force, 2006). The parish school model relied heavily upon the support and involvement of the pastor. Although principals are typically the administrative head of schools, in the parish model, the pastor maintains supervisory authority over the principal and over the finances of the school. When parishes are strong and pastors are stable, this is strength of the Catholic educational system. As smaller parishes are increasingly unable to fund a school and as pastors often have to manage, administer, and troubleshoot several parishes, educators have been designing governance models that place the responsibility for operating the school in the hands of professionals who are familiar with the business side of education.

School boards or commissions have adopted models of specified or limited jurisdiction, which give significant oversight responsibility to the board, while preserving some specific, limited powers for the pastor or bishop. The idea behind such a model is that fuller participation will result in more thorough cooperation and eventual success for the school.

Bishops, too, exercise a similar jurisdiction in the realm of diocesan high schools. Although all such schools have a principal or president as the executive head, the current diocesan structure gives the diocesan bishop ultimate authority over the school curriculum, budget, staff, and operations. New models of shared governance are emerging at this level as a way to seek out broader participation and ownership in the school and to ensure a stable future.

Long-established practices nationwide have led every diocese in the United States to operate as its own independent school district, thereby losing the leverage that the Catholic Church's national scope has in relation to purchasing power, federal funding, and investment opportunities. Every diocese, for example, does all of its purchasing separately and independently of every other diocese in the country. This is true for purchases such as computers for schools and health care for teachers and other employees. It is likewise true for the purchase of utilities such as natural gas, electricity, and water. Because of this arguably unsound business practice, Catholic schools and dioceses are most likely paying much more for electronics, insurance, utilities, and other supplies and commodities when compared to other organizations of similar size and scope. Governance models with deeper lay participation and less clergy control have the potential to remedy these errors.

On the investment side, individual Catholic institutions such as parishes and schools often handle their own investments or, at best, invest with the diocesan central office. The investment leverage of the nationwide reach of the Catholic Church is lost in such an arrangement, as is the access to investment vehicles that are historically high yield-producing, because many such instruments require large sums of money not typically found in any one investor. Economies of scale questions, therefore, will be at the forefront in designing governance models for schools that support and encourage purchasing and investing in ways that take full advantage of the economic power of a national Catholic school system and a national church. *See also:* Anti-Catholicism in Education; Drexel, Katherine; Hughes, John; National Catholic Educational Association; Plenary Councils of Baltimore; Seton, Elizabeth.

Further Reading: John Augenstein, Christopher J. Kauffman, and Robert J. Wister, eds., *One Hundred Years of Catholic Education: Historical Essays in Honor of the Centennial of the National Catholic Educational Association* (Washington, DC: NCEA, 2003); Harold A. Buetow, *Of Singular Benefit: The Story of U.S. Catholic Education* (New York: Macmillan, 1970); David Campbell, "What Is Education's Impact on Civic & Social Engagement?" in *Measuring the Effects of Education on Health and Civic/ Social Engagement,* ed. Richard Desjardins and Tom Schuller (Paris: Centre for Educational Research and Innovation/Organisation for Economic Cooperation and Development, 2006).Congregation for Catholic Education, *The Religious Dimension of Education in a Catholic School* (Vatican City: Congregation for Catholic Education, 1988); John J. Convey, *Catholic Schools Make A Difference: Twenty-Five Years of Research* (Washington, DC: NCEA, 1992); Maureen Hallinan, ed., *Sector Effects and Student Outcomes* (Notre Dame, IN: University of Notre Dame Press, 2006); Thomas C. Hunt, Ellis A. Joseph, and Ronald J. Nuzzi, eds., *Catholic Schools in the United States: An Encyclopedia* (Westport, CT: Greenwood Press, 2004); Thomas C. Hunt, Ellis A. Joseph, and Ronald J. Nuzzi, eds., *Catholic Schools* Still *Make A Difference: Ten Years of Research 1991–2000* (Washington, DC: NCEA, 2002); Thomas C. Hunt, Ellis A. Joseph, and Ronald J. Nuzzi, *Handbook of Research on Catholic Education* (Westport, CT: Greenwood Press, 2001); Jacques Maritain, *Education at the Crossroads* (New Haven, CT: Yale University, 1943); Dale McDonald, *United States Catholic Elementary and Secondary Schools 2006–2007* (Washington, DC: NCEA, 2007); National Catholic Educational Association, *2006 Annual Report: Leadership, Direction, and Service* (Washington, DC: NCEA, 2007); *The Official Catholic Directory 2006* (New Providence, NJ: P. J. Kenedy & Sons, 2006); Sacred Congregation for Catholic Education, *The Catholic School* (Vatican City: Sacred Congregation for Catholic Education, 1977).University of Notre Dame, *Making God Known, Loved and Served: The Future of Catholic Primary and Secondary Schools in the United States* (Notre Dame, IN: University of Notre Dame, 2006); Timothy Walch, *Parish School: American Catholic Parochial Education from Colonial Times to the Present* (New York: Crossroad Publishing, 1996); James Youniss and John J. Convey, eds., *Catholic Schools at the Crossroads: Survival and Transformation* (New York: Teachers College Press, 2000).

Ronald J. Nuzzi

Center for Reclaiming America

The Center for Reclaiming America (CFRA) was founded in 1996 by James Kennedy (1930–2007) as the political advocacy arm of his conservative Presbyterian Coral Ridge Ministries, and was based out of Fort Lauderdale until its closure in the spring of 2007. The CFRA was known primarily for its annual conferences, which drew an impressive array of powerful evangelical and conservative leaders (in 2006, speakers included Richard Land of the Southern Baptist Convention, Rick Scarborough of Vision America, Alan Sears of the Alliance Defense Fund, and Tim Wildmon of the American Family Association). The CFRA used these conferences to build grassroots support for five concerns: religious liberty, pro-life, creationism, challenging the "homosexual agenda," and battling pornography, all concerns that mirrored Kennedy's personal political activism. He was one of the original board members of the Moral Majority, a founder of the Alliance Defense Fund, one of the advisory board of the Abstinence Clearinghouse, and a member of the advisory committee of the National Committee on Bible Curriculum in the Public Schools. He was a prominent member of the theologically conservative Presbyterian Church in America, which broke with mainline Presbyterianism in the mid-1970s over what it saw as its increasingly liberal theology.

Though Kennedy was politically active, he is most notable for his theological innovations per his conception of Dominion Theology. Dominion Theology refers to a range of beliefs that are based upon the postmillennialist concept that Christ will not return to earth until most of society has converted to Christianity, as compared to the more prevalent view of evangelical premillennialists, who believe that Christ's second coming is imminent. Dominionists contend that human society, starting with America (a "Christian nation"), must first be realigned with the law of the Hebrew Scriptures (Coral Ridge Ministries, at www.coralridge.org). In 2005, Kennedy elaborated on this point for the CFRA conference attendees: "We are to exercise godly dominion and influence over our neighborhoods, our schools, our government...our entertainment media, our news media, our scientific endeavors—in short, over every aspect and institution of human society." This belief has clear implications for public education, and the CFRA's involvement in the schools followed the course of other contemporary conservative Christian groups. CFRA challenged the appropriateness of Darwinism in the science classroom and advocated teachings based upon Genesis; it opposed sex-education courses that address homosexuality or alternatives to abstinence; and it was a forceful advocate of the Christian student's right to proselytize, pray, and advance her religious viewpoint on campus.

Kennedy has served on the advisory committee for the National Council for Bible Curriculum in Public Schools, whose curriculum has been criticized as inaccurate and promoting a sectarian perspective. He has also served on the advisory board of the Abstinence Clearinghouse, which has worked for the Department of Health and Human Services under the second Bush administration to develop guidelines for effective abstinence education programs. While Kennedy's Coral Ridge Ministries has been active in trying to reshape public education, it also supports sending students to private church-run schools, itself operating a K–12 private school with attendance of over 1,000 students.

The CFRA abruptly announced its closure in April 2007, a development that was assumed to be due to Kennedy's poor health (he retired from the ministry in August of the same year and died a month later). Coral Ridge Ministries maintains, however, that the closure of the CFRA was part of a major internal restructuring of the whole organization. The ministry claims to have stepped back from explicit political engagement and rededicated itself to its original mission of evangelizing. Nevertheless, Coral Ridge continues to exert influence on and cultivate working relationships with more politically active Christian organizations. For example, in 2007 it produced *Censoring the Church and Silencing Christians,* a video challenging hate crimes legislation in partnership with the Family Research Council. *See also:* Alliance Defense Fund; American Family Association.

Further Reading: Center for Reclaiming America, at www.reclaimamerica.org; "Ailing Rev. Kennedy Retires from Coral Ridge Presbyterian Church," *South Florida Sun-Sentinel,* August 27, 2007, sec. A, p. 1; "Coral Ridge Puts Politics Aside for Now," *Miami Herald,* August 28, 2007, sec. B, p. 1; "For Evangelicals, a Bid to 'Reclaim America,'" *Christian Science Monitor,* March 16, 2005, p. 16; Michelle Goldberg, *Kingdom Coming* (New York: Norton, 2007); William Martin, *With God on Our Side* (New York: Broadway Books, 1996).

Shipley Robertson Salewski

Chamberlin v. Dade County Board of Public Instruction

This case concerned an establishment clause challenge to a Florida statute requiring daily readings from the Bible, the recitation of the Lord's Prayer, singing of religious hymns, and holding of baccalaureate programs. Other practices challenged in the school district were distribution of sectarian literature to schoolchildren, after hours Bible instruction, religious observance of the Christmas, Hanukkah, and Easter holidays, including instruction in the dogma of the Nativity and Resurrection, and display of religious symbols. A Florida trial court denied injunctive relief to prohibit the alleged constitutional violations, finding no violation of the no establishment clause or state constitutional provisions pertaining to religious freedom and religious preferences. The Supreme Court of Florida in 1962 affirmed the trial court decision opining that the Establishment Clause applies to government setting up a particular religious belief or church, not to government recognizing religion where it might be done without drawing any invidious distinctions between different religious beliefs or sects.

On direct appeal to the U.S. Supreme Court, the Court in 1963 vacated and remanded the *Chamberlin* case back to the Supreme Court of Florida in light of the U.S. Supreme Court's decisions in *Murray v. Curlett* (1963) and *School District of Abington Township v. Schempp* (1963). *Murray* and *Schempp* were companion cases decided by the Court on the same day, invalidating state statutes in Pennsylvania and Maryland, the first of which provided for Bible reading in public schools, and the second of which provided for opening exercises in public schools embracing reading of the Bible or recitation of the Lord's Prayer. Both *Murray* and *Schempp* had been preceded by the Supreme Court's 1962 decision in *Engel v. Vitale* invalidating use of the New York Board of Regent's prayer at lunchtime to invoke God's blessings. The Supreme Court in *Schempp* and *Murray* rejected the notion that the Establishment Clause forbids only governmental preference of one religion over another. Referencing an earlier Supreme Court decision, *Everson v. Board of Education* (1947), permitting public transportation of religious school students on public school buses, the Court in *Schempp* and *Murray* observed the purpose of the Establishment Clause as creating a complete and permanent separation of the spheres of religious activity and civil authority by comprehensively forbidding every form of public aid or support for religion. In sum, a violation of the no establishment provision occurs even if, as in the government requirements in *Schempp* and *Murray,* students are permitted to absent themselves with parent permission.

On remand, the Supreme Court of Florida (1964) affirmed its prior decision, holding that the state statute relating to reading of the Bible was enacted in the interest of good moral training and, thus, the statute was founded upon secular rather than sectarian considerations and did not offend the establishment of religion clause of the U.S. Constitution. The Florida Supreme Court's decision was again appealed to the U.S. Supreme Court and the Court, this time, with only a one sentence statement, held, on the basis of *Schempp,* the Florida statute to be a violation of the Establishment Clause. In a final remand to the Supreme Court of Florida (1965), that court found prayer and devotional Bible reading in state public schools pursuant to statute or as sponsored by school authorities to be a violation of the no establishment of religion clause of the U.S. Constitution.

Although *Chamberlin v. Dade County Board of Instruction* had an interesting pedigree of two visits to the U.S. Supreme Court within the span of two years, the case made no contribution to the law regarding the relationship between public schools and religion. As is apparent, the Supreme Court's second decision regarding *Chamberlin* was really just a replay of its earlier *Schempp* and *Murray* decisions, which became, by virtue of their earlier appearance, the mainstay in establishment clause jurisprudence. Other than presenting an interesting historical record of a conflict between a state Supreme Court and the U.S. Supreme Court, *Chamberlin* has virtually faded from all substantive discussions regarding the interpretation of the Establishment Clause. *See also:* Academic Freedom; *Engel v. Vitale.*

Further Reading: *Chamberlin v. Dade County Board of Public Instruction,* 143 So.2d 21 (Fla. 1962); *Chamberlin v. Dade County Board of Public Instruction,* 374 U.S. 487 (1963); *Chamberlin v. Dade County Board of Public Instruction,* 160 So.2d 97 (Fla. 1964); *Chamberlin v. Dade County Board of Public Instruction,* 377 U.S. 402 (1964); *Chamberlin v. Dade County Board of Public Instruction,* 171 So.2d 535 (Fla. 1965); *Engle v. Vitale,* 370 U.S. 421 (1962); *Everson v. Board of Education,* 330 U.S. 1 (1947); *Murray v. Curlett,* 374 U.S. 203 (1963); *School District of Abington Township v. Schempp,* 374 U.S. 203 (1963).

Ralph D. Mawdsley

Christian Coalition

In 1988, religious broadcaster M.G. ("Pat") Robertson, founder and head of the Christian Broadcasting Network, made a serious run for the U.S. presidency. To support his campaign, he created an effective grassroots organization, known as Freedom Council, in several states. Though defeated, he made a credible showing and determined to build a permanent political organization that could help elect Christian candidates to office and gain a decisive voice in the Republican Party. The result was Christian Coalition, which he founded in 1989. Its first—and most effective—leader was a skilled young conservative activist and organizer, Ralph Reed.

To recruit members, the fledgling organization raised money by using one of the Christian Right's most dependable ploys: outraging its constituency with sensational accounts of offenses against religion and morality committed by homosexuals, liberals, or the government. The initial campaign hit all these buttons at once, attacking the National Endowment for the Arts for subsidizing exhibits of the work of Andres Serrano, whose "Piss Christ" photo featured a crucifix submerged in the artist's urine, and of Robert Mapplethorpe, who specialized in sadomasochistic and homoerotic images. Addressed to people who had supported Robertson's campaign, the letters not only sought funds and members, but encouraged recipients to volunteer to start state and local chapters of the new organization. The money raised in that first effort went toward full-page ads in the *New York Times, Washington Post, USA Today,* and other newspapers, calling on Congress to prohibit the use of taxpayer money to underwrite pornography, obscenity, or attacks on religion, and warning legislators that, if they did not do so, they would face the wrath of voters in 1992. The ads brought Christian Coalition its first national publicity and additional income and enabled Reed to go on the road to start organizing chapters.

Disappointed by the failure of the Reagan administration and Congress to deliver strong support for the Christian Right's social agenda, Reed concentrated on teaching Coalition members how to exert pressure closer to home, with school boards and city councils, and, crucially, how to gain power in Republican precinct organizations. Beginning in cities where response to the organization's mailings had been greatest, Reed conducted "Leadership Schools," offering detailed instruction on how to participate in local politics and how to form local, state, and regional organizations throughout the country.

After consolidating the base of previous Robertson supporters, Reed and Guy Rodgers, who had been active in the campaign and had come on board as Christian Coalition's first national field director, began to recruit people who had not been part of the campaign effort. Predictably, many of these came from other segments of the "pro-family" movement, such as James Dobson's Focus on the Family or Beverly LaHaye's Concerned Women for America. They had developed a taste for politics and a desire to be more effective, but lacked the nuts-and-bolts knowledge of how to be effective. Christian Coalition promised to fill that gap. It not only stressed the importance of organization, but taught its members to avoid using "Christianese" and to learn to speak in the language of the people they were trying to influence. It advised them to hold preliminary meetings in settings other than their own churches, to avoid the appearance of proselytizing; to reserve rooms half the size of the expected crowd, to create an appearance of an unanticipated groundswell of interest and enthusiasm; and to make sure that name tags were written in bold block letters, to enable leaders to call people in the first few rows by their first names, creating a greater sense of community.

By the fall of 1991, Christian Coalition had more than 82,000 members and was financially secure. A year earlier, it had proved its effectiveness in a major election when it distributed 750,000 voter guides in North Carolina just before Election Day, helping rescue Jesse Helms from what appeared to be probable defeat. Now, it applied its young muscles on the national level during Senate hearings regarding the nomination of Clarence Thomas to the Supreme Court, identifying senators it regarded as swing votes and mobilizing members to make tens of thousands of phone calls to them. When Thomas was confirmed, it gave Coalition members a sense that they were no longer a voice crying in the wilderness but people who could influence public policy and who had to be taken seriously in the halls of power.

At the 1992 Republican National Convention in Houston, Reed spoke before the Platform Committee on behalf of Christian Coalition, reminding its members of the strong support evangelical voters had given President George Bush in the 1988 election. He proved persuasive. Despite opposition from abortion-rights Republicans, the platform retained the antiabortion plank, as well as planks in support of the Religious Right's positions favoring public prayer, providing vouchers that parents could use to send their children to parochial schools, and opposing same-sex marriage, programs in public schools that provide birth control information, and the use of public funds to subsidize "obscenity and blasphemy masquerading as art." On the floor of the convention itself, Pat Robertson gave a hard-line speech in line with Coalition goals, and Pat Buchanan reinforced his message by speaking of a cultural war for America's soul. After the convention, Vice President Dan Quayle addressed a Christian Coalition God and Country rally in Houston and President Bush spoke to the organization's annual Road to Victory in Virginia Beach and gave Robertson's "700 Club" broadcast an exclusive interview. The Christian Right was never as enthusiastic about Bush as they had been about Reagan, but they once again offered the Republican ticket strong support. Though Bush lost badly to Bill Clinton, 60 percent of evangelical voters cast their ballots for him; only 28 percent voted for Clinton, with most of the remainder voting for Ross Perot. Moreover, Republicans gained ten seats in the House and an estimated 500 "pro-family" candidates were elected at the local level, mostly to school boards and state legislatures.

Under Reed's leadership, the organization grew steadily until, in 1996, it claimed a membership of 1.9 million in 2,000 chapters across the country, and a budget of $26.5 million. Critics question the membership figures, but no one doubted the organization was having significant influence and impact on American politics, and particularly on the Republican Party. A 1995 survey conducted by *Campaigns and Elections* magazine found that Christian right forces had "dominant strength" in the Republican Party in 18 states and "substantial influence" in 13 others. (A later survey raised the number of states in the substantial influence category to 26.) Christian Coalition was widely regarded as the political organization most responsible for this development, and its annual "Road to Victory" conference was considered an important opportunity for conservative politicians to establish or strengthen ties to evangelical supporters.

Ralph Reed resigned his position with the organization in 1997. Under a succession of new leaders, including Pat Robertson himself for a time, Christian Coalition steadily lost influence until, by 2007, it was a shadow of its former self. It claimed to have distributed 70 million voter guides during the 2004 campaign, but it had active organizations in only a handful of states and exhibited little grassroots clout. It did, however, maintain an active Web site that continued to provide information and "action alerts" on a legislative agenda that included trying to confirm as many conservative judges as possible, opposing embryonic stem cell research, removing limits on evangelical chaplains in the military, maintaining tax cuts implemented by the Bush administration, and pushing for a federal Defense of Marriage Amendment that would outlaw same-sex marriage.

In founding Christian Coalition, Robertson asserted that atheistic and humanistic forces had transformed America from a Christian nation into an "anti-Christian pagan nation" and that he hoped the new organization could help reverse that change. The charge itself is a dubious one, and evidence of the hoped-for success even harder to measure. Without doubt, however, Christian Coalition played a critical role in helping religious conservatives become an enduring and important part of the social, cultural, and political landscape of America. *See also:* Concerned Women for America; Focus on the Family; Moral Majority.

Further Reading: Christian Coalition, at www.cc.org; William Martin, *With God on Our Side: The Rise of the Religious Right in America* (New York: Broadway Books, 1996; 2004); People for the American Way, at www.pfaw.org; Ralph Reed, *Contract with the American Family* (New York: Random House, 1995).

William Martin

Christian Day Schools

Protestant-sponsored weekday schooling is not new to American education. Prior to the advent of state common school systems in the middle decades of the nineteenth century, the rich religious diversity that characterized overwhelmingly Protestant early America was manifested in an equally rich diversity of Protestant Christian schools. Throughout this period, the Lutherans, Friends, Moravians, Baptists, German and Dutch Reformed, Presbyterians, Methodists, and Anglicans established elementary schools and academies for their children and charity schools for children of the poor. Most of the so-called town schools of colonial New England and the quasi-public district schools and charity schools of the early 1800s were also de facto Protestant schools.

The 1830s, 1840s, and 1850s, however, marked an era of intense debate and reform focusing on issues of control, finance, and curriculum that led to a major alteration in the American educational landscape. By the 1850s in the North and the 1870s in the South, states had established the general framework for a free, tax-supported, state-regulated common school system. Student enrollment shifted to the free "common schools," the earlier practice of distributing tax dollars and land to schools under private or religious control for the accomplishment of public purposes was sharply curtailed in many states, and nonpublic schools, Protestant and Catholic alike, were often criticized as undemocratic, elitist, and divisive. During this period several Protestant denominations, such as the Methodist and Episcopal, considered creating alternative school systems, and in the case of the latter, a number of dioceses, mostly in the South, encouraged establishment of schools. In the 1840s and 1850s, the Old School Presbyterians under the leadership of Cortlandt Van Rensselaer and Charles Hodge, among others, attempted to establish a system of schools to transmit orthodox beliefs. Although this Presbyterian body founded a total of about 260 schools by 1870, a lack of enthusiasm and schism bred by intersectional strife doomed the experiment. Individual churches continued to maintain schools, but, with the exception of the Lutheran Church–Missouri Synod, major Protestant denominations and most of their members accepted government provision of elementary schooling, though not without occasional expressions of concern regarding secularization of the public schools. They embraced them because nineteenth century "common" schools were, for the most part, general Protestant schools and thought to be a principal means to creating a moral, disciplined, and unified Protestant citizenry. Furthermore, as Roman Catholics asked for tax dollars to support their schools and complained about offensive practices in the common schools, such as Bible reading without comment, most Protestants set aside their denominational differences and united behind the purportedly "nonsectarian" common school.

Protestant leaders were often in the vanguard of the common school movement as a means of fashioning a Christian, by which they meant Protestant, America. In the words of Robert T. Handy, a noted church historian, elementary schools did not need to be under the control of particular denominations because "their role was to prepare young Americans for participation in the broadly Christian civilization toward which all evangelicals were working" (Handy, 1971, p. 102). While the common school, by means of Bible reading, prayers, hymns, Protestant teachers, and the ubiquitous *McGuffey Readers,* inculcated the mutually reinforcing dispositions and beliefs of nondenominational Protestantism, republicanism, and capitalism, many Protestant leaders expected the Sunday school to stress the particular tenets of the various denominations. This educational arrangement of "parallel institutions" satisfied most Protestants in the last half of the nineteenth century. Indeed, by 1900, about 15,500,000, or nearly 92 percent of the approximately 16,850,000 elementary and secondary students, attended public institutions, while only about 1,350,000 students, or about 8 percent, attended private institutions. Eight hundred fifty-four thousand, or 63 percent of these students were enrolled in the burgeoning Catholic schools, while most of the remaining 496,000 souls were scattered among Lutheran, Christian Reformed, Baptist, Presbyterian, Adventist, Episcopal, and secular private schools.

Much has changed since the formulation of the "parallel institutions" strategy. Evangelical Protestantism no longer shapes American culture and the public schools as it did in the 1800s. The twentieth century witnessed its gradual decline as the dominant culture-shaping force and the growing influence of secularism, particularly among social elites. On the other hand, the public outcry following the 1962 and 1963 U.S. Supreme Court decisions declaring state-sponsored prayer and devotional Bible reading in tax-supported schools unconstitutional, the resurgence of evangelicalism amidst the cultural and political crises of the 1970s, and the political activism of conservative Protestants at the national, state, and local levels suggest that a significant minority of the general public is very uncomfortable with a quasi-official secular worldview and a public square devoid of symbols of America's Christian heritage.

Profoundly dissatisfied with what they perceive to be the secularistic—not neutral—belief system embodied in the public school curriculum, unsatisfactory behavioral and academic standards, and the centralized control of public education, a growing number of conservative Protestants, though hardly a majority, many of whom see the state school system as a mission field, have tried to regain control of their children's education that they believe has been usurped by, among others, secular elites, the courts, teacher unions, federal government, and "educrats." Since the 1960s, they have utilized several strategies. For example, some evangelical and fundamentalist Protestants have sought to incorporate theistic symbols and perspectives in the public schools through, for example, urging consideration of creationism or Intelligent Design in science classes, posting Ten Commandments plaques, and advocating history texts that recognize the influence of Christianity on the development of the United States and sex education curricula that stress abstinence. Others have either protested the use of curricular materials that they believe advance secularism, e.g., certain home economics and literature texts, or sought to have their children exempted from exposure to the offending materials or their complete removal from the school curriculum. Still other conservative Protestants have forsaken their historic commitment to public schools and either looked to the private institutions to provide an education congruent with their beliefs or opted for homeschooling.

Contemporary Christian Schooling

Since the mid-1960s, a small but growing number of fundamentalist and evangelical Protestants and their churches, few of which are affiliated with "mainline" denominations, such as the United Methodist Church, have been establishing and patronizing alternatives to public education that are usually referred to as Christian day schools or fundamentalist academies (so-called in order to distinguish them from schools sponsored by Protestant denominations, for example, the Lutheran Church–Missouri Synod). Between 1920 and 1960, independent fundamentalist churches and conservative parachurch organizations founded approximately 150 of these institutions. The vast majority of conservative Protestants, however, remained wedded to public schooling during this period and crusaded for daily Bible reading and restrictions on the teaching of Darwinian evolution. In the aftermath of intradenominational battles between fundamentalists and modernists and the Scopes "Monkey Trial" in 1925, fundamentalist leaders concentrated on developing their own radio stations, colleges, Bible schools, camps, missionary societies, and publishing houses. Their withdrawal from American culture, however, did not lead to the creation of a significant number of separate elementary and secondary schools. Liberal and conservative Protestants alike considered the public school "theirs." By the mid-1960s, however, growing disenchantment with the ongoing secularization of public education, deepening concern about trends in American culture related to drugs, sex, and disorder, a resurgent evangelical faith, and, in some cases, fears related to desegregation sparked a significant increase in the number of Christian day schools.

Assessing the growth of these modern-day Christian institutions was initially difficult. Some schools were of such a separatist persuasion that they refused to report enrollment data to state and federal education agencies. For similar reasons, others chose not to affiliate with any of the national or regional associations of Christian schools, the primary sources of statistics on these institutions. Nevertheless, most students of the Christian day school movement now estimate that between 8,000 and 12,000 of these schools have been founded since the mid-1960s. In 2007, these institutions enrolled between 1.0 and 1.2 million students (pre-K–12) or approximately 20 percent of all private school students. Some of these schools have closed their doors. Institutions founded with more enthusiasm than resources and leadership have had short lives. Estimating the number of schools that have closed since the 1960s is as difficult as determining the exact number of schools that have been established. Many are simply invisible and pass from the educational landscape unnoticed. In the mid-1990s, however, the Association of Christian Schools International (ACSI) estimated that about 1,100 schools had closed since the mid-1960s.

The most concrete evidence of the growth of the independent Christian school movement is readily apparent in the membership figures of the two major associations that provide, among other things, legal and legislative services, administrator and teacher support, curriculum, certification and accreditation, and early childhood services to their member schools. The Western Association of Christian Schools, which in 1978 merged with two smaller organizations—the National Christian School Education Association and the Ohio Association of Christian Schools—to form ACSI, claimed a membership in 1967 of 102 schools (K–12) with an enrollment of 14,659. By 1973, the figures were 308 and 39,360, respectively. In 1983, ACSI figures were approximately 1,900 (pre-K–12) and 270,000; in 1989, 2,347 and 340,626; in 1993, 2,801 and 463,868; in 2000, 3,849 and 707,928; and in 2005, 3,957 and 746,681. The American Association of Christian Schools (AACS), a rival organization of a more fundamentalist nature, was founded in 1972 with 80 schools enrolling 16,000 students. By 1983, the association claimed a membership of more than 1,100 schools and 160,000 students, and in 1991, 1,200 and 187,000. In 2004, AACS reported about 1,050 schools with approximately 175,000 students (part of the recent decline is likely due to the withdrawal of a state organization and its schools in the early 1990s). Despite the fact that some of these schools appeared long before they affiliated with either ACSI or AACS, these figures testify to the vigor of the Christian day school movement since the 1960s (American

Association of Christian Schools, at www.aacs.org; Association of Christian Schools International, at www.acsi.org).

Though the growth of evangelical Christian schools has outpaced that of other types of schools in the private sector since the 1970s, their expansion has apparently slowed since the early 2000s. Aside from the increasing cost of competing with the government sector and a soft economy, anecdotal evidence suggests that an increasing number of parents are opting for homeschooling in lieu of private schooling. While the number of Christian day schools and their enrollments are unlikely to increase as fast as they did in the last three decades of the twentieth century, the Christian school movement remains one of the more dynamic segments of the American educational enterprise and represents the first widespread and lasting institutional dissent from the public school paradigm since the establishment of large numbers of Roman Catholic schools during the latter part of the nineteenth century. Furthermore, along with the explosive growth of homeschooling since the mid-1980s, which, though becoming more diverse demographically, is still dominated by evangelical Protestants, this movement marks a significant erosion of conservative Protestants' once nearly universal loyalty to public education.

Characteristics

Researchers have shown considerable interest in these schools since the early 1980s. They have examined, among other things, the relationship of the aforementioned growth pattern to the evangelical revival and concomitant alienation from American culture and its educational institutions, charges of racial discrimination against these schools, clashes with government officials regarding the legitimacy of state licensing and teacher certification requirements, the quality of Christian day schools compared to their public counterparts, curriculum formats, parent and student characteristics, and various features of these schools.

They have discovered that although all Christian day schools profess the centrality of Jesus Christ and the authority of the Bible in their educational endeavors, they are quite different in many respects. For example, though most of these schools are attached to a local church (ACSI reports that about 85 percent of its schools fall into this category), a significant minority, often the largest and/or most prestigious, are governed by a local school society or foundation. Facilities range from poorly equipped church basements to modern multibuilding campuses. While a majority are elementary schools, an increasing number are offering prekindergarten and secondary education as well. Programs of study vary considerably from standardized and narrow to the most comprehensive available anywhere. Enrollments also vary from school to school from fewer than ten students to over 2,000. In general, these schools are smaller and more intimate than their state-controlled counterparts. The average enrollment is currently between 150 and 200.

Educational environments also differ among these institutions. Some Christian school classrooms are reminiscent of those of the public schools of the 1950s, while others resemble Skinnerian learning labs where students work independently through a series of curriculum packets without benefit of a teacher in a conventional sense (the Accelerated Christian Education program or ACE). Many schools use Christian curricula published by Bob Jones University Press, A Beka, or ACSI, while others use secular materials and expect instructors to provide Christian perspectives. Some schools mix healthy doses of patriotism with religious instruction. Others shun this practice. Some have very relaxed codes of conduct. Others require uniforms and forbid physical contact between boys and girls during school-related activities.

Several excellent studies testify to the diversity of institutional climates manifest in Christian day schools. For example, Alan Peshkin's pioneering study of a fundamentalist Christian high school in central Illinois described the attitudes and behavior of parents, students, teachers, administrators, and pastors who shaped the institution. He concluded that the school served the educational needs of a fundamentalist Christian community, particularly its emphasis on salvation, social separation, and missions, but expressed concern about the separatist, authority-oriented nature of the school that he opined discouraged exploration of America's cultural riches and bred intolerance. Susan Rose compared and contrasted the climate of a fundamentalist Baptist school and that of a school sponsored by a charismatic Christian fellowship. While the former school stressed strict rules, routinization, drill, and individual work, the latter emphasized creativity, flexibility, and group work. In a similar vein, Peter Lewis examined the ethos of a free school and that of a Christian school. He found that though their cultures differed significantly from the climate of the public school, the former valued creativity and freedom, while the latter stressed discipline, basics, and religious instruction. After studying a variety of Christian schools affiliated with fundamentalist, charismatic, and mainline evangelical fellowships, Melinda Wagner claimed that the schools had to some extent compromised with American culture and were not as separatist as their rhetoric often suggests. Likewise, David Sikkink identified and described a variety of Christian day schools, including an example of a growing number of classical Christian schools whose distinctives often include rigorous instruction in a trivium of grammar, dialectic, and rhetoric (often with a base in Latin). In sum, although all Christian day schools are committed to transmitting a Christian worldview, this commitment is embodied in institutions that are remarkably diverse in structure, program, and climate.

Increasing minority enrollment and the growing number of what Christian school advocates frequently call black Christian academies are also contributing to diversity within the Christian school movement. Although often viewed as stalwart supporters of public education—the arena in which many early civil rights battles were fought and won—Americans of African descent have often resorted to private or quasi-public schools when public education was either unavailable or inadequate.

Since the 1980s, black enrollment in private schools has increased steadily. By the late 1990s, approximately 6 percent of black elementary and secondary school students enrolled in nonpublic schools. Though a majority of these students were in Catholic schools, some of the recent increase is evident in the Christian day school sector. Although often stereotyped as "white flight academies," particularly in the South, these institutions do enroll minority students and their number, though still comparatively small, has grown in recent years. Christian day schools are, to some extent, interracial. In 2007, Americans of African descent accounted for about 11 percent of their enrollment and minorities for approximately 24 percent.

Of greater significance to both the Christian day school movement and urban public education is the rapid growth of black Christian academies, most of which are located in metropolitan areas. Americans of African descent initiate, sustain, and govern these schools, which usually are not dependent upon organizations outside the black community. Such schools, however, do identify themselves with the contemporary evangelical school movement. Indeed, many are members of ACSI. Most black Christian schools stress racial heritage, discipline, and academic achievement as well as a Christian worldview.

Although the creation of Afro-centric schools has sparked some interest in the scholarly community, only a handful of researchers have paid close attention to the growth and ethos of black Christian schools. This oversight is, at least in part, due to their "invisibility." Like the predominantly white evangelical schools founded in the 1960s and 1970s, their black counterparts have been springing up out of the public eye since the early 1980s. They are often unknown to government agencies, public school districts, religious associations, and other usual sources of school statistics.

Jack Layman, a veteran student of independent Christian schools, documented at least 200 black Christian schools located in cities throughout the United States by the early 1990s. He found, for example, over a dozen each in Atlanta, Philadelphia, and Washington, D.C.; eight in Baltimore; six in Jackson, Mississippi; and over 30 in greater Los Angeles. During the 1990s, this segment of the Christian school movement continued to expand. In Philadelphia, for example, these schools now number better than 50. As was the case with the schools founded in the 1960s and 1970s, diversity of facilities, size, and climate characterize the newer black Christian schools. Whatever their characteristics, these institutions represent a significant dissent from a long-standing faith in public education among a growing number of African Americans.

Future Directions

In the 1970s, when Christian schools were multiplying at a rate of better than one per day, leaders focused on seemingly routine problems such as how to get started, adequate facilities, and methods of discipline. More critical matters, such as articulating a positive philosophy of Christian school education and combating legal and legislative efforts to impose state accreditation and teacher licensing requirements on these schools, also consumed an immense amount of time, energy, and resources.

As the Christian school movement has matured, many of those issues have been at least partially resolved. Weaker schools have closed, while others have developed better administrative processes and educational programs. Christian schools know why they exist and are able to articulate clearly their philosophy of education. Furthermore, conflicts with government authorities regarding accreditation and teacher certification requirements based on free exercise of religion and parental rights claims have been largely resolved in favor of the schools in most states. Legal and legislative concerns have shifted to issues such as employment policies, state and federal involvement in child care, and, most recently, the acceptability of courses informed by Christian perspectives by state universities.

In the early years of the movement, advocates were confident that Christian schools would contribute to a robust revival of Christian life in the United States, as an army of young people benefited from the combined nurturing of home, church, and Christian school. Indeed, some went as far as to claim that Christian schools were the hope of the increasingly "Godless" American republic. Evidence of this revival, particularly in regard to teenage lifestyles, is scanty. Some observers argue that Christian education per se is no more a panacea for America's real and perceived ills than public schooling, and that Christian schools are just as likely to reflect as to determine the spiritual levels of their constituency.

Though their growth rate has slowed in the new millennium and time and experience have tempered earlier messianic expectations, Christian day schools still make up the most robust segment of the private school sector. While enrollments in other religious schools have either stagnated or declined, these schools continue to grow and are now a fixed feature of the educational landscape. Whether this segment of the increasingly pluralistic American educational enterprise will continue to expand remains to be seen. *See also: Common School; State Regulation of Religious Schools.*

Further Reading: American Association of Christian Schools, at aacs.org; Association of Christian Schools International, at www.acsi.org; James C. Carper and Thomas C. Hunt, *The Dissenting Tradition in American Education* (New York: Peter Lang, 2007); Robert T. Handy, *A Christian America: Protestant Hopes and Historical Realities* (New York: Oxford University Press, 1971); Jack Layman, "Black-Flight: The Rise of Black Christian Schools" (Ph.D. diss., University of South Carolina, 1992); Peter S. Lewis, "Private Education and the Subcultures of Dissent: Alternative/ Free Schools (1965–1975) and Christian Fundamentalist Schools (1965–1990)" (Ph.D. diss., Stanford University, 1991); Alan Peshkin, *God's Choice: The Total World of a Fundamentalist Christian School* (Chicago: University of Chicago Press, 1986); Susan Rose, *Keeping Them Out of the Hands of Satan: Evangelical Schooling in America* (New York: Routledge, Chapman and Hall, 1988); David Sikkink, "Speaking in Many Tongues," *Education Matters* 1 (Summer 2001): 36–45; Melinda B. Wagner, *God's Schools: Choice and Compromise in American Society* (New Brunswick, NJ: Rutgers University Press, 1990).

James C. Carper

Christian Educators Association International

The Christian Educators Association International (CEAI), formerly National Educators Fellowship, was founded in 1953 by two Los Angeles educators as the first national organization of professional Christian educators, and it continues to serve teachers and administrators in public, private, and charter schools. Its mission is to "encourage, equip, and empower Christian educators," and to promote teaching as a form of ministry, excellence as an expression of faith, and God's word as the source of wisdom (Christian Educators Association International, at www.ceai.org). The CEAI also partners with churches to provide curricular, fellowship, and after-school support and to actively promote Judeo-Christian heritage as the foundation of American culture. Though it is not a union, it supplies some of the services unions typically provide and has therefore come to be considered a union alternative in some regions. The CEAI educates its members as to their Constitutional rights, especially as persons of faith in the public school classroom, and provides members benefits such as personal liability insurance. It also sends members copies of its *Teachers of Vision* magazine and offers them the benefits of its strategic partnership with lawyers from the Liberty Council and Liberty University School of Law (founded by Jerry Falwell), whose lawyers are well-versed in the religious freedom cases. The CEAI is supported by membership fees, donations, and grants, and maintains close ties to powerful conservative Christian organizations such as Focus on the Family and Concerned Women for America. It claimed some 65,000 members in 2007.

The CEAI markets itself to teachers who say they feel trapped in the secular school system or unions that do not necessarily share their particular Christian values. While it is not opposed to Christian day schools (and does serve some teachers within such schools), its focus is on the public schools where the vast majority of teachers work and where it says conservative values are less likely to be shared. The association provides teachers with practical and inspirational resources. It provides free classroom Bibles for teachers who request them, pamphlets designed to promote Intelligent Design (such as "10 Questions to Ask Your Biology Teacher about Evolution"), and guidelines for how to witness to students without preaching or defying the law.

The CEAI received a boost in membership after the National Education Association endorsed civil unions and same-sex marriages in 2006, a decision that was unpopular with many conservative Christian educators. The CEAI is careful in its language on this topic: while it embraces the "ex-gay perspective," it also encourages its members to promote this perspective in a public and accountable way. It urges teachers to oppose Gay-Straight Alliances in schools and offers ten steps for how to do so, encouraging prayer and transparency throughout (CEAI, at ceai.org).

While paying attention to the practical realities of the school day and the letter of constitutional law, the CEAI offers detailed guidance on how educators who view teaching as missionary activity can walk the fine line between witnessing and proselytizing. For instance, in guidelines for starting a Bible club in a public school, the CEAI recommends not only the time of day and organization of meetings most likely to work for teenage students, but also how to make sure that the club is recognized by the school and enjoys the full rights it is owed under the law. It also emphasizes that the club must be student-initiated and student-led, but explains that this does not prohibit teachers from fund-raising or spiritually mentoring the student leadership. It directs teachers with further concerns to legal documents published on its Web site and legal organizations, such as the American Center for Law and Justice, that specialize in questions about religious liberty and free speech in the public schools. *See also:* Concerned Women for America; Episcopal Schools; Liberty Counsel.

Further Reading: Christian Educators Association International, at www.ceai.org.

Shipley Robertson Salewski

Christian Legal Society

Founded in 1961 by four lawyers, the Christian Legal Society (CLS) is a national network of lawyers, judges, law professors, and students that exists to provide fellowship among members and promote the practice of law as an avenue for Christian ministry. The CLS devotes itself to advocating biblical conflict reconciliation, providing legal assistance to the needy, and affirming religious freedom and the sanctity of life from conception. To these ends, it partners with organizations such as the Salvation Army to assist the poor, legally represents parties involved in "test case" litigation, and writes *amicus curiae* briefs, especially to the U.S. Supreme Court. Materials on its Web site emphasize that the organization does not cater to particular political groups or denominations but instead provides "strategic networks for the common good with organizations on the political left and right" (Christian Legal Society, at www.clsnet.com). In 2006, it reported membership of more than 3,400 attorneys and a budget of $2.2 million, raised from membership dues, conference fees, and contributions. It publishes the quarterly magazine *The Christian Lawyer* and in 2001 founded the Institute for Christian Legal Studies in cooperation with Pat Robertson's Regent Law School, with which it maintains close ties.

In 1975, the CLS established the Center for Law and Religious Freedom, an advocacy arm of the organization, to litigate cases and advise legislatures and other government offices (often school boards) on legal concerns. Its declared mission is "to remove obstacles to the propagation of the Good News of Jesus Christ." In 1993, the Center added "life advocacy" to its prior focus on religious freedom, though religious freedom remains the issue for which the Center is known and the primary issue through which it is involved in the public schools. The Center supports "opt-out" rights and the promotion of Intelligent Design as an appropriate perspective within the science classroom. It also supports a vigorous conception of free speech that allows religious students to proselytize in schools and openly express their points of view on issues such as sexual orientation, even when those points of view run contrary to antidiscrimination policies within schools.

The Center is a prominent defender of the use of state-funded vouchers to pay tuition at religious schools. In 1999, in partnership with the Union of Orthodox Jewish Congregations of America and the National Association of Evangelicals, it filed an *amicus* brief urging the Supreme Court to hear the case of Vermont parents who wished to use existing vouchers to send their children to a Catholic School. In 2002, it supported a Cleveland voucher program, which the Court ultimately upheld, in *Zelman v. Simmons-Harris.*

The Center has worked to protect and expand the rights of Christians in schools with arguments based on free speech and equal access law. In 2003, it successfully pressured a school district to change its policy in order to let a fifth-grade student distribute fliers for the Child Evangelism Fellowship at his school. In 2007, it filed suit, along with the Alliance Defense Fund, against Arlington Public Schools in Virginia on behalf of Parents and Friends of Ex-Gays for the right to distribute fliers about the "ex-gay position" on homosexuality. This is part of an ongoing and national effort to challenge antidiscrimination policies aimed at protecting GLBTQ (Gay, Lesbian, Bisexual, Transgender, and Questioning) youth, which CLS argues often end up discriminating against the viewpoints of conservative Christians. In a related case, the Center filed an *amicus* brief in support of the speech rights of Joseph Frederick, an Alaska high school student, in *Morse v. Frederick* (2007), contending that though it disagreed with the content of Frederick's message ("Bong Hits 4 Jesus"), any limitation on his right to express himself might also result in the limitation of Christian students' free speech rights.

Representatives of CLS have been active as drafters of policy and legislative documents, notably the *Religious Freedom Restoration Act* (1993), and have shown a willingness to work with groups that hold competing views. In 1999, for example, the CLS coauthored, along with the First Amendment Center and the American Jewish Congress, the 12-page "Public Schools and Religious Communities," outlining the acceptable functions religious communities may play in the life of the schools. Acceptable services include providing after-school day care and mentoring on church grounds and offering clergy for counseling during crisis situations. The CLS also helped draft "Public Schools and Sexual Orientation: A First Amendment Framework for Finding Common Ground," with the First Amendment Center and The Gay, Lesbian and Straight Education Network, which proposes a set of principles to guide the process of finding policies that groups with widely divergent positions can support. *See also:* Common Ground Documents; First Amendment Center; National Association of Evangelicals.

Further Reading: Joan Biskupic, "Court Rejects Case on School Subsidy Curb," *Washington Post,* December 14, 1999, sec. A, p. 6; David Cho, "Religious Fliers to Be Allowed in Schools,"

Washington Post, January 16, 2003, sec. T, p. 9; Christian Legal Society, at www.clsnet.com; Charles C. Haynes, "A Moral Battleground, a Civil Discourse," *USA Today,* March 20, 2006, sec. A, p. 15.

Shipley Robertson Salewski

Civic Education

Civic education prepares students to become members of their society. Knowledge about government and politics is a fundamental aspect of civic education, but the concept is more inclusive. Civic education involves more than simply transmitting knowledge to a student; it also includes shaping the student by promoting values conducive to constructive participation in society. The goal of civic education broadly understood is the creation of good citizens. In the modern United States, many educators believe that the purpose of civic education is to prepare students to become productive members of a pluralistic democracy.

Throughout much of American history, civic education was largely a communitarian enterprise. It sought to forge a common nation from people with different heritages, albeit predominantly European. From the emergence of the common schools in the mid-nineteenth century and continuing well into the twentieth century, civic education focused on patriotic nationalism and the assimilation of new immigrants into American society.

Civic education during this period also was distinctly religious in nature. The values of Protestant Christianity, for example, were woven throughout the fabric of the common school movement. Students were exposed to these values both directly, such as through daily readings of the Bible without comment, and indirectly, such as through the famed *McGuffey Readers,* which taught Protestant virtues along with reading, writing, and arithmetic. Although some groups, most notably Catholics, objected, their objections were not to the religious nature of public education, but rather to the preference for Protestantism. The solution for Catholics was to form their own parochial schools.

The nature of civic education, however, changed fundamentally in the twentieth century, especially as the United States became more socially secular and religiously diverse. With the rise of secularism, demands for the separation of church and state increased. In the realm of education, these demands emerged most prominently in the conflict over evolution and creationism. Although the Tennessee Supreme Court upheld John Scopes's conviction for teaching evolution in 1925, the U.S. Supreme Court would redefine the role of religion in American education in the 1960s. In *Engel v. Vitale* (1962), for example, the Supreme Court prohibited mandatory prayer in public school; and in *Abington School District v. Schempp* (1963), the Court prohibited mandatory Bible readings. Later, in *Epperson v. Arkansas* (1968), the Supreme Court struck down a state law prohibiting the teaching of evolution.

The increase in religious diversity begun with the influx of Catholic immigrants in the nineteenth century continued throughout the twentieth. By the middle of the century, the emphasis of Protestant values in civic education had evolved into a broader concept of Judeo-Christian values. This concept encompassed much, albeit not all, of the religious diversity in the United States. Robert Bellah's 1967 essay "American Civil Religion," for example, reflected how America had developed a common public framework based on Judeo-Christian traditions.

In 1965, however, the United States significantly altered its immigration policies, facilitating a dramatic increase in non-European immigration. With greater geographic diversity came greater religious diversity. Muslims, Hindus, Sikhs, Jains, Buddhists, and others entered the country in greater numbers than ever before. Although Protestant Christians still represent the largest religious demographic group in America, the United States is now arguably the most religiously diverse country in the world. Today, even the concept of Abrahamic traditions, much less Judeo-Christian, is insufficient to reflect the country's religious diversity.

With the rise of social secularism and religious diversity, civic education became the subject of renewed attention in the late twentieth century and continued to evolve. Some educators stressed a return to the virtues of classical republicanism, including the idea that the virtuous citizen places the common good before individual interest. The goal of civic education was to cultivate students who will consider their public responsibilities. Others, in contrast, stressed the ideals of political liberalism, including autonomy and individualism. Civic education for these educators focused on civil liberties and rights. In addition, critiques of traditional approaches to civic education have emerged. Some feminist scholars, for example, charge that the traditional paradigms of educational socialization are inherently patriarchal and call for a greater emphasis on relationships and care.

Regardless of the philosophical perspective, civic education in the twenty-first century has shifted from the previously dominant communitarian focus to a multicultural one. The essential project of civic education for many educators is no longer the formation of a shared culture, but rather an inclusive society. For these educators, modern pluralistic democracy requires the fostering of inclusive values such as mutual toleration and respect.

The relationship between civic education and religion also has changed in recent decades. Although devotional religion is no longer a fundamental element of civic education in the public schools, the study of religion still is present. The Supreme Court's decisions in *Engel* and *Abington School District* did not preclude the study of religion in public schools. On the contrary, schools may teach religion as an academic as opposed to a devotional subject. The Court even indicated that civic education may require the academic study of religion.

The increased emphasis on pluralism as a central element of civic education also supports the academic study of religion. As explained above, religion is a rapidly expanding form of social diversity in the United States. Civic education in America thus needs to prepare students to live in a religiously diverse society. At a minimum, living in such a society requires mutual toleration of different religious beliefs as well as nonbelief. While not always sufficient, knowledge and understanding help to promote mutual toleration. The multicultural study of diverse religions should be an essential element of American civic education.

Although civic education and religious belief in a pluralistic democracy are entirely compatible, they are not without the potential for conflict, especially where the goal of civic education is not merely tolerance but also respect. Some religions are fundamentally exclusive in nature, as are some secular worldviews. Adherents of both extremes do not regard other faiths or beliefs as valid or true. Civic education designed to promote mutual tolerance and respect can be threatening to such beliefs.

Adherents of religious beliefs incompatible with civic education in a pluralistic society have two fundamental alternatives. They can withdraw from the public education system or seek accommodation within the public education system. Withdrawing from the public school system for religious reasons has a long history dating back to the formation of Catholic schools in the nineteenth century. Today, many conservative Protestant Christians either homeschool their children or send them to private religious schools. Religious objectors have even been allowed to withdraw their children from public education without substituting another form of traditional education. In *Wisconsin v. Yoder* (1972), the U.S. Supreme Court held that a group of Old Order Amish parents could withdraw their children from school after the eighth grade. The Court emphasized that continued enrollment was a threat to Amish beliefs.

Accommodations can take many forms, but commonly involve excusing religious objectors from particular classes or activities. Schools, however, do not always have to grant such accommodations. In *Mozert v. Hawkins County Board of Education* (1987), for example, a group of evangelical parents objected to a public school reading program. The parents asserted that the program exposed their children to ideas inconsistent with their religious faith and sought to have their children exempted from the program. Though the federal district court granted the parents an accommodation, the U.S. Court of Appeals for the Sixth Circuit overturned that ruling, holding that the school could compel participation in the reading program. Following this ruling, many parents withdrew their children from the public education system and enrolled them in Christian private schools.

Cases such as *Yoder* and *Mozert* raise complex issues involving the balancing of well-recognized rights such as the Free Exercise Clause of the First Amendment with legitimate state interests such as preparing students to participate in a pluralistic democracy through civic education. Scholars are deeply divided on how to balance these rights. Some categorically favor one interest over the other, while others try to honor both. Regardless, the relationship between civic education and religion in the United States continues to evolve and to be the subject of significant disagreement. *See also:* Civil Religion and Education; Secularism.

Further Reading: Diana L. Eck, *A New Religious America: How a "Christian Country" Has Become the World's Most Religiously Diverse Nation* (New York: HarperCollins, 2001); Amy Gutmann, *Democratic Education* (Princeton, NJ: Princeton University Press, 1987); Charles L. Glenn, Jr., *The Myth of the Common School* (Amherst: University of Massachusetts Press, 1988); Stephen Macedo, *Diversity and Distrust: Civic Education in a Multicultural Democracy* (Cambridge, MA: Harvard University Press, 2000); Diane L. Moore, *Overcoming Religious Illiteracy: A Cultural Studies Approach to the Study of Religion in Secondary Education* (New York: Palgrave Macmillan, 2007); Richard John Neuhaus, *The Naked Public Square: Religion and Democracy in America* (Grand Rapids, MI: Eerdmans, 1984); Nel Noddings, *Educating Moral People: A Caring Alternative to Character Education* (New York: Teachers College Press, 2002); George M. Thomas, Lisa R. Peck, and Channin G. De Hann, "Reforming Education, Transforming Religion, 1876–1931," in *The Secular Revolution: Power, Interests, and Conflict in the Secularization of American Public Life,* ed. Christian Smith (Berkeley: University of California Press, 2003).

Brendan Randall and Diane L. Moore

Civil Religion and Education

A search for "civil religion" nets many references; most debate the validity and uniqueness of the phenomenon. Here it is understood as beliefs, rituals, and behaviors that impact the social and political life of a nation, transcending specific religious traditions. Though most discussions of civil religion focus on manifestations in the political realm, the role of civil religion in school settings has also received considerable attention.

A term originally coined by Jean Jacques Rousseau in *The Social Contract*—"civil religion"—garnered attention in the United States of America after 1967 when sociologist Robert Bellah used it to describe how America's upheavals, especially Vietnam, were justified by politicians. Why did Bellah's 1967 article attract such attention? Some argue that the times contributed greatly. Among his chief examples of civil religion were three quotations from the inaugural address of assassinated President John F. Kennedy, as well as references to many other presidential inaugural speeches. He considered Abraham Lincoln, the martyred president, as the foremost example of a public theologian (p. 12).

In the two decades following Bellah's 1967 article, his analysis was both highly praised for its insightfulness and debunked for its inaccuracies. In addition to arguments regarding its efficacy, a second debate ensued regarding its universality. In the third and fourth decades after Bellah's watershed article, the scholarly community has made fewer references to civil religion. Those who write about the term fall into two camps, those who accept its reality or those who object, offering counter arguments and new terminology.

Is civil religion universal, as Rousseau and later Durkheim believed, or is it a phenomenon in some but not all industrialized countries like the United States? G.K. Chesterton observed that America was "a nation with the soul of a church" (Richey and Jones, 1974, p. 45). Sidney Mead concurred, calling America a "religious republic." Will Herberg, in *Protestant, Catholic, Jew,* posited there was "an American way of religion," while Martin Marty has chosen the terms, "public religion" or "public church."

If America does not allow an establishment of religion (a much debated concept), how can it be said the country has a civil religion? Those arguing that it does exist conclude that what it is not is "church religion"; that is, its practices and pronouncements are not so associated with Protestant or Catholic languages and practices, for example, that persons of other faith traditions are offended. First, what is religion? Marty posits that it has an ultimate concern, common myths and stories, rites and ceremonies, and behavioral correlates. Pierard and Linder (1998) describe civil religion as "beliefs, values, rituals and ceremonies that unite the nation, providing a shared sense of history and destiny and linking people to some sense of absolute meaning" (pp. 22–23).

The following are frequently cited as examples of civil religion; most are from the political arena. Most common is the political speech when a divine power is invoked, ending with the line, "God bless America." Often cited is Supreme Court Justice William Douglas's remark in *Zorach v. Clausen,* 343 U.S. 306 (1952), "We are a religious people whose institutions presuppose a Supreme Being." What few recall is that Justice Douglas was receiving media consideration as a presidential candidate then. A related practice is having a scriptural text placed on a public monument or on a public building. A common practice, for example, is to have libraries engraved with "the truth shall set you free." Sometimes, religious symbols are placed on buildings or on the nation's currency, for example, "In God We Trust." The preambles to almost all state constitutions have a reference to God or a Supreme Being or deity. A similar practice is to quote from a religious text or historical religious event, such as Ronald Reagan's reference to America being a "city upon the hill." National holidays, especially Thanksgiving, Memorial Day, and the Fourth of July, have embedded religious sentiments.

The stories told of founding fathers and mothers often include religious dimensions, i.e., a godly parent or divine intervention (George Washington escaping injury or death in battle). Another example is that political leaders have sponsored prayer breakfasts or call for public buildings to be used for community worship services. The singing of the national anthem at sports events and displays of the flag at community events is another sign of civil religion, as is the practice of prayers before Friday night high school football games.

There appear to be two principal areas of continuing discussion among scholars still writing about civil religion. The first is on what to name it and the second is on the scope of investigation. Derek Davis provides a helpful framework for the complex relationship of religion and state in the United States of America, noting three crosscurrents—the separation of church and state, the integration of religion and politics, and the accommodation of civil religion make it difficult to be precise to keep such forces separate.

Those who accept civil religion as ritual expressions of patriotism are content with the term, although some prefer "civic religion" as an alternative. For some observers, including Bellah, the nation has lost much of its political civility. New terms suggested include: "public religion," "public theology," "public piety," "cultural deism," and "civic faith." The term "ceremonial deism" was used in *Lynch v. Donnelly*, 465 U.S. 668 (1984) and *County of Allegheny v. A.C.L.U.*, 492 U.S. 573 (1989).

Recent publications giving extensive coverage to civil religion focus more on comparative studies of civil religion and how civil religion impacts specific groups. Aldridge, Bellah, and Odell-Scott analyze it in other countries. Some scholars explore civil religion for specific groups, such as minorities and sexual orientation. Others question whether civil religion's role is supportive and integrative for the wider society or more openly critical of the nation's political leadership and commercial business practices.

As historian of education Henry Perkinson has argued, American common schools and later public schools have frequently been asked to remedy the nation's perceived social ills and problems, especially after wars. Kniker has found that American public schools emphasize values in the curriculum within a decade following a major war. In their formal curriculum and perhaps more much in their informal curricula, the public schools' enterprise reflects civil religion. Some authors consider public schools America's "established church," offering a "common faith." These interpreters agreed, however, that the public schools act more as receptors of civil religion than as instigators. The sourcebook, *Finding Common Ground*, provides helpful information on how public schools may deal with different perspectives based on religious diversity that are occurring today in the areas described.

Perhaps the most frequent practice of civil religion is the daily recitation of the Pledge of Allegiance. Just prior to World War II (circa 1940), students held their right hands out in a salute similar to that used by Hitler. That changed quickly after the war began. During the 1940s, the U.S. Supreme Court heard two cases brought by Jehovah's Witness families, because such a pledge (to the flag) was regarded as idolatrous. In the first case, the justices decreed that the children could be forced to say the pledge. In the second case, at war's end, the justices reversed the previous verdict. During President Dwight Eisenhower's administration, the words, "under God," were added to the pledge.

Throughout much of the twentieth century, the American school calendar was sensitive to the major holidays celebrated by Christians, Christmas and Easter. Occasionally, some suburban districts with large numbers of Jewish students also accommodated their holidays. Toward the end of the century, as religious diversity increased, public schools renamed the break times as "administrative holidays" or "spring break." The actual school vacation days still coincide, however, with the two Christian holidays.

The public schools of America are in a difficult position. A calendar produced by the former National Conference of Christians and Jews compiled a list of well over 200 religious and ethnic holidays per year. To observe all such events would seriously impact instructional time. To omit all caused criticisms such as schools are "godless" or "in the hands of secular humanists." The inclusion of some holidays, like Halloween, angers some religiously conservative parents. The growing influence of Muslims in the country now means that Islamic holidays are noted in some school calendars.

Choral groups and orchestra/band concerts are still a staple of schools. Titles such as "The Christmas Concert" or "Easter Concert" have given way to "Winter Concert" or "Spring Festival" or "Holiday Concert." Depending upon the school district's background, these musical productions may not include any religious selections or only a few.

A fading practice nationally, but still widely used in some schools, are baccalaureate services. They are clearly religious, usually led by local clergy. Participants sing hymns, scriptural texts are read, and sermons or meditations are given either by the students or ordained clergy. Prayers for the graduates are common. Attendance at these services is voluntary for the graduates. In part, such services are popular because they relieve pressure on graduation services, especially at the high school level, to minimize if not eliminate religious elements. Over the years, graduates who are from minority (in their community) faith traditions, with the assistance of groups like the American Civil Liberties Union, have objected to sectarian prayers at such ceremonies.

One of the most divisive church-state areas is prayer. The U.S. Supreme Court and lower courts have been deluged with cases, most often about prayers in the classroom, but in more recent years about student prayer groups prior to or after school and prayers at school sports events. Citing the Establishment Clause of the First Amendment, the Courts have consistently concluded that teachers or administrators cannot lead prayers. That said, voluntary prayers by students that are not disruptive (examples: praying at lunch, or quietly before a test) are permissible. The Muslim faith requires multiple prayer times per day. More anecdotes than reality may exist, but there are accounts of some school districts setting aside certain spaces for "prayer rooms." The Council on American-Islamic Relations has become an active advocate for Islam.

The appropriateness of teaching about religion and the evolution of religion in textbooks are covered in other selections of this reference work. Here, it bears repeating that the U.S. Supreme Court (*Abington v. Schempp*) in 1963 endorsed studying the role of religion in history, the use of religious imagery and themes in literature, and gaining knowledge of the role of religion in cultures. How might civil religion specifically be studied in the curriculum? A history class might analyze presidential inaugural addresses. That same class or a literature class could study such "sacred texts" as the Declaration of Independence, the Constitution, and Lincoln's Gettysburg Address. Faculty organizing musical performances might examine with students such songs as "Battle Hymn of the Republic" and "America the Beautiful." Student homework assignments on famous religious figures can be appropriate.

Currently, various states either have passed or are considering legislation mandating a form of Bible study in public schools. One dimension of the statehouse debates is the adoption of two available curricula, one viewed as very conservative. Even the more "liberal" curriculum is criticized for emphasizing only the positive impact of religion.

Finding Common Ground summarizes a number of other religiously related activities in public schools. It offers guidelines that point out how and under what conditions students and teachers may discuss religious matters outside the classroom, but somewhere on school premises. For example, schools may provide opportunities for students to distribute invitations to religious events or religious literature at specific sites in the building at designated times. There have been controversies about certain groups (e.g., Christian rock bands, athletic teams, or fitness organizations) that are brought for programs at school assemblies. The controversy comes because, while the groups may not make any public testimonies about their faith at the assembly, they invite the youth to an off-campus meeting that is religious.

One area that deserves more attention concerns specialized staff. One example is the use of "grief counselors" in public schools. Following school shootings or the death of several students in a car accident, media report that grief counselors will be present. Who are these counselors? Are they only licensed specialists trained at secular universities and hospitals or do they include ordained clergy from the area? An emerging trend at the postsecondary level is having a chaplain for sports teams at public universities. Even when privately funded, debate is intense. At one institution, the position was renamed as a "life skills assistant" and detailed guidelines were provided for what could and could not be done as a spiritual adviser to college athletes.

Civil religion is a phenomenon that does exist in the United States of America. It is not something new, nor is it unique to this country. Granted, the form it takes in the United States is different in tone and texture, because of such factors as the so-called doctrine of separation of church and state while citizens still expect the blending of religion and politics. A review of the literature finds that direct treatment of the topic of civil religion is waning. As noted, there is relatively little research on civil religion within public school and public higher education contexts. What there is suggests that religion, generally, and civil religion, specifically, can be perceived to be both a positive or a negative force, and are viewed as either important or insignificant. *See also:* Civic Education; Common Ground Documents; The Pledge of Allegiance; Religious Holidays.

Further Reading: Alan Aldridge, *Religion in the Contemporary World: A Sociological Introduction* (Cambridge, England: Polity Press, 2000); Robert Bellah, *Beyond Belief: Essays on Religion in a Post-Traditional World* (New York: Harper & Row, 1970); Robert Bellah, "Civil Religion in America," *Daedalus* 96 (Winter 1967): 1–21; Robert Bellah, "New Time Religion," *Christian Century,* May 22–26, 2002, pp. 20–26; Robert Bellah, Robert Greenspahn, and Frederick Greenspahn, eds., *Uncivil Religion: Interreligious Hostility in America* (New York: Crossroad, 1987); Stephen Carter, *Civility: Manners, Morals, and the Etiquette of Democracy* (New York: Basic Books, 1998); Jose Casanova, *Public Religions in the Modern World* (Chicago: University of Chicago Press, 1994); Mark Chancey, "Bible Bills, Bible Curricula, and Controversies of Biblical Proportions: Legislative Efforts to Promote Bible Courses in Public Schools," *Religion & Education* 34 (Winter 2007): 28–47; John Murray Cuddihy, *No Offense: Civil Religion and Protestant Taste* (New York: Seabury Press, 1978); Mary Doak, *Reclaiming Narrative for Public Theology* (Albany: State University of New York Press, 2004); Charles Haynes and Oliver Thomas, *Finding Common Ground* (Nashville, TN: The Freedom Forum, First Amendment Center, 2006); Will Herberg, *Protestant, Catholic, Jew: An Essay in American Religious Sociology* (New York: Doubleday and Company, 1955); Charles Kniker, *Teaching About Religion in the Public Schools* (Bloomington, IN: Phi Delta Kappa, 1985); Barry Lynn, *Piety & Politics: The Right-Wing Assault on Religious Freedom* (New York: Harmony Books, 2006); Martin Marty, with Jonathan Moore, *Education, Religion, and the Common Good* (San Francisco: Jossey-Bass, 2000); Barbara McGraw, *Rediscovering America's Sacred*

Ground: Public Religion and Pursuit of the Good in a Pluralistic America (Albany: State University of New York Press, 2003); Sidney Mead, *The Nation with the Soul of a Church* (New York: Harper & Row, 1975); Warren A. Nord, *Religion & American Education: Rethinking a National Dilemma* (Chapel Hill: University of North Carolina Press, 1996); David Odell-Scott, ed., *Democracy and Religion: Free Exercise and Diverse Visions* (Kent, OH: Kent State University Press, 2004); Gerald Parsons, *Perspectives on Civil Religion* (Burlington, VA: Ashgate, 2002); Henry Perkinson, *The Imperfect Panacea: American Faith in Education 1865–1990,* 3rd ed. (New York: McGraw-Hill, 1991); Richard Pierard and Robert Linder, *Civil Religion and the American Presidency* (Grand Rapids, MI: Zondervan, 1998); Stephen Prothero, ed., *A Nation of Religions: The Politics of Pluralism in Multireligious America* (Chapel Hill: University of North Carolina Press, 2006); Russell E. Richey and Donald G. Jones, eds., *American Civil Religion* (New York: Harper and Row, 1974); Jean Jacques Rousseau, *Social Contract,* ed. C.M. Andrews (New York: William H. Wise, 1901); James Sears, with James C. Carper, eds., *Curriculum, Religion, and Public Education* (New York: Teachers College Press, 1998); Robert Wuthnow, *Christianity and Civil Society: The Contemporary Debate* (Valley Forge, PA: Trinity Press International, 1996).

Charles R. Kniker

Cochran v. Louisiana State Board of Education

Acts No. 100 and No. 143 of the 1928 Louisiana legislature allowed the expenditure of state funds to purchase secular textbooks for all schoolchildren, regardless of whether the school attended was public or religious. Act No. 100 mandated that, after allowing funds and appropriations as the state constitution required, the severance tax fund monies should first be devoted to supplying textbooks for schoolchildren without cost. The State Board of Education was charged with the implementation of the act. Act No. 143 made appropriations that were in accordance with Act No. 100.

Appellant citizens and taxpayers brought suit to keep the State Board of Education and government officials from using any money in the severance tax fund to purchase schoolbooks and supply them without cost to the schoolchildren of Louisiana. Appellants alleged that the laws violated certain provisions of the state constitution as well as Section 4 of Article 4 of the Fourteenth Amendment of the U.S. Constitution. The trial court refused to issue an injunction.

The Supreme Court of Louisiana upheld the denial of an injunction. Relying on its earlier decision in *Borden v. Louisiana State Board of Education,* the court found no violation of either the state or the federal constitution. It also found that appellants presented no substantial federal question under Section 4 of Article 4 of the U.S. Constitution, which guarantees to each state a republican form of government since any issues under that section are political, not judicial. Therefore, the court had no jurisdiction over the issues since there was no federal question.

Appellants claimed that the use of the severance tax fund for the purchase of schoolbooks was "a taking of private property for a private purpose." They argued that the purpose of the statutes was to aid private, religious, and other nonpublic schools.

The U.S. Supreme Court upheld the decision of both the trial and state supreme courts and cited the latter's reasoning in its written opinion. The acts say nothing about religious or sectarian schools or churches. Nowhere in the act is money designated for the support of any church or religion. The sole purpose of the act was to purchase textbooks for the state's schoolchildren to use without any cost. All schoolchildren were to be given textbooks, regardless of the school attended; expenditure of funds was not limited to benefit only those students attending public schools. The child, not the school, is the beneficiary of the provisions of the act. The state, which has an interest in the development of an educated citizenry, benefits by the assurance that all children will have appropriate textbooks.

The U.S. Supreme Court agreed with the state court that there was nothing in the statutes that mandated or permitted the supplying of religious books to schoolchildren; only secular textbooks were provided. It cannot be reasonably inferred from the statute that its intent is to in any way promote private or religious instruction; the intent is to promote an educated citizenry. Thus, it is the child who benefits. The state court also found that the books were only lent to the student, but the U.S. Supreme Court found that irrelevant to the federal question.

Therefore, the Supreme Court found that the statute's mandate that the severance tax fund, the money that comes from the taxing power of the state, is being used for a public, not a private purpose. There is no segregation of private schools or their pupils nor is there any evidence of interference in any matters of private concern, such as may properly be found in a private institution such as a religious school. The statute's purpose is education and the method chosen to achieve the purpose, the court found, is comprehensive. The common interest is safeguarded and individual interests are accommodated only as a result of the achievement of the primary interest.

The *Cochran* case is generally considered the one that created the child benefit theory. If whatever is provided by statute or regulation is neutral, primarily benefits the child, and is not directly intended to benefit a particular religion or religion in general, provision of the aid mandated by the statute is not a violation of the U.S. Constitution. Unless a state constitution specifically forbids students in private and/or religious schools from receiving state-supplied aid, the provision of aid that primarily benefits the child should not be a violation of the state constitution. For example, the government provides Medicaid and many hospitals, including religious ones, accept Medicaid patients. The fact that Medicaid payments are made to a religious hospital does not make the payments a type of aid to religion or religious institutions. The purpose of Medicaid is to provide medical benefits for persons who would not otherwise have them. The fact that a religious institution is the recipient of the funds does not make promotion of, or aid to, religion a purpose of Medicaid.

Cases in which Catholic school students alleged a deprivation of constitutional due process rights often attempted to make the case that since education is a public function that the state performs, anyone who performs a public function is a state actor. This argument was never accepted by courts, which routinely held that unless the state was present in the contested activity to such an extent that the activity could fairly be said to be that of the state, no state action was present. To date, no court has found state action present in the disciplinary actions of private schools. Analogously, then, the mere fact that a religious institution receives state funds does not make it a state actor nor is the state subsidizing or promoting religion if the main purpose of the aid is to benefit an individual, not a religious institution. Should a statute only allow aid to religious institutions, it would then, of course, violate the U.S. Constitution, as it would respect an establishment of religion and favor religious institutions over purely secular ones.

Cochran set the stage for many other cases involving aid to students. In *Everson v. Board of Education* (1947) the U.S. Supreme Court ruled that a state could provide reimbursement to parents for transportation costs incurred in getting their children to religious schools, since the primary beneficiaries of the reimbursement would be the parents and the student, not the religious institution even if, without the reimbursement, a parent could not afford the cost of a religious education for his or her child. Any benefit to the religious institution is indirect and not a result intended by a statute that authorizes the giving of aid for specific, nonreligious purposes to students and/or their parents.

In 1968, the U.S. Supreme Court held in *Board of Education v. Allen* that a New York statute mandating the use of government funds for the purchase of secular textbooks to be loaned to all schoolchildren regardless of the school attended did not violate the Establishment Clause of the First Amendment in the absence of any evidence that the loaned textbooks were used to promote religion. Since the state law is neutral on its face and does not allow the provision of religious textbooks from state funds, there is no impermissible entanglement of the state in religious affairs or in the promotion of religion.

Religious schools then are seen as having a dual function: the provision of (1) a secular education and (2) a religious education. So long as state aid promotes secular education and not religious education, there is no impermissible break in the First Amendment "wall" separating church and state. Nonetheless, the U.S. Constitution does not require state-provided aid/benefits to students in religious schools and their parents; such benefits are simply allowed. No state is required to provide benefits, but may if its legislature so chooses. *See also: Board of Education v. Allen; Wolman v. Walter.*

Further Reading: *Board of Education v. Allen,* 392 U.S. 236 (1968); *Borden v. Louisiana State Board of Education,* 168 La. 1005, 123 So. 655; *Cochran v. Louisiana Board of Education,* 320 U.S. 1 (1947); *Everson v. Board of Education,* 330 U.S. 1 (1947).

Mary Angela Shaughnessy

Committee for Public Education and Religious Liberty v. Nyquist

In *Committee for Public Education and Religious Liberty v. Nyquist* (1973), the U.S. Supreme Court, in an opinion authored by Justice Lewis Powell, addressed a dispute from New York with significant implications for religiously affiliated nonpublic schools. As part of its analysis, the Court expanded on its rationale in *Sloan v. Lemon* (1973), handed down on the same day, wherein it struck down a program from Pennsylvania that granted parents whose children attended nonpublic schools tuition reimbursement on the ground that it impermissibly singled out a class of citizens for a special economic benefit. In the interim, the Court has essentially repudiated its holdings on the first two, and arguably more important based on later developments, of the three issues in *Nyquist.*

At issue in *Nyquist* was an expansive statute from New York that offered a variety of forms of aid for eligible parents who sent their children to religiously affiliated nonpublic schools. After a federal trial court struck down only part of the statute for violating the First Amendment Establishment Clause by providing state aid to religious schools, the Supreme Court ruled that the entire law was unconstitutional.

On the first of the three issues, tuition reimbursement, the Court found that even though the funds went directly to parents rather than to the schools that their children attended, they were unacceptable. The Court acknowledged that while the parents would have used the money to pay for tuition, the law's failure to separate secular from religious uses had the impermissible effect of providing financial support for the religious schools. To this end, the Court rejected the state's claim that the parents were not simply conduits because they were free to spend the money in any manner they chose since they paid the tuition and the law merely provided for reimbursements. The Court asserted that even if the funds were offered as incentives to have parents send their children to religious schools, the law violated the Establishment Clause even had the money not been passed on to the schools, a position that the Court later rejected in upholding a voucher program from Cleveland, Ohio, in *Zelman v. Simmons-Harris* (2002).

The second issue in *Nyquist* addressed sections in the statute that provided parents with state income tax deductions as long as they did not receive tuition reimbursements under another part of the law. The Court invalidated this part of the statute in pointing out that there was little difference, when considering whether the aid had the effect of advancing religion, between a tax benefit and a tuition grant. The Court maintained that under both programs parents received the same form of encouragement and reward for sending their children to nonpublic schools. Ten years later, in *Mueller v. Allen* (1983), in upholding a state income tax plan for parents, the Court was satisfied that the program at issue was constitutionally permissible because it was part of a larger system of deductions for parents.

In the final issue in *Nyquist,* the Court vitiated the statute's maintenance and repair provision for nonpublic schools since it placed almost no restrictions on how funds were used. According to the Court, since the government is forbidden from erecting buildings in which religious activities, including schooling, is conducted, public funds could not be used to renovate facilities that were in need of repairs.

Two dissenting opinions, which disagreed with the parts of the majority's decision that struck down the statute, were issued by Justices Byron White and William Rehnquist. Both were essentially satisfied that the statute did not provide impermissible aid. These justices dissented because they were of the view that since the aid was available to all eligible children, not simply those who attended religious schools, it was constitutional. *See also:* Government Aid to Religious Schools; *Lemon v. Kurtzman* and *Earley v. DiCenso; Mueller v. Allen.*

Further Reading: *Committee for Public Education and Religious Liberty v. Nyquist,* 413 U.S. 756 (1973); *Levitt v. Committee for Public Education and Religious Liberty,* 413 U.S. 472 (1973); *Mueller v. Allen,* 463 U.S. 388 (1983); *Sloan v. Lemon,* 413 U.S. 825 (1973); *Zelman v. Simmons-Harris,* 536 U.S. 639 (2002).

Charles J. Russo

Committee for Public Education and Religious Liberty v. Regan

Committee for Public Education and Religious Liberty v. Regan (1980) involved an establishment clause challenge to a New York statute authorizing the use of public funds to reimburse church-sponsored and secular nonpublic schools for costs incurred by them in complying with certain state-mandated requirements, including requirements related to testing (pupil evaluation, achievement, and scholarship and college qualification tests) and to reporting and record keeping. *Regan* was a sequel to an earlier U.S. Supreme Court decision, *Levitt v. Committee for Public Education and Religious Liberty* (1973), where the Court had invalidated a New York statute reimbursing nonpublic schools for the expenses of administering, grading, compiling, and reporting the results of both state-mandated and teacher-prepared tests as long as the teacher-prepared tests were free of religious instructions so as to avoid inculcating students in the religious precepts of the sponsoring church. The Supreme Court in *Levitt* found the reimbursement for teacher-prepared tests to be an infringement of the Establishment Clause of the First Amendment because such tests are an integral part of the teaching process and because the state statute's lump sum reimbursement left no way to separate state-mandated from teacher-prepared tests. The statute litigated in *Regan* had addressed *Levitt* by providing reimbursement only for state-mandated tests.

Regan, occurring as it did in 1980, came after a decade of Supreme Court decisions invalidating a wide variety of state efforts to provide financial assistance to nonpublic (including religious) schools. Three years prior to *Regan,* a badly divided Court, in *Wolman v. Walter* (1977), had upheld the use of public monies for purchases of secular textbooks for loan to the students, for use of standardized test and scoring services that were the same as those used by the public schools, and for the provision of diagnostic and therapeutic services to the students, but had invalidated the use of public monies for purchases of instructional materials and equipment for the students and for transportation for field trips. In the same year as the *Wolman* decision, the Supreme Court remanded a revised *Levitt* case for reconsideration in light of the Court's just-handed-down *Wolman* decision. The Court's decision in *Regan* became the vehicle for rationalizing acceptable public expenditure of funds for nonpublic religious schools.

The *Regan* Court's majority decision, unlike the badly fractured majority opinion in *Wolman,* represented agreement among the five majority members. The tripartite *Lemon v. Kurtzman* (1971) test that had been applied in the 1970s in such a way as to invalidate almost all of the nonpublic school aid cases that came before the Court, now was viewed more flexibly. New York's reimbursement scheme was viewed as having a secular purpose of assuring that all students, including those in nonpublic schools, would have access to quality educational opportunities. Since the tests measured academic and not religious subjects, the risk of the tests being used for religious purposes was nonexistent. Some of the tests were graded on-site by nonpublic school employees but this was not considered to be an establishment clause concern since the tests consisted largely or entirely of objective questions with multiple choice answers. The majority, likewise, found no problem with some of the comprehensive tests including an essay question or two. The chance that grading the answers to state-drafted essay questions in secular subjects would be used to gauge a student's grasp of religious ideas was minimal, especially in light of state procedures designed to guard against serious inconsistencies in grading and misuse of essay questions.

More significant in terms of appreciating the sea change represented by *Regan* in interpreting the no establishment clause was the broad common sense approach the majority took towards the subject of reimbursing nonpublic school personnel to grade tests. The alternative, the Court reasoned, would be paying the nonpublic school to do the grading and paying state employees or some independent service to perform that task, even though the grading function would be the same regardless of who performs it and would not have the primary effect of aiding religion whether or not performed by nonpublic school personnel. The Court, in cryptic, yet prophetic, fashion, declared that "We decline to embrace a formalistic dichotomy that bears so little relationship either to common sense or to the realities of school finance." This moderating approach to government funds and nonpublic religious schools accelerated in the 1980s and 1990s as more funding state arrangements were upheld. *See also:* Government Aid to Religious Schools; *Lemon v. Kurtzman* and *Earley v. DiCenso.*

Further Reading: *Committee for Public Education and Religious Liberty v. Regan,* 444 U.S. 646 (1980); *Lemon v. Kurtzman,* 403 U.S. 602 (1971); *Levitt v. Committee for Public Education and Religious Liberty,* 413 U.S. 472 (1973); *Levitt v. Committee for Public Education and Religious Liberty,* 433 U.S. 902 (1977); *Wolman v. Walter,* 433 U.S. 229 (1977).

Ralph D. Mawdsley

Common Ground Documents

Common ground documents are a series of agreements reached since the late 1980s by coalitions of civil liberties, religious, and educational groups on the constitutional role of religion in the public schools. The first of these agreements was negotiated in 1987 in a process co-chaired by the Americans United Research Foundation (an arm of Americans United for Separation of Church and State) and the Baptist Joint Committee on Public Affairs (now the Baptist Joint Committee for Religious Liberty). This effort to reach consensus about religion in the curriculum was triggered by the controversy surrounding a court case in Alabama, *Smith v. Board of School Commissioners of Mobile County* (1986). In his decision, Federal District Judge Brevard Hand ordered the removal of history and home economics textbooks from Alabama public schools because they unconstitutionally promoted the religion of "secular humanism." Hand supported his ruling by citing the virtual silence about religion in American history texts.

Although Judge Hand's decision was later overturned by the Court of Appeals for the Eleventh Circuit, it underscored for many educational and religious groups the need for a new approach to religion in the curriculum. Concern over the neglect of religion in textbooks was reenforced by two studies published by the liberal People for the American Way and Paul Vitz, a conservative scholar. Groups on the left and right did not agree on the constitutionality of excluding religion from the curriculum. But they did agree that ignoring religion was educationally unsound and that public schools could—and should—do better.

After more than a year of discussion and debate, agreement was reached in the spring of 1988 on "Religion in the Public School Curriculum: Questions and Answers," the first common ground statement in U.S. history on the importance of teaching *about* religion in public schools. Seventeen national organizations endorsed the document, including religious groups such as the National Association of Evangelicals, the American Jewish Congress, the Christian Legal Society, and the Islamic Society of North America and educational organizations such as the National Education Association, the National School Boards Association, and the American Association of School Administrators. The agreement states in part:

> Because religion plays a significant role in history and society, study about religion is essential to understanding both the nation and the world. Omission of facts about religion can give students the false impression that the religious life of humankind is insignificant or unimportant. Failure to understand even the basic symbols, practices and concepts of the various religions makes much of history, literature, art and contemporary life unintelligible.

Study about religion is also important if students are to value religious liberty, the first free-dom guaranteed in the Bill of Rights. Moreover, knowledge of the roles of religion in the past and present promotes cross-cultural understanding essential to democracy and world peace. (Haynes and Thomas, 2007, p. 98)

Over the next two years, the same coalition produced two additional consensus statements framed as questions and answers: "Religious Holidays in Public Schools" (1989) and "The Equal Access Act" (1991).

Despite a long history of conflict over the "December dilemma," the organizations involved in the religious holiday negotiations agreed that under the First Amendment public schools should not sponsor devotional celebrations in December or at any other time of the year. At the same time, however, all sides agreed that study about religious hol-idays could be included in the curriculum as opportunities for learning about religions.

The process of drafting the third agreement regarding equal access for student religious clubs was complicated by the fact that organizations at the table were divided about the wisdom and, in some cases, the constitutionality of the Equal Access Act (EAA) passed by Congress in 1984 and upheld as constitutional by the U.S. Supreme Court in 1990 (*Westside Community Schools v. Mergens*). The act ensures that students in secondary public schools may form religious clubs if the school allows other student clubs not related to the curriculum. The clubs must be student-initiated and student-led. Outsiders may not direct or regularly attend student religious clubs, and teachers acting as monitors may be present at the meetings in a nonparticipatory capacity only.

Soon after Congress enacted the EAA, a coalition of religious and civil liberties groups chaired by the Baptist Joint Committee wrote guidelines explaining the act's key provi-sions. After the Supreme Court's decision in *Mergens,* a larger coalition met to expand the guidelines and develop a consensus on how the EAA should be applied in a school setting. After several months of discussion, the coalition reached agreement on answers to 29 frequently asked questions about the act.

Since the release of these three agreements in 1988, 1989, and 1991, respectively, hundreds of thousands of copies of these three documents have been disseminated to public schools throughout the nation. The guidance they offer, supported as it is by a broad range of national groups, has been quoted and adopted in many state and local school policies.

In April 1995, a different, but overlapping, coalition of 35 religious and civil liberties groups released "Religion in the Public Schools: A Joint Statement of Current Law." Chaired by the American Jewish Congress, the drafting committee spanned the religious and ideological spectrum from the Christian Legal Society to the American Civil Liberties Union. Although the drafters disagreed about what the law should be, they were able to reach agreement of what then-current law said about religious expression in public schools.

The Joint Statement addresses the widespread confusion among school officials and the public about what is and is not legally permissible in public schools regarding such divi-sive issues as student prayers, distribution of religious literature, and student garb. Contrary to the popular perception that God had been banned from public schools, the statement outlines a variety of ways in which students may express their faith under the First Amendment and teachers may teach about religion in the classroom.

The significance of the Joint Statement was not lost on the administration of President Bill Clinton. Eager to dispel misconceptions about religion in public schools and anxious to head off congressional efforts to pass a "school prayer" amendment, U.S. Secretary of Education Richard Riley welcomed the statement as a common ground approach that could serve as the basis for presidential guidelines. Drawing on the Joint Statement, the Department of Education issued guidelines entitled "Religious Expression in Public Schools" and, at the President's directive, sent a copy to every school superintendent in the nation in August 1995.

That same year, 23 major educational associations and religious organizations sought agreement on guiding principles for addressing conflicts in public education over educational philosophy, school reform, and the role of religion and values. Co-chaired by the First Amendment Center and the Association for Supervision and Curriculum Development (ASCD), the initiative was an attempt to bring more civility to the culture-war debates then taking place in many school districts.

In March 1995, the group released "Religious Liberty, Public Education, and the Future of American Democracy: A Statement of Principles," a civic framework for negotiating differences and, where possible, reaching common ground. The agreement was extraordinary not only for what it said, but also for who said it. Among the endorsing groups were the Christian Coalition, People for the American Way, the Catholic League for Religious and Civil Rights, the Council on Islamic Education, and the Union of American Hebrew Congregations, the broadest coalition to support any of the common ground documents.

Although it is difficult to gauge the impact of the Statement of Principles, it is fair to say that some of the signatories did not always model the civil debate and constructive dialogue called for in the document. Nevertheless, the language of the agreement has been influential in helping local communities articulate a shared understanding of religious liberty in their schools. The most widely quoted part of the statement, Principle IV, offers consensus language on the constitutional and educational role of religion in public education:

> Public schools may not inculcate nor inhibit religion. They must be places where religion and religious conviction are treated with fairness and respect. Public schools uphold the First Amendment when they protect the religious liberty rights of students of all faiths or none. Schools demonstrate fairness when they ensure that the curriculum includes study *about* religion, where appropriate, as an important part of a complete education. (Haynes and Thomas, 2007, p. 12)

Encouraged by the progress made toward finding common ground, Secretary Riley urged the First Amendment Center to create consensus guidelines aimed specifically at parents and teachers. In 1996, the Center and the National PTA jointly published "A Parent's Guide to Religion in the Public Schools," a question and answer format built on the consensus reached in earlier guidelines. Two years later, the Center released "A Teacher's Guide to Religion in the Public Schools," providing classroom teachers with guidance on protecting religious liberty rights of students, teaching about religions, and presenting the rights and obligations of public school employees. Twenty-two major religious and educational organizations endorsed the teacher's guide.

The improved environment for addressing religion in schools in the late 1990s encouraged some school districts to create new partnerships with local faith communities to offer tutoring, mentoring, and after-school programs. The Chicago school system, for example, asked the Christian Legal Society and the American Jewish Congress to provide legal guidance for such cooperative programs. In 1998, the Chicago guidelines were adapted for national use and published by the First Amendment Center as "Public Schools and Religious Communities: A First Amendment Guide." The document encourages partnerships between schools and religious institutions but cautioned that cooperative activities must be wholly secular in nature.

This agreement on the constitutional framework for partnerships was sponsored by 15 educational and religious groups, including the U.S. Catholic Conference, the National School Boards Association, and the Baptist Joint Committee. But a number of separationist groups, notably Americans United for Separation of Church and State, declined to endorse the document out of concern that the guidelines would be ignored and partnerships might become opportunities for religious indoctrination.

In December 1999, President Clinton directed the U.S. Department of Education to once again inform school districts about the constitutional role of religion in public schools. This time, however, the president decided to send a packet of consensus documents to every principal in the nation. Included in the mailing were two Department of Education publications: an updated version of "Religious Expression in the Public Schools" and "How Faith Communities Support Children's Learning in Public Schools," a description of successful partnerships between local schools and religious institutions. Also included were three publications from the First Amendment Center: "A Teacher's Guide to Religion in the Public Schools," "A Parent's Guide to Religion in the Public Schools," and "Public Schools and Religious Communities: A First Amendment Guide."

The mailing of these guidelines in January 2000 marked the first time that every public school received directives on permissible student religious expression, guidance for teachers on study about religion in the curriculum, legal ground rules for cooperative relationships between religious communities and public schools, and advice to parents on a range of issues involving religion and values in schools. Because the various guides were endorsed by broad coalitions, they provided a legal safe harbor (or at least the closest thing to it) for school boards, administrators, and teachers.

Just weeks prior to Clinton's directive, 21 educational, religious, and civil liberties groups reached agreement on the place of the Bible in schools, one of the longest-running conflicts in public-school history. The negotiations on the Bible guide began in 1998 when the First Amendment Center and the National Bible Association convened a drafting committee that included representatives from People for the American Way, the Christian Legal Society, the American Jewish Committee, the Baptist Joint Committee, and the American Jewish Congress. The deliberations took place during a time of heightened controversy regarding the constitutionality of Bible electives being offered in Florida, Mississippi, and other states.

After a year of discussion, the coalition found common ground and published "The Bible and Public Schools: A First Amendment Guide" in December 1999. The document neither encourages nor discourages Bible electives, but rather provides legal and educational guidance for school districts interested in offering such a course. The agreement also outlines the rights of students to express their faith in a public school, including the right to form Bible clubs in secondary schools if the school allows other extracurricular clubs. Following its release, the Bible guide was widely disseminated and used by state offices of education and local districts to help determine the constitutionality of proposals for Bible courses. An organization called "The Bible Literacy Project" used the Bible agreement as a framework for developing a student textbook, *The Bible and Its Influence,* for use in public schools.

The consensus statements on the place of religion in public education encouraged the First Amendment Center in 2004 to seek common ground on how to address conflicts over issues regarding homosexuality in schools, a debate that implicates deeply held religious and philosophical convictions on all sides. Two groups with very divergent views on homosexuality, the Christian Educators Association International and the Gay, Lesbian and Straight Education Network, collaborated with the center and BridgeBuilders (an organization that mediates disputes over religion in schools) to draft "Public Schools and Sexual Orientation: A First Amendment Framework for Finding Common Ground." Released in May 2005, the statement was also endorsed by the American Association of School Administrators and the Association for Supervision and Curriculum Development. The guide is not prescriptive, but rather outlines a process for dialogue within the guiding principles of the First Amendment.

The common ground agreements reached since 1987 were intended to provide a First-Amendment alternative to two failed models that have dominated the history of public schooling. On one end of the spectrum are schools where one religion (the majority faith) is preferred in school policies and practices. On the other end, are schools where religion is largely ignored as though public schools were intended to be religion-free zones. A third model, as envisioned in the agreements, provides for protecting student religious expression and including religious perspectives in the curriculum while simultaneously rejecting state endorsement or promotion of religion.

By 2007, almost 20 years after the first agreement on religion in schools, many districts had moved closer to the third model advocated in the various common ground documents. State social studies standards and textbooks included considerable discussion of religion; student religious clubs met on hundreds of high school campuses; the sight of students praying or reading their Scriptures was commonplace. Many factors contributed to bringing about this change: Passage of the Equal Access Act of 1984; advocacy and litigation by conservative Christian parents and organizations; and the groundbreaking inclusion of study about religions in the California social-science history framework of 1987, to cite just a few. But the common ground documents on religion in schools have played a critical role in helping many school districts translate these developments into new policies and practices consistent with the First Amendment and widely accepted by the community. *See also:* First Amendment Center; Haynes, Charles C.; Religion and the Public School Curriculum; U.S. Department of Education Guidelines on Religion and Public Education.

Further Reading: American Jewish Congress et al., "Religion in the Public Schools: A Joint Statement of Current Law" (1995); Ronald D. Anderson, *Religion and Spirituality in the Public School Curriculum* (New York: Peter Lang, 2004); BridgeBuilders, at www.Bridge-Builders.org; California Department of Education History–Social Science Curriculum Framework and Criteria Committee, *History–Social Science Framework for California Public Schools* (Sacramento: Author, 1987); O. L. Davis et al., *Looking at History: A Review of Major U.S. History Textbooks* (Washington, DC: People for the American Way, 1986); David S. Doty, "Maelstrom in Modesto: Developing a Common Ground Policy for the Protection of Gay and Lesbian Students in Public Schools," *California Social Studies Review* 40 (Spring 2001): 32–36; First Amendment Center, at www.firstamendmentcenter.org; Charles C. Haynes and Oliver Thomas, *Finding Common Ground: A First Amendment Guide to Religion and Public Schools* (Nashville: First Amendment Center,

2007); Emile Lester and Patrick S. Roberts, *Learning about World Religions in Public Schools: The Impact on Student Attitudes and Community Acceptance in Modesto, Calif.* (Nashville: First Amendment Center, 2006); Warren A. Nord, *Religion and American Education: Rethinking a National Dilemma* (Chapel Hill, NC: University of North Carolina Press, 1995); Warren A. Nord and Charles C. Haynes, *Taking Religion Seriously Across the Curriculum* (Alexandria, VA: ASCD, 1998); Paul Vitz, *Censorship: Evidence of Bias in Our Children's Textbooks* (Ann Arbor, MI: Servant Books, 1986).

Charles C. Haynes

Common School

The term "Common School" has for us the status of a historical artifact; it is not commonly heard in discussions of American education (or that in other English-speaking countries), nor was it much in use in other Western nations except in reference to schooling in the United States. For a time, however, the term had great evocative power in the debates in the United States over the extension of schooling in a uniform fashion to the entire rising generation.

What did the American educational reformers of the first part of the nineteenth century mean by the "common school"? The meaning of the term seems to have evolved from a statement of fact to a statement of a program. Initially the common school was simply the school that taught what was considered the common skills and knowledge that all children should acquire before entering the world of work; it was distinguished from the Latin school and the academy that offered more advanced schooling for the relatively small number of youth who aspired to the learned professions on the one hand and to a variety of other occupations—including schoolteaching—on the other. Thus the common school was simply the school that taught everything that was regarded as the common foundation of life in society. This included biblical knowledge and essential Christian beliefs from a Protestant perspective.

What was new about the "common school program" was not the provision of local schools providing elementary instruction and supported by varying combinations of local taxation and tuition charges; that had been the norm in New England and areas to the west settled from New England for two centuries, and was increasingly common in the Mid-Atlantic states in communities where no one church was sufficiently dominant to provide for the schooling of all the local children. Ad hoc arrangements were worked out and proved more or less satisfactory depending on local leadership and the commitment of parents to the schooling of their children.

The new element introduced by Horace Mann and his counterparts in other states was to make schooling—not just its availability but its nature and function—a matter of state concern and policy, with the explicit intention of shaping the future of American society through its youth. This agenda emerged contemporaneously with similar developments in France, the Netherlands, Canada, Ireland (under British rule), and England, and, like them, explicitly influenced by earlier state-led efforts in Prussia and other German states to use schooling as an instrument of public policy.

In the early national period of the United States—and, it is important to note, before immigration became a significant factor in policy debates—there were a few voices calling for a more expansive version of what the common school should achieve, and what the role of the state should be in bringing this about. James Carter wrote in his influential *Essays on Popular Education* (1824–1825) that "Upon this topic of popular education, a *free* government must be *arbitrary.*" The objective of educational action by government had little to do with economic or egalitarian goals; it was to shape future citizens to a common pattern. Like Jean-Jacques Rousseau and educational theorists during the French Revolution, Carter turned to the model of Sparta to illustrate what the state could and should do. "If the Spartan could mold and transform a nation to suit his taste, by means of an early education, why may not the same be done at the present day?" (Glenn, 1988, p. 75).

A crucial step was taken by the Massachusetts legislature in 1837, when it voted to create a state board of education to collect information about schools and to provide advice on how schools could be improved (Michigan and Ohio created administrative positions that year with a similar mandate). Although several states had earlier given one of their officials responsibility for overseeing the distribution of the (limited) state funds provided to local schools and to academies, this was the first instance in which a state official had been charged with seeking to improve the quality of the education provided.

The new board was "granted no direct authority over the schools; its primary function was enlightenment" (Cremin, 1957, p. 6). Governor Edward Everett appointed Horace Mann (1796–1859), an attorney and state senator, to the board, from which he soon resigned to take the paid position of board secretary. "Having found the present generation composed of materials almost unmalleable," Mann wrote at the time, "I am about transferring my efforts to the next. Men are cast-iron, but children are wax. Strength expended upon the latter may be effectual which would make no impression on the former" (Messerli, 1971, p. 249).

In the first issue of his *Common School Journal* (1838), through which he sought to influence public opinion in general as well as teachers, Mann wrote that "If we would have improved men, we must have improved means of educating children.... Of all the means in our possession, the common school has precedence, because of its universality." Even more boldly, in 1841, he claimed that

> the Common School is the greatest discovery ever made by man.... Other social organizations are curative and remedial; this is preventive and an antidote.... Let the Common School be expanded to its capabilities, let it be worked with the efficiency of which it is susceptible, and nine tenths of the crimes in the penal code would become obsolete; the long catalogue of human ills would be abridged. (Glenn, 1988, p. 80)

It was Mann, above all, who transformed the essentially neutral term "common school" into a program for state leadership in the creation of a uniform and—by intention, at least—monopolistic system of schooling in which all of the children in a community would receive a common education. In effect, common came to refer to the experience and its intended effects rather than to the curriculum to be mastered. From an essentially modest project, it became the unlimited one of social transformation and nation building, parallel in its ambitions to the efforts taking shape during the 1830s in France and other Western nations.

Horace Mann and his American allies, and their counterparts in other countries, were successful in large part because they were able to persuade their respective publics that the purpose of their efforts was no threat to the religious character of popular schooling but was, in fact, intended to make it more consistent and effective. Clothing the "common school project" in the vocabulary of Protestantism, something that had not been the case of the proposals a generation earlier by Thomas Jefferson and his allies in their similar but unsuccessful proposals, did a great deal to disarm suspicion about state interference with the supremely local business of educating children.

Mann's successor, Barnas Sears, wrote in his official report for 1852 that

> The most perfect development of the mind, no less than the order of the school and the stability of society, demands a religious education. Massachusetts may be regarded as having settled, at least for herself, this great question of the connection of religion with the Public Schools. She holds that religion is the highest and noblest possession of the mind, and is conducive to all the true interests of man and of society, and therefore she cannot do otherwise than seek to place her schools under its beneficent influence. (Glenn, 1988, p. 173)

The effect of this emphasis on the religious character of the common public school was to make it unacceptable, as "Protestant," to many among the growing Catholic population resulting from German and Irish immigration. Ironically, though, it was a much attenuated Protestantism that found expression in public schools, at least as intended by Horace Mann, and his fiercest critics were among the more orthodox Protestants (Glenn, 1988, pp. 180–196). The evidence suggests that the actual practices of religious instruction, Bible reading, and prayer at the opening or closing of the school day were in decline throughout the nineteenth century, with religious themes increasingly replaced, in schoolbooks, by moral ones (Dunn, 1958). Despite this weakening of its religious character, the panic over Catholic immigration and growing Catholic political power produced a Protestant united front in support of the common public school.

The common school and the vision of American life that it embodied came to be vested with a religious seriousness and exaltation, becoming the core institution of American society, the definer of meanings, and the only way to higher life—spiritually as well as materially—for generations of immigrant and native-born children alike. In close alliance with but never subordinate to the Protestant churches, the common public school occupied a "sacred space" where its mission was beyond debate and where to question it was a kind of blasphemy. That the power of this idea has not faded is evident from the deep-rooted and often irrational resistance to proposals that parents be allowed to choose the schools that their children attend. *See also:* The Bible in the Public Schools; Hughes, John; Mann, Horace; *McGuffey Readers;* Prayer in the Public Schools.

Further Reading: Lawrence Cremin, ed., *The Republic and the School: Horace Mann on the Education of Free Men* (New York: Teachers College Press, 1957); Raymond B. Culver, *Horace Mann and Religion in the Massachusetts Public Schools* (New Haven, CT: Yale University Press, 1929); William Kailer Dunn, *What Happened to Religious Education? The Decline of Religious Teaching in the Public Elementary School, 1776–1861* (Baltimore, MD: Johns Hopkins University Press, 1958); Charles L. Glenn, Jr., *The Myth of the Common School* (Amherst: University of Massachusetts Press, 1988); Benjamin Justice, *The War that Wasn't: Religious Conflict and Compromise in the Common Schools of New York State, 1865–1900* (Albany: State University of New York Press, 2005); Carl F. Kaestle, *Pillars of the Republic: Common Schools and American Society, 1780–1860* (New York: Hill and Wang, 1983); Jonathan Messerli, *Horace Mann: A Biography* (New York: Alfred A. Knopf, 1972).

Charles L. Glenn, Jr.

Concerned Women for America

Concerned Women for America (CWA) was founded in San Diego in 1979 by Beverly LaHaye as a conservative alternative to the National Organization for Women (NOW). LaHaye is the wife of Tim LaHaye, a leading conservative Christian activist who was on the founding board of Moral Majority, established the same year. (He is also coauthor of the phenomenally successful *Left Behind* series of novels.) Now headquartered in Washington, the organization claims to have more than 500,000 members in 500 state and regional groups. Membership, however, is extended to anyone making a contribution of any dollar amount, making it difficult to assess the strength of commitment. Still, the organization appears to be about the size of NOW and can generate a deluge of telephone calls, e-mails, letters, and faxes to members of Congress they hope to influence on issues of concern.

Unlike such organizations as Moral Majority, which purported to welcome any who supported its broad goals, regardless of religious affiliation, CWA's statement of faith forthrightly affirms belief in the Bible as "the verbally inspired, inerrant word of God and the final authority on faith and practice," in the virgin birth, and in the grace extended through the atoning death of Jesus as the only path to salvation. Its stated mission is "to protect and promote Biblical values among all citizens—first through prayer, then education, and finally by influencing our society—thereby reversing the decline in moral values in our nation." In the service of this mission, the organization publishes *Family Voice* magazine and houses the Beverly LaHaye Institute, which provides speakers and a plethora of multimedia materials pertinent to the organization's agenda.

While it can be counted on to affirm the panoply of positions favored by the Christian Right, CWA concentrates on six "core issues," each of which it sees as part of "a battle over worldviews."

(1) *Family.* Although articles on its Web site and in its publications address such matters as prostitution, sex slavery, child marriage, children born out of wedlock, and divorce, the overwhelming concern under this rubric is homosexuality and, by extension, same-sex marriage. It supports Defense of Marriage Amendments, which define marriage as between one man and one woman.

(2) *Sanctity of Human Life.* Its stated commitment to "protection of all innocent human life from conception until natural death" includes fervent opposition to abortion, embryonic stem cell research, and the morning-after pill. (The inclusion of "innocent" permits an exception for capital punishment.)

(3) *Pornography.* In its effort to reverse a tide of coarseness in American culture, CWA campaigns against all forms of pornography and obscenity, including offerings on the Internet, cable and network broadcasts, and hotel televisions.

(4) *Religious Liberty.* CWA speaks out when Christians are persecuted or restricted in foreign lands. Domestically, they support prayer and other religious expressions in schools and public venues and decry what they regard as the secularization of Christmas.

(5) *National Sovereignty.* Like other groups on the Christian Right, CWA is critical of international organizations perceived to have some authority over the United States, with particular animus for the United Nations, which it regards as advocating measures contrary to its beliefs, such as those relating to sexuality and gender equality. Concern for national sovereignty also inclines CWA to support stricter control of immigration.

(6) *Education.* Some CWA publications criticize the National Education Association, decry political correctness, speak favorably of vouchers and homeschooling, and oppose the Harry Potter series, charging that the books promote acceptance of the occult and promotion of witchcraft.

But the overwhelming preponderance of attention focuses on the superiority of abstinence-only sex education, purported efforts by schools to make homosexuality appear normal and acceptable, and the need to allow the teaching of Intelligent Design as an alternative to Darwinian evolution. In one of its best-known efforts, CWA provided legal counsel (Michael Farris, founder of Home School Legal Defense Association and Patrick Henry College, established especially for homeschooled students) for the case of *Mozert v. Hawkins County* [Tennessee] *Board of Education* (1986), representing parents who wanted their children exempted from reading school texts they believed demeaned their religious convictions. After a five-year struggle in the courts, the parents lost the case—but the controversy essentially killed the popular texts and made publishers wary of offending conservative Christians.

In addition to keeping its members informed on these issues, CWA's Legislative Action Committee provides instruction on how to lobby officials at all levels of government, providing regular alerts on bills of interest, together with talking points and supportive information to help volunteers be more effective in their contacts with government representatives. Each month, intensively trained volunteer members of "Project 535"—one for each member of Congress—travel to Washington to lobby their representatives and senators on behalf of legislation supported by CWA. Shortly afterward, reports of their visits are communicated to members in each legislative district, who are then urged to contact their representatives in Congress about the legislation in question. It is this level of organization, political savvy, and ideological commitment that has, since the rise of the Christian Right in the late 1970s, helped make that movement a formidable and enduring part of the American political landscape. *See also:* Secularism; Sex Education and Religion.

Further Reading: Concerned Women for America, at www.cwfa.org; William Martin, *With God on Their Side: The Rise of the Religious Right in America* (New York: Broadway Books, 1996; 2004); People for the American Way, at www.pfaw.org.

William Martin

Council for American Private Education

The Council for American Private Education (CAPE), a coalition of national organizations and state affiliates serving private elementary and secondary schools, was founded in 1971 to provide a coherent and unified voice for private K–12 education in the United States. CAPE is dedicated to fostering communication and cooperation within the private school community and with the public sector to improve the quality of education for all of the nation's children.

CAPE speaks as one voice on behalf of its members as it promotes the vital role of private schools in American education and their significant contributions to educating the public and promoting the common good. The United States is blessed by a rich diversity of private schools—some rooted in religious tradition, some that provide intensive academic experiences, and some that are specialized for specific populations. Together these schools offer parents, a child's primary educators, a wide range of options, enabling them to select a setting that reflects their values and best meets their child's needs.

CAPE member organizations are diverse, representing a host of religious and pedagogic traditions. In 2003, according to the National Center for Education Statistics, the nation's 28,384 private schools enrolled 5.1 million students, approximately 10 percent of the nation's K–12 enrollment. Most private school students (82 percent) attended religious schools in 2003, and those schools were affiliated with an array of religious traditions. Catholic schools enrolled 46.2 percent of private school students; Conservative Christian schools enrolled 15.1 percent; 5.3 percent were in Baptist schools; 4 percent in Lutheran schools; 3.9 percent in Jewish schools; 1.9 percent in Episcopal schools; 1.2 percent in Assemblies of God schools; and 1.1 percent in Seventh-day Adventist schools; as well as smaller percentages in schools affiliated with other denominations (Broughman and Swaim, 2006).

To provide some historical context, in 1970, the year before CAPE's founding, private schools had an estimated overall enrollment of 5.4 million students, about 10.5 percent of the country's 51.3 million K–12 students—figures very close to the enrollment levels and market share of 2003. As is the case today, the vast majority of private school students attended religious schools in 1970; in fact, 81 percent of private school students were in Catholic schools (Snyder and Hoffman, 2003).

CAPE's founding members reflected the religious nature of the private school land-scape in 1971. Indeed, six of CAPE's seven original members represented religious schools: the Board of Parish Education of the Lutheran Church–Missouri Synod, Christian Schools International, the Friends Council on Education, the National Association of Episcopal Schools, the National Catholic Educational Association, and the National Society for Hebrew Day Schools. Only the National Association of Independent Schools did not have an overtly religious mission, though many of its member schools did.

By September 2007, CAPE's membership had expanded to 17 organizations represent-ing a broad spectrum of the nation's private schools: Agudath Israel of America, American Montessori Society, Association Montessori International–USA, Association of Christian Schools International, Association of Christian Teachers and Schools, Association of Waldorf Schools of N.A., Christian Schools International, Evangelical Lutheran Church in America, Friends Council on Education, Lutheran Church–Missouri Synod, National Association of Episcopal Schools, National Association of Independent Schools, National Catholic Educational Association, National Christian School Association, Oral Roberts University Educational Fellowship, Seventh-day Adventist Board of Education, United States Conference of Catholic Bishops, Wisconsin Evangelical Lutheran Schools. As was the case in 1971, most of those organizations represented religious schools. CAPE also had a robust state CAPE network, with CAPE-like affiliates in 31 states and jurisdictions, including the District of Columbia and Puerto Rico.

As it did in 1971, CAPE promotes the rights of parents to educate their children in the schools of their choice, encourages excellence and pluralism in education, and promotes the right of private schools to fulfill their unique missions. It also monitors and analyzes legislation and regulations affecting private schools, provides information about private education to policy makers and the public, and keeps the private school community informed on issues and programs. On the public policy front, CAPE fosters the participa-tion of the private school community in shaping the nation's education agenda, develops and promotes positions on education policy, and advocates the equitable opportunity of private school students to participate in appropriate state and federal education programs.

In the nation's earliest days, private schools helped establish the country's foundation for education. Today, private schools help fulfill the American ideal of educational plural-ism. CAPE serves as the voice of the country's religious and independent schools and continues to advance its mission to preserve and promote educational pluralism so that parents have a choice in the schooling of their children. More information about CAPE is available at www.capenet.org. *See also:* Government Aid to Religious Schools; State Regulation of Religious Schools.

Further Reading: Stephen P. Broughman and Nancy L. Swaim, *Characteristics of Private Schools in the United States: Results from the 2003–2004 Private School Universe Survey* (Washington, DC: U.S. Department of Education, National Center for Educational Statistics, 2006); Thomas D. Snyder and Charlene M. Hoffman, *Digest of Education Statistics, 2002* (Washington, DC: U.S. Department of Education, National Center for Educational Statistics, 2003).

Joseph McTighe

Council for Spiritual and Ethical Education

The Council for Spiritual and Ethical Education (CSEE) is an association of independent schools from throughout the United States and Canada. It was founded in 1898 as the National Preparatory School Committee, a branch of the Young Men's Christian Association (YMCA), and was composed primarily of New England preparatory schools for the purpose of collaboration in the formation of young men into upstanding Christian gentlemen. The Committee separated from the YMCA after World War II under a new name, the Council for Religion in Independent Schools (CRIS). Throughout the latter half of the twentieth century, CRIS grew in diversity, expanding to include boarding schools and day schools, both schools that were religiously affiliated and schools that were not, and schools with grade levels from kindergarten through grade 12. The primary foci of the Council's mission were religious education (including education about religions) and ethical growth. Schools without religious affiliations that were members tended to affiliate because some of the early discussions in independent schools about the development of ethical leaders—what has come to be known as character education—began under its leadership.

The Council for Spiritual and Ethical Education came into being with a second name change in the mid-1990s. The majority of member schools were simultaneously affiliated with the National Association of Independent Schools (NAIS), although even today there are a number of institutions (primarily religious schools) affiliated with CSEE that are not NAIS members. Membership roles in the first decade of the twenty-first century included schools primarily in the United States and some in Canada. About half of the schools have no religious affiliation; the others include a small number of Jewish and Muslim schools, and a much greater number of Christian schools (primarily Episcopal, Roman Catholic, Presbyterian, Methodist, and Friends schools). Even before the name change from CRIS to CSEE the organization began work with schools on sensitive teaching about the world's religious traditions and interfaith dialogue.

CSEE is singular as a national educational association in that it addresses issues of religious diversity, moral/ethical growth, and spiritual formation without advocating a specific religious affiliation or orientation. In 2006, CSEE began a project developing a manual of activities and resources to address the issue of spiritual growth in children and adolescents. The manual was intended for use in schools that wished to nurture spiritual development where the student population consisted of children from a variety of religious traditions, as is so often the case in North America. The spiritual development project entailed the collaborative efforts of a group of educators from all grade levels

(K–12); team members represented Episcopal, Jewish, Roman Catholic, Muslim, and Friends schools, and a couple of nonaffiliated independent schools.

The spiritual development project began shortly after CSEE's Working with the Best program, through which a team of administrators and educators committed to a series of training sessions with some of North America's best known character education researchers and trainers. Late in their training they began doing workshops and working as resources to increase the breadth and effectiveness of moral development and ethical leadership in their own and other independent schools.

CSEE runs a number of national and regional workshops in areas of its mission to support "the moral and spiritual development of children by providing resources and educational opportunities to elementary, middle, and secondary schools." Workshops are primarily for educators, and only occasionally involve students. A number of workshops are cosponsored or have worked collaboratively with other organizations, like the Program in Religion and Secondary Education at Harvard Divinity School, Religious Studies in Secondary Schools, the New England Independent School Spiritual Council, and the Curriculum Initiative. CSEE also publishes a monthly newsletter for its member schools as well as a variety of PDF or Web-based periodical publications for religion teachers, community service directors, parents, and student advisors. Its other publications include resources, and a few curricular items, for moral and spiritual development in schools. *See also:* Spirituality.

Further Reading: The Council for Spiritual and Ethical Education, at www.csee.org; Robert A. Moss, *Voices of Religion in Independent Schools: The Evolution of the Council for Religion in Independent Schools* (Portland, OR: CSEE, 1993).

David Streight

Creationism

Scholars from every side of the debate over creationism agree that it minimally entails the belief that a supernatural creator is responsible for the universe. In this sense, a creationist is anyone who believes that a supernatural being created the universe. Since this definition could encompass even a theistic evolutionist who embraces all of neo-Darwinism, "creationism" may be better understood by breaking it down into subgroups.

The most well-known form of creationism is biblical young earth creationism, which adheres to a literal interpretation of Genesis and postulates that the universe was created by the Judeo-Christian God on the order of 6,000 to 10,000 years ago. Under this view, the "days" of the Genesis creation account are considered to be actual 24-hour periods. Young earth creationists generally hold that the Noahic flood in Genesis was a global event that generated many of the earth's geological features, including much of the fossil record. They believe that humans and animals were specially created supernaturally by God only a few thousand years ago, "according to their kind." Most also contend that much small-scale "microevolution" has occurred since the creation of life. In 1981, one federal court judge described this form of young earth "creation science" taught under an Arkansas law:

Creation-science includes the scientific evidences and related inferences that indicate:
(1) Sudden creation of the universe, energy, and life from nothing; (2) The insufficiency of

mutation and natural selection in bringing about development of all living kinds from a single organism; (3) Changes only within fixed limits of originally created kinds of plants and animals; (4) Separate ancestry for man and apes; (5) Explanation of the earth's geology by catastrophism, including the occurrence of a worldwide flood; and (6) A relatively recent inception of the earth and living kinds. (*McLean v. Board of Education,* 1982)

Another contingent of "biblical old earth creationism" believes that the Judeo-Christian God created the universe and life on earth on the order of millions or billions of years ago. This view accepts the mainstream geological timescale and paleontological record. Nonetheless, many old earth creationists claim to adhere to a literal interpretation of Genesis where they understand the Hebrew word "yom" is best translated as an indefinite period of time rather than a 24-hour day. They often assert that the events in Genesis are separated by unspecified long periods of time. As for the Noahic flood, they typically hold it was a localized, nonglobal event of minimal geological consequence. Old earth creationists share with young earth creationists a skepticism of Darwinian evolution, but they believe God progressively and specially created life-forms over millions, or even billions of years. They often maintain that microevolution has occurred since the creation of original "kinds" of life.

Like biblical old earth creationists, Hindu creationists accept that the earth and universe are on the order of billions of years old. Hindu creationists base their views upon the Vedic scriptural texts, and their creator is typically the supreme consciousness Brahman. Hindu creationists sometimes question Darwinian evolution, and in some cases assert that humans have existed on earth for many millions of years, existing far before the date typically given the mainstream scientific view for the origin of humans.

These forms of creationists share key similarities that distinguish them from theistic evolutionists (who are creationists in the general sense): they all believe that there exists real scientific evidence to support their views. Such creationists have been referred to as "scientific creationists," even by those who believe their views ultimately are not scientific. In contrast, a theistic evolutionist would not say that there is scientific data capable of proving her own belief that God created the universe. In contrast, biblical creationists or Hindu creationists would claim that empirical data can in some real sense directly validate their religious creation account.

Some have maintained that the controversial idea of "intelligent design" (ID) is a form of creationism. Most proponents of ID maintain that it is not a form of creationism because ID does not require that life-forms were specially created in their present form, ID does not base its claims upon any religious text, and ID does not address questions about the identity or nature of the designer. Indeed, many biblical creationists point out similar distinction between ID and creationism, sometimes even criticizing ID because it does not enter religious discussions about the identity of the designer.

During the 1970s and 1980s, creationists pushed for schools to grant "equal time" to teaching creationism whenever evolution was taught. After a series of cases, the U.S. Supreme Court found in *Edwards v. Aguillard* (1987) that "creation science" entailed the view that "a supernatural creator was responsible for the creation of humankind." The Court held this is a religious viewpoint and unconstitutional to teach in public schools. Whether teaching young earth creation science or presenting the general creationist view that a "supernatural creator" created life, courts have consistently held these are religious viewpoints that are unconstitutional to advocate in public schools. Precedent suggests that schools have freedom to teach *about* such religious viewpoints in comparative religion or philosophy courses.

School districts have the power to prevent a teacher from advocating creationism. In *Hazelwood School District v. Kuhlmeier* (1988), the U.S. Supreme Court held that a district may impose "reasonable restrictions" on teacher speech during classroom instruction. According to the Court, the test of

> whether speech of a government employee is constitutionally protected expression...entails striking a balance between the interests of the teacher, as a citizen, in commenting upon matters of public concern and the interest of the State, as an employer, in promoting the efficiency of the public services it performs through its employees.

The Court of Appeals for the Fifth Circuit applied this reasoning and held that "the question of whether a public employee's speech is constitutionally protected turns upon the 'public' or 'private' nature of such speech." Under such a rule, some curricular materials not authorized by the district might not be a matter of "public concern," and districts may sanction a teacher for teaching outside of the proscribed curriculum. The Court of Appeals for the Seventh Circuit has held a similar view, stating: "There is a compelling state interest in the choice and adherence to a suitable curriculum...[and] [i]t cannot be left to individual teachers to teach what they please." Teacher speech may therefore be restricted when such regulations are "reasonably related to legitimate pedagogical concerns." Administrators who are seeking to prevent violations of the Establishment Clause regarding advocating creationism would normally have such "legitimate pedagogical concerns."

Teachers do not normally have the academic freedom to endorse creation science. In the case *Webster v. New Lenox School District No. 122* (1990), a student complained that junior high teacher Ray Webster had violated the Establishment Clause by advocating creationism in his social science classroom. After the district investigated the teacher's activities, Webster acknowledged that he had promoted creation science. The district's superintendent instructed him to stop teaching creation science because that would advocate religion in the classroom. Webster then sued the district, alleging it was inhibiting his freedom of speech, and demanded the right to teach "a nonevolutionary theory of creation."

The lower court in *Webster* declared that the school district held a "responsibility of ensuring that the Establishment Clause is not violated." On appeal, the Seventh Circuit affirmed that obligation. It was particularly concerned with the impressionable age of junior high students, which "imposes a heightened responsibility upon the school board to control the curriculum." The U.S. Supreme Court took a similar view in *Edwards,* observing that "[t]he State exerts great authority and coercive power through mandatory attendance requirements, and because of the students' emulation of teachers as role models and susceptibility to peer pressure." Following the Supreme Court's *Edwards* holding that creation science is religion, the Seventh Circuit required that "[g]iven the school board's important pedagogical interest in establishing the curriculum and legitimate concern with possible Establishment Clause violations, the school board's prohibition on the teaching of creation science to junior high students was appropriate."

The school district in *Webster* did not enact a policy prohibiting the teaching of creationism until after a student complained. Yet even in the absence of such a restriction, courts have agreed that teachers who advocate creation science are establishing religion and violating the Constitution. Under cases like *Webster,* school districts have not only the ability to prevent a teacher from teaching creation science, they have the obligation to ensure that religion is not established. *See also:* Evolution; Intelligent Design; Science and Religion.

Further Reading: *Edwards v. Aguillard,* 482 U.S. 578 (1987); Norman Geisler, *Creation and the Courts: Eighty Years of Conflict in the Classroom and the Courtroom* (Wheaton, IL: Crossway Books, 2007); *Hazelwood School District v. Kuhlmeier,* 484 U.S. 260 (1988); *Kirkland v. Northside Independent School District,* 890 F.2d 794 (5th Cir. 1989); Phillip Kitcher, *Abusing Science: The Case Against Creationism* (Cambridge, MA: MIT Press, 1983); Edward J. Larson, *Trial and Error: The American Controversy over Creation and Evolution* (New York: Oxford University Press, 2002); *McLean v. Board of Education,* 529 F. Supp. 1255, 1264 (E.D. Ark.1982); Henry Morris, *Scientific Creationism* (Green Forest, AR: Master Books, 1985); National Academy of Sciences, *Science and Creationism: A View from the National Academy of Sciences,* 2nd ed. (Washington, DC: National Academy Press, 1999); Ronald L. Numbers, *The Creationists: The Evolution of Scientific Creationism* (Berkeley and Los Angeles: University of California Press, 1992); *Palmer v. Board of Education,* 603 F.2d 1271 (7th Cir. 1979); Eugenie C. Scott, *Evolution vs. Creationism: An Introduction* (Berkeley and Los Angeles: University of California Press, 2004); *Webster v. New Lenox School District No. 122,* 917 F.2d 1004 (7th Cir. 1990); Kurt Wise, *Faith, Form and Time: What the Bible Teaches and Science Confirms About Creation and the Age of the Universe* (Nashville: B & H Publishing Group, 2002). Parts of this entry are adapted from Casey Luskin, "Alternative Viewpoints about Biological Origins as Taught in Public Schools," *Journal of Church and State* 47 (Summer 2005): 583–617, and used by permission.

Casey Luskin

D

Dabney, Robert L.

Robert Lewis Dabney (1820–1898) was born in Louisa County, Virginia. Young Dabney imbibed class and racial attitudes common in the Old South on his parents' modest plantation, and his formal education was typical of that afforded to children of the small planter class, including "old field schools" and tutors. After attending Hampden-Sidney College in 1836–1837, where a revival cemented his commitment to the Christian faith, Dabney taught school briefly before continuing his education at the University of Virginia, where he completed work for a master's degree. In 1844, he entered Union Theological Seminary, a staunchly Old School Presbyterian institution then located at Hampden-Sidney. While at Union, Dabney embraced the same tenets of Calvinism held by the well-known Charles Hodge and his Princeton colleagues, including the absolute authority of the Bible and God's sovereignty. Upon graduation in 1846, he accepted a call from Tinkling Spring Church located near Staunton, Virginia. During his pastorate, he established a reputation for sharp, conservative social and religious commentary that earned him an appointment to the Union faculty in 1853, where he taught church history and theology until 1883. He declined an appointment at Princeton Seminary in 1860, despite the fervent recruiting efforts of Hodge, preferring to stay in the South. In 1883, he left Union due to ill health and accepted an appointment at the University of Texas where he taught philosophy until 1894 and helped found Austin Theological Seminary.

Like Hodge, Dabney was a man of considerable intellectual depth and breadth who enjoyed the respect of friends and enemies alike and penned essays on a wide variety of topics, including race, capitalism, geology, unions, the southern cause, ethics, slavery, religion, and education. Indeed, most scholars recognize him as the preeminent Southern Presbyterian theologian after the War Between the States. While Hodge addressed education throughout his public life, most of Dabney's work on education appeared between 1875 and 1880.

Dabney's most trenchant commentary on religion and education appeared in two lengthy essays published in *The Princeton Review* in 1879 and 1880. The first of these, his complex, provocative, and often prescient educational credo entitled "Secularized Education," addresses questions regarding the nature of a proper education and the control of education. Like Hodge, Dabney argued that true education required moral culture and moral culture could not exist apart from Christianity. In his words, "Every line of true knowledge must find its completeness in its convergency to God." True education should be based on God's word, the Bible, and the doctrines derived from it, such as sin, redemption, and God's sovereignty. Mere reading from the Scriptures and instruction in "natural theology" would not suffice.

Though Dabney agreed with Hodge regarding the nature of a true education, he departed from his fellow Calvinist on the role of the state in education. Dabney disagreed with Hodge's proposal that the common school should teach the beliefs of the Protestant majority with appropriate safeguards for religious minorities. Maintaining that the state was a secular entity, Dabney claimed that it should not prefer any religious propositions over others. To do so would inevitably violate an individual's or a group's civil rights. He rejected as simply unjust the imposition of the beliefs of the majority on the minority via a state school system. He also criticized plans to distribute the school fund to various schools because some taxpayers would inevitably end up subsidizing beliefs with which they disagreed.

The Union seminary professor also dissented from Hodge's contention that the family, church, and state should share responsibility for the proper education of the young. Dabney posited that God had designated the family, which antedated both the church and the state, as the agency in charge of the education of children. Only parents could train the intellect and educate the conscience, which, he believed, were inextricably intertwined. He warned Christians that they should not depend on the state to accomplish this task by means of pan-Protestant common schooling. With remarkable prescience, he pointed out that they should prepare themselves for the eventual removal from the public schools all prayers, catechisms, and Bibles. The church, Dabney opined, could not counteract the influence of an increasingly powerful and expansive secular state school system. As far as he was concerned, the Sunday school was no match for Monday through Friday school. In sum, he urged that

> both State and Church recognize the parent as the educating power; that they assume towards him an ancillary instead of a dominating attitude; that the State shall encourage individual and voluntary efforts by holding a shield of legal protection over all property devoted to education; that it shall encourage all private efforts; and that it shall aid those whose poverty and misfortune disable them from properly rearing their own children.

Such an approach, he believed, would solve all the problems touching on religion in public schools because parents, not the state, would create schools.

A year later, in 1880, Dabney's "Popular Education as a Safeguard for Popular Suffrage" appeared in *The Princeton Review*. After revisiting several themes he discussed in "Secularized Education," he warned his readers about the potential tyranny of an increasingly centralized, government-controlled school system. He worried that those in control would be tempted to use the schools as "propaganda for the rulers' partisan opinions instead of useful knowledge and virtue." Like many current critics, Dabney thought a powerful state system was a threat to competition among parties and viewpoints, which he deemed a necessary condition for free government. Better to leave education in the hands of parents, he believed, than in the hands of either a parental and powerful state or a potentially dogmatic church.

Dabney's views regarding the nature and control of education placed him at odds with most public school patrons and advocates. Moreover, most of his fellow Presbyterians save for a few unreconstructed Southerners, paid scant attention to his criticism of the general direction of American education. In recent years, however, Dabney's work has gained an audience among Christian homeschool leaders and advocates of separating school and state. *See also:* Alliance for the Separation of School & State; Hodge, Charles; Homeschooling; Presbyterian Schools.

Further Reading: James C. Carper and Thomas C. Hunt, *The Dissenting Tradition in American Education* (New York: Peter Lang, 2007); Robert L. Dabney, "Popular Education as a Safeguard for Popular Suffrage," *The Princeton Review* 56 (September 1880): 186–206.Robert L. Dabney, "Secularized Education," *The Princeton Review* 55 (September 1879): 377–400; David Henry Overy, "Robert Lewis Dabney: Apostle of the Old South" (Ph.D. diss., University of Wisconsin, 1967); Jerry Robbins, "R.L. Dabney, Old Princeton, and Fundamentalism" (Ph.D. diss., Florida State University, 1991); Clark D. Stull, "Education at Home and School: The Views of Horace Bushnell, Charles Hodge, and Robert Dabney" (Ph.D. diss., Westminster Theological Seminary, 2005).

James C. Carper

Dewey, John

John Dewey (1859–1952) did not think of himself as an educator, and indeed confessed that his brief career as a schoolteacher was unsuccessful. His academic lecturing was, by all accounts, uninspiring. Indeed, Dewey's most influential disciple wrote in his diary as he began his graduate studies at Teachers College, "Hear Dewey, very good. I am wondering, however, whether I might not come to be an interpreter of Dewey," adding bluntly, "He needs one" (Beineke, 1998, p. 60).

It was as an academic psychologist and then philosopher that Dewey exercised a profound influence on how the purpose and the methods of education were and are understood, an influence extending to China, Turkey, and the Soviet Union as well as across the United States. It is safe to say that few young Americans complete a teacher education program without reading something by Dewey and hearing one or more lectures about him.

Like Horace Mann and like a number of leading European education reformers, Dewey grew up in a church in the Calvinist tradition and then rejected that for a form of Protestantism so liberal that it was no longer distinctively Christian. It is intriguing to wonder what it is about the "cultural mandate" as understood within Calvinism that translates into a project to use state authority to reshape a nation through its schools.

Like Mann, Dewey made adroit use of traditional religious language and imagery to promote an educational agenda which, while in some sense religious, had little in common with the religious views of most of their fellow citizens. Thus Dewey's most frequently anthologized essay, first published in 1897, was entitled "My Pedagogic Creed," and insisted that "the teacher always is the prophet of the true God and the usherer in of the true kingdom of God" (Dewey, 1974, p. 439).

A decade later, in "Religion and Our Schools" (1908), Dewey appears to suggest that religion could and should be taught in the schools, but only after it had been transformed so that "the non-supernatural view is more completely elaborated in all its implications." He is characteristically evasive about what precisely that nonsupernatural religion would be, but calls for educators to "labor persistently and patiently for the clarification and development of the positive creed of life implicit in democracy and in science, and to work for the transformation of all practical instrumentalities of education till they are in harmony with these ideas." Only when such views are "more completely in possession of the machinery of education" would it be safe to abandon the strict neutrality of schools toward all systems of belief. Meanwhile, the emphasis in schools should be upon "the state life, the vitality of the social whole, [which] is of more importance than the flourishing of any segment or class," and he called therefore for "the subordination of churches to the state" (Dewey, 1977, pp. 167–169). This emphasis on the state as the summary and instrument of social unity is not often mentioned by Dewey or by his admirers, but it is a continual theme, often counterposed to what he saw as the divisive and antiprogress influences of families and local communities.

In an anticipation of the *Humanist Manifesto* of 1933, of which he was a primary author, Dewey called upon educators to

> do what they can to prevent all public educational agencies from being employed in ways which inevitably impede the recognition of the spiritual import of science and of democracy, and hence of that [new] type of religion which will be the fine flower of the modern spirit's achievement. (Dewey, 1977, p. 177)

Dewey's experience in Soviet Russia in 1928, reported in a series of articles for *The New Republic,* gave him a heightened sense of how schools could possess a religious character that was not derived from traditional or theistic religion, but rather from commitment to a "progressive" and "scientific" determination to shape the future. He wrote enthusiastically that "the movement [that is, communism] in Russia is intrinsically religious," and that he had experienced for the first time "what may have been the moving spirit and force of primitive Christianity" (Dewey, 1988, p. 245–246). The following year he argued that "under certain conditions schools are more religious in substance and in promise without any of the conventional badges and machinery of religious instruction than they could be in cultivating these forms at the expense of a state-consciousness" (Dewey, 1929, p. 515).

The preamble to the *Humanist Manifesto* in 1933 was explicit about the religious character of Humanism, stating that "any religion that can hope to be a synthesizing and dynamic force for today must be shaped for the needs of this age. To establish such a religion is a major necessity of the present" (Kurtz, 1973, p. 8).

Dewey returned to this theme in a short book that he called *A Common Faith* (1934), making the case for a nontheistic, nonsupernatural "religion" that could serve as an uncontroversial basis for social unity around common goals. It should be noted that Dewey was writing this during the early years of the Depression and New Deal, when he and many other intellectuals firmly believed that only some form of socialism could reconcile America's social classes and diverse immigration-derived groups to address the urgent problems that the nation faced. That point had been made in the *Humanist Manifesto* the previous year:

> humanists are firmly convinced that existing acquisitive and profit-motivated society has shown itself to be inadequate and that a radical change in methods, contours, and motives must be instituted. A socialized and cooperative economic order must be established to the end that the equitable distribution of the means of life be possible. (Kurtz, 1973, p. 10)

The emphasis in *A Common Faith* was upon religious experience (experience was a favorite word with Dewey), which he defined not in terms of worship or traditional mysticism but as something that later Progressive educators would refer to as "life adjustment." "The actual religious quality in the experience," Dewey wrote, "is the effect produced, the better adjustment in life and its conditions, not the manner and cause of its production" (Dewey, 1986, p. 11).

This required abandonment of any idea of revealed religion, since "the religious function in experience can be emancipated only through surrender of the whole notion of special truths that are religious by their own nature, together with the idea of peculiar avenues of access to such truths." Dewey insisted that he was, in fact, only clearing away the effects of millennia of priestcraft and superstition to reveal what had, in fact, "always been implicitly the common faith of mankind. It remains to make it explicit and militant" (Dewey, 1986, pp. 23, 58).

Consistently, then, John Dewey understood the mission of public schools in religious terms, though applying his own understanding of the nature of religion. The progressive and scientific religion that schools should promote was by no means to be neutral toward traditional faiths. Early in his career as a philosopher and would-be reformer of education, in 1908, he argued that schools would have to be neutral until the time was right to place this emerging new religion at the center of the educational process. Twenty-five years later, in the wake of the rise of the Soviet Union and in the crisis situation created by the Depression, he was convinced that the time had come to make it "explicit and militant." *See also:* Humanism and the Humanist Manifestos; Secularism.

Further Reading: John A. Beineke, *And There Were Giants in the Land: The Life of William Heard Kilpatrick* (New York: Peter Lang Publishing, 1998); James Campbell, *Understanding John Dewey* (Chicago: Open Court, 1995); John Dewey, *Character and Events: Popular Essays in Social and Political Philosophy* (New York: Henry Holt, 1929); John Dewey, "My Pedagogic Creed" (1897), in *John Dewey on Education,* ed. Reginald D. Archambault (Chicago: University of Chicago Press, Phoenix Edition, 1974); John Dewey, "Religion and Our Schools" (1908), in *Essays on Pragmatism and Truth, 1907–1909* (Carbondale, IL: Southern Illinois University Press, 1977); John Dewey, "A Common Faith" (1934), in *John Dewey: The Later Works, 1925–1953,* ed. Jo Ann Boydston (Carbondale, IL: Southern Illinois University Press, 1986); John Dewey, "Impressions of Soviet Russia, VI: The Great Experiment and the Future" (1928), in *John Dewey: The Later Works, 1925–1953,* ed. Jo Ann Boydston (Carbondale, IL: Southern Illinois University Press, 1988); Paul Kurtz, *Humanist Manifestos One and Two* (Amherst, NY: Prometheus Books, 1973); Steven C. Rockefeller, *John Dewey: Religious Faith and Democratic Humanism* (New York: Columbia University Press, 1991); Alan Ryan, *John Dewey and the High Tide of American Liberalism* (New York: W. W. Norton & Company, 1995); Robert B. Westbrook, *John Dewey and American Democracy* (Ithaca, NY: Cornell University Press, 1991).

Charles L. Glenn, Jr.

Drexel, Katharine

The daughter of a wealthy Philadelphia investment banker, Katharine Drexel (1858–1955) was one of the most important women religious in the history of American Catholic parochial education. Indeed, it would not be too much to say that Drexel ranks with Elizabeth Ann Seton as one of the driving forces in the movement to establish

Catholic schools across the United States. Both women later would be canonized as saints for their work in this regard.

Katharine Drexel was born in Philadelphia on November 26, 1858, the third daughter of Francis A. Drexel and Hanna Jane Langstroth. Although the family was wealthy, tragedy was an early visitor; shortly after Katharine's birth, her mother died. Katharine's father quickly remarried and the three Drexel girls were raised and homeschooled by their stepmother and private tutors. The family traveled widely in Europe as well as in the United States.

Katharine and her sisters lost their stepmother in 1883 and two years later their father passed away. These two tragic losses caused Katharine to turn to her faith for solace and comfort. She was guided in her quest by a family friend, the Reverend James O'Connor, and by a visit from Bishop Martin Marty and Monsignor Joseph Stephan. Marty and Stephan encouraged Drexel to focus her energy and inheritance on the plight of American minorities, particularly Native Americans and African Americans.

Drexel and her sisters traveled to Europe in 1886 and 1887 and had a private audience with Pope Leo XIII. The pope listened to the three women discuss the plight of the American poor and challenged the sisters to become missionaries themselves. The Drexel sisters returned to the United States in the spring of 1887 and toured a number of Catholic missions in the Dakotas. The Drexels saw firsthand the immense poverty of the Plains Indians and were deeply moved.

With counsel from O'Connor, Katharine Drexel decided to establish a religious order to minister to minorities. Before taking such a bold step, she became a novice of the Sisters of Mercy in 1889. After completing her religious formation, she sought the approbation and sponsorship of Archbishop Patrick Ryan of Philadelphia in the establishment of the Sisters of the Blessed Sacrament for Indians and Colored People. By the end of 1891, Drexel had 28 novices in her congregation and in 1892 she opened a motherhouse in Cornwell, Pennsylvania.

By June 1894, Drexel was able to send forth her congregants to fulfill the mission of educating Native Americans. In that year, four Blessed Sacrament sisters opened St. Catherine's School in Santa Fe, New Mexico. This would be the first of dozens of such enterprises that Drexel built and sustained with her inheritance. Over the course of her career, Drexel directed the creation of convents, social service agencies, schools, and clinics on Native American reservations in Arizona, North Dakota, South Dakota, Washington State, and Wisconsin, among other states.

In addition to this work among Native Americans, Drexel and the members of her congregation built numerous schools for African Americans in New England, the Midwest, and the South. The first of these schools was the Institute of St. Francis de Sales in Rock Castle, Virginia, for African American girls. The capstone of her work on behalf of African Americans came in 1925 when Drexel contributed the critical funds needed to transform a New Orleans high school into Xavier College and thereby established the first historically black Catholic college for the education of African American parochial school teachers. Xavier became a university in 1931 and remains today the only historically black Catholic college in the United States.

In all of these efforts, Drexel was fortunate to have at her disposal the enormous assets of her family's fortune. Over the course of her lifetime it is estimated that she donated more than $12 million to the construction of Catholic institutions. She also contributed funds to the Bureau of Catholic Indian Missions, the Catholic Interracial Council, and the National Association for the Advancement of Colored People. Many of these financial contributions were made without fanfare as Drexel wanted no publicity for her generosity.

Drexel suffered a heart attack in 1935 and retired from active leadership of her order in 1937. She would live until 1955, devoting the balance of her life to contemplation and prayer. Her cause for sainthood was advanced shortly after her death, and she was canonized by Pope John Paul II on October 1, 2000. *See also:* Catholic Schools; Seton, Elizabeth.

Further Reading: Katherine Burton, *The Golden Door: The Life of Katharine Drexel* (New York: P.J. Kenedy, 1957); Consuela Marie Duffy, *Katharine Drexel* (Cornwall Heights, PA: Mother Katharine Drexel Guild, 1966); Ellen Terry, *Katharine Drexel: Friend of the Neglected* (New York: Farrar, Straus, Cudahy, 1958).

Timothy Walch

E

Eagle Forum

A woman's organization that claims to have approximately 80,000 members, Eagle Forum was founded in 1972 by conservative activist Phyllis Schlafly for the express purpose of opposing the Equal Rights Amendment, which Congress had passed and which seemed headed for sure ratification by at least the 38 states necessary for incorporation into the U.S. Constitution. Schlafly and her "Stop ERA" brigades contended that the amendment was unnecessary, since the Fourteenth Amendment already offers equal protection to "all persons." Moreover, they argued, enforcing such a provision would be prohibitively expensive and would lead inevitably to unisex toilets, legal homosexual marriages, women on the battlefield, and husbands freed of responsibility to support their families. Joined by other forces, many of them Protestant fundamentalists, the anti-ERA movement managed to stop the amendment in its tracks, three states short of ratification, even after Congress extended the deadline by two years.

Headquartered in Alton, Illinois, Schlafly's hometown, Eagle Forum also has offices in Washington, D.C. In 2007, its Web site listed at least 40 state organizations but fewer than 20 had Web sites, suggesting a low level of development. Schlafly's numerous books include *A Choice Not an Echo,* reported to be one of the ten best-selling conservative books of all time. Eagle Forum has published her monthly *Phyllis Schlafly Report* and *The Eagle's Voice*. She has also written a syndicated newspaper column and a steady stream of articles for the Eagle Forum Web site. An effective speaker, Schlafly has long been in high demand at conservative political gatherings, and her weekly radio commentaries have been carried by hundreds of stations.

Having gained legitimacy and stature from its successful opposition to the ERA, Eagle Forum expanded the scope of its interests and activities to include a number of the issues dear to both "movement conservatives," particularly those sometimes referred to as "paleoconservatives," and the Christian Right. It counts among its several missions the support of American sovereignty and is regularly critical of organizations such as the United Nations and the International Criminal Court, which it regards as threatening that sovereignty. It supports a strong defense system, but opposes sending U.S. troops to war unless national security is clearly at stake. It affirms a high regard for the Constitution and decries the "Imperial Judiciary" and "activist judges." It favors minimal regulation of commerce, reduction in taxes, secure borders, and tightened immigration laws and is highly critical of many trade agreements made between the United States and global competitors, charging that they regularly place American companies at a severe disadvantage. It regards global warming as a bogus issue supported by fake science.

As a key pioneer in the "pro-family" movement, Eagle Forum extols the role of "the fulltime homemaker" and opposes "radical feminists," abortion, and same-sex marriage. It also focuses heavily on issues related to education. Phyllis Schlafly played a major role in convincing conservative Christians that "Secular Humanism" was a rampant and corrosive ideology being forced on their children by godless educators, depicting it as a crucial weapon in a "Culture War" that threatened to undermine the nation and, indeed, western civilization. Eagle Forum's wide-ranging critique of American education, from pre-K through university graduate levels, is detailed in books, position papers, and the monthly publication, *The Education Reporter—The Newspaper of Education Rights*. It regards pre-K programs as largely ineffective for educational purposes and recommends that taxpayer funds go to more productive programs. It opposes mental-health screening of children in schools and widespread prescription of behavior-controlling drugs such as Ritalin. It champions homeschooling and vouchers that would enable low-income parents to send children to private schools, including faith-based schools. It opposes bilingual education and calls for a rigorous, traditional curriculum, beginning with an early emphasis on phonics-based reading. It regards Darwinian evolutionary theory as erroneous and criticizes textbooks that give more attention to America's faults than to its strengths. It decries the use of values clarification techniques, charging that they encourage a relativism that undercuts morality. Conversely, it supports an abstinence-only approach to education regarding sex and drugs. It regards the National Education Association as a key source of problems in the schools and is critical or highly skeptical of such approaches and initiatives as Outcome-Based Education, Goals 2000, and No Child Left Behind.

Attention to education at the college level focuses heavily on the liberal bias of professors, discrimination against students who espouse views other than those deemed politically correct, and neglect of courses on American history and government in favor of offerings considered insubstantial or corrosive, particularly those relating to feminism and sexuality. Eagle Forum Collegians offers conservative students an opportunity to network with each other, culminating in an annual Collegians Summit in Washington, D.C., where students hear and meet with a range of conservative activists, including members of Congress. *See also:* Humanism and the Humanist Manifestos; Secularism; Sex Education and Religion.

Further Reading: Eagle Forum, at www.eagleforum.org; William Martin, *With God on Our Side: The Rise of the Religious Right in America* (New York: Broadway Books, 1996; 2004); People for the American Way, at www.pfaw.org.

William Martin

Edgerton Bible Case

Devotional Bible reading in public schools was a mainstay of public education in the United States in the mid-nineteenth century. Strongly advocated by Protestant churches,

Baptist, Congregational, Methodist, and Presbyterian, the practice was seen as the bulwark of Christianity and of the nation.

Wisconsin joined the union in 1848. The framers of the state's constitution did not view the practice as sectarian instruction; rather, they viewed it as the fundamental book that undergirded the very basic beliefs of the citizens of the nation and the state. It made the schools' mission religious, but not sectarian. The Bible was every citizen's birthright and its reading was absolutely necessary for infusing the spirit of Christianity in the young and indispensable for the country's moral health.

The practice of Bible reading (King James Version) in the state's primary schools remained as the nineteenth century progressed, but it was challenged more frequently as reports from the state's school superintendents reflect. The influx of persons with diverse backgrounds, especially Catholic, into Wisconsin made the state's population become more religiously heterogeneous. Catholics believed that the Church was the guardian and interpreter of God's revelation; hence, the Bible (the Catholic or Douay Version) was under its guidance and protection.

In the 1880s a group of Catholics in the town of Edgerton brought suit against the practice in the public school of that town, charging that the practice constituted sectarian instruction, and thus was in violation of their children's rights of conscience. The Edgerton School Board denied the charge, pointing out that the children had the right to leave the room during the reading of the Bible, and that each person had the right to read and interpret the Bible for himself or herself. The Board also stated that it had the authority to choose textbooks for use in the schools, and that the Bible was on a list recommended for that purpose by the state superintendent for general, not sectarian, purposes. Lastly, the Board averred that the overwhelming majority of the people in Edgerton were Protestants, and they desired to have the King James Version read in the school.

Circuit Court Judge John R. Bennett ruled in favor of the defendant, adjudging that Bible reading did not constitute sectarian instruction, that its devotional reading did not make the school a place of worship, and that other citizens (the majority) besides the Catholics had rights of conscience. The Bible, Bennett maintained, held a unique place in the nation's history.

The plaintiffs, aided by funds that resulted from a campaign by the lay-run, English newspaper in Milwaukee, *The Catholic Citizen,* appealed the decision to the Wisconsin Supreme Court. Counsel for the plaintiffs claimed that the practice was sectarian instruction and both violated the Catholic students' rights of conscience and made the public schoolhouse a place of worship. Counsel for the defense denied these allegations, declaring that the students had the right to interpret the Bible for themselves, that the nation had been Christian since its beginning, and that the Bible was the foundation of Christianity, which in turn constituted the grounds for the public school system and American civil liberties. The school board had no right to keep such a book, upon which the teaching of morals and the fundamentals of the Christian religion were based, from the schools.

On March 17, 1890, the Supreme Court, in a unanimous decision, ruled that Bible reading constituted sectarian instruction and made the school a place of worship. Consequently, the practice was in violation of the Wisconsin constitution on both counts.

Catholics generally rejoiced at the decision, which made the public schools free from official Protestant domination. Unitarians joined Catholics, seeing the decision as a victory for the rights of conscience of a religious minority. *The Catholic Citizen,* in particular, was especially gleeful. The Catholic bishops of the state, however, paid little attention to the decision, being involved in the conflict over the Bennett Law, which in their eyes threatened the very existence of Catholic schools.

Protestant leaders and the Protestant press were highly critical of the decision. The decision was looked on as a renunciation of the nation's past, which would lead to the moral decay of Wisconsin society. The state's highest court had outlawed the use of the very book in its schools that next to the church itself, had laid the foundations of intelligence, virtue, and freedom in the nation. The Bible, in their eyes, was not a sectarian book. In fact, it was the book that created the public school institution itself. As a consequence, students were now deprived of its salutary influence.

Some Protestants decried the role of Catholicism in this legal battle. The state's Baptists, Congregationalists, Methodists, and Presbyterians denounced the decision at their official state meetings and at some regional gatherings. Several denominations called for an alliance of Protestant denominations to overturn the decision. Such an action was not forthcoming, however, and the decision stood. The Edgerton decision was the first of its kind by a state supreme court in the country. It presaged the *Abington Township v. Schempp* decision of the U.S. Supreme Court by 73 years. It not only ended symbolic Protestant domination of the public schools in Wisconsin, it attested to the fact that these schools were no longer "nonsectarian Christian" but would, in time, become secular. *See also: Abington School District v. Schempp* and *Murray v. Curlett*; The Bible in the Public Schools.

Further Reading: J.J. Blaisdell, *The Edgerton Bible Case: The Decision of the Wisconsin Supreme Court* (Madison: State Historical Society of Wisconsin, 1890); Harry H. Heming, *The Catholic Church in Wisconsin* (Milwaukee: T.J. Sullivan, 1896); Thomas C. Hunt, "The Edgerton Bible Case: The End of an Era," *The Catholic Historical Review* 67 (October 1981): 589–619; W.A. McAtee, "Must the Bible Go?" *Minutes of the Synod of Wisconsin of the Presbyterian Church 1891* (Madison: Tracy, Gibbs, and Co., 1891); *Wisconsin Reports,* 76 Wis., 177.

Thomas C. Hunt

Edwards v. Aguillard

In 1981 the Louisiana legislature passed legislation titled "Evolution-Science in Public School Instruction." The legislation required a balanced treatment of creation science and evolution science in public schools. The act did not require any instruction in the "subject of origins but simply permits instruction in both scientific models (evolution-science and creation-science) if public schools choose to teach either" and then both must be presented. In other words the "Creationism Act" forbids the teaching of evolution unless the theory of "creation science" is also taught. The legislature stated the act's purpose was "protecting academic freedom." The bill also stated:

"Balanced treatment" means providing whatever information and instruction in both creation and evolution models the classroom teacher determines is necessary and appropriate to provide insight into both theories in view of the textbooks and other instructional materials available for use in his classroom.

"Creation-science" means the scientific evidences for creation and inferences from those scientific evidences.

"Evolution-science" means the scientific evidences for evolution and inferences from those scientific evidences.
"Public schools" mean public secondary and elementary schools.

Parents, leaders, and religious leaders challenged the act's constitutionality. A federal district court ruled that the act violated the Establishment Clause of the First Amendment of the U.S. Constitution. The district court "held that the Creationism Act violates the Establishment Clause...because it prohibited the teaching of evolution [and also] because it requires the teaching of creation-science with the purpose of advancing a particular religious doctrine."

The court stated "that the statute's avowed purpose of protecting academic freedom was inconsistent with requiring, upon risk of sanction, the teaching of creation science whenever evolution is taught." The court found that the Louisiana legislature's actual intent was "to discredit evolution by counterbalancing its teaching at every turn with the teaching of creationism, a religious belief." The Fifth Circuit Court of Appeals also held that the law violated the Establishment Clause.

The U.S. Supreme Court in a 7-2 ruling written by Justice William Brennan affirmed the appellate court in holding the act unconstitutional, stating that it had no secular purpose and the primary purpose was to promote a specific religious belief. Justices Brennan, Thurgood Marshall, Harry Blackmun, Lewis Powell, John Paul Stevens, and Sandra Day O'Connor composed the majority, while Justice Antonin Scalia wrote a dissenting opinion in which Chief Justice William Rehnquist joined.

The Court used the three-pronged *Lemon* test in evaluating the Louisiana legislation. The Establishment Clause forbids a legislature from passing any law "respecting an establishment of religion." The *Lemon* test is used to determine whether legislation meets the Establishment Clause standard. The first prong is whether the law has a secular purpose, the second prong is whether the law's principal or primary effect neither advances nor inhibits religion, and the third prong is whether the result fosters excessive entanglement. If the legislation fails any of these three prongs, then the act violates the Establishment Clause.

The Court stated that the first prong of the *Lemon* test was violated because the act did not have a secular purpose. The Bill stated the purpose was to promote academic freedom. Requiring schools to teach creation science along with evolution did not advance academic freedom. Teachers already had the flexibility of teaching any scientific theory they chose and "any scientific theory...based on...facts [could] be included in [the] curriculum already, and no legislation...[was] necessary." Also evolution does not need to be taught but if taught then creation science must be taught. The Court then added, "[T]he Act does not serve to protect academic freedom, but has the distinctly different purpose of discrediting 'evolution by counterbalancing its teaching at every turn with teaching of creationism.'"

The Court then looked at the legislature to see if secular purpose for passing the law could be determined. The act's patron had explained during the legislative hearings "that his disdain for the theory of evolution resulted from his belief that evolution...views (were) contrary to his own religious beliefs." Therefore the historic record showed that the purpose of the act was not secular. The Supreme Court opined, "Because the primary purpose of the Creationism Act is to advance a particular religious belief, the Act endorses religion in violation of the First Amendment." *See also:* Creationism; Evolution; Science and Religion; Scopes Trial.

Further Reading: *Edwards v. Aguillard,* 482 U.S. 578 (1987); *Lemon v. Kurtzman,* 403 U.S. 602 (1971).

M. David Alexander

Elk Grove Unified School District v. Newdow

The Elk Grove (California) Unified School District required all elementary school classes to recite the Pledge of Allegiance daily. Michael Newdow, an atheist, filed suit on behalf of his daughter alleging that the words "under God" in the Pledge violated the Establishment and Free Exercises Clauses of the U.S. Constitution. Since he was divorced from his daughter's mother, he claimed standing to sue on his daughter's behalf as "next friend." The magistrate judge ruled the Pledge constitutional as did the U.S. Federal District Court. The Ninth Circuit Court of Appeals reversed. The Ninth Circuit ruled that Newdow had standing as a parent and the district's policy requiring the Pledge violated the Establishment Clause, specifically the phrase "under God," which was added to the Pledge in 1954.

The child's mother filed a motion to intervene and dismiss the suit, stating she had exclusive legal custody. The Ninth Circuit ruled that Newdow as a noncustodial parent under California law had a right to seek redress in court on behalf of his child.

The U.S. Supreme Court ruled that

> This case...concerns...[the mother's] right under the custody orders and, most important, their daughter's interests upon finding herself at the center of a highly public debate. Newdow's standing derives entirely from his relationship with his daughter, but he lacks the right to litigate as her next friend.

After the Supreme Court decision that Newdow did not have judicial standing to sue on his daughter's behalf, the case was remanded to the lower federal court. After the U.S. Supreme Court ruled Newdow did not have standing, upon rehearing, the U.S. Federal District Court ruled that the Ninth Circuit previous decision ruling the Pledge unconstitutional was binding in that jurisdiction. The court said that notwithstanding the fact the Supreme Court reversed the Ninth Circuit on lack of standing for the father, the ruling that the Pledge was unconstitutional was still binding. *See also:* The Pledge of Allegiance; *West Virginia State Board of Education v. Barnette.*

Further Reading: *Elk Grove Unified School District v. Newdow,* 542 U.S. 1 (2004); *Newdow v. The Congress of the United States of America,* 383 F. Supp. 2d 1229 (ED Calif. 2005).

M. David Alexander

Engel v. Vitale

The Board of Education of Union Free School District, No. 9, New Hyde Park, New York, acting in its role as authorized by state law, directed the district's principal to require that a particular prayer be said aloud by students in all classrooms before the school day began. The prayer, which was accepted on the recommendation of the State Board of Regents, an agency established by the state constitution and which had broad powers over the state's public schools, was a simple one: "Almighty God, we acknowledge our dependence upon Thee, and we beg Thy blessings upon us, our parents, our teachers and our Country." The Board of Regents had both composed and recommended the prayer, which was published as a part of the Regents' "Statement on Moral and Spiritual Training in the Schools." The Board of Regents stated a belief that everyone of good will would support the statement.

Soon after the reciting of the prayer was begun in the school district, the parents of ten students brought action in a New York state court alleging that the reciting of the official prayer was contrary to their and their children's beliefs and/or religious practices, and thus was a violation of the Establishment Clause of the First Amendment, which mandates "Congress shall make no law respecting an establishment of religion." The American Civil Liberties Union joined the group of parents in the suit. Plaintiffs argued that the prayer requirement favored the Christian religion over others and/or religious belief in general. The parents alleged that the state constitution could not support a law directing the use of prayer in public schools and that the school district's implementation of the law violated the Establishment Clause of the First Amendment of the U.S. Constitution, which was made applicable to the state of New York and all states by the Fourteenth Amendment to the Constitution. The American Ethical Union, the American Jewish Committee, and the Synagogue Council of America, all of which filed briefs of *amici curiae*, joined plaintiffs. The state court and the New York Court of Appeals found no violation of the Establishment Clause.

In *Engel v. Vitale* (1962), however, the U.S. Supreme Court by a 6-1 vote (Justices Felix Frankfurter and Byron White did not participate in the decision) declared that it was unconstitutional for any government agency such as a public school or government agents such as employees of a public school to require students to recite prayers. Writing for the majority, Justice Hugo Black quoted extensively from Thomas Jefferson's writings on the "wall of separation" protected by the First Amendment and from James Madison's "Memorial and Remonstrance against Religious Assessments." Black also compared the prayer recitation in public schools to the creation of the English *Book of Common Prayer* developed for the state religion of Anglicanism. State religion, Black observed, is exactly what the First Amendment was enacted to prevent.

In response to the Regents' argument that no student was forced to recite the prayer, Black held that neither the fact that the prayer may be denominationally neutral nor the fact that its observances on the part of students is voluntary can serve to free it from the limitations of the Establishment Clause. The fact that recitation of prayer is a religious activity cannot be denied and indeed, no party to the case attempted to argue otherwise. Black stated that the majority decision was intended to show respect, not hostility, for religion.

Justice Byron White offered a brief summary of the history surrounding government officials' practice of developing prayers for religious services. England had a state religion and required that the Book of Common Prayer, created under the direction of the government and ratified by Acts of Parliament, be used. Taxes supported the Church of England. Disagreements over prayer and religious ceremonies threatened the national peace. Religious practice could be altered by the whim of the presiding monarch. Changes to practice had to be presented as amendments to the Book of Common Prayer, and Parliament had to approve the amendments. Thus, church and state were almost completely entwined and entangled. Much of the legislative body's, as well as the monarch's, time was spent on religious matters, sometimes to the detriment of nonreligious issues.

England's insistence upon a state religion and a particular manner of practicing it, even down to seeming minutiae, led many colonists to seek religious freedom in the colonies. White stated, however, at least 8 of the 13 colonies enacted laws making the majority's religion the state religion; four of the remaining five established religions. The success of the colonies in the Revolutionary War encouraged those who were not members of the majority or "state" religion to vehemently protest any state religion. In Virginia, in which religions other than the Episcopal Church constituted a greater force than that constituted by the Episcopalians, a growing movement to give religious freedom the source of law for which many came to the colony took hold. James Madison and Thomas Jefferson opposed all religious institutions established by law on the basis of principle. Ultimately, they procured the passage of the "Virginia Bill for Religious Liberty" in which all religious groups were viewed as equal.

Thus, the history of the relationship of government and religion in the United States is a rich one. The First Amendment was enacted, not to harm religion, but to guarantee the rights of all people to worship or not worship as they chose. The majority opinion held that by the time the Constitution was adopted, many Americans realized the dangers of a union of church and state; indeed, many had personally experienced the results of such a union. The Founding Fathers ensured that government would be democratic, of the people and by the people, rather than one dominated by a monarch. To protect the people from a state religion, the First Amendment was added to guarantee that the national government could not "control, support or influence the kinds of prayer the American people can say."

The Court rejected the argument of the Board of Regents that maintained that the practice of the mandated daily prayer did not violate either the Establishment or the Free Exercise Clauses of the First Amendment, as the prayer was nondenominational and did not reflect any particular religion, and, since no student was compelled to participate in the recitation of the prayer, it could not be argued that any student's rights were violated by being forced to participate in a religious exercise. According to the Court: "Neither the fact that the prayer may be denominationally neutral nor the fact that its observance on the part of the students is voluntary can serve to free it from the limitations of the Establishment Clause," and if the Establishment Clause is violated, the practice cannot be permitted even if one were to accept the argument that the Free Exercise Clause is not violated because students are not required to participate.

The state legislature of New York allowed by law school districts to implement a policy requiring daily recitation of a prayer which, at the very least, acknowledges the existence of God and a person's dependence on that God. While it is true that no one particular religion is promoted by this prayer, the fact that it is recited daily in public schools demonstrates a preference for religion over no religion. The prayer does not take into account the fact that some persons practice religions that do not acknowledge one God and/or do not refer to a supreme being as "God."

Most of all, the Court continued, the state had enacted a policy that clearly indicates a preference for the practice of prayer over the absence of prayer in its public schools. This law violates the First Amendment rights of all public school students and must be struck down.

Acknowledging that some people would not view the prayer as any danger to religious freedom since it is "so brief and so general," Justice White concluded his opinion by quoting James Madison, who held that notice of any preference for religion must be taken at the first alarm; for he writes if a government can require a citizen to contribute three pence to the support of a religion, it can require so much more. So, no breach, no matter how small or seemingly insignificant, can ever be permitted. *See also:* Moments of Silence; Prayer in the Public Schools; *Wallace v. Jaffree.*

Further Reading: *Engel v. Vitale,* 370 U.S. 421 (1962); *School District of Abington Township School District v. Schempp* and *Murray v. Curlett,* 374 U.S. 203 (1963).

Mary Angela Shaughnessy

Episcopal Schools

The over 2-million-member Episcopal Church in America is part of the 80-million-member Worldwide Anglican Communion. The earliest known Episcopal school in the United States, Trinity, was founded in New York City in 1709. More schools were founded throughout the eighteenth century and early nineteenth century as parish-based charity schools in cities such as New York and Philadelphia. Independently governed schools with a variety of missions, often serving more affluent students, developed from the 1840s to the First World War, though some did not survive the financial constraints brought on by the Depression. After the Second World War, the Episcopal school movement, along with the Church, expanded westward, with parishes planting both a church and a school in a location. In the South, the Episcopal schools were among the first to provide racial integration to their communities.

Today Episcopal schools consist of a wide variety of institutions, including early childhood, Montessori, day schools, elementary schools, secondary, single-sex, boarding, military, religious order, and college preparatory. The schools range from small to large, tuition-based to well-endowed, classical to progressive, and they are found throughout the Episcopal Church in the United States, the Caribbean, Central and South America, and the Pacific Rim. Of the over 1,000 schools, over 900 are connected to parishes and cathedrals. Presently Episcopal school growth continues across all spectrums, with a budding interest in the *Nativity Miguel* Network of Schools model, which seeks to provide tuition-free education to underserved urban populations.

The National Association of Episcopal Schools (NAES) was created in 1965 as an independent, separately incorporated membership services organization when the Episcopal Church could no longer fund a staff member that had supported the schools since 1956. It is not an official department of the Episcopal Church in America, does not assume to speak for the church, and does not set or define policy or pedagogy. The NAES provides professional development and other resources for school leaders. Of the roughly 1,100 Episcopal education institutions, serving over 160,000 children and employing over 15,000 staff, about 500 schools belong to the NAES. The National Center for Education Statistics estimates that in 2005–2006, there were 334 Episcopal schools in the United States with an enrollment of 100,691 taught by 11,533 instructors.

The theological foundation of the schools is the Baptismal Covenant found in the Book of Common Prayer. The Covenant calls individuals and institutions to certain fundamental disciplines and dispositions in order to embody their identities as people of faith. Episcopal schools are created to be communities that honor, celebrate, and worship God, that model God's love and grace, and that serve God in all persons, regardless of origin, background, ability, or religion.

Oversight of the schools is multilayered. In parish day schools, the rectors, wardens, and vestry govern either directly or by delegation. Diocesan schools are governed by a more traditional Board of Trustees. Both groups follow the Constitution and Canons of the Diocese and the national Church. Most of the schools seek accreditation from independent secular agencies. Many schools in the Southwest, for example, choose accreditation by the Southwestern Association of Episcopal Schools, an independent regional association, separately incorporated from the NAES. Because, on average, no more than 25 percent of the student body is Episcopal, the schools are referred to as "parish day schools," meant to serve the entire reachable community, rather than "parochial schools," attended only by parishioners.

Most of the early childhood education programs and elementary schools have teachers certified by the state. Some teachers in some schools may not have teaching certificates, but they have terminal degrees in their academic specialty. High standards are maintained through annual reviews of teacher performance. Excellence is not just appreciated, but expected. There is generally no faith requirement for teachers, although some schools and dioceses require Episcopal Church membership for the head of school and/or board membership.

While the Episcopal schools vary greatly in emphasis and approach, certain themes are characteristic. They strive to combine spiritual formation with all aspects of the educational experience. They celebrate the life of the mind, rationality, and excellence. Because of their Baptismal Covenant understandings about God's love for all and the dignity of all human beings, they desire to be strongly inclusive, ecumenical, and open to a diversity of ethnic and socioeconomic and religious backgrounds. Nondiscrimination is mandatory in NAES member schools and the schools "seek justice and peace among all people." All faiths and backgrounds are welcomed into these ministries of education and human formation.

While welcoming to all and eschewing indoctrination, the Episcopal schools do seek to integrate Episcopal religious and spiritual formation into the curriculum and life of the school. They seek to be clear, yet "graceful," in their declarations of their ecclesiastical identity so that all—Episcopalians and non-Episcopalians, Christians and non-Christians, and people of no faith tradition—find a community in which to clarify their own beliefs while honoring those who think and believe differently. Based fully in Christian love and the belief that all human beings have unique worth and beauty, the schools challenge all who attend to discover a life of meaning, purpose, and service to the world.

While varying broadly, certain distinctives can be found in the institutional lives of Episcopal schools. There is a commitment to communal worship as set out by the Book of Common Prayer and other models and modes that are developed to engage the students in developmentally appropriate worship and prayer. Episcopalian or not, Christian or not, most students, staff, and faculty are expected to participate in the times of worship, which maintain an atmosphere of love and discipline in a graceful and inclusive way.

Episcopal schools also have a commitment to developmentally appropriate religious studies. The lower grades have chapels and times of character education. The upper grades may study religion in history, religion and culture, sacred texts, world religions, ethics, moral reasoning, or biblical studies. Whether the school offers preparation for baptism or confirmation usually depends on the type of school. Boarding schools often offer students preparation for these milestones of church membership. The parish day schools generally do not because they consider their mission to be the whole community and because students daily return to their homes and their own houses of worship.

Finally, Episcopal schools seek to exemplify and pursue social justice in their institutional lives and in their outreach to the community. Community projects and service learning are common features of Episcopal schools. Students are taught that the reason for helping others is not simply social responsibility or good citizenship; it is an expectation from God, a response to his love for humanity. *See also:* Council for American Private Education.

Further Reading: Jonathan T. Glass, *A Dual Accountability: The Experience of Episcopal Schools* (New York: National Association of Episcopal Schools, 2003 and 2007); Governing Board, NAES, *Principles of Good Practice for Furthering Episcopal Identity in Episcopal Schools* (New York: National Association of Episcopal Schools, 2005); National Association of Episcopal Schools, at episcopalschools.org; National Center for Education Statistics, at nces.ed.gov; Religious Life Committee, Board of Trustees, Oregon Episcopal School, *The Idea of an Episcopal School* (New York: National Association of Episcopal Schools, 2002).

Steven C. Vryhof

Epperson v. Arkansas

In 1928 the Arkansas legislature adopted a statute, which was the result of a popular initiative, prohibiting the teaching of evolution. This statute made it unlawful for a teacher in public education, whether it was at the elementary, secondary, or university level to teach that mankind ascended or descended from lower life-forms or to use textbooks that taught the theory of evolution. The law stated that

> It shall be unlawful for any teacher or other instructor in any University, College, Normal, Public School, or other institution of the State, which is supported in whole or in part from public funds derived by State and local taxation to teach the theory or doctrine that mankind ascended or descended from a lower order of animal and also it shall be unlawful for any teacher, textbook commission, or other authority exercising the power to select textbooks for above mentioned educational institutions to adopt or use in any such institution a textbook that teaches the doctrine or theory that mankind descended or ascended from a lower order of animals....Any teacher or other instructor or textbook commissioner who is found guilty of violation of this act by teaching the theory...or by using, or adopting any such textbooks in any such educational institution shall be guilty of a misdemeanor and upon conviction shall be fined not exceeding five hundred dollars; and upon conviction shall vacate the position thus held in any educational institutions of the character above mentioned or any commission of which he may be a member.

The Arkansas Legislation was modeled after the "Monkey Law" passed in 1925 by the Tennessee Legislature, which led to the famous 1927 Scopes trial (*Scopes v. Tennessee*).

Before 1965–1966 the biology textbook at the high school in Little Rock did not have a section on the Darwinian Theory of Evolution. Then for the academic year 1965–1966, on recommendation of the biology teachers, a textbook was selected that taught evolution.

Susan Epperson was employed to teach biology in the fall of 1964. Since the new textbook had a section on evolution and state statute made it a criminal offense to teach evolution, she found herself in a moral dilemma. She therefore filed suit, seeking to have the state statute declared void and enjoining local officials from dismissing her for teaching evolution, which was a violation of state law.

The Chancery Court found the statute to be unconstitutional. On appeal the Supreme Court of Arkansas reversed the Chancery Court. The entire Supreme Court of Arkansas's opinion was only two sentences. The state's high court stated:

> Upon the principal issue, that of constitutionality, the court holds that Initiated Measure No. 1 of 1928, Ark.Stat.Ann, s 80-1627 and s 80-1628 (Repl. 1960), is a valid exercise of the state's power to specify the curriculum in its public schools. The court expresses no opinion on the question whether the Act prohibits any explanation of the theory of evolution or merely prohibits teaching that the theory is true; the answer not being necessary to a decision in the case, and the issue not having been raised. The decree is reversed and the cause dismissed.

The U.S. Supreme Court ruled that the Arkansas statute violated the Establishment Clause of the First Amendment. The Court noted that the state had the right to control the curriculum and that the Bible may be studied from a literary and/or from a historic viewpoint, but the prohibition on violating the Constitution by fostering a religious viewpoint through the curriculum is prohibited and absolute. The Arkansas statute prevented teachers from teaching evolution because it was contrary to the Book of Genesis's presentation on the origin of man, therefore unconstitutional. *See also:* Creationism; *Edwards v. Aguillard;* Evolution; Science and Religion.

Further Reading: *Epperson v. Arkansas,* 393 U.S. 97 (1968); *Epperson v. Arkansas,* 416 S.W. 2d 322 (1967); *Kitzmiller v. Dover Area School District,* 400 F. Supp. 2d 707, 205 Ed. Law Rep. 250 (M.D. (PA) 2005) (Intelligent Design); *Scopes v. Tennessee,* 289 S.W. 2d 363 (1927); *Selman v. Cobb School District,* 449 F. 3d 1320 (Call (GA) 2006) (Evolution textbook stickers).

M. David Alexander

Equal Access Act

The Equal Access Act (EAA) was signed into law by President Ronald Reagan on August 11, 1984, after passing Congress by a vote of 88-11 in the Senate and 337-77 in the House. The act requires public secondary schools receiving federal funds to give equal access to students who wish to form religious groups if the school allows other student groups not related to the curriculum to meet on campus during noninstructional time. Under the provisions of the act, these groups or clubs must be entirely student-initiated and student-led. Outsiders may not direct or regularly attend student religious clubs, and school employees acting as monitors may be present at the meetings as nonparticipants only.

By enacting the EAA, Congress sought to end what many in the House and Senate perceived as discrimination against student religious speech in public schools. At the urging of many evangelical and mainline Christian organizations (with the Christian Legal Society playing a leading role), a bipartisan coalition in both houses drafted legislation in the early 1980s designed to ensure that students could meet together to express their faith while simultaneously prohibiting school sponsorship or promotion of student religious activities. Early opponents of the legislation included many educational associations and separationist groups such as the American Civil Liberties Union, the Anti-Defamation League, and Americans United for Separation of Church and State.

Although congressional supporters of the EAA were primarily concerned to give equal access to student religious expression, they expanded the act to include political, philosophical, and other forms of student speech in order to win support from members of Congress who opposed singling out religious speech for special treatment. They also agreed to limit the application of the act to secondary schools, as defined by state law, to address the concern that younger students could not form or run religious groups without help from school staff or outside adults.

When the EAA was first proposed, opponents in Congress supported by various civil liberties, religious, and educational groups were concerned that the law would open high schools to proselytizing by religious groups and create the appearance of school endorsement of religion. But in recent years, many of the law's harshest critics have acknowledged that the problems predicted during the congressional debate have not materialized. By 2007, students were forming religious clubs on thousands of high school campuses with little controversy or conflict.

In the early years after passage of the EAA, however, some school leaders resisted student religious clubs, often declaring a wide variety of student groups curriculum-related in order to avoid having to permit religious groups. After a number of conflicting lower-court rulings about what the act means by "noncurriculum-related" student groups and other issues surrounding the wording of the EAA, a lawsuit reached the U.S. Supreme Court in 1989.

The case, *Board of Education of the Westside Community Schools v. Mergens* (1990), involved a Nebraska high school that refused to recognize a Bible club even though the school had a chess club, a scuba diving club, and other student activities that the school claimed were related to the curriculum. By a vote of 8-1, the Court ruled against the school, interpreting "noncurriculum-related student club" to mean any student group that does not directly relate to the courses taught by the school. The Court upheld the constitutionality of the Equal Access Act and underlined the "crucial difference between government speech endorsing religion, which the Establishment clause forbids, and private speech endorsing religion, which the Free Speech and Free Exercise clauses protect."

The Court's decision in *Mergens* made it easier for students in most school districts to form religious clubs (mostly Christian). And in 1991, a coalition of some 20 religious and educational organizations issued "The Equal Access Act: Questions and Answers," consensus guidelines that helped local schools implement the act consistent with the Court's ruling.

These developments, however, did not end all disputes over the application of the EAA. In a series of lower court decisions in the 1990s, student religious groups won the right to be treated in the same way as secular student groups on such issues as meeting times and use of school media. And in one decision, *Hsu v. Roslyn,* a Christian group won the right to require that some of its officers be Christians. More recent conflicts have involved mostly unsuccessful attempts by some school districts to bar controversial secular student clubs, especially Gay/Straight Alliances. *See also: Board of Education of the Westside Community Schools v. Mergens; Lamb's Chapel v. Center Moriches Union Free School District.*

Further Reading: *Board of Education of the Westside Community Schools v. Mergens,* 496 U.S. 226 (1990).Joan DelFattore, *The Fourth R: Conflicts Over Religion in America's Public Schools* (New Haven, CT: Yale University Press, 2004); Charles C. Haynes and Oliver Thomas, *Finding Common Ground: A First Amendment Guide to Religion and Public Schools* (Nashville: First Amendment Center, 2007); Allen D. Hertzke, *Representing God in Washington: The Role of Religious Lobbies in the American Polity* (Knoxville: University of Tennessee Press, 1998);

Charles C. Haynes

Everson v. Board of Education of the Township of Ewing

Everson v. Board of Education (1947) echoed the earlier *Cochran* decision (1930) in which the U.S. Supreme Court applied what later came to be known as the "child benefit" theory; namely, if the intended beneficiary of state aid is the child and not a religion, the aid is permissible even if there is an ancillary benefit to religion in general or one religion in particular. New Jersey enacted a statute authorizing local school districts to enter into contracts to provide transportation for children to and from schools. The Ewing Township Board of Education, in accordance with the law, decided to give reimbursement of school busing costs to the parents of students utilizing the transportation. Some money was allocated for the payment of transportation costs of students to and from Catholic parochial schools, the curriculum of which included both secular instruction and regular instruction in the religious beliefs and types of worship of the Roman Catholic Church.

The appellant, Arch Everson, a taxpayer living in the district, challenged the board's reimbursement of transportation costs to parents whose children were being transported to Catholic schools. Arguing that the New Jersey statute and the resolution passed by the local board authorizing reimbursement to parents of parochial students violated both the New Jersey and U.S. Constitutions, the appellant maintained that the law was one "respecting an establishment of religion," which is prohibited by the First Amendment to the Constitution, "Congress shall make no law respecting an establishment of religion, or prohibiting the free exercise thereof. . . ."

Prior to the passage of the Fourteenth Amendment to the Constitution, which made the First Amendment applicable, albeit over time, to the states, some states adopted laws that guaranteed the First Amendment protections. Some states, however, continued to restrain the free exercise of religion and to discriminate against particular religious groups. The Fourteenth Amendment made the First Amendment applicable to the states; thus, argued appellant, if the reimbursement of transportation costs with tax dollars violates the First Amendment, New Jersey, bound by the strictures of the Fourteenth Amendment, had no authority to pass the state statute and local government had no authority to implement it.

Justice Hugo Black, writing for the 5-4 majority, observed that early Americans fought for the passage of the First Amendment because of the religious intolerance they encountered in their individual colonies. Even though colonists came to the New World in search of religious freedom, adherents of different religions struggled against each other. In most cases, Black wrote, these struggles were efforts by established religious groups to maintain absolute political and religious supremacy. He noted:

With the power of government supporting them, at various times and places, Catholics had persecuted Protestants, Protestants had persecuted Catholics, Protestant sects had persecuted other Protestant sects, Catholics of one shade of belief had persecuted Catholics of another shade of belief, and all of these had from time to time persecuted Jews.

Charters granted by the English Crown to individuals and companies authorized these same individuals and companies to build religious institutions and compel all believers and nonbelievers to attend the services and support the church, Justice Black continued, "and all of these dissenters were compelled to pay tithes and taxes to support government-sponsored churches whose ministers preached inflammatory sermons designed to strengthen and consolidate the established faith by generating a burning hatred against dissenters."

Eventually, colonists rose up in protest. They were vehemently opposed to paying taxes to fund ministers' salaries and to build and maintain churches. Although the movement to have a religiously neutral government grew in several colonies, Virginia took the lead in opposing an established church. Black discussed the development that reached a crisis point in 1785–1786 when the Virginia legislative body was ready to renew the tax levy for support of the established state church. Thomas Jefferson and James Madison were the leaders of the opposition to the tax. The proposal to renew the tax died in committee.

Justice Black recognized that modern day Americans had not experienced the persecution that those who lived in the colonies, before, during, and immediately after the Revolutionary War did. The cases alleging a violation of the Establishment Cause of the First Amendment reaching the Supreme Court in more recent times concerned proposed state aid to church schools and efforts to provide religious instruction in public schools according to the beliefs of one religion.

Additionally, some religious institutions had either tried to secure or have accepted state financial support for the operation of their schools. None of these cases alleged a preference for one particular faith over another, but rather the preference for religion over no religion. State court decisions evidence an effort to remain true to their state constitutional provisions protecting religious freedom and separating religions and government. These decisions, however, can be problematic when one is attempting to determine the line between taxes providing funds for the welfare of the public and those intended to support the teaching of religion in religious schools. Nonetheless, Black wrote, the Court was charged with determining whether the New Jersey law violated the Establishment Clause, particularly with regard to the imposition of taxes that would provide the monetary support for the actions authorized by statute.

Earlier cases dealing with the Free Exercise Clause of the First Amendment, even before the enactment of the Fourteenth Amendment, resulted in Supreme Court decisions supporting individuals' right to practice the religion of their choice or to practice no religion at all. Thus, Justice Black claimed, the same broad interpretation should be made when considering "establishment of religion" cases: "The structure of our government has, for the preservation of civil liberty, rescued the temporal institutions from religious interference. On the other hand, it has secured religious liberty from the invasion of the civil authority."

Ultimately, Black asserted, the establishment of religion clause means the following: (1) neither state nor federal governments can set up a church or make one religion a state religion; (2) no government can enact laws aiding all religions, a particular religion, or preferring one religion over another; (3) governments cannot force a person to attend or refrain from attending a church or to evidence belief in any religion, and no person can be punished for his religious beliefs or nonbeliefs; (4) no tax can be imposed to support religious activities or institutions; and (5) no government can participate in the governance or affairs of religious organizations. Quoting Jefferson, Black stated, the "wall of separation between church and State" must be observed. The smallest breach of the wall cannot be condoned.

The Court recognized that the reimbursement of transportation costs benefits the parents of students attending religious schools. It is possible that some children would not be able to attend religious schools if their parents did not receive transportation reimbursement, as the cost would be prohibitive. Nonetheless, the Court pointed out, the statute in question simply provides a program to help parents get their children to school, even religious schools, so long as the schools are accredited. Since there is no direct aid to religion or to religious institutions, there is no breach of the "wall" separating religion and government, and thus no violation of the Establishment Clause of the First Amendment.

Justice Robert Jackson's lengthy dissent argued that the New Jersey statute, which did have a public purpose, namely the protection of education and those being educated, exceeded the bounds of the Establishment Clause because it also, however indirectly, benefited religion. For example, parents might find it easier to afford parochial education because they did not have to pay the cost of transporting their children to the schools. Parochial schools might then experience increased enrollment and receive more tuition.

It should be noted, however, that just because a state *may* give aid, it does not *have* to give the aid. *See also: Cochran v. Louisiana State Board of Education;* First Amendment Religion Clauses and the Supreme Court; Separation of Church and State/Wall of Separation between Church and State.

Further Reading: *Cochran v. Louisiana State Board of Education,* 281 U.S. 370 (1930); *Everson v. Board of Education,* 330 U.S. 1 (1947).

Mary Angela Shaughnessy

Evolution

Evolution as a scientific theory is a central organizing principle of biology and predictive theory for the diversity of life on Earth. In biology, evolution specifically refers to a change in the features of a specific population (a group of a species living together in one place) over time. Introduced to the public by naturalist Charles Darwin's *On the Origin of Species,* published in 1859, evolution presupposes that all life on Earth came from a common ancestor, with mutations giving certain organisms characteristics that allowed them to better survive (and have more chance to reproduce), thus leading to changes in a group of that species. All cells can mutate—some mutations are lethal and lead to death (of the cell or organism), while others may confer advantages to an organism—advantages such as better chances of reproduction (higher, richer sperm count or more attractive features to potential mates). Some mutations may affect only a single or small group of cells, while others affect the entire organism. Evolution does not happen within a single individual—it is a phenomenon that is seen in populations over time.

Charles Darwin (who had originally intended to become a clergyman but changed his mind after a two-year trip to South America and the Galapagos Islands off the western coast of Ecuador, where he encountered animals that pushed him on his path to discover the laws governing nature) was neither the first nor the only scientist to conceive of evolution in the mid-1800s, but his book did put the theory on the map. Further evidence elevated evolution to the status of a well-established scientific principle. While further research may lead to the development of a new, more complex scientific theory to explain the diversity of life, and scientists have certainly disagreed among themselves about some of the details of evolutionary theory, any new theory of evolution would need to be able to explain how evolution passed previous tests to its veracity (in other words, any such theory would include most of the elements—if not all—of the theory).

In the first decades after Darwin published his book, many people played down any conflict between the book's conclusions and the beliefs of Christianity. In fact, some proponents of the theory even emphasized God's role in evolution. While in England, Darwinian advocate and biologist T.H. Huxley immediately began to draw a line between Darwin's theory and Christianity (becoming known as "Darwin's Bulldog" for his defense of evolution in a debate with Archbishop Samuel Wilberforce); in the United States, Harvard botanist Asa Gray, who arranged for the American publication of *On the Origin of Species,* saw no conflict between evolution and his own Protestant faith. University of California geologist Joseph LeConte, who published one of the earliest high school science textbooks, also saw no conflict. LeConte was the leading proponent of evolution in the United States in the late 1800s, having reconciled for himself that the evidence for evolution showed its accuracy and, therefore, that the religion in which he believed deeply needed to accommodate this concept. Given the lack of widespread religious resistance to evolution in the nineteenth century, evolution became a more prominent concept in the emerging public school science curriculum, as education became more formalized and larger numbers of school (and schools in more rural areas) began to use textbooks that included information about evolution.

As evangelical Christianity developed in the United States in the late nineteenth century, there was a shift from efforts at accommodation to deeper hostility to evolution in many quarters of the religious community, especially among those known as fundamentalists. Whereas early leaders in the evangelical movement, such as Dwight L. Moody and James Orr, either declined to admit a rift between science and religion or even left open the possibility of evolution (by, for example, taking each of the days in Genesis not as a literal 24-hour day but rather as an epoch), some religious leaders now began hardening their attitudes towards evolution and even attacked Darwinian evolutionary theory as a direct opposition to Christianity.

Hostility toward evolutionary theory led to the infamous Scopes "monkey" trial, in which a high school teacher was prosecuted for teaching evolution in violation of Tennessee law. Tennessee was one of only three states that had existing measures to prevent the teaching of evolution. After the Scopes trial, 20 states considered antievolution bills, with three states passing laws forbidding the teaching of evolution. Antievolution resolutions were also introduced to—and were passed by—many local school boards and district administrations. The teaching of evolution dramatically declined in most parts of the United States until the 1960s, as textbooks removed references to evolution in order to not lose markets due to the controversy.

In the 1960s, however, the national mood toward evolution shifted again for a variety of reasons. Most important was the launching of the Soviet satellite *Sputnik* in 1957. The result of the Soviets' feat in the United States was a strong interest in developing Americans' scientific abilities in order to best the Russians. The National Defense Education Act of 1958 aimed to revitalize science education in the United States by providing funding to update science education and to develop rigorous curriculum in all of the sciences. To meet this new demand, textbooks began to include ample information on evolution and a stress on the primacy of evolution in biology. The newly created National Science Foundation funded the development of the Biological Sciences Curriculum Study, which emphasized the centrality of evolution to biology.

Challenges to the teaching of evolution changed over the course of the last century. While in the 1920s, the challenge focused primarily on opposing the teaching of human evolution, challenges in the 1970s focused on a loophole seemingly created by the ruling of the Supreme Court in the landmark *Epperson v. Arkansas* (1968) case that declared laws banning the teaching of evolution to be unconstitutional. Antievolutionists argued that the Supreme Court's majority opinion in that case allowed the teaching of creationism along with evolution in science classrooms. This argument was based on the claim that creationism represented an alternative scientific explanation and was therefore due its own fair share of classroom time. The early 1980s saw bills passed in Arkansas and Louisiana that gave creationism equal time in science classrooms. These laws were struck down, as judges asserted that creationism did not meet scientific standards. The Supreme Court ruled in *Edwards v. Aguillard* (1987) that Louisiana's law, which carefully avoided religious references, nevertheless had quite clearly been designed to promote one religious point of view and therefore violated the U.S. Constitution.

The list of arguments against evolution that has been put forth by critics of Darwinism, including a few scientists, legal theorists, and philosophers, since the 1970s is long, ranging from claims that evolution is not testable to attacks on some hypotheses of the evidence of evolution to moral and religious attacks on scientists and the scientific community. The current challenge to the teaching of evolution in U.S. schools, however, is different from that of the Scopes trial era or even the creationist challenge of the 1970s. Proponents of Intelligent Design (ID) argue that their plea for fundamental change in the way biology is taught, especially in high school, is not being made on a religious basis but rather from a scientific one. Proponents of ID contend that some intelligent agent designed life on Earth. Further, they assert that American school children should learn about the idea that they promote as an alternative scientific theory. Evolution, ID proponents contend, is a controversial topic and should be taught as such. Because of the stance that ID proponents are taking, they are also promoting the idea that teaching evolutionary biology alone, without reference to ID, is bad science because it does not include the skepticism that is essential to all scientific research.

Thus, the current educational debate over the teaching of evolution pits those who support ID against most of the scientific community. Some might see this debate as one between religious ID proponents and secular evolutionists. In fact, many scientists hold deep religious convictions, but recognize that science does not seek to address the same questions as religion. Religion goes beyond naturalistic explanations of the world and offers answers to questions about the meaning of life—but critics of ID assert that such explanations do not qualify as science and so should not be taught in science classrooms.

It is also important to understand that many in both the scientific and religious communities today believe that there is no inherent conflict between religion and science including the scientific understanding of evolution. Paleontologist and noted author Stephen J. Gould argued in his book *Rock of Ages: Science and Religion in the Fullness of Life* that science and religion look at two different aspects of the same things and that they need not conflict—each answers its own questions and does not and need not tread on the other. Indeed, scientific theories such as evolution need not diminish religious beliefs or interfere with what children are taught in their homes or religious communities. In the United States, public schools must focus on the knowledge used by participants in a large and diverse society; and changing science education for religious purposes fails the larger goals of a democratic society in which religion has thrived, to a unique degree in the Western world, because of the separation of church and state. *See also:* Creationism; *Edwards v. Aguillard; Epperson v. Arkansas;* Intelligent Design; *Kitzmiller v. Dover Area School District;* Science and Religion.

Further Reading: Charles Darwin, *On the Origin of Species* (London: Murray, 1859); Committee on Revising Science and Creationism: A View from the National Academy of Sciences, National Academy of Sciences and Institute of Medicine of the National Academies, *Science, Evolution, and Creationism* (Washington, DC: National Academies Press, 2008); *Edwards v. Aguillard,* 482 U.S. 578 (1987); *Epperson v. Arkansas,* 393 U.S. 97 (1968); Stephen J. Gould, *Rock of Ages: Science and Religion in the Fullness of Life* (New York: Ballantine Books, 1999).

Rebecca P. Lewis and James W. Fraser

Exodus Mandate Project

Founded in 1997 by E. Ray Moore, Jr., a retired Army Lt. Colonel and Chaplain, and headquartered in Columbia, South Carolina, the Exodus Mandate Project is part of Frontline Ministries, a nonprofit ministry that endeavors to influence American culture with the Christian faith. The stated vision of the Project is to

> encourage and assist Christian families to leave Pharaoh's school system (i.e. government schools) for the Promised Land of Christian schools or home schooling. It is our prayer and hope that with this fresh obedience by Christian families in educating their children according to Biblical mandates will prove to be a key for revival in our families, our churches and our nation. (Exodus Mandate Project, at www.exodusmandate.org)

Pursuant to this goal, Moore, the current director of the Exodus Mandate Project, urges Christian parents to remove their children from the public schools rather than to try to reform them or "take them over."

Like some other conservative Christian groups and leaders, e.g., the late D. James Kennedy and James Dobson, on occasion, Moore's organization views public school education as academically deficient, saturated with secular humanism, and incapable of providing a biblically based education with moral absolutes for Christian children. As Moore put it in his book, *Let My Children Go* (2002), "With God almost nowhere to be found in public schools, morality was left with the false foundations of secular humanism which offers only various forms of relativism" (p. 45). In addition to its concern about secularism, the Project often warns Christian parents about the promotion of homosexuality and "dogmatic Darwinism" in the public schools. Indeed, concern about recent legislation touching on "gender" issues in the Golden Bear State's public schools (no doubt exacerbated by the controversial 2008 California Supreme Court decision legitimizing same-sex relationships, which was nullified by a state constitutional amendment adopted by popular vote in November 2008) prompted the Project to launch "California Exodus 2008," a campaign to energize conservative Christians and like-minded organizations in the state and cause as many as 10 percent of Christians in California to remove their children from the state school system.

Given its commitment to the belief that parents, not the state, are responsible for the education of their children, the Project eschews vouchers and tuition tax credits as means for promoting educational choice. Such mechanisms, Moore believes, will lead to government interference with the educational prerogatives of parents and subvert the independence of Christian schools. On this and related educational choice issues, the Project is closely aligned with the position of the Alliance for the Separation of School & State and several activists within the Southern Baptist Convention (SBC), who have attempted since 2004 to get the SBC to pass a resolution at its annual meeting urging parents to remove their children from the public schools. One of the major figures in this effort, Bruce N. Shortt, serves as a member of the Board of Directors of the Exodus Mandate Project.

The Exodus Mandate communicates its message through its Web site, e-mail, mass mailings, articles, interviews, and conferences. It has volunteer coordinators in ten states, including California, Texas, West Virginia, and Michigan. *See also:* Alliance for the Separation of School & State; Focus on the Family; Sex Education and Religion; Southern Baptists and Education.

Further Reading: Exodus Mandate Project, at www.exodusmandate.org; E. Ray Moore, Jr., *Let My Children Go* (Columbia, SC: Gilead Media, 2002); Bruce N. Shortt, *The Harsh Truth about Public Schools* (Vallecito, CA: Chalcedon Foundation, 2004).

James C. Carper

F

Faribault–Stillwater Plan

The Faribault–Stillwater Plan was an educational experiment to resolve the conflict between the Catholic Church and the American public school system. Sponsored by John Ireland, the controversial Archbishop of St. Paul, the plan called for the cities of Faribault and Stillwater, Minnesota, to provide publicly funded education for Catholic children in parish school buildings. No religious symbols or instructional materials would be present in the buildings until the school day ended. In form and content, the Faribault–Stillwater Plan closely mirrored a similar plan that had been in use in Lowell, Massachusetts, Pough-keepsie, New York, and other American communities in the middle of the nineteenth century.

The Faribault–Stillwater Plan came to national attention when Archbishop Ireland trumpeted the experiment at the 1890 meeting of the National Education Association. By shining a spotlight on the plan, Ireland also precipitated a controversy among Catholic educational leaders about the future of parochial education.

Conservative Catholics were particularly suspicious of Ireland and his friendship with Cardinal James Gibbons of Baltimore, the foremost American Catholic leader of the last quarter of the nineteenth century. Conservatives wanted a clear statement of support for Catholic education without compromise and, to that end, the American archbishops discussed the merits of the Faribault Plan at their annual conference in November 1891. Unfortunately, they did not resolve the conflict. The issues raised by the Faribault Plan were front page news in the Catholic press in 1892 and received extensive coverage in the secular press as well.

In response to the simmering conflict over the Faribault Plan, Ireland and Gibbons appealed directly to Pope Leo XIII. Gibbons sent the pope a lengthy summary of the proceedings of the conference of archbishops held in 1891 and indicated that there had been no criticism of Ireland or his Faribault Plan. The letter bolstered Ireland's case and the early word from members of the Curia was that Ireland would be completely vindi-cated. After months of consideration, the pope issued a statement acknowledging the fundamental righteousness of the school legislation of the Third Plenary Council of Baltimore, but noted that, after considering all of the facts and circumstances, the Faribault Plan could be "tolerated."

Perhaps it was inevitable that such a subtle message would be open to misinterpretation. The liberals interpreted the message as a vindication of Ireland and the concept of cooperative education. The conservatives countered by arguing that the pope had upheld the Third Plenary Council mandate that every parish should have a school. The Faribault Plan, argued the conservatives, was to be *tolerated* only as a *special* case.

Rather than calming the waters, the pope's message stirred up the acrimony between the two sides. But the matter became moot when tension in Faribault and Stillwater over the use of nuns as teachers led to a termination of the cooperative agreements between the public and parochial schools in those two communities. Ireland's well-publicized plan, therefore, was no longer a "threat" to parish school development. The Faribault Plan, as it was known, was at an end in 1892.

But the initial controversy did not die and exposed a larger controversy within American Catholicism between liberal and conservative perspectives on the future of Catholic education. Efforts by the Vatican to end the matter only created more tension that came to a head at the 1892 meeting of the American archbishops.

The revised Vatican decision still permitted Catholic children to attend public schools and forbade clergy from withholding the sacraments from parents who sent their children to public schools. Another point in the decision noted the Church's general support for public education, but also noted the Church's objection to the lack of Christian denominational instruction in public schools. The Vatican plan also proposed that the bishops make special provision for the religious education of Catholic children enrolled in public schools. Finally, the document maintained the earlier acceptance of the compromise plan implemented in Faribault and Stillwater, Minnesota.

The conservatives protested to the pope but it was all for naught. In May 1893, the pope wrote to Gibbons to tell him and the other American archbishops that the Vatican saw no conflict between the Vatican propositions and the mandates of the Third Plenary Council of Baltimore. Rome had spoken and the great Catholic school controversy was at an end.

The pope's decision was more than a vindication of the Faribault Plan. The Vatican had outlined and emphasized the harmony that existed between the Catholic Church and the American ideals of public education. The pope himself had confirmed that the Church had no fundamental disagreements with the principles of public education. *See also:* Catholic Schools; Gibbons, James Cardinal; Ireland, John; Lowell Plan; Poughkeepsie Plan.

Further Reading: Harold A. Buetow, *Of Singular Benefit: The Story of U.S. Catholic Education* (New York: Macmillan, 1970); Mary A. Grant and Thomas C. Hunt, *Catholic School Education in the United States* (New York: Garland Publishing, 1992); Marvin R. O'Connell, *John Ireland and the American Catholic Church* (St. Paul, MN: Minnesota Historical Society Press, 1988); Daniel Reilly, *The School Controversy, 1891–1893* (New York: Arno Press, 1969); Timothy Walch, *Parish School: American Catholic Parochial Education from Colonial Times to the Present* (Washington, DC: National Catholic Educational Association, 2003).

Timothy Walch

Farrington v. Tokushige

This case involved a challenge to a statute enacted by the legislature of the Territory of Hawaii imposing requirements on foreign language schools operating in Hawaii, a foreign language school defined as one taught in any language other than English or Hawaiian. At the time of this litigation, 163 foreign language schools were operated in the territory, nine being conducted in the Korean language, seven in Chinese, and the remainder in Japanese. These schools that received no public funds enrolled 20,000 students and employed 300 teachers. Although the statute was directed broadly at all foreign language schools, the greatest impact was on Japanese schools where enrollment had increased from 1,320 in 1900 to 19,354 in 1920.

The statute required that all foreign language schools secure annually an operating permit from the department of public instruction; that the schools furnish the department with a list of the name, sex, parents or guardians, place of birth, and residence of each child; and that all persons teaching in the schools obtain an annual permit. No school would be issued a permit unless the department was satisfied that it could direct the minds and studies of pupils in such a way as to make them good and loyal American citizens, and no teacher would be issued a permit unless the department was satisfied that the applicant was possessed of the ideals of democracy, had knowledge of American history and institutions, and knew how to read, write, and speak the English language. The statute further authorized the department to determine the courses to be taught and the textbooks to be used. While the statute permitted foreign language instruction in first through third grades, instruction in fourth grade and above was to be in English. The most onerous of the statutory requirements were that no foreign language school could operate at the same time as a public school and no student could attend a foreign language school for more than one hour per day. Failure of the school to follow the statutory requirements would result in the department revoking immediately its permit, and a teacher's instructing in any language other than English could result in his or her conviction for a misdemeanor.

In 1925, an owner of one of the Japanese schools filed a lawsuit alleging that the statute violated the rights of parents to direct the education of their children, observing that parents were afraid to pay tuition fees to the foreign language school because of the statute's provisions and, as a result, the schools were unable to pay teacher salaries and other expenses. A federal district court in Hawaii granted a temporary injunction, prohibiting the governor, attorney general, and superintendent of public instruction from enforcing the statute. On appeal, the Ninth Circuit Court of Appeals affirmed, finding that the statute violated the Fourteenth Amendment liberty right of parents to direct the education of their children, a right recently asserted by the Supreme Court in *Meyer v. Nebraska* (1923) and *Pierce v. Society of Sisters* (1925). The Ninth Circuit further assailed the defendants' ungrounded fears underlying enactment of the statute, that "within the next fifteen years a majority of the electorate [would] be American citizens of Japanese extraction" and that "the Japanese do not readily assimilate with other races and especially with the white race," with a response eloquent in its directness and simplicity: "You cannot make good citizens by oppression, or by a denial of constitutional rights, and we find no such conditions there as will justify a departure from the fundamental principles of constitutional law."

The Supreme Court granted certiorari but failed to reach the merits of the case. While the Court agreed that the plaintiff's affidavit supporting his complaint stated a claim under the Fourteenth Amendment, the case had been appealed from an interlocutory order and, thus, defendant public officials had not had an adequate opportunity to present facts justifying their position. Thus, the case was remanded back to the federal district court so that the territory could present their reasons why their deliberate plan to bring foreign language schools under a strict governmental control did not violate the plaintiff's constitutional rights.

No recorded case exists as to the eventual outcome of this litigation. Because the Supreme Court decision never addressed the merits of the case, it has no precedent value as to constitutional rights, but does have historical interest when considered in light of the Supreme Court's later decision upholding the internment of Japanese Americans during World War II (*Korematsu v. United States*, 1944). *See also: Meyer v. Nebraska; Pierce v. Society of Sisters;* State Regulation of Religious Schools.

Further Reading: *Farrington v. Tokushige*, 273 U.S. 284 (1927); *Farrington v. Tokushige*, 11 F.2d 710 (9th Cir. 1926); *Korematsu v. United States*, 323 U.S. 214 (1944); *Meyer v. Nebraska*, 262 U.S. 390 (1923); *Pierce v. Society of Sisters*, 268 U.S. 510 (1925).

Ralph D. Mawdsley

First Amendment Center

The First Amendment Center, with offices at Vanderbilt University in Nashville, Tennessee, and Washington, D.C., is an independent affiliate of the Freedom Forum, a nonpartisan foundation, and the Newseum, the interactive museum of news. The center was founded December 15, 1991, by John Seigenthaler on the 200th anniversary of the ratification of the first ten amendments to the U.S. Constitution.

The First Amendment Center's mission is to preserve and protect First Amendment freedoms through information and education. The center provides a forum for the exploration of issues concerning freedom of speech, of the press, and of religion, and the right to assemble and to petition the government.

The center's work in K–12 education began in the mid-1990s when the center hired a director for religious freedom and First Amendment education initiatives. The center helps local schools and communities address issues regarding religious liberty in public schools through conflict resolution, dissemination of consensus guidelines, and First Amendment training workshops.

At the national level, the First Amendment Center convenes coalitions of religious, civil liberties, and education organizations to seek agreements on how public schools can address religious liberty issues without fights and lawsuits. Three of these agreements, "A Teacher's Guide to Religion in the Public Schools," "A Parent's Guide to Religion in the Public Schools," and "Public Schools and Religious Communities: A First Amendment Guide" were distributed to every public school principal in the United States by the U.S. Department of Education in 2000. Two additional guides, "The Bible and Public Schools: A First Amendment Guide" (1999) and "Public Schools and Sexual Orientation: A First Amendment Framework for Finding Common Ground" (2006), are widely used by local school districts.

Initiatives regarding religious liberty in public schools supported by the center on the state and local levels are inspired by the vision of the Williamsburg Charter, a restatement of First

Amendment religious liberty principles signed by nearly 200 leaders from every sector of American life in 1988. Drawing on the charter's definition of the principles of rights, responsibilities, and respect that flow from the First Amendment, the center founded statewide "Three Rs" projects in Utah and California as well as local projects in other states. In California, the program is cosponsored by the California County Superintendents Educational Services Association. The Utah project is cosponsored by the Utah Office of Education. In 2007, the California Three Rs was underway in all 11 educational regions of the state and the Utah 3Rs project had reached most of the state's school districts.

Endorsed by education, civil liberties, and religious groups from across the religious and ideological spectrum, Three Rs projects prepare teams of parents, community leaders, school board members, teachers, and administrators from local districts to understand and apply religious liberty principles in schools. The programs also help teachers to teach about religions in ways that are constitutionally permissible and educationally sound. Three Rs training has enabled school districts to develop policies and practices that have broad support in the community and protect the religious liberty of all parents and students.

On March 16, 2001, the 250th anniversary of James Madison's birth, the First Amendment Center joined with the Association for Supervision and Curriculum Development (ASCD) to launch a nationwide program, "First Amendment Schools: Educating for Freedom and Responsibility." The goal of this initiative is to transform how schools model and teach the rights and responsibilities of the First Amendment. Schools in the program commit to provide all members of the school community with daily opportunities to exercise their First Amendment freedoms with responsibility. From 11 project schools in 2001, the ASCD-led network of First Amendment Schools grew to over 100 public and private schools by 2007.

The First Amendment Center is known for helping local school districts resolve conflicts concerning religion in schools without litigation. Since the early 1990s, the center has been asked to mediate a wide range of disputes from fights over how to deal with religion in the curriculum to controversies over school policies regarding sexual orientation.

A typical example of the center's mediation work took place in Mustang, Oklahoma, after a debate erupted in 2004 over school holiday programs in December. When the fight broke out, the district had no policies addressing religion in December or at any other time of the year. With advice from the center, the superintendent and school board formed a community task force of religious leaders, parents, and educators to develop a comprehensive religious liberty policy. After months of deliberation, the school board accepted the recommendations of the task force and adopted guidelines that focus on how to teach about religion throughout the year and outline in detail the religious liberty rights of students and parents. The district followed up with in-service training for administrators and teachers. A year after the initial conflict, the Mustang schools had moved from battleground to common ground.

Some of the conflicts addressed by the center involve social issues that often divide school districts along religious and ideological lines. For example, the center helped mediate a conflict that broke out in Modesto, California, in the mid-1990s over homosexuality and public schools. The fight erupted when the school board added "sexual orientation" to a policy on safe schools. Many religious conservatives in the community were concerned that language in the policy about "tolerance" meant that the district was endorsing homosexuality. After months of argument, the district asked for assistance from the First Amendment Center. Working with the 115-member committee of educators, students, parents, and religious leaders, the center helped the community reach agreement on a First Amendment framework of shared rights and responsibilities. As a result, the district was able to adopt a safe schools policy that included all students without undermining the religious convictions of any parent or student.

Christian pastors on the committee discovered that school officials were not advocating acceptance of homosexuality by including sexual orientation in the statement on safe schools. And gay students and parents of gay students discovered that conservative Christians on the committee favored taking measures to ensure an end to bullying and harassment of gay students. Once agreement was reached on how to make the schools safer without taking sides in the culture-war debate over homosexuality, school officials followed up with in-service training for administrators and teachers on the new policy as well as on religious liberty issues long neglected by the district.

The agreement in Modesto led the First Amendment Center to develop consensus guidelines for dialogue that could be used in other districts. In collaboration with the Christian Educators Association International (CEAI) and the Gay, Lesbian and Straight Education Network (GLSEN), the center drafted "Public Schools and Sexual Orientation: A First Amendment Framework for Finding Common Ground." The statement was co-drafted by BridgeBuilders, an organization that mediates disputes in local school districts, and endorsed by CEAI, GLSEN, the American Association of School Administrators, and the Association for Supervision and Curriculum Development. Since its release in 2005, the statement has been disseminated throughout the nation.

The First Amendment Center sponsors conferences on religious liberty in K–12 education and publishes books and monographs on religious liberty in public schools. It also disseminates *Inside the First Amendment,* a newspaper column that frequently addresses religion and schools issues. *See also:* California 3 Rs Project: Rights, Responsibilities, Respect; Common Ground Documents; Haynes, Charles C.; Utah 3 Rs Project: Rights, Responsibilities, Respect.

Further Reading: BridgeBuilders, at www.Bridge Builders.org; David S. Doty, "Maelstrom in Modesto: Developing a Common Ground Policy for the Protection of Gay and Lesbian Students in Public Schools," *California Social Studies Review* 40 (Spring 2001): 32–36; First Amendment Center, at www.firstamendmentcenter.org; Charles C. Haynes and Oliver Thomas, *Finding Common Ground: A First Amendment Guide to Religion and Public Schools* (Nashville: First Amendment Center, 2007); Charles C. Haynes, Sam Chaltain, John E. Ferguson, Jr., David L. Hudson, Jr., and Oliver Thomas, *The First Amendment in Schools* (Alexandria, VA: ASCD, 2003); James Davison Hunter and Os Guinness, eds., *Articles of Faith, Articles of Peace: The Religious Liberty Clauses and the American Public Philosophy* (Washington, DC: The Brookings Institution, 1990); Emile Lester and Patrick S. Roberts, *Learning about World Religions in Public Schools: The Impact on Student Attitudes and Community Acceptance in Modesto, California* (Nashville, TN: First Amendment Center, 2006); Warren A. Nord and Charles C. Haynes, *Taking Religion Seriously Across the Curriculum* (Alexandria, VA: ASCD, 1998).

Charles C. Haynes

First Amendment Religion Clauses and the Supreme Court

"Congress shall make no law respecting an establishment of religion, or prohibiting the free exercise thereof." These 16 words comprise the First Amendment religion clauses.

They have been the federal law of the land since 1791 and the subject of nearly 200 religious liberty cases issued by the Supreme Court since 1817. Many of the more recent religious liberty cases have also drawn in the First Amendment Free Speech Clause and the Fourteenth Amendment Due Process and Equal Protection Clauses.

Nearly a third of the Supreme Court's 200 odd cases on religious liberty have been on issues of religion and education. Nearly all of them have raised one of three questions: What role may religion play in public education? What role may government play in religious education? And what constitutional rights do private citizens—parents and students especially—have in public and private schools. The Supreme Court has worked out a set of rough logics to address these questions, which lower federal courts have refined and extended a bit. While government has the power to mandate education for children, the Supreme Court has held repeatedly, parents have the right to choose between public and private school education for their children, and government may now facilitate that choice. While the First Amendment forbids most forms of religion in public schools, it protects most forms of religion in private schools. While the First Amendment forbids government from funding the core religious activities of private schools, it permits delivery of general governmental services and subsidies to public and private schools and students alike. While the First Amendment forbids public school teachers from religious expression in their classes and school functions, it permits public school students to engage in private religious expression. It now further requires that religious students and other private parties get equal access to public school facilities, forums, and even funds that are open to their nonreligious peers for nonschool functions.

The Court has worked out much of this logic only since 1940. From 1776 to 1940, most constitutional issues involving religion and education were governed by state and local governments. The First Amendment applied by its terms only to the federal government, and neither Congress nor the federal courts were particularly active on these issues until the twentieth century. Most issues of religious liberty, including those dealing with religion and education, were left to the states to resolve, each in accordance with its own state constitution. In the 1940s, however, as part of a broader national response to the Depression, World War II, and budding Cold War, the federal courts assumed principal control of religious liberty questions. In *Cantwell v. Connecticut* (1940) and *Everson v. Board of Education* (1947), the U.S. Supreme Court for the first time applied the First Amendment Free Exercise and Establishment Clauses to state and local governments. It did so by "incorporating" these First Amendment guarantees into the general liberty guarantee of the Fourteenth Amendment: "No state shall deprive any person of…liberty …without due process of law." Since 1940, the Court has sought to create a national law on religious liberty binding on all federal, state, and local officials. Religion and education questions have been a prominent part of this new legal exercise.

These First Amendment cases have not always followed clean logical lines. The Supreme Court has sometimes digressed and occasionally reversed itself. Several of its religion and education cases have featured brilliant rhetorical and judicial fireworks in majority and dissenting opinions. Part of this back-and-forth is typical of any constitutional law in action. "Constitutions work like clocks," American founder John Adams once put it. To function properly, their pendulums must swing back and forth, and their mechanisms and operators get wound up from time to time.

But part of this back-and-forth is peculiar to the First Amendment religion clauses. The religion clauses were among the most contested provisions of the new Bill of Rights, pitting many strong theological and political voices of the 1780s against each other. Two theological views on religious liberty were critical to the formation of the First Amendment: those of New England Congregational Puritans (like Fisher Ames and Charles Livermore) and those of Free Church Evangelicals (like Isaac Backus and John Leland). Two political views were equally influential: those of Enlightenment Libertarian thinkers (like Thomas Jefferson and James Madison) and those of Civic Republicans (like John Adams and George Washington). Exponents of these four views often found common cause and used common language, particularly during the constitutional convention and ratification debates over religious liberty. Yet each group offered its own distinct teachings on religious liberty and had its own preferences for their implementation at law. Together, these groups held up the four corners of a wide canopy of opinion about religious liberty in the eighteenth century.

Beneath this canopy of opinions, these diverse founding groups ultimately came to embrace six main principles of religious liberty that they incorporated into the First Amendment: (1) liberty of conscience; (2) freedom of religious exercise; (3) religious pluralism; (4) religious equality; (5) separation of church and state; and (6) no federal establishment of religion. The First Amendment religious liberty guarantees were designed to balance these principles. The First Amendment Free Exercise Clause outlaws government *proscriptions* of religion—actions that unduly burden the conscience, restrict forms of religious exercise and expression, discriminate against religion, or invade the autonomy of churches and other religious bodies. The First Amendment Establishment Clause, in turn, outlaws government *prescriptions* of religion—actions that unduly coerce the conscience, mandate forms of religious exercise and expression, discriminate in favor of or against religion, or improperly ally the government with churches or other religious bodies. Both clauses thereby provide complementary protections to the first principles of religious liberty that the eighteenth-century American founders championed.

In the twin cases of *Cantwell v. Connecticut* (1940) and *Everson v. Board of Education* (1947) that opened the modern era of the religious liberty, the Supreme Court worked hard to balance these basic principles of religious liberty, and thereby to render the free exercise and no establishment clauses complementary guarantees of religious liberty. In *Cantwell,* the Court effectively read each of these principles into the Free Exercise Clause, as well as the Free Speech Clause as applied to religion. This First Amendment, Justice Owen Roberts wrote for the *Cantwell* Court, protects "[f]reedom of conscience and freedom to adhere to such religious organization or form of worship as the individual may choose."

It "safeguards the free exercise of the chosen form of religion," the "freedom to act" on one's beliefs. It protects a "plurality of forms and expressions" of faith, each of which deserves equal protection under the law. It ensures the "basic separation" of religious and political authorities and entities. For in "the realm of religious faith, and in that of political belief," the Court wrote, "sharp differences arise." Furthermore,

> But the people of this nation have ordained in light of history, that, in spite of the probability of the excesses and abuses, these liberties are, in the long view, essential to enlightened opinion and right conduct on the part of the citizens of the democracy. The essential characteristic of these liberties is, that under their shield many types of life, character, opinion and belief can develop unmolested and unobstructed. Nowhere is this shield more necessary than in our own country for a people composed of many races and of many creeds.

Similarly, in *Everson v. Board of Education* (1947), despite its famously strong language on strict separation of church and state, the Court struck a judicious balance among these founding principles of religious liberty. "The 'establishment of religion' clause of the First Amendment means at least this," Justice Hugo Black wrote for the *Everson* court. No federal or state government (1) "can set up a church"—a violation of the core disestablishment principle; (2) "can force or influence a person to go or to remain away from church against his will or force him to profess a belief or disbelief in any religion"—a violation of liberty of conscience; (3) can "punish [a person] for entertaining or professing religious beliefs or disbeliefs, for church attendance or non-attendance"—a violation of both liberty of conscience and religious equality; or (4) "can, openly or secretly, participate in the affairs of any religious organizations or groups, or *vice versa*"—a violation of the principle of separation of church and state. Justice Black also underscored the founders' principle of religious pluralism and equality, declaring that government may not exclude "individual Catholics, Lutherans, Mohammedans, Baptists, Jews, Methodists, Nonbelievers, Presbyterians, or the members of any faith, *because of their faith, or lack of it,* from receiving the benefits of public welfare legislation." Liberty of conscience, freedom of exercise, religious equality, religious pluralism, separation of church and state, and no establishment of religion were all considered part of First Amendment religious liberty in the Court's initial formulation.

In recent years, however, the Supreme Court has narrowed its focus to principles of neutrality and equality, and has weakened the Free Exercise and Establishment Clause guarantees respectively. In *Employment Division v. Smith* (1990), the Court held that neutral, generally applicable laws will pass free exercise scrutiny, even if they happen to impose substantial burdens on a party's free exercise rights. Similarly, in *Zelman v. Simmons-Harris* (2002), the Court held that government programs that are neutral on their face and neutral in application will pass no establishment inquiry, even if they happen to impart substantial benefits to religion. This recent "neutralization" of the First Amendment religion clauses has pressed religious liberty advocates to seek freedom for and from religion under other federal constitutional guarantees of free speech, equal protection, and due process, under various state constitutional guarantees of religious liberty, and under a growing number of federal and state statutes on discrete aspects of religion—all of which have emphasized the need for equal treatment and protection of religious and nonreligious parties.

The constitutional law on religion and education are part and product of these general patterns of religious liberty protection in this country. On each of the three main questions—the place of religion in public education, of government in religious education, and of private constitutional rights within schools—the Court has moved among several of the main principles of religious liberty, and in recent years has been increasingly deferential to the states and to the legislatures.

Religion and Public Education

In its first generation of modern cases on religion and public education, the Supreme Court emphasized the principle of separation of church and state. This was a natural forum for the firm application of separationist logic, for most states had already accepted this logic in dealing with local issues of religion and education. Between 1848 and 1921, 33 state constitutions explicitly prohibited state and local governments from granting funds and other aid to religious schools. Fifteen state constitutions insisted further that state schools remain free from "sectarian influence" or from the control of religious officials and institutions. At the turn of the twentieth century and thereafter, various Christian groups had led campaigns to reinvigorate traditional forms of religion in the public schools—calling for the enhancement of biblical teaching, the appointment of Christian teachers, the establishment of religious ceremonies and symbols, and much else. By 1947, these issues had occupied state courts and constitutional conventions for more than a half century—with widely varying results. With the 1947 Everson case, the Supreme Court took firm control of these controversies and systematically outlawed the use of religious teachers, texts, ceremonies, and symbols in the public schools.

Separation of Church and State

In its early cases on religion and public schools, the Court developed a general argument that dominated its reasoning for the next four decades. The public school is a government entity, the Court argued, one of the most visible and well-known arms of the government in any community. One primary purpose of the public school is to stand as a model of constitutional democracy and to provide a vehicle for the communication of democratic norms and practices to its students. The state mandates that all able students attend schools, at least until the age of 16. These students are perforce young and impressionable. Under such circumstances, the public schools must cling closely to core constitutional and democratic values. One such core value is the separation of church and state taught by the First Amendment. Some relaxation of constitutional values, even those of the First Amendment, might be possible in other public contexts—where mature adults can make informed assessments of the values being transmitted. But no such relaxation can occur in public schools with their impressionable youths who are compelled to be there. In public schools, if nowhere else in public life, strict separation of church and state must be the norm.

The case that opened this series was *McCollum v. Board of Education* (1948). The state action at issue was a "release time" program, adopted by a local public school board for fourth through ninth grade students. For 30 to 45 minutes once a week, students were released from their regular classes to be able to participate in religious classes if their parents consented to their participation. Students could choose among three such religious classes, taught, respectively, by qualified Protestant, Catholic, or Jewish teachers. These religious teachers were not employed by the school but were approved by its superintendent. Students whose parents did not consent to their participation continued their "secular studies" during this release time period.

A parent of one student challenged the release time program as a violation of the First Amendment Establishment Clause. The *McCollum* Court agreed. Writing for the majority, Justice Black declared that this was precisely the kind of conflation of church and state that *Everson* sought to outlaw—using "tax-supported property for religious instruction and the close cooperation between school authorities and the religious council in promoting religious education." Black continued:

> The operation of the State's compulsory education system thus assists and is integrated with the program of religious instruction carried on by separate religious sects. Pupils compelled by law to go to school for secular education are released in part from their legal duty upon the condition that they attend the religious classes. This is beyond all question a utilization

of the tax-established and tax-supported public school to aid religious groups to spread their faith. And it falls squarely under the ban of the First Amendment [that]...had erected a wall of separation between Church and State.

In *Engel v. Vitale* (1962), the Court extended this separationist reasoning to outlaw government-sponsored prayer in state schools. The State Board of Regents of New York had adopted a nondenominational prayer to be recited by public school teachers and their students at the commencement of each day: "Almighty God, we acknowledge our dependence upon Thee, and we beg Thy blessings upon us, our parents, our teachers, and our Country." Students who did not wish to participate in the prayer could remain silent or be excused from the room during its recitation. Parents challenged both the state's creation of the prayer and its use in the public school classroom, as violations of the Establishment Clause. The *Engel* Court agreed. Again Justice Black wrote for the majority:

> It is no part of the business of government to compose official prayers for any group of the American people to recite as part of a religious program carried on by government...There can be no doubt that New York's state prayer program officially establishes the religious beliefs embodied in the Regents prayer...Neither the fact that the prayer may be denominationally neutral nor the fact that its observance on the part of the students is voluntary can serve to free it from the Establishment Clause...When the power, prestige, and financial support of government is placed behind a particular religious belief, the indirect coercive pressure upon religious minorities to conform to the prevailing officially approved religion is plain.

This prohibition on prayer in public schools remains the law of the land, as the Court underscored more recently, albeit in part with different logics, in *Lee v. Weisman* (1992) and again in *Santa Fe Independent School District v. Doe* (2000).

In *Abington Township School District v. Schempp* (1963), the Court extended this reasoning to outlaw Bible reading in the public schools. Following general state law, a public school district mandated that each school open its day with the reading of ten Bible verses. Either a teacher or a volunteer student would read the text. Each reader was permitted to choose the text of the day. No commentary or discussion of the Bible reading was allowed. In some schools, a common reading was broadcast throughout the school; in other schools, the reading was done in individual classrooms. In some schools, this reading was followed by public recitation of the Lord's Prayer and of the Pledge of Allegiance. Students whose parents did not consent could again refuse to participate or leave the room during these religious exercises.

After *Engel v. Vitale,* the *Schempp* Court found this case an easy violation of the First Amendment Establishment Clause. The policy in question was an overtly religious exercise, mandated by the state, for impressionable youths required to be in school, with no realistic opportunity for the average student to forgo participation. "[I]t is no defense that the religious practices here may be relatively minor encroachments on the First Amendment," Justice Tom Clark wrote for the Court. "The breach of neutrality that is today a trickling stream may all too soon become a raging torrent."

In an important aside, however, Justice Clark emphasized that to ban confessional religion from the public school was not to ban religion from the curriculum altogether. Responding to Justice Potter Stewart's sharply worded dissent that the Court had effectively established "secularism" as the religion of the public school, Justice Clark offered a conciliatory word about the objective value of religion in public education:

We agree of course that the State may not establish a "religion of secularism" in the sense of affirmatively opposing or showing hostility to religion...We do not agree, however, that this decision in any sense has that effect. In addition, it might well be said that one's education is not complete without a study of comparative religion or the history of religion and its relationship to the advancement of civilization. It certainly may be said that the Bible is worthy of study for its literary and historic qualities. Nothing we have said here indicates that such study of the Bible or of religion, when presented objectively as part of a secular program of education, may not be affected consistently with the First Amendment.

In two subsequent cases, however, the Court closed the door quite firmly against even symbolic and objective forms of religion in the public school during instructional time. In *Stone v. Graham* (1980), the Court struck down a state statute that required the posting of a plaque bearing the Ten Commandments on the wall of each public school classroom. The plaques were donated and hung by private groups in the community. There was no public reading of the commandments nor any evident mention or endorsement of them by teachers or school officials. Each plaque bore a small inscription that sought to immunize it from charges of religious establishment: "The secular application of the Ten Commandments is clearly seen in its adoption as the fundamental legal code of Western Civilization and the Common Law of the United States." The *Stone* Court struck down the displays as a form of religious establishment. It found the statute mandating the Decalogue display had no "secular legislative purpose" but was "clearly religious." The Ten Commandments are sacred in Jewish and Christian circles, and they command "the religious duties of believers." It made no constitutional difference, said the Court, that the Ten Commandments were passively displayed rather than formally read or that they were privately donated rather than purchased with state money. The very display of the Decalogue served only a religious purpose and was thus per se unconstitutional.

In *Edwards v. Aguillard* (1987), the Court pressed this logic further to strike down a Louisiana act requiring a "Balanced Treatment for Creation-Science and Evolution-Science in Public School Instruction." The statute mandated that a public school teacher could not teach "evolution-science" without teaching "creation-science" and vice versa. Teachers were not required to teach a theory of origins, but if they did, they had to give equal time to "the scientific evidences" for both evolutionary and creationist accounts of origins. The stated legislative purpose of the act was "to promote academic freedom" in allowing teachers to explore various theories of origins, including religious theories.

The *Edwards* Court declared the act unconstitutional. After rehearsing the legislative history at length, the Court concluded that the act had no real secular purpose but was a thinly veiled attempt to import religious teachings into the curriculum. The act evinced a "discriminatory preference for the teaching of creation and against the teaching of evolution," Justice Brennan wrote for the Court. Its "preeminent purpose" was "clearly to advance the religious viewpoint that a supernatural being created humankind. The term 'creation science' was defined as embracing this particular religious doctrine... In this case, the purpose of the Creationism Act was to restructure the science curriculum to conform with a particular religious viewpoint." This was not a proper objective teaching of religion but an unconstitutional establishment of religion. Lower federal courts have recently used this precedent to strike down the teaching of scientific theories of "intelligent design" alongside the teaching of evolution in public schools.

In *Wallace v. Jaffree* (1985), the Court stretched its separationist logic to its furthest point. At issue in the case was a state statute that authorized a moment of silence at the beginning of each school day for "meditation or voluntary prayer." On rehearsing the legislative history, the Court found that the statute revealed no secular purpose but a "legislative intent to return prayer to the public schools." "The addition of 'or voluntary prayer'" to the statute, Justice Stevens wrote for the Court, "indicates that the State intended to characterize prayer as a favored practice."

Liberty of Conscience

While separation of church and state was the major key in which the Supreme Court played in its early orchestrations on religion and public schools, liberty of conscience and freedom of exercise was a minor key that periodically sounded as well. *West Virginia State Board of Education v. Barnette* (1943) was a case in point. The children of Jehovah's Witnesses were expelled from a public school, and their parents threatened with fines, because the children refused to salute the American flag or recite the Pledge of Allegiance—important acts in the middle of World War II. The Bible, as the Witnesses understood it, prohibited such acts as forms of false worship of idols. To compel the students to perform such acts, their parents argued, was a violation of their liberty of conscience rights. The *Barnette* Court agreed, overruling the 1940 case of *Minersville School Board v. Gobitis* that held against the Witnesses on similar facts. While acknowledging the importance of teaching national loyalty and unity in public schools, the *Barnette* Court held that the compulsory participation in such civic ceremonies violated the liberty of conscience. As Justice Robert Jackson wrote for the Court:

> If there is any fixed star in our constitutional constellation, it is that no official, high or petty, can prescribe what shall be orthodox in politics, nationalism, religion, or other matters of opinion or force citizens to confess by word or act their faith therein. If there are any circumstances which permit an exception, they do not now occur to us.

In *Zorach v. Clauson* (1952), the Supreme Court again accommodated the religious needs of public school students and their parents. New York City allowed students to be released from public school, at their parents' request, to attend important religious functions. These functions were off school grounds and involved no school officials or expenses. Taxpayers objected that this program violated the First Amendment Establishment Clause and its mandate of strict separation of church and state. The *Zorach* Court disagreed. "We would have to press the concept of separation of Church and State to... extremes to condemn the present law on constitutional grounds," Justice William O. Douglas wrote. "When the state encourages religious instruction or cooperates with religious authorities by adjusting the schedule of public events to sectarian needs, it follows the best of our traditions."

The concern to accommodate religious scruples of conscience also informed the Court's reasoning in the more recent school prayer case in *Lee v. Weisman* (1992). A public school principal engaged a local rabbi to offer prayers at a middle school graduation ceremony. He instructed the rabbi to be "nonsectarian" and furnished him with published guidelines to illustrate an appropriate prayer. The graduation ceremony took place on public school grounds. The prayer followed the public recitation of the Pledge of Allegiance, with participants standing. Although students were not required to participate in the graduation ceremony, or in the prayer, most did. The *Weisman* Court found the state action doubly coercive and intrusive upon religious conscience. The state was dictating to the rabbi the content of his prayer. It was also effectively coercing all students to participate in its recitation. Although it adduced earlier cases that outlawed prayer in schools, the Court did not repeat their separationist reasoning, but focused instead on the coercive aspects of the prayer. A similar concern informed the Court's majority opinion in *Santa Fe Independent School District v. Doe* (2000), which outlawed student prayer at public high school football games.

Equal Access

While official prayers and overt forms of religious expression remain prohibited in public schools, private religious expression by public school students and others, outside of formal school hours, has come to be protected. The Supreme Court has reached this conclusion in a series of cases that have often pitted the principle of equality against that of separation of church and state.

The opening case in this series was *Widmar v. Vincent* (1981). The state University of Missouri had a policy of opening its facilities to voluntary student groups to use outside of formal instructional time. More than 100 student groups organized themselves in the year at issue. A voluntary student group, organized for private religious devotion and charity, sought access to the university facilities. The group was denied access, in application of the university's written policy that its buildings and grounds were not to be used "for purposes of religious worship or religious teaching." The student group appealed, arguing that this policy violated their First Amendment free exercise and free speech rights as well as their Fourteenth Amendment equal protection rights. The university countered that it had a compelling state interest to maintain a "strict separation of church and state."

The *Widmar* Court found for the religious student group. The Court held that where a state university creates a limited public forum open to voluntary student groups, religious groups must be given "equal access" to that forum. Justice Lewis Powell wrote for the Court that the university "has discriminated against student groups and speakers based on their desire to use a generally open forum to engage in religious worship and discussion. These are forms of speech and association protected by the First Amendment. In order to justify discriminatory exclusions from a public forum based on the religious content of the group's intended speech" the university must show that "its regulation is necessary to serve a compelling state interest and that it is narrowly drawn to achieve that end." In the Court's view, a general desire to keep a strict separation of church and state was not a sufficiently compelling state interest. The religious groups would enjoy only "incidental benefits" from this ruling. The values of "equal treatment and access" outweighed the hypothetical dangers of a religious establishment.

The *Widmar* Court bracketed the question whether this equal access principle could be extended from the state university to the public school. Lower courts refused this extension, arguing that state universities, with more mature students who were not compelled to be there, were fundamentally different from lower public schools, with their young and impressionable students under compulsory school attendance laws. Congress responded with the Equal Access Act of 1984 that required that in public high schools voluntary religious student groups be given equal access to classrooms available to nonreligious student groups after school hours. Taxpayers challenged this act as a violation of the First Amendment Establishment Clause. The Court upheld the act in *Westside*

Community Schools v. Mergens (1990), arguing that Congress had legitimately protected the First and Fourteenth Amendment rights of religious students to "equal treatment" and "equal protection."

In *Lamb's Chapel v. Center Moriches Union Free School District* (1993), the Court extended the "equal access" principle to other religious groups besides students. A local school board, pursuant to state policy, opened its public school facilities after hours to local private groups for various "social, civic, recreational, and political uses." The policy stated explicitly, however, that the "school premises shall not be used by any group for religious purposes." Lamb's Chapel, an evangelical group, applied for use of the facilities to show a film series that discussed traditional family values from a Christian perspective. When their application was twice denied, they filed suit arguing that such exclusion violated their free speech rights. The *Lamb's Chapel* Court agreed. Relying on *Widmar* and other free speech cases, the Court found that the school had engaged in religious discrimination in denying access to this limited public forum. Again, the school district's concern to avoid an establishment of religion was not considered a sufficient reason for denying equal access to this religious group.

In *Rosenberger v. Rector and Visitors of the University of Virginia* (1995), the Court extended this equal access logic to hold that a voluntary group of religious students in a state university was entitled to the same funding made available to nonreligious student groups. The state University of Virginia encouraged student groups to organize themselves for extracurricular activities. Each student group had to register with the university and to include in all its communications a disclaimer that the group and its activities were acting independently of the university. Properly registered student groups were permitted to apply for funding from a general student activity fund to pay for their activities, including costs for printing and distributing their literature. These funds had to be paid to outside contractors. Of the 343 properly registered student groups the year in question, 118 received funds, 15 were denied funds.

One of the groups denied funds was a properly registered religious student group that printed an overtly religious newspaper for circulation on the state university campus. The group's request for funds to defray printing costs was denied on grounds that the student activity fund could not be used for "religious activities." The group appealed, arguing that such discriminatory treatment violated their First Amendment free speech rights. The *Rosenberger* Court agreed. The state university policy, Justice Anthony Kennedy wrote for the Court, improperly "selects for disfavored treatment those student journalistic efforts with religious editorial viewpoints." This, too, was "viewpoint discrimination," in violation of the Court's equal access precedents.

In *Good News Club v. Milford Central School* (2001), the Court extended this equal access logic from the state university and public high school to the public grade school. Authorized by state statute, a local public school enacted a policy for qualified local residents to use public school facilities after school hours for "instruction in any branch of education, learning, or the arts" and for "social, civic and recreational meetings." The policy, however, prohibited use of the facilities by any group "for religious purposes," for fear of establishing religion. The Good News Club, a private Christian organization that instructed 6- to 12-year-old children in Christian morality and practice, sought permission to hold the club's weekly after-school meetings in the cafeteria of a public grade school and to involve children who attended that school. Their lesson plans indicated that these meetings would involve adult-led prayers, the collective singing of religious songs, and the children's recitation of Bible verses, among other activities. Denied permission, they appealed, arguing that Milford's policy of excluding them from this limited public forum violated their First Amendment free speech rights.

The *Good News* Court agreed. Writing for a plurality, Justice Clarence Thomas declared that, while a state may restrict its forum to and for certain purposes, its "power to restrict speech" within such a forum "must not discriminate against speech on the basis of viewpoint." The school district was not obliged to create this "limited public forum," but once it did, any restriction had to be viewpoint-neutral and reasonable in light of the forum's purpose. The Good News Club's intended use fit easily within this public forum's stated purpose of facilitating "instruction in any branch of education, learning, or the arts," Justice Thomas wrote for the majority. "[S]peech discussing otherwise permissible subjects cannot be excluded from a limited public forum on the ground that the subject is discussed from a religious viewpoint." That a program of instruction might be "quintessentially religious" in inspiration or "decidedly religious in nature" does not prohibit it from being characterized as a proper teaching of morals and sound cultivation of character. "The Good News Club seeks nothing more than to be treated neutrally and given [equal] access to speak about the same topics as are other groups." This is not the kind of coercion, endorsement, or indoctrination of religion that violates the First Amendment establishment clause.

Government and Religious Education

While the principles of liberty of conscience, freedom of expression, and religious equality have come to prominence only in more recent cases on religion and public schools, they were central considerations from the start in Supreme Court cases on government and religious education. These principles formed the premises of a general Supreme Court logic about the role of government in private religious school education. Private schools of all sorts, the Supreme Court repeatedly held, are viable and valuable alternatives to public schools. Private religious schools in particular allow parents to educate their students in their own religious tradition, a right that they must enjoy without discrimination or prejudice. Given that public education must be secular under the Establishment Clause, private education may be religious under the Free Exercise Clause. To be accredited, all private schools must meet minimum educational standards. They must teach reading, writing, and arithmetic, history, geography, social studies, and the like so that their graduates are not culturally or intellectually handicapped. But these private schools may teach these subjects from a religious perspective and add religious courses beyond them. They may discriminate in favor of hiring teachers who share their faith and must be free from some of the usual requirements of teachers' unions. And these religious schools are presumptively entitled to the same government services that are made available to their counterparts in public schools—so long as those services are not used for core religious activities.

The Supreme Court began formulating its accommodationist logic respecting religious education already before World War II and continued to apply it in the first generation of cases after the 1947 *Everson* case. The Court abruptly reversed this logic in a series of cases from 1971 to 1986 that insisted on a strict separation of church and state. Since 1986, the Court has returned to a new variant of accommodationism, framed mostly in "equal access" terms.

Accommodation of Religion

Many of the Supreme Court's early cases on religious education came from the frontier states and territories, where Congress and the federal courts were of necessity more active. *Quick Bear v. Leupp* (1908) was the Court's very first case on religion and education. In treaties with the Sioux Indians, Congress had agreed to hold money in trust to be used later for the Indians' education—as partial consideration for the tribal lands that the federal government had confiscated. The treaties entitled the Sioux to designate the schools for which the money should be spent. The Sioux requested that the funds be spent on the Catholic schools that had long been serving their communities. Taxpayers objected, arguing that such payments violated the "spirit of the Constitution" that required that government must "always be undenominational [and] never act in a sectarian capacity." The *Quick Bear* Court rejected this argument, and held that Congress was not establishing religion or prohibiting its free exercise but simply discharging its treaty obligations to pay for the schools that the Sioux had chosen.

In *Meyer v. Nebraska* (1923), the State of Nebraska, like other states in the aftermath of World War I, began to clamp down on German Protestants, exposing them to a number of increasingly onerous registration and taxation policies and often turning a blind eye to private violence against them. At issue in *Meyer* was a new state law that mandated English instruction in all grade schools. Teachers in private Protestant grade schools were convicted under this statute for reading Bible stories in German. The Court reversed the conviction, holding that this violated the rights of the parent to direct the education of his children, and "to worship God according to the dictates of his own conscience."

The most important of these early cases was *Pierce v. Society of Sisters* (1925). Oregon had passed a law mandating that all eligible students must attend public schools. The law was transparently designed to eliminate Catholic and other private religious schools and to give new impetus to the development of the state's public schools. The Society of Sisters, which owned and operated several private Catholic schools, challenged this law as a violation of the educational rights of the parents, children, schools, and schoolteachers alike. The *Pierce* Court struck down the Oregon law and upheld the rights of the parents and of the religious schools. Such "rights guaranteed by the Constitution may not be abridged by legislation which has no reasonable relation to some purpose within the competency of the state," the Court opined. "The fundamental theory of liberty upon which all governments in this Union repose excludes any general power of the state to standardize its children by forcing them to accept instruction from public teachers only." It also forecloses "unwarranted compulsion—over present and future patrons" of the religious schools. Extending *Pierce's* logic in *Farrington v. Tokushige* (1927), the Court held that states could not impose unduly intrusive and stringent accreditation and regulatory requirements on religious and other private schools. In *Cochran v. Board of Education* (1930), it upheld a Louisiana state policy of supplying textbooks to all students, including religious school students.

This accommodation of religious schools and students continued into the early 1970s. *Everson* itself, for all its sweeping separationist dicta, nonetheless held that it was no establishment of religion for states to provide school bus transportation to religious and public schoolchildren alike. Moreover, it was no establishment of religion for the state to reimburse the parents of religious and public schoolchildren alike for the costs of using school bus transportation. "[C]utting off church schools [and their students] from these services, so separate and indisputably marked off from the religious function, would make it far more difficult for the schools to operate," Justice Black wrote. "But such obviously is not the purpose of the First Amendment. The Amendment requires the State to be neutral in its relations with groups of religious believers and non-believers; it does not require the state to be their adversary."

The Court struck a similar tone in *Board of Education v. Allen* (1968). The State of New York had a policy of lending prescribed textbooks in science, mathematics, and other "secular subjects" to all students in the state, whether attending public or private schools. Many of the private school recipients of the textbooks were religious schools. A taxpayer challenged the policy as a violation of the Establishment Clause. Citing the 1930 *Cochran* case, the Court upheld this policy, emphasizing that it was the students and parents, not the religious schools, that directly benefited. "Perhaps free books make it more likely that some children choose to attend a sectarian school," Justice White wrote for the Court, "but that was true of the state-paid bus fares in *Everson,* and does not alone demonstrate an unconstitutional degree of support for a religious institution."

The Court continued this accommodationist reading of the First Amendment Establishment Clause in a trio of cases upholding the payment of government construction grants and revenue bonds to religious colleges and universities. In the first of these cases, *Tilton v. Richardson* (1971), the Court rebuffed a no establishment challenge to federal grants that supported construction of library, science, and arts buildings at four church-related colleges. The grants were made as part of the federal Higher Education Facilities Act (1963), which sponsored new college and university buildings throughout the nation. Chief Justice Warren Burger wrote for the *Tilton* Court: "The Act itself was carefully drafted to ensure that the federally-subsidized facilities would be devoted to the secular and not the religious functions of the recipient institution." This feature, together with the reality that most funding was directed to state, not religious, universities and colleges was sufficient to save them from charges of religious establishment. The Court held to this precedent in *Hunt v. McNair* (1973) and *Roemer v. Maryland Board of Public Works* (1977).

The Court went even further in accommodating religious education in the 1972 case of *Wisconsin v. Yoder.* Wisconsin, like all states, mandated that able children attend school until the age of 16. A community of Old Order Amish, who were dedicated to a simple agrarian lifestyle based on biblical principles, conceded the need to send their children to grade school—to teach them the basic fundamentals of reading, writing, and arithmetic that they would need. But the community leaders and parents refused to send their children to higher schools, lest they be tempted by worldly concerns and distracted from learning the values and skills they would need to maintain the Amish lifestyle. When they were fined for their defiance of the school attendance laws, the parents and community leaders filed suit, arguing that the State had violated their free exercise and parental rights. The *Yoder* Court agreed, and ordered that they be exempted from full compliance with these laws. What seemed to impress the Court was that the Amish "lifestyle" was "not merely a matter of personal preference, but one of deep religious conviction, shared by an organized group, and intimately related to daily living" and that these "religious beliefs and attitudes towards life, family and home...have not altered in fundamentals for centuries." In the Court's view, compliance with the compulsory school attendance law "carries with it a very real threat of undermining the Amish community and religious practice as they exist today; they must either abandon belief and be assimilated into society at large, or be forced to migrate to some other and more tolerant region." To exempt them was not to "establish the Amish religion" but to "accommodate their free exercise rights." This case would later become a *locus classicus* for the homeschooling movement, which lower federal and state courts have upheld in a number of states.

Separation of Church and State

In *Lemon v. Kurtzman* (1971), the Supreme Court abruptly reversed course. Drawing on the strict separationist logic of its earlier public school cases, the *Lemon* Court crafted a three-part test to be used in all future cases arising under the First Amendment Establishment Clause, including those dealing with religious schools. To meet constitutional objections, the Court held, any challenged government law must: (1) have a secular purpose; (2) have a primary effect that neither advances nor inhibits religion; and (3) not foster an excessive entanglement between church and state. Incidental religious "effects" or modest "entanglements" of church and state are tolerable, the Court allowed. But defiance of any of these three criteria is constitutionally fatal.

The *Lemon* Court used this three-part test to strike down a state policy that reimbursed Catholic and other religious schools for some of the costs of teaching secular subjects that the state prescribed. The challenged state policy was restricted to religious schools that served students from lower-income families. Reimbursements were allowed only for clearly specified secular subjects and were limited to 15 percent of the costs. The *Lemon* Court held that this policy fostered an "excessive entanglement between church and state." The Catholic schools in question were notably religious—closely allied with nearby parish churches, filled with religious symbols, and staffed primarily by nuns who were under "religious control and discipline." "[A] dedicated religious person, teaching at a school affiliated with his or her faith and operated to inculcate its tenets, will inevitably experience great difficulty in remaining religiously neutral." She will be tempted to teach secular subjects with a religious orientation in violation of state policy. "A comprehensive, discriminating, and continuing state surveillance will inevitably be required to ensure that these restrictions are obeyed and the First Amendment otherwise obeyed." This is precisely the kind of excessive entanglement between church and state that the First Amendment Establishment Clause outlaws.

Lemon left open the question whether the state could give aid directly to religious students or to their parents—as the Court had allowed in earlier cases. Two years later, the Court closed this door tightly. In *Committee for Public Education v. Nyquist* (1973) and *Sloan v. Lemon* (1973), the Court struck down state policies that allowed low-income parents to seek reimbursements from the state for some of the costs of religious school tuition. *Nyquist* further struck down a state policy that allowed low-income parents to take tax deductions for the costs of sending their children to private schools. In *Nyquist*, Justice Powell characterized such policies as just another "of the ingenious plans of channeling state aid to sectarian schools." Responding to the state argument that "grants to parents, unlike grants to [religious] institutions, respect the 'wall of separation' required by the Constitution," the Court declared that "the effect of the aid is unmistakably to provide desired financial support for non-public, sectarian institutions." This violates the second prong of the *Lemon* test that outlaws any policy whose primary effect is to advance religion.

Lemon also left open the question of whether the state could give textbooks, educational materials, or other aid to religious schools for the teaching of mandatory secular subjects, or the administration of state-mandated tests and other programs. The Court struck down most such policies, save the lending of textbooks, which had been upheld since the 1930 *Cochran* case in a long series of increasingly tedious cases, from 1973 to 1985. By 1985, these cases seemed to "partake of the prolixity" of a Byzantine code, in Justice William Rehnquist's phrase uttered in dissent in *Wallace v. Jaffree* (1985). Rehnquist summarized the prevailing law thus:

> [A] State may lend to parochial school children geography textbooks that contain maps of the United States, but the State may not lend maps of the United States for use in geography class. A State may lend textbooks on American colonial history, but it may not lend a film of George Washington, or a film projector to show it in history class. A State may lend classroom workbooks, but may not lend workbooks in which the parochial school children write, thus rendering them nonreusable. A State may pay for bus transportation to religious schools, but may not pay for bus transportation from the parochial school to the public zoo or natural history museum for a field trip. A State may pay for diagnostic services conducted in the parochial school but therapeutic services must be given in a different building; speech and hearing "services" conducted by the State inside the sectarian school are forbidden, but the State may conduct speech and hearing testing inside the sectarian school. Exceptional parochial school students may receive counseling, but it must take place outside of the parochial school, such as in a trailer parked down the street. A State may give cash to a parochial school to pay for administration of State-written tests and State-ordered reporting services, but it may not provide funds for teacher-prepared tests on secular subjects. Religious instruction may not be given in public school, but the public school may release students during the day for religion classes [in the sectarian school], and may enforce attendance of those classes with its truancy laws.

Equal Treatment and Freedom of Choice

These fine-grained distinctions eventually proved to be unworkable in practice. Accordingly, in a series of cases from the mid-1980s forward, the Supreme Court softened these separationist holdings, and reversed several of the harsher cases on point. Many of these more recent cases adduced the principle of equality as well as the principle of liberty of conscience, now in the form of the freedom of parents and students to choose the form of education that suited them best.

The first case of these cases was *Mueller v. Allen* (1983), where the Court upheld a Minnesota law that allowed parents of private schoolchildren to claim tax deductions from state income tax for the costs of "tuition, transportation, and textbooks." Ninety-five percent of the private schoolchildren in the state attended religious schools. Most of their parents availed themselves of this tax deduction. A taxpayer in the state challenged the law as an establishment of religion. The *Mueller* Court disagreed. The tax deduction policy had a secular purpose of fostering quality education, Justice Rehnquist wrote for the Court, applying the first step of the *Lemon* test. The motives of the legislature should not be considered: Laws should be upheld against charges of establishment "when a plausible secular purpose for the state's program may be discerned from the face of the statute." Moreover, the law fostered no entanglement between church and state.

The "more difficult" question for the *Mueller* Court was whether the law had "the primary effect of advancing the sectarian aims of the non-public schools"—the principal ground on which the *Nyquist* Court a decade before had struck down such tax deduction policies. The *Mueller* Court distinguished *Nyquist* rather tendentiously. The saving features of the Minnesota law, Justice Rehnquist reasoned, were that this was a deduction for educational costs, not religious education; that it allowed deductions for the costs of "private" education, not "nonpublic" education; and that the deductions for religious education allowed by this law were sufficiently diluted by the many other deductions, for medical, charitable, and other causes. The *Nyquist* Court had characterized all such arguments as "ingenious schemes." The *Mueller* Court found that these features sufficiently "reduced the Establishment Clause objections" to the law. The state aid to sectarian schools, Justice Rehnquist concluded, "becomes available only as a result of numerous, private choices of individual parents of school-age children." This saves it from constitutional infirmity.

In *Witters v. Washington Department of Services for the Blind* (1986), the Court upheld a state program that furnished aid to a visually impaired student attending a Christian college. The program provided funds "for special education and/or training in the professions, business or trades" for the visually impaired. Money was to be paid directly to eligible recipients, who were entitled to pursue education in the professional schools of their choice. Witters's condition qualified him for the funds. His profession of choice was the Christian ministry. He sought funds to attend a Christian college in preparation for the same. The state agency denied funding, on grounds that this was a direct funding of religious education prohibited by *Lemon* and its progeny.

The *Witters* Court disagreed. Applying the *Lemon* test, the Court found the policy, and its application to Witters, to be constitutional. The policy served a secular purpose of fostering educational and professional choice for all, including the handicapped. It involved no entanglement of church and state. Its primary purpose was to facilitate this student's professional education, which happened to be religious. This "is not one of 'the ingenious plans for channeling state aid to sectarian schools that periodically reach this Court,'" Justice Thurgood Marshall wrote for the *Witters* Court.

> It creates no financial incentive for students to undertake sectarian education. It does not provide greater or broader benefits for recipients who apply their aid to religious education …In this case, the fact that aid goes to individuals means that the decision to support religious education is made by the individual not by the State.

In *Zobrest v. Catalina Foothills School District* (1993), the Court extended this logic from a college student to a high school student. Both federal and state disability acts required that a hearing-impaired student be furnished with a sign-language interpreter to accompany him or her to classes. The state furnished the interpreters at its own costs. Zobrest's hearing impairment qualified him for an interpreter's services. But he enrolled at a Catholic high school. The state refused to furnish him with an interpreter, on grounds that this would violate the *Lemon* rule that the state could give no direct aid to a religious school; moreover, the presence of a state-employed interpreter in a Catholic high school would foster an excessive entanglement between church and state. Following *Mueller* and *Witters,* the *Zobrest* Court upheld the act as "a neutral government program dispensing aid not to schools but to handicapped children." "If a handicapped child chooses to enroll in a sectarian school," Chief Justice Rehnquist wrote for the Court, "we hold that the Establishment Clause does not prevent the school district from furnishing him with a sign-language interpreter."

In *Agostini v. Felton* (1997), the Court extended this logic from the high school to the grade school, overturning the controversial case of *Aguilar v. Felton* (1985). In the earlier

Aguilar case, the Court had declared unconstitutional New York City's program that sent public school teachers into religious schools to offer remedial services to disadvantaged students. The remedial services in question in *Aguilar* were authorized and funded by Congress in the Elementary and Secondary Education Act (1965), known as the Title I program. The act set detailed standards both for student eligibility and for the education to be offered eligible students. More than 20,000 students in Catholic, Jewish, Protestant, and other religious schools in the city annually availed themselves of these Title I services. Lacking sufficient space in existing public buildings, and lacking sufficient land to build new public buildings adjacent to religious schools, New York City had chosen to offer the remedial services on site to eligible religious school students. State-funded public school teachers with materials were sent into the religious schools to teach the eligible religious school students. Field supervisors were sent out monthly to ensure compliance with the law, in particular to ensure that the Title I funds were directed to remedial, not religious, education in these schools. The program had been in place for 19 years.

In the early 1980s, local taxpayers had challenged the program as a violation of the disestablishment clause. The *Aguilar* Court had agreed. Though "well-intentioned," Justice William Brennan wrote for the Court in 1985, the program fosters an excessive entanglement of church and state. The religious schools receiving the Title I instructors are "pervasively sectarian," having as a "substantial purpose, the inculcation of religious values." Because of this, "ongoing inspection is required to ensure the absence of a religious message. In short, the scope and duration of New York's Title I program would require a permanent and pervasive State presence in the sectarian schools receiving aid." This, Justice Brennan concluded, is precisely the kind of excessive entanglement between church and state that the disestablishment clause outlaws.

Four justices wrote bitter dissents in *Aguilar.* Justice Rehnquist charged that the Court "takes advantage of the 'Catch 22' paradox of its own creation, whereby aid must be supervised to ensure no entanglement, but the supervision itself is held to cause an entanglement." Justice Sandra Day O'Connor denounced the majority opinion as "wooden," "formalistic," and "lacking in common sense." In the 19 years of the program, she wrote, quoting the record, "there has never been a single incident in which a Title I instructor 'subtly or overtly' attempted to 'indoctrinate the students in particular religious tenets at public expense.'" The real losers, she wrote, are disadvantaged children who happen to live "in cities where it is not economically or logistically feasible to provide public facilities for remedial education adjacent to the parochial school...For these children, the Court's decision is tragic."

In 1997, the *Agostini* Court, led by Justice O'Connor, overruled *Aguilar.* The ample procedural subtleties of the case aside, the *Agostini* Court declared that its establishment law had changed sufficiently to offset the *Aguilar* holding. Citing *Zobrest,* Justice O'Connor wrote that the mere presence of a state employee in a religious institution is not a per se unconstitutional means of state inculcation of religion or the kind of "symbolic union of church and state" that violates the excessive entanglement prong. Citing *Witters,* she wrote that "we have departed from the rule...that all government aid that directly aids the educational functions of religious schools is invalid." The *Aguilar* Court had been "unduly zealous and mechanical" in its application of the *Lemon* test, the Court concluded. In particular, it had used the "excessive entanglement prong" to enforce a form of separatism that could not be squared with other constitutional values. Children in religious schools are just as entitled to Title I benefits as children in public schools. They cannot be denied these benefits simply for the sake of upholding "the abstract principle" of separation of church and state.

In *Mitchell v. Helms* (2000), the Court extended *Agostini* to uphold the constitutionality of direct government aid to the secular functions of religious schools. Chapter 2 of the federal Education Consolidation and Improvement Act (1981) channels federal funds to state and local education agencies for the purchase of various educational materials and equipment. The legislation permits states to loan such materials directly to public and private elementary and secondary schools, provided that the state retain title in those materials and that the recipient schools use them only for programs that are "secular, neutral, and nonideological." The amount of aid for each participating school depends on the number of students it matriculates. In accordance with the act, Louisiana distributed materials and equipment to public and private schools within various school units in the state. In one county, some 30 percent of the Chapter 2 aid was allocated to private schools, most of which were Catholic. The aid was distributed properly per the federal formula. There was no allegation that the private religious schools used the aid for anything but "secular, neutral, and nonideological" programs. Local taxpayers brought suit, however, arguing that such "direct aid" to such "pervasively sectarian" schools constituted an establishment of religion.

The *Mitchell* Court disagreed, and held the Chapter 2 program constitutional both on its face and as applied in this case. Six justices found that the law did not advance religion using the three criteria that *Agostini* had distilled: There was no governmental indoctrination of religion because the aid was "offered to a broad range of groups or persons without regard to their religion" and was used for "secular, neutral, and nonideological programs." The act did not define its recipients by reference to religion; all accredited public and private schools and students were eligible. And there was no excessive entanglement between religious and governmental officials in the administration of the program. Accordingly, the Court upheld Chapter 2. The Court also overruled two earlier cases— *Meek v. Pittenger* (1975) and *Wolman v. Walter* (1977)—that held unconstitutional similar aid programs distributing materials directly to religious schools, acknowledging that the separationist principles at work in these decisions had become unworkably rigid.

In *Zelman v. Simmons-Harris* (2002), the Court upheld another form of state aid to religious schools, now using a logic of equality and neutrality. At issue in *Zelman* was the State of Ohio's Pilot Project Scholarship Program, which Ohio had adopted to address a "crisis of magnitude" in its public school system. The program gave parents a choice to leave their children in the local Cleveland public school district or to enroll them in another public or private school that participated in the school voucher program. For those parents who chose to remove their children, the program provided them with a voucher to defray tuition costs at the private school to which they chose to send their children. In the 1999–2000 academic year, 82 percent of the private schools participating in the voucher program were religiously affiliated; 96 percent of the students participating in the voucher program enrolled in these private religious schools.

The Court concluded that there was no dispute that the program was enacted for a "valid secular purpose of providing educational assistance to poor children in a demonstrably failing public school system." Thus the Court addressed the sole issue of whether the Ohio program has the "effect" of advancing religion in violation of the disestablishment clause. Writing for the majority, Chief Justice Rehnquist drew a distinction between government programs that provide aid directly to religious schools (*Mitchell, Agostini,* and

Rosenberger) and programs of "true private choice" (*Mueller, Witters,* and *Zobrest*). To the Court, the latter trio of cases

> make[s] clear that where a government aid program is *neutral* with respect to religion, and provides assistance directly to a *broad class of citizens,* who, in turn, direct government aid to religious schools wholly as a result of their own genuine and independent *private choice,* the program is not readily subject to challenge under the Establishment Clause. A program that shares these features permits government aid to reach religious institutions only by way of the deliberate choices of numerous individual recipients. The incidental advancement of a religious mission, or the perceived endorsement of a religious message is reasonably attributable to the individual, not the government, whose role ends with the disbursement of the funds.

The Court found that the Ohio voucher program is one of "true private choice" that is neutral to religion, and is thus constitutional. As in *Mitchell,* the majority stressed that there is a broad range of educational choices and the program did not define its recipients by reference to religion. Moreover, the Court distinguished its holding from that in *Nyquist,* where the program provided incentives for students to attend religious schools and prohibited public schools from participating. Here there are no financial incentives for parents to choose a religious school; rather there are disincentives for choosing religious schools since under the program private schools receive only a portion of the government assistance that public community and magnet schools receive.

While these recent "equal access" cases remain the federal law of the land, their future has been cast in some doubt by the Court's most recent case of *Locke v. Davey* (2004). The State of Washington established a "Promise Scholarship" program for its college-bound students. The program required students to meet clear criteria for high school grades and family income. They were free to use the scholarship at any accredited college. But the program explicitly stated that the student could not pursue a degree in theology. Davey met all the eligibility criteria and received a Promise Scholarship. He chose to attend Northwest College, an accredited college affiliated with Assemblies of God that teaches a liberal arts curriculum from a decidedly Christian perspective. Davey declared a double major in business and in pastoral ministry. Because of this latter interest, the state withdrew his scholarship.

Davey appealed, arguing that the state law targets religion students for special exclusions in violation of the principle of neutrality demanded by both the free exercise and the disestablishment clause. Moreover, it forces him to choose between two rights: if he accepts the scholarship, he may not study theology; if he studies theology, he must give up his scholarship. The State of Washington countered that it was not obstructing Davey's free exercise rights, but merely refusing to subsidize his exercise of them in violation of its state constitution that provided: "No public money or property shall be appropriated for or applied to any religious worship, exercise, or instruction, or the support of any religious establishment."

The *Locke* Court agreed with the State of Washington and found no violation of Davey's free exercise rights. Writing for a 7-2 majority, Chief Justice Rehnquist characterized this as a case that involves the "play in the joints" between the free exercise of religion and disestablishment clauses. The Free Exercise Clause does not require the state to pay for Davey's scholarship, and the Establishment Clause does not prevent the state from doing so. Distribution of scholarship money was a state legislative decision, and the state's decision to exclude theology majors from funding cast only "a relatively minor burden on Promise Scholars." Eligible students could still go to any accredited college, including a religious college. They could still take any courses, including religion courses. They simply could not be theology majors. This is not the kind of facial discrimination, the Court concluded, that requires inquiry into a compelling state interest or least restrictive alternative. It is a sensible, neutral, and generally applicable law that states are and must be fully empowered to make.

The Supreme Court has not yet extended this holding into lower public schools, and, as of the time of this writing, most lower federal courts have read *Locke v. Davey* quite narrowly as further evidence of the Court's newfound respect for federalism and state rights. Whether this case signals the end of "equal access" logic and the start to a new First Amendment understanding of religion and education remains to be seen. *See also:* Jefferson, Thomas; Madison, James; Separation of Church and State/Wall of Separation between Church and State.

Further Reading: Appendix I with detailed case citations; Michael S. Ariens and Robert Destro, *Religious Liberty in a Pluralistic Society,* 2nd ed. (Durham, NC: Carolina Academic Press, 2002); Sol Cohen, ed., *Education in the United States,* 4 vols. (New York: Random House, 1974); Philip Hamburger, *Separation of Church and State* (Cambridge, MA: Harvard University Press, 2002); Michael W. McConnell, John H. Garvey, and Thomas C. Berg, *Religion and the Constitution,* 2nd ed. (New York: Aspen, 2006); John Witte, Jr., *Religion and the American Constitutional Experiment,* 2nd ed. (Boulder: Westview Press, 2005).

John Witte, Jr.

Focus on the Family

Focus on the Family (FOF), founded by James C. Dobson, is the largest and one of the most influential evangelical institutions in America. Reared in the deeply conservative Nazarene Church, Dobson earned a doctorate in child development at the University of Southern California (USC) and taught for a time at the USC medical school. His 1976 book, *Dare to Discipline,* assuring parents that children needed firm discipline as well as love, met with such overwhelming success that he resigned from USC, began a radio show, and, in 1977, founded FOF, with a stated aim to help create, sustain, and defend strong families. He wrote other best-selling books, steadily expanded his radio outreach, and produced a set of family-focused films that were shown in churches across America. In 1993, the organization moved to Colorado Springs, where it functions as the "anchor store" among more than a hundred smaller church and parachurch organizations. Although Dobson ceded the position of president and CEO to the first of several successors in 1993, he remains chairman of the Board of Directors and retains an active role. His daily half-hour radio program is aired over more than 3,000 stations in the United States and more than 6,000 stations in 164 countries worldwide. The organization also produces other radio programs, including the "FOF Radio Theatre" and, for children, "Adventures in Odyssey." In addition, FOF publishes ten monthly magazines, produces a plethora of audio and video recordings, and maintains an elaborate set of Web sites. With a staff of more than 1,300 and annual income above $130 million, its extensive facilities, set on a 49-acre campus, have become a major tourist attraction in Colorado Springs.

Dobson has viewed FOF as both a bulwark and aggressive force in what he has called a "Civil War of Values," the product of deliberate attempts by secular humanists to destroy a culture built on traditional values. Like most of his colleagues on the Christian Right, he favors vouchers that can be used in private schools. Unlike many of them, he has not voiced strenuous opposition to public schools, but generally speaks positively of most teachers and school administrators, acknowledging that many parents have no viable alternative to public schools. Because he sees children as the real prize in the culture war, however, FOF concentrates heavily on issues related to education. To combat problems of unsafe environments, epitomized by school shootings, bullying, drug abuse, and the presence of gangs and weapons in schools, FOF calls on school administrators to establish increased structure, exercise strong discipline, and instill a respect for authority, beginning in early grades. It criticizes the professional educational establishment, particularly the National Education Association, which it claims has abandoned interest in the classroom in favor of supporting liberal political candidates and advocating liberal social views such as acceptance of homosexuality and multiculturalism. It has also criticized the PTA on similar grounds. Charging that the educational establishment has squandered taxpayer money, FOF favors giving parents a stronger hand in the education of their children, including the right to protect their children from exposure to ideas they regard as harmful, and provides materials parents can use to challenge materials in textbooks. It also pushes for the teaching of Intelligent Design as an alternative to Darwinian Evolution. FOF argues that schoolchildren are being denied their religious freedoms by limits placed on their ability to express themselves openly about their religious faith and frequently provides examples of repressive rules, many of which do, in fact, go beyond what the law requires. The organization also publishes a magazine, *Teachers in Focus,* which contains advice as to how Christian teachers can work Christian teaching into their presentations.

Like virtually all organizations on the Christian Right, FOF focuses great attention on matters related to sexuality. Dobson has not only refused to concede an exception for abortion in cases in which the life of the mother is endangered but has fiercely criticized those conservative Christians who regard that as a reasonable stance. FOF opposes any form of sex education that is not abstinence-based and is relentless in its opposition to homosexuality and same-sex marriage. On several occasions, Dobson has become so exercised about California directives forbidding negative discussion of homosexuality in public schools that he has recommended that, if possible, parents keep their children out of the public schools.

Because of an extensive following, to which his broadcasts and publications provide regular communication, Dobson has become a major player in Republican politics. Major Republican candidates for high office recognize that his approval can be important and his opposition deadly to their campaigns. As a 501(c)(3) nonprofit organization, FOF is legally limited with respect to engagement in partisan politics, but the political implications of its views are transparent, and one of its magazines, *Citizen,* deals specifically with political issues. Dobson and his colleagues also regularly urge listeners to contact their political representatives regarding civic issues. To avoid legal complications, Dobson established Focus on the Family Action, a 501(c)(4) organization subject to fewer restraints in pushing its political agenda. Dobson also played a major role in establishing the Family Research Council, a key representative of the Christian Right in Washington. *See also:* School Choice; Sex Education and Religion.

Further Reading: Focus on the Family, at www.family.org; William Martin, *With God on Their Side: The Rise of the Religious Right in America* (New York: Broadway Books, 1996; 2004); People for the American Way, at www.pfaw.org.

William Martin

Friends (Quaker) Schools

The Religious Society of Friends was originated by George Fox (1624–1691) during a period of political upheaval and social change in England. The established churches, Catholic and Anglican, were caught up in conflicts and preoccupied with forms and power struggle rather than religious witness. Amid this turmoil, thousands of "seekers" were looking for something that they could believe in and that would give meaning to their lives. One such seeker, George Fox, after years of spiritual questioning, had a revelation that led to the founding of the Religious Society of Friends and has since been central to its life and witness. From this revelation, George Fox derived his essential insight, which was that there is "that of God" in everyone and that one can gain access to the God within through stillness and the practice of silence. The belief that there is "that of God" in every person led to the Quaker practices of silent worship, careful listening, compassion, nonviolence, full equality of women, and social action in pursuit of social justice. Fox also believed that decisions in the religious community should be made by the "sense of the meeting," a nonvoting, spiritual consensus process.

As a result of the persecution of Quakers in England, many Friends emigrated to the American colonies. William Penn arrived in America in 1681 and founded Pennsylvania as the "Holy Experiment," a colony governed on the ideals of religious tolerance and participatory government. Under Penn, who believed a moral, educated citizenry was necessary for a participatory democracy, Friends schools were founded in Philadelphia in the late 1600s for both boys and girls to provide "useful knowledge, such as is consistent with Truth and Godliness." By the late eighteenth century, the schools emphasized providing a "guarded education," protecting youth from influences that might draw them away from the "Light" and the peculiarities of the Friends.

During the nineteenth century, the Quaker movement split again and again. Although the 100,000 Quakers in America today share a common heritage, they span the spectrum from biblical authority fundamentalists to New Age universalists, from those who adhere to biblical understandings of sin, the divinity of Christ, and his atonement to those who believe all religions hold important truths. The "unprogrammed" Friends have no preordained order of worship, no appointed or paid main speaker, and no agenda for meeting. They see God or the Divine as "Inward Teacher," a spirit or light that can be experienced by all humanity. The idea of "Inner Light," or "that of God in everyone," requires that all be heard and all be respected. "Programmed" Friends, about two-thirds of American Quakers, resemble American evangelical churches with orders of worship, singing, preaching, and talk of accepting Christ and expecting help through faith. Some of the programmed churches have schools that, like the churches themselves, resemble their evangelical Christian counterparts.

After World War II, a renaissance occurred in "unprogrammed" Quaker education. Although Friends schools do not seek to inculcate a particular set of beliefs or doctrines, non-Quakers were and are attracted by the moral atmosphere and quality education. Quaker schools were seen as outposts of conscientious objectors, laboratories for experimentation and progressive education. Today, more than 80 Friends schools are members of the Friends Council on Education, the national association of Quaker schools. Friends Council member schools exist in mostly eastern seaboard states, serving more than 27,000 students from diverse backgrounds, mostly non-Quaker. The attraction is the unique Quaker pedagogy, as well as the schools' "atmosphere of sincerity" and the "subtle aura which pervades them," their focus on truth and the spiritual dimension of life, the emphasis on valuing and making space for students to explore and think critically about values and to take action with integrity.

The Quaker belief in the Inner Light leads to faith in the ability of every member of the school community to reach his or her full potential. Children are expected to grow and change in an environment that nurtures their spirits and challenges them to develop inner resources for discipline and achievement. Children learn to respect and practice truth and to know the various ways it can be found—through scientific investigation, through creative expression, through worship, through service within the school community and beyond. They are encouraged to respect the talents and perspectives of others, and include them in a cooperative, rather than competitive, search for knowledge.

Friends education strives to be socially responsible. Believing that the spiritual, social, and intellectual aspects of education are closely linked, Friends have always stressed the importance of an education that supports the overall development of the child. Because Friends believe that faith requires action in the world, Friends schools emphasize the development of a caring community, peaceful resolution of conflict, and service to others. As in the Quaker saying, "let your life speak," the Quaker principles of equality, community, peace, simplicity, and stewardship are reflected in curricular and community programs.

A basic tenet of Quakerism is that spiritual insight emerges from ongoing reflection within a gathered community. At Friends schools, this belief is reflected in an open-minded approach to curriculum and teaching, in an emphasis on critical thinking skills, and in a developmental approach to children and learning. Work on individual skills and knowledge is balanced with group learning, in which each person's insights contribute to a collective understanding.

As the only national organization of Friends schools, the Friends Council on Education assists member Quaker schools and their teachers, students, and families by providing consultation, publications, and programs to support the implementation of Friends values in the classroom and in the life of Friends school communities. The Council helps Friends schools maintain their Quaker identity and ethos, and their relationship with the Religious Society of Friends. *See also:* Council for American Private Education.

Further Reading: Howard Brinton, *Friends for 300 Years* (Wallingford, PA: Pendle Hill Publications, 1964); Friends Council on Education, at friendscouncil.org; Thomas D. Hamm, *The Quakers in America* (New York: Columbia University Press, 2003); Paul A. Lacey, *Growing into Goodness: Essays on Quaker Education* (Philadelphia: Pendle Hill Publications, 1998); Irene McHenry, Jane Fremon, Nancy Starmer, and J. Harry Hammond, *Readings on Quaker Pedagogy: Philosophy and Practice in Friends Education* (Philadelphia: Friends Council on Education, 2004).

Steven C. Vryhof

G

Gibbons, James Cardinal

As the Archbishop of Baltimore from 1877 until his death, Cardinal James Gibbons (1834–1921) was the nominal leader of the Catholic Church in the United States. In this capacity, he represented Roman Catholicism to the American people and American Catholic values to the Vatican. Gibbons also brokered the evolution of American Catholic education from a defensive response to Protestant-oriented common schools in the nineteenth century to a religious alternative to a secular public education system in the twentieth century.

Gibbons was born in Baltimore in July 1834, but he was taken to Ireland three years later. He returned to the United States in 1847 with his widowed mother and spent the next eight years as a grocer in New Orleans. In 1855, he returned to Baltimore where he entered the seminary. Ordained in 1861, he rose quickly through the ranks of the Church, and by 1868 he was the youngest bishop in the United States. After short stays in North Carolina and Virginia, Gibbons was elevated to Archbishop of Baltimore in 1877.

He became deeply involved in the issue of parochial education as the presiding prelate at the Third Plenary Council of Baltimore in 1884. The Council decrees clearly advocated the need for parish schools, but stopped short of condemning Catholic parents who sent their children to public schools.

Gibbons's most prominent role in the history of Catholic education came in 1891 when he came to the defense of his friend, Archbishop John Ireland of St. Paul, over the matter of a collaborative educational experiment in Faribault and Stillwater, Minnesota. Much to the dismay of conservative bishops, Gibbons refused to condemn public education and encouraged efforts to find a common ground between the two systems.

In fact, Gibbons defended Ireland's efforts to develop specific plans for cooperative schools in those two Minnesota communities and obtained official approval for Ireland's plans from the Vatican. On education, as on other social issues, Gibbons sought ways of harmonizing the tenets of the Catholic faith with the principles of American democracy.

After more than a year of investigation and consideration, the pope issued a decision on Archbishop Ireland, his educational philosophy, and his school plan. The statement acknowledged the fundamental righteousness of the school legislation of the plenary councils of Baltimore, but noted that after considering all of the facts and circumstances, that the Faribault Plan could be "tolerated." The statement was carefully nuanced so as not to offend either liberals or conservatives with the intention of ending the controversy. Unfortunately, the conflict had gone too far for either faction to drop the matter, and both the liberals and the conservatives claimed victory after the statement was made public.

The conservatives countered that Gibbons had misinformed the pope about the condition of the Church in the United States. The pope responded to the conservatives with a plea for unity and a call for the bishops to work together for public funding for denominational institutions.

Gibbons was in total agreement with the pope in praying for an end to the controversy. The Cardinal was a realist, however. He knew that neither faction would accept such a neutral statement. Matters continued to deteriorate during the summer, and it was clear to Gibbons that the school controversy would again be the main topic of discussion at the upcoming November conference of the archbishops.

But the conservatives were in no mood to find common ground and resisted proposals made by the Vatican at the meeting. The pope's personal representative, Archbishop Francis Satolli, proposed that the American hierarchy "tolerate" the enrollment of Catholic children in public schools. The proposal was met with stony silence.

The conservatives later protested to Rome with great vigor, but the response from the pope badly disappointed them. In early January 1893, the pope announced the appointment of Satolli to be the first permanent apostolic delegate to the United States. And in May, the pope wrote to Gibbons to tell him and the other American archbishops that the Vatican saw no conflict between Satolli's propositions and the mandates of the Third Plenary Council of Baltimore.

The great Catholic school controversy had ended. But after more than three years of acrimony, the differences between the liberals and conservatives remained. More important, the conservatives felt betrayed. The conservatives feared, with some justification, that Catholic children by the thousands would drift away from parish schools.

But the pope's decision in favor of Satolli's propositions was more than a vindication of Gibbons or a victory for the liberals. Satolli had outlined and emphasized the harmony that existed between the Catholic Church and the American ideals of public education. It was an important day when the pope confirmed that the Church had no fundamental disagreements with the principles of public education. It was an extraordinary achievement for Gibbons and marked an end to the combative educational policy instituted by John Hughes more than 50 years earlier. *See also:* Catholic Schools; Faribault-Stillwater Plan; Ireland, John.

Further Reading: John Tracy Ellis, *The Life of James Cardinal Gibbons, Archbishop of Baltimore, 1834–1921,* 2 vols. (Milwaukee, WI: Bruce Publishing, 1951); Thomas W. Spalding, *The Premier See: A History of the Archdiocese of Baltimore, 1789–1989* (Baltimore, MD: Johns Hopkins University Press, 1989).

Timothy Walch

Good News Club v. Milford Central School

The U.S. Supreme Court decided *Lamb's Chapel v. Center Moriches Union Free School District* in 1993; eight years later an almost identical issue was litigated in *Good News Club v. Milford Central School.* The issue was whether religious groups could use school facilities for various activities. The Supreme Court ruled in *Good News* that it violated the free speech rights of individuals to allow facilities to be used by one group and not another; this constituted viewpoint discrimination. The Supreme Court in *Good News* stated, " [t]hat exclusion is indistinguishable from the exclusions held violative of the [Free Speech] clause in *Lamb's Chapel*" where the school district discriminated against the group because of its religious viewpoint.

The *Lamb's Chapel* case arose out of New York Education Law § 414 (*McKinney* 2000) and a local school district policy. The local policy concerned implementing New York State Law Section 414, which authorized the use of school property for various purposes, such as elections and civic use, but prohibited the facilities from being used "by any group for religious purposes." In accordance with § 414, the Milford School Board enacted a policy that school district residents may use facilities after school hours "for among other things, (1) instruction in education, learning, or the arts and (2) social, civic, recreational and entertainment uses pertaining to the community welfare," but not for religious purposes.

Two residents applied to use the school facilities after school hours for the Good News Club, a private Christian organization for children aged 6 to 12. The Good News Club would use the facilities to gather to sing songs, listen to Bible lessons, memorize Scripture, and pray. The organizations's lesson plans included the teachers leading "a child to Christ" and gave "unsaved children" the opportunity to know God's word and be saved. The school district denied the Good News request because its activities were religious and not a secular subject that was discussed from a religious perspective. The Good News Club filed suit, claiming a violation of free speech rights under the First and Fourteenth Amendments, equal protection under the Fourteenth Amendment, and right of religious freedom under the Religious Freedom Restoration Act (RFRA). The RFRA was ruled unconstitutional in *City of Boerne v Flores* (1997).

A federal district court ruled for the school district because the activities were of a religious nature. The Second Circuit Court of Appeals affirmed the lower court because "the Club's subject matter was quintessentially religious and its activities fell outside the bounds of pure moral and character development."

The U.S. Supreme Court reversed the Second Circuit and held the school board's exclusion of a children's Christian club was unconstitutional viewpoint discrimination. The Court stated that "viewpoint discrimination was not required to avoid violating the Establishment Clause."

The Supreme Court was guided by previous cases, specifically *Lamb's Chapel* and a 1995 decision, *Rosenberger v. Rector and Visitors of University of Virginia* (where a student organization was denied funding to print a publication that offered a Christian viewpoint). *Lamb's Chapel* and *Rosenberger* found that when a state establishes a limited public forum, "the State is not required to and does not allow persons to engage in every type of speech. The State may be justified 'in reserving [the forum] for certain groups or for the discussion of certain topics.'" This power given to the State is not without limits; these limits are that speech cannot be discriminated against based on the viewpoint and any restrictions must be reasonable in light of the forum's purpose. The Court in *Rosenberger* held the refusal to print a publication because it addressed religious issues and violated free speech principles, and the school district's exclusion of the Good News Club "based on its religious nature is indistinguishable" from the exclusion of *Rosenberger*.

When applying the *Lamb's Chapel* decision, the Court said that there was no difference between the *Lamb's Chapel* and *Good News*. It concluded the only possible difference was that the activity in *Lamb's Chapel* was that moral lessons were taught using films and in *Good News* moral lessons were presented live through storytelling and prayer. Therefore the "distinction is inconsequential. Both modes of speech used religious viewpoint."

The school district proffered the argument that even if the restriction constitutes viewpoint discrimination, the interest in not violating the Establishment Clause outweighed the groups' right to access of facilities. The Court again cited *Lamb's Chapel,* saying the Club's meetings were after school, not school sponsored, and open to any child who obtained parental permission, not just the Good News Club members; therefore the activities did not violate the Establishment Clause.

Justices David Souter and John Paul Stevens who voted with the majority in *Lamb's Chapel* both wrote dissenting opinions in *Good News*. They distinguished *Good News* from *Lamb's Chapel* because it constituted religious activities to the point of "worship." Justice Stevens opined:

> This case is undoubtedly close. Nonetheless, regardless of whether the Good News Club's activities amount to "worship," it does seem clear, based on the facts in the record, that the school district correctly classified those activities as falling within the third category of religious speech and therefore beyond the scope of the school's limited public forum. In short, I am persuaded that the school district could (and did) permissibly exclude from its limited public forum proselytizing religious speech that does not rise to the level of actual worship. I would therefore affirm the judgment of the Court of Appeals.

Justice Souter asserted that since the lesson plans were to "Lead the Child to Christ," students were instructed that "[t]he Bible tells us we can have our sins forgiven by receiving the Lord Jesus Christ. It tells us how to live to please Him. . . . If you have received the Lord Jesus as your Savior from sin, you belong to God's special group . . . His family." Justice Souter concluded this was an evangelical service of worship for conversion and therefore distinguishable from *Lamb's Chapel*. *See also:* First Amendment Religious Clauses and the Supreme Court; *Lamb's Chapel v. Center Moriches Union Free School District*.

Further Reading: *City of Boerne v. Flores,* 521 U.S. 507 (1997); *Good News Club v. Milford Central School,* 533 U.S. 98 (2001); *Lamb's Chapel v. Center Moriches Union Free School District,* 508 U.S. 384 (1993); *Rosenberger v. Rector and Visitors of University of Virginia,* 515 U.S. 819 (1995).

M. David Alexander

Government Aid to Religious Schools

Religious schools in the United States face constant pressure to maintain their financial viability. In many countries of the world religious schools are fully funded by the central government in the same manner as public schools are funded. This is not so in the United States. Here, the federal Constitution as well as state constitutions and statutes provide restrictions on the amount and type of aid that can be given to religious schools. On the federal level the First Amendment states in part "Congress shall make no law respecting an establishment of religion or prohibiting the free exercise thereof." This restriction was applied to actions by state government through the Fourteenth Amendment. Thus, both state and federal funds are prohibited in direct support of religious schools.

The First Amendment prohibition on funding religious schools has been well tested in the courts. In its landmark decision, *Everson v. Board of Education* (1947), the U.S. Supreme Court determined that payments by the state to parents for transportation costs of their children attending a parochial school did not violate the Constitution. It based its decision, in part, on the "child benefit" theory, namely, that funding is given for the direct benefit of the child, not the school. Thus, there is no direct aid to the religious school. Some 20 years later in the *Allen* decision, the Court arrived at the same conclusion regarding the provision of textbooks for children in parochial schools.

In 1971 the Supreme Court in *Lemon v. Kurtzman* developed a judicial test for determining if government aid to religious schools would be considered constitutionally appropriate. The three-part test required that first, any aid must have a secular legislative purpose; second, the primary effect of the aid must not advance religion; and finally, such aid must not foster excessive entanglement between government and religion. This *Lemon* test has been the basis for numerous decisions in the ensuing years, although its application has been somewhat diminished by the Court in more recent times.

In *Lemon,* the Court reviewed legislation in two states that would provide funding for a variety of needs in the parochial schools. The legislation was carefully written so as not to violate either the secular purpose or the primary effects tests. The court determined, however, that application of the funds would excessively involve the government in the parochial schools to ensure that funds were not being spent for a religious purpose. Thus, the attempted funding of religious schools violated the excessive entanglement prong of the *Lemon* test.

The State of Minnesota attempted to provide financial support to religious schools through a more indirect method by allowing parents to take a deduction on their income tax returns for the expenses incurred by their children in attending both public and private schools. The Court had previously struck down a similar provision in another state that was focused entirely on parochial schools. Because the Minnesota plan included all schools both public and private (including religious schools), the Supreme Court ruled that it did not violate the no establishment clause of the First Amendment.

Federal law provides that funds be made available for the support of children with a variety of special needs. It also provides that these funds should be provided for children in private as well as public schools. As a result, in many places public school teachers would go to the parochial school to provide special education services. In a stunning Supreme Court decision, *Aguilar v. Felton* (1985), the provision of such services on the premises of a religious school was determined to be in violation of the excessive entanglement prong of the *Lemon* test. As a result, children in parochial schools had to go to either a public school or a neutral site off the grounds of their own school for such services. The result was a good bit of chaos and disorganization as public school administrators tried to find an efficient way to provide services without violating the Supreme Court ruling. Several years later the Court determined that its decision in *Aguilar* was not good law. Its ruling in *Agostini v. Felton* (1997) allowed public school employees to provide services to children on the site of a religious school. Thus, it drew back from a rigid application of the three-part test in *Lemon.*

The Court's decision in *Agostini* should not have been surprising. A few years earlier it had allowed a much more intrusive form of government aid to religious schools in its decision in *Zobrest* (1993). Here a hearing-impaired student at a Catholic high school had requested that a sign-language interpreter be provided at government expense. He was entitled to services under federal law. Having a public school employee assist him during the school day at a religious school, however, seemed to be a violation of the excessive entanglement provision of *Lemon*. The high court, however, thought the interpreter would be merely a neutral figure in assisting the student in his education even though that would include religious education. The Court further weakened restrictions on aid to religious schools in its decision in *Mitchell v. Helms* (2000), which allowed federal funds for instructional materials provided to religious schools.

Of special interest to those who support government funding for parochial schools is the matter of school vouchers. In such a scheme, the state government provides funding to specified children to attend any school they desire, public or private. The parents simply present the school administration with a voucher provided by the state, which can be redeemed for the cost of tuition at the school. The inclusion of religious schools in such plans has been quite controversial and many deemed it to be a violation of the First Amendment. In its *Zelman* decision, however, the Supreme Court upheld the Cleveland, Ohio, voucher plan. Previously the Supreme Court of Wisconsin upheld that state's voucher program, which included religious schools, for the city of Milwaukee. It was held not to be in violation of the state constitution, which prohibits direct aid to private and religious schools.

It appears then, that the Supreme Court has moderated its stance restricting government funds to religious schools. How much further it will go remains to be seen. While some have found hope in the voucher rulings that more direct aid may be made available to support religious schools, others point to the very narrowness of those rulings in achieving a particular educational purpose. Thus the Court's move from a more separationist stance to one more accommodating to religious schools may be at an end.

An additional consideration is the matter of state law. States have the right to be more restrictive than the federal Constitution and frequently are. For example, the Constitution of Michigan specifically prohibits any "Public monies…credit, tax benefit, exemption or deductions, tuition voucher" from being provided, directly or indirectly, for the support of a nonpublic school. Many other states have similar provisions. Thus, regardless of the accommodating nature of the federal decisions, aid to religious schools may be blocked by state restrictions.

There is also the matter of political viability of government aid to support religious schools. Especially in times of scarce resources where public schools are struggling to maintain financial stability, the provision of state funds to private and religious schools may not be politically possible. As religious school enrollment declines, especially among the Catholic schools, political support for their funding at public expense has waned.

A further consideration is that many leaders of religious schools are concerned about the entanglement of government funds with private school operation. They feel there should be a wall of strict separation between government and religious schools. The fear is that with government aid comes government control and that such control may negate the very purpose of a religious school. Thus many religious schools refuse to accept even the aid that is currently available. Private schools have a great deal of freedom in employment matters, which is especially important to religious schools as they attempt to inculcate their students with a particular set of religious values. In doing so they must be able to carefully choose personnel who are committed to those values. They also have much freedom in selecting the student body, which contributes to the religious ethos of the school. Leaders in religious schools must determine to what extent they are willing to jeopardize their future freedom of operation in the search for government aid. *See also:* First Amendment Religious Clauses and the Supreme Court; *Lemon v. Kurtzman* and *Earley v. DiCenso;* Tuition Tax Credits; Vouchers.

Further Reading: *Agostini v. Felton,* 521 U.S. 203 (1997); *Aguilar v. Felton,* 473 U.S. 402 (1985); Kern Alexander and M. David Alexander, *American Public School Law,* 6th ed. (Belmont, CA: Thomson West, 2005); *Board of Education v. Allen,* 392 U.S. 236 (1968); *Everson v. Board of Education,* 330 U.S. 1 (1947); Ronald B. Flowers, *That Godless Court,* 2nd ed. (Louisville: Westminster John Knox Press, 2005); *Lemon v. Kurtzman,* 403 U.S. 602 (1971); *Mitchell v. Helms,* 530 U.S. 793 (2000); *Zelman v. Simmons-Harris,* 536 U.S. 639 (2002); *Zobrest v. Catalina Foothills School District,* 509 U.S. 1 (1993).

Lyndon G. Furst

Grand Rapids School District v. Ball

School District of City of Grand Rapids v. Ball (1985), a companion case with *Aguilar v. Felton* (1985), involved the constitutionality of the school district's Shared Time and Community Education programs. The district's Shared Time program offered a variety of remedial and enrichment mathematics, reading, art, music, and physical education courses in nonpublic elementary schools. Shared Time teachers, who often moved from classroom to classroom during the course of the school day, were public school full-time employees hired in accordance with its normal hiring procedures of the public schools. The public school district paid a nominal amount of money to rent the nonpublic school classrooms, which had to be free of religious symbols and artifacts. All of the supplies, materials, and equipment used in connection with Shared Time instruction were supplied by the public school district. The public school's Community Education program offered a wide range of classes available to students and adults taught in nonpublic elementary schools at the conclusion of the regular school day. Among the courses offered were Arts and Crafts, Home Economics, Spanish, Gymnastics, Yearbook Production, Christmas Arts and Crafts, Drama, Newspaper, Humanities, Chess, Model Building, and Nature Appreciation. Forty of the 41 schools participating in both programs were characterized as pervasively religious.

The plaintiffs in this case were taxpayers who challenged both programs as violating the Establishment Clause of the First Amendment. The federal district court in which the complaint was filed found the programs to be violations of the Establishment Clause and issued an injunction prohibiting their operation. The Sixth Circuit Court of Appeals affirmed and, after granting a writ of certiorari to review the case, the U.S. Supreme Court affirmed the Sixth Circuit.

The Supreme Court relied on the tripartite *Lemon v. Kurtzman* (1971) test as the basis for its analysis of the school district's programs. Both the district court and Sixth Circuit Court had found that the programs satisfied the *Lemon v. Kurtzman*'s secular purpose test, in this case of improving the quality of students' education, a conclusion that the Supreme Court saw no reason to disturb.

The Supreme Court found that the two programs violated the second part of the *Lemon* test in that they had the primary effect of advancing religion. In addition to 40 of the 41 schools participating in the Shared Time program being characterized as pervasively sectarian, the Court found three ways the programs had the primary effect of advancing religion: (1) the state-paid instructors, influenced by the pervasively sectarian nature of the religious schools in which they work, could subtly or overtly indoctrinate the students in particular religious tenets at public expense; (2) the symbolic union of church and state inherent in the provision of secular, state-provided instruction in the religious school buildings threatened to convey a message of state support for religion to students and to the general public; and (3) the programs in effect subsidized the religious functions of the parochial schools by taking over a substantial portion of their responsibility for teaching secular subjects. In effect, the Court found that the challenged governmental action in *School District of City of Grand Rapids v. Ball* amounted to a symbolic union of church and state and was sufficiently likely to be perceived by adherents of the controlling denominations as an endorsement, and by the nonadherents as a disapproval, of their individual religious choices. The Supreme Court determined that even the signs placed outside nonpublic school classrooms declaring that the room was being used for public school educational activities could constitute for students viewing the signs a powerful symbol of state endorsement and encouragement of the religious beliefs taught in the same class at some other time during the day.

Although the Supreme Court did not question the professional dedication of teachers providing instruction in the two programs and even though no evidence existed of the teachers engaging in indoctrination while teaching in the public school programs, the Court nonetheless found that a teacher placed in a pervasively religious setting may knowingly or unwillingly tailor the content of the course to fit the school's announced goals. Worth noting is that 12 years later in *Agostini v. Felton* (1997), the Supreme Court, in overruling *School District of City of Grand Rapids v. Ball,* expressly abandoned the presumption in *Ball* that the placement of public employees on parochial school grounds inevitably results in the impermissible effect of state-sponsored indoctrination or constitutes a symbolic union between government and religion. *See also: Agostini v. Felton; Aguilar v. Felton.*

Further Reading: *Agostini v. Felton,* 521 U.S. 203 (1997); *Aguilar v. Felton,* 473 U.S. 402 (1985); *Lemon v. Kurtzman,* 403 U.S. 602 (1971); *School District of City of Grand Rapids v. Ball,* 473 U.S. 373 (1985).

Ralph D. Mawdsley

H

Harvard Program in Religion in Secondary Education

In 1972, Harvard University's Divinity School established a unique program in religion and secondary education. While the program has seen several structural changes in its 35-year history, the core has remained consistent. Students in the program earn a master's degree—either a Master of Theological Studies or a Master of Divinity degree and also gain State of Massachusetts' licensure as secondary school teachers in a variety of fields, including history, English, chemistry, foreign language, or political science, depending in large part on their undergraduate major. While completing all of the state-required course work in education, including substantial student teaching, and course work in the specific field in which they will teach, students in the Program in Religion and Secondary Education (PRSE) also focus especially on the teaching of religion in public schools. In the process they develop unique expertise in the academic study of religion from a nonsectarian perspective and also find ways to develop curriculum in a range of secondary school subjects in ways that attend to religion and the diverse religious worldviews of today's students.

There are a number of sources for curricular materials on the teaching of religion in public schools in the United States, either as part of specialized courses in religion or religious topics, or as an infusion into other courses in history, English, or other more traditional public school fields. Harvard's PRSE is unique, however, in having a specialized focus on the preparation of teachers who will be both state-licensed subject matter experts in traditional middle and high school fields, but also experts in the teaching of religion in these schools.

The PRSE students interact regularly with other divinity school students and faculty, including Divinity School students preparing for ordination in church ministries and those seeking to teach in religion at both the secondary and the college and university levels. They also have opportunities to interact with and take courses in the Harvard Graduate School of Education. In addition, Harvard is the home to the Center for the Study of World Religions and a number of other centers and institutes of interest to students pursuing careers in which public school teaching and attention to issues of religion intersect. The program is currently directed by Professor Diane L. Moore, Professor of Practice in Religious Studies and Education. *See also:* Religion and Public Education Resource Center.

Further Reading: Harvard Program in Religion and Secondary Education, at www.hds.harvard.edu/prse.

James W. Fraser

Haynes, Charles C.

For the past two decades, Charles C. Haynes (b. 1949) has been the most influential spokesman and advocate regarding issues relating to religion, religious liberty, and public schools. Haynes graduated from Emory University, received an MTS in Religion and Education from Harvard University, and took his doctorate in Theological Studies at Emory. Since 1995, he has been a Senior Scholar at the Freedom Forum's First Amendment Center. Haynes's work falls into three overlapping areas.

First, he has been the principal organizer and drafter of a series of "common ground" statements on religion and public schools that have been endorsed by a wide range of national religious, educational, and civil liberties groups. The first of these statements, "Religion and the Public School Curriculum" (1988) made several important claims: that it is constitutional to teach about religion; that *teaching about* religion must be done neutrally; that it is important to teach about religion; and that textbooks are deficient in their treatment of religion. The endorsing organizations (Christian, Jewish, and Muslim, along with the major national educational organizations) made it clear that a *new consensus* about religion and public schools was forming.

Between 1988 and 2006 Haynes engineered eight additional common ground statements, addressing, among other themes, religious holidays, equal access to school facilities, the Bible, and sexual orientation. *A Teacher's Guide to Religion and Public Schools,* which Haynes drafted, was endorsed by more than 20 religious and educational organizations. Hundreds of thousands of copies of these documents have been distributed, and in 1999, President Bill Clinton had several of them, including the *Teacher's Guide,* sent to every public school in the country. Cumulatively, the statements demonstrate that there is much more agreement than disagreement about how to deal with religion in public schools. They have helped provide a "safe haven" for teachers and administrators who deal with issues that may still be controversial in their districts.

Second, Haynes has spent much of his time crisscrossing the United States, giving talks, leading workshops, and mediating disputes (including, on occasion, court-ordered remediation). He has organized major, ongoing, statewide projects on religion and public education for educators in Utah and California. (These "3 Rs" projects have emphasized the principles of rights, respect, and responsibilities that flow from the First Amendment.) He is the national expert to whom educators, reporters, and legislators turn to understand controversies regarding religion and public education.

Haynes's remarkable success in finding common ground amid the battles in our culture wars, both in national and in local communities, is testimony to his extraordinary tact, patience, empathy, persuasiveness, and, perhaps most important, fairness (which has generated trust on all sides). He has been able to work effectively with both secular liberals and religious conservatives in finding common ground.

Third, Haynes is the author, coauthor, or editor of seven books, and since 1996 he has written a biweekly newspaper column, "Inside the First Amendment," printed in papers across the country. His most important book, *Finding Common Ground: A First Amendment Guide to Religion and Public Schools* (edited and written with Oliver Thomas), is an invaluable collection of common ground statements, court rulings and analyses, sample school policies, and advice for teachers and administrators. It has been widely used.

A number of overlapping themes run through Haynes's writing and his work more generally:

(1) *Religious Liberty.* The religion clauses of the First Amendment and the Supreme Court's interpretation of them are the central texts for his understanding of the proper role of religion in public schools, though he has also emphasized the theological roots of the idea of religious liberty, particularly in the life and writings of Roger Williams.

(2) *Common Ground.* Understood rightly, the First Amendment provides a framework for *living with our deepest differences.* Finding common ground, he argues, is not simply a matter of political compromise, but of recognizing that our constitutional and religious traditions provide principles on which we can agree in negotiating our differences.

(3) *Civil Schools.* Haynes argues that two models of public schooling have failed: *sacred* schools, which privileged Protestantism; and *naked* schools, which have become religion-free zones. The ideal, by contrast, is the *civil public school,* which protects the religious liberty rights of all students, treating religion with fairness and respect.

(4) *Taking Religion Seriously.* Given the importance of religion in our history and culture, religion must be taken seriously in the public school curriculum. He has been particularly concerned with how to deal with religion in teaching history.

See also: Common Ground Documents; Religion and the Public School Curriculum; U.S. Department of Education Guidelines on Religion and Public Education.

Further Reading: Charles C. Haynes and Oliver Thomas, *Finding Common Ground: A First Amendment Guide to Religion and Public Schools* (Nashville: First Amendment Center, 1994, 2002, 2007); Charles C. Haynes et al., *Religion in American Public Life: Living with Our Deepest Differences* (New York: W. W. Norton, 2001); Charles C. Haynes and Warren A. Nord, *Taking Religion Seriously Across the Curriculum* (Alexandria, VA: ASCD and First Amendment Center, 1998); Charles C. Haynes et al., *First Freedoms: A Documentary History of First Amendment Rights in America* (New York: Oxford, 2006).

Warren A. Nord

Hodge, Charles

Historians have often pointed out that most Protestants supported the creation of common school systems in the mid-1800s. They did so because they believed that the public school with its pan-Protestant character evidenced by Bible reading without comment, for example, would help maintain a Protestant Christian culture in the face of increasing religious pluralism spurred in large measure by the growing number of Roman Catholics. Protestant support for public education, however, was neither unanimous nor unequivocal. Some heirs of the Reformation expressed reservations about the extent of the government's role in education and the gradual secularization of common schooling. One such Protestant was Charles Hodge (1797–1878), a well-known

Presbyterian theologian, who taught at Princeton Seminary throughout a great portion of the nineteenth century.

Born in Philadelphia and immersed in Calvinism, otherwise known as Reformed theology, from his childhood education through his collegiate and seminary studies, Hodge was appointed Professor of Oriental and Biblical Literature at Princeton Seminary in 1822. Three years later he founded the *Biblical Repertory and Princeton Review* (hereafter cited as *BRPR*). During his tenure as editor for more than 40 years, Hodge transformed it into a highly respected theological journal that spoke to a wide range of contemporary issues, including popular education, Darwinism, Kant, revivalism, church-state matters, and the role of religion in the public schools. Of the 140 plus essays and commentaries Hodge contributed to the journal, at least a dozen focused on education-related topics.

Though a strong supporter of Presbyterian parochial schools and the absolute necessity of religious instruction, not mere moral education, in any worthwhile education, Hodge often asserted that the state shared responsibility with parents and the church to ensure the proper education of all children. He conditioned his support for public schooling, however, on the inclusion of meaningful religious instruction, including the use of the Bible as a textbook. The Princeton scholar dissented vigorously from the position that the state could only offer secular instruction and that Protestant Christian doctrines of sin, redemption, and salvation had no place in the common schools. Indeed, he often argued that education without biblical religion was not "neutral" but in fact irreligious or atheistic and ultimately destructive of the individual and society.

In his early essays on education, Hodge asserted that the Bible was authoritative and should be taught, not merely read, in the state schools. To neglect such instruction, he believed, would be destructive of public virtue. Parents and pastors alone could not accomplish this task. If the public schools were unwilling or unable to teach children the doctrines of sin and salvation and the "facts" of the Bible, Hodge suggested the creation of Christian schools. In 1833, for example, he wrote that if the common schools included a proper arrangement for "imparting...sound moral and religious instruction, there would be but little for us to desire in the matter of common schools." If the common schools developed in a different direction, however, Christian schools were absolutely essential.

As the state became more involved in schooling and proposals to remove religious instruction from the common schools more pressing, Hodge expressed concern that the common schools might be purged of meaningful religious instruction, that is, essential doctrines of Protestant Christianity. He was particularly critical of Horace Mann's proposal to "introduce sublime truths of ethics and natural religion." Despite his concern about the direction of common schooling, however, Hodge still embraced the public school system and hoped that all Protestants would unite behind the "doctrines of the Reformation, including inspiration of the Scriptures, justification through the atonement of Christ alone, and the resurrection of the just and the unjust."

By the mid-1840s, however, Hodge believed that the common schools were becoming increasingly "anti-Christian," that Presbyterians and others had to pay for schools that did not teach their beliefs, that secular education enforced by exclusion from public funds was unjust, and that the increasing centralization of control of common schools was "tyrannical." In an 1847 address to the General Assembly of the "Old School" Presbyterian Church, he asserted that the "time is fast coming in which all denominations of Christians will address themselves in earnest to the establishment of schools" and urged each Presbyterian congregation to establish a common school. Hodge even commended Roman Catholics for discerning the need for parochial schools before his fellow Protestants.

Eight years later, in what Lewis Sherrill calls Hodge's most mature thinking on the education question, the Princeton don published a lengthy essay in *BRPR* in which he returned to his hope that the state would play a role in the religious education of the young, especially those from unchurched families. Common schools, he maintained, should teach basic doctrines on which all Protestants agreed. For those who objected, such as Roman Catholics, Hodge recommended that they found their own schools and that as a matter of fairness parents patronizing these schools should be exempted from public school taxes or receive a share of the school fund. In essence, he proposed nineteenth-century equivalents of tax credits and vouchers as a means of addressing the growing religious pluralism of the United States. Despite his strong reservations about Roman Catholic Church and its theology, Hodge thought its schools would contribute to the public good. For those who objected to the Protestant public school but did not have access to an alternative, Hodge suggested that students be released from school when offensive material was presented or provided with alternative religious instruction. In sum, Hodge envisioned a common school system that transmitted basic Protestant beliefs and doctrines of the majority as well as various mechanisms for accommodating minorities.

Nevertheless, Hodge seemed to be coming to the realization that public schools would probably fall short of his expectations, thus requiring the creation of Christian schools with or without state support. Unfortunately, Presbyterian efforts to establish a system of parochial schools between the mid-1840s and the 1860s yielded only about 265 institutions. Greatly disappointed with this result, Hodge said very little about alternative schools after the Civil War. He seemed content to discuss the role of parents, the church, and the state in the education of the young; to urge ministers and elders to scrutinize common schools in their neighborhoods and attempt to secure Christian teachers and use of the Bible; and to establish Christian schools when common schools became unacceptable.

Charles Hodge's views on education did not change significantly over his half-century of public life. He consistently championed Presbyterian parochial schools, yet realized that the government had a significant role to play in the education of children. He objected strenuously to the elimination of regular religious instruction from public education, but came to grips with the fact that having Bible reading and Christian teachers might be all that could be expected in the common schools. That being the case, however, Hodge remained adamant that education could never be "neutral" on matters of religion. When matters of conscience arose in the context of religious instruction, he argued for accommodations and options for dissenters rather than elimination of instruction approved by the Protestant majority. Moreover, unlike most of his fellow Protestants, Hodge consistently supported distribution of tax dollars to religious schools, even those operated by the Roman Catholic Church, because such schools contributed to the education of the public.

Though Charles Hodge's carefully articulated and balanced objections to the secularization of education, the centralization of state control, and the public school system's exclusive claim on tax dollars for education and his arguments for shared educational responsibility engaged nineteenth-century readers, his work is largely overlooked in most educational circles today. Only scholars firmly rooted in the Reformed theological tradition explore his voluminous writings. *See also:* The Bible in the Public Schools; Common Ground Documents; Hughes, John; Mann, Horace; Presbyterian Schools.

Further Reading: *Biblical Repertory and Princeton Review,* 1–40 (1825–1868); James C. Carper and Thomas C. Hunt, *The Dissenting Tradition in American Education* (New York: Peter Lang, 2007); Lewis Joseph Sherrill, *Presbyterian Parochial Schools, 1846–1870* (New Haven, CT: Yale University Press, 1932); Clark D. Stull, "Education at Home and School: The Views of Horace Bushnell, Charles Hodge, and Robert Dabney" (Ph.D. diss., Westminster Theological Seminary, 2005).

James C. Carper

Homeschooling

Parent-led, home-based education (often called homeschooling), a centuries-old practice throughout the world, surprised the public and the education establishment by mushrooming from only about 13,000 K–12 students in the early 1970s to roughly 2 million in 2008 in the United States. Homeschooling has been revived in nations as disparate as Australia, Canada, Hungary, Germany, Japan, Mexico, New Zealand, the United Kingdom, and the United States. Both early writings and other public presentations related to homeschooling reveal religion as a crucial element in home education's resurgence, development, and current life.

Religion—in the broad sense of being the values, ideas, and beliefs that motivate persons' thoughts, reasoning, and actions—is behind the homeschool movement, just as it is behind all educational or schooling endeavors, whether led by atheists, evangelical Christians, Muslims, or Roman Catholics. More specifically, religion in the conventional sense of matters pertaining to metaphysics, epistemology, and axiology that center around a revelatory God has played an essential and explicit role for a majority of home-education families during the past three decades.

Origins of Modern Home-Based Education

Numerous persons involved in the early part of the homeschool movement held that their reasons for home-based education were not religious but many of the thinkers with whom they identified touched upon the religiously philosophical. For example, John Holt, a well-known pioneer of the homeschool movement, professed in a 1980 *Mother Earth News* interview that children are, by nature, smart, curious, and eager to learn and simply need to be put in the right environment where they may choose what to do. "Students who are placed in an environment where they feel safe to explore and receive help when they need it will do fine," Holt said (p. 12). He promoted a child-centered pedagogy and implicitly placed children's innate good qualities at the center of right education while relegating teaching, the purposeful and planned impartation of metaphysically correct propositions, to a lower level of importance.

Simultaneous to secular-sounding voices critiquing institutional schooling and promoting what came to be called homeschooling (or unschooling), clearly religious voices in the 1970s and 1980s were beginning to advocate home-based education. Some shared with the other homeschoolers certain pedagogical methods that were not common in institutional schools run by university-trained and state-certified teachers, but the Christians' view of the nature of humans and reasons for educating their children generally stemmed from a biblical worldview. They thought the God of the Bible gave to parents—not the state in its schools (i.e., public schools) or those operating privately run schools—the authority over and the responsibility for the teaching, training, indoctrination, and upbringing of their children, with assistance from their brethren in the church.

Pioneers of the Christian homeschool movement such as author Ray Ballmann; attorney, author, and speaker Michael Farris; speaker and author Gregg Harris; speaker, attorney, and author Christopher Klicka; program founder Paul D. Lindstrom; author and magazine publisher Mary Pride; and magazine publisher Roberta Sue Welch clearly linked parent-led education to biblical prescriptions. For example, Ballmann wrote in *The How and Why of Home Schooling* regarding reasons to homeschool: "First and foremost is the fact that the Bible states that educational responsibility lies firmly in parental hands. Deuteronomy 6 is one of the many biblical passages that explicate the child-rearing and education responsibilities of parents" (1987, p. 16). Pride, in *The Way Home,* concluded that scripture prescribes parents to be the main educators of children and wrote that as she reads "the Scriptures, *public education is not a legitimate function of government* at all" (1985, p. 98).

Development of the Movement

The homeschool population was small enough in the early 1980s that parents from a wide array of religious backgrounds needed to work together to affect public policy and legal decisions without focusing on their religious differences. As the movement advanced and grew remarkably in numbers, the homeschool community had the luxury of being able to compartmentalize in the late 1980s. That is, along with more practitioners and leaders in the movement came more local, statewide, and national networking organizations, serial publications, books, and businesses. During this time, the strongly biblical "believer" Christian voice grew significantly in visibility, numbers, percentage of the homeschool population, organization, and influence.

Since the late 1980s, research estimates have placed self-proclaimed secular, humanist, or nonreligious homeschoolers at about one-fifth of the movement's population. A small minority of homeschoolers, on the other hand, would shy away from discussions of things both philosophical and religious. But most studies show that since the mid-1990s roughly three-fourths of home-educating parents are clearly religious in the conventional sense, and the large majority of these are self-proclaimed Bible-believing Christians (e.g., evangelical, fundamentalist, or reformed Protestants) or, as a much smaller portion, Roman Catholics. Mitchell Stevens, in *Kingdom of Children,* notes that while homeschool families and advocates are not homogeneous, there is clearly a majority and dominant group of "conservative Protestants" or Christian "believers" engaged in homeschooling. The remaining families are "inclusives" or the "other homeschoolers," including Buddhists, Jews, Mormons, Muslims, New Agers, pagans, Taoists, and other religious groups, and people from a wide range of lifestyles.

Research substantiates that religious thought underlies reasons for home education for a majority of families. A government-backed study published in 2006, *Homeschooling in the United States,* found that 30 percent of parents said their most important reason for homeschooling was "to provide religious or moral instruction" to their children, and 31 percent reported the top reason was "concern about environment of other schools" that included value- and belief-related issues such as "safety, drugs, or negative peer pressure." In Brian Ray's nationwide study *Home Educated and Now Adults* of over 5,000 Americans,

77 percent of the adults reported one reason they were home educated was "religious reasons," 74 percent said one reason was so their parents could teach them "particular values, beliefs, and worldview," and 69 percent said one reason was so their parents were able "to develop character/morality" in them as children. In-depth probing in other studies shows that religious belief systems and specific values were and continue to be clearly at the root of most reasons given by parents for home education. At the same time, most parents also think they can give their children a better academic education via homeschooling than they would get in a public school. There is also some evidence that homeschooling is growing in popularity, for spiritual reasons, with minority religious groups in the United States such as Muslims (Ray, 2004).

Current Status of the Home-Education Movement

Carper and Hunt's chapter, "Homeschooling *Redivivus*" in *The Dissenting Tradition in American Education,* provided a pithy history of the modern homeschool movement as follows:

> Though initially led and dominated by parents who embraced the progressive, child-centered pedagogy espoused by critics of institutional education such as John Holt, Paul Goodman, and Ivan Illich, conservative Protestants, deeply troubled by the de facto secularism and inflexibility of mass of [sic] public education and desirous of a reinvigorated family structure, accounted for most of the explosive growth as well as the leadership of the homeschooling "movement" in the 1980s and 1990s, and the concomitant clashes with state officials regarding the right of parents to teach their own children. In the new millennium, however, parents with increasingly diverse educational philosophies/confessions/worldviews, including Jews, Catholics, Muslims, and assorted secularists, have joined the ranks of the "Anabaptists" of American education whose legal right to homeschool is now recognized in all fifty states. (2007, p. 239)

It appears the homeschool movement was continuing to grow in early 2008. In addition to homeschool families finding themselves a part of an "increasingly diverse" movement, they are recognizing that they are potentially part of a movement that increasingly recognizes the religious (and sociopolitical) nature of public schools and is not fond of what is being done in them. Related to this, four elements will likely engender further growth in the portion of Americans who home educate their children rather than send them away to a place and enterprise called school.

First, distance education initiatives in various forms are expanding in the United States. Technology, such as personal computers, and the Internet have made connections between teachers and students, who are separated by great distances, much easier and more effective than in the past. This ease and efficiency has greatly enhanced opportunities to those engaged in home education, and an above-average percentage of homeschool households use the Internet.

Second, questioning the democratic, moral, philosophical, and religious rightness of state-compelled schooling seems to be increasing. This interest has recently appeared in conventional forums in fresh ways. For example, Tom Burkard and Dennis O'Keeffe made a "case against compulsory school attendance laws" in *Home Schooling in Full View,* an easily accessible book aimed at a broad general audience, academics, and university students. And Barry Grant addressed "education without compulsion" in a widely read professional serial publication, the *Mensa Research Journal*. His thesis that compelled schooling is not well suited to a freedom-based, democratic republic has resonated with the homeschool community for decades.

The third element bolstering homeschooling is the fact that religiously conservative citizens—and others who might call themselves reasonable, socially moderate Americans—are noticeably alarmed at the continued move of public schools toward teaching increasingly younger students about value-laden topics such as human sexual orientation, family structures, premarital sexual behavior, abortion, origins of life and species, and the mention of God or gods in schools. Some have responded by fortifying their efforts to presumably "take back" the schools and make them more Christian friendly. During the first decade of the millennium, however, others are making notable efforts to urge parents to abandon the state-run school system. The reasons are clearly religious and political. For example, several members of Southern Baptist Convention (SBC) submitted various pro-Christian education resolutions to the 2004, 2005, 2006, and 2007 SBC Annual Meetings urging, among other things, that all Southern Baptists remove their children from government schools. The Exodus Mandate Project is aggressively advancing its message nationwide that "Christian children need Christian education." And the Alliance for the Separation of School and State has been promoting since 1994 the thesis that parents, and not the state at all, should be in charge of their children's education.

The fourth factor that will likely increase growth of the homeschool movement is that key organizations and individuals have become more consciously proactive, since the turn of the millennium, at spreading the philosophy and practice of parent-led home-based education. For example, the National Alliance of Christian Home Education Leadership (the Alliance) is a vibrant system of networking and support for Christian homeschool organizations and leaders involved in them. As of 2007, the Alliance had established a Web site, promotional public-relations materials, a database of articles to help home-school organizations advance homeschooling, and a new emphasis on proselytizing for parent-led education. Considering Homeschooling Ministry, an organization devoted to strengthening the reach of the private, biblical homeschooling movement in the United States, vigorously promotes parent-led education especially to parents of preschool-age children and posits the following: "It is never too early for a family to begin researching homeschooling and the importance of providing a child with a Biblical education" that leads children to a lifetime of giving glory to Jesus the Christ. And the Home School Legal Defense Association, the largest homeschool organization in the United States with over 80,000 member families, actively recruits families into the ranks of home education.

Many wondered during the 1990s whether homeschooling was a passing fad. Evidence to date shows it was not and is not an ephemeral craze. Parent-led home-based education now consists of about one-fourth of all students in private educational settings in the United States, and it continues to gain momentum as a robust and principally religious educational movement. *See also:* Dabney, Robert L.; *Pierce v. Society of Sisters.*

Further Reading: Raymond E. Ballman, *The How & Why of Homeschooling* (Wheaton, IL: Crossway Books, 1987).James C. Carper and Thomas C. Hunt, *The Dissenting Tradition in American Education* (New York: Peter Lang, 2007); Bruce S. Cooper, ed., *Home Schooling in Full View* (Greenwich, CT: Information Age Publishing, 2005); Barry Grant, "Education Without Compulsion: Toward New Visions of Gifted Education," *Mensa Research Journal* 38 (Fall 2007): 7–17; John Holt, "Teach your own children…at home," *Mother Earth News,* July/August 1980, pp. 11–14; Home School Legal Defense Association, at www.hslda.org; Christopher J. Klicka, *Home Schooling:*

The Right Choice (Nashville, TN: Broadman & Holman Publishers, 2001); National Alliance of Christian Home Education Leadership, at www.beginninghomeschooling.com; Mary Pride, *The Way Home: Beyond Feminism, Back to Reality* (Westchester, IL: Crossway Books, 1985); Daniel Princiotta, Stacey Bielick, and Christopher Chapman, *Homeschooling in the United States* (Washington, DC: U.S. Department of Education, 2006); Brian D. Ray, *Home Educated and Now Adults* (Salem, OR: National Home Education Research Institute, 2004); Brian D. Ray, *Worldwide Guide to Homeschooling* (Nashville, TN: Broadman & Holman, 2005); Mitchell Stevens, *Kingdom of Children* (Princeton, NJ: Princeton University Press, 2001).

Brian D. Ray

Hughes, John

John Hughes (1797–1866) was the foremost leader of the Catholic education movement in the middle decades of the nineteenth century. As Bishop and later Archbishop of New York, Hughes defended the right of Catholics to educate their children in parish schools. Indeed, Hughes was sufficiently confrontational that he led a highly publicized effort to gain public funds for the support of Catholic schools in the 1840s.

Born in June 1797 in County Tyrone in the north of Ireland, Hughes and his family emigrated to Philadelphia in 1816 just as young John reached manhood. Determined to become a priest, he worked as a gardener to pay for his seminary education.

In January 1838, the pope selected Hughes to assist and eventually succeed John DuBois, the aging bishop of New York. With this appointment, Hughes became the key figure in the transformation of the Church into an important force in urban educational affairs.

His combative style and unwillingness to compromise made it inevitable that Hughes would clash with city leaders over education. In fact, the bishop's campaign against the Public School Society between 1840 and 1842 received national attention in the press, and it is often considered by historians to be a turning point in the Church's effort to establish parish schools.

Hughes objected to the Protestant-oriented schools on doctrinal and cultural grounds. The public schools sponsored by the Public School Society, a charitable organization that received public funds, used only the King James Version of the Bible and taught that Catholicism was a backward, and in some cases depraved, religion.

In fact, Hughes believed that these public schools were an effort to wean Catholic children from the religion of their parents and encourage them to become Protestants. In response, he succeeded in establishing eight free schools and a few pay schools enrolling about 5,000 children, one-fourth to one-third of the Catholic children of school age in New York at that time.

Hughes realized that Catholic education for every Catholic child in New York would not be possible until he obtained additional support, most particularly a share of the state school fund. With the support of the governor, who had supported the establishment of schools taught by teachers who shared the immigrants' language and religion, Hughes petitioned the New York City Common Council for a share of the state school funds allocated to the city. The Public School Society challenged the petition as a threat to the very notion of a common school system. The Council agreed, rejected the Hughes petition, but also decided to purge anti-Catholic passages from the Public School Society textbooks. He was not satisfied, however, and wanted a share of the state school funds.

Hughes petitioned the state legislature for relief. The resulting law did not distribute funds to Catholic schools but it did end the control of state school funds by the Public School Society, put the public schools under the control of publicly elected ward commissioners, provided for a central board of education, and prohibited sectarian teaching in the schools.

The new law was no victory for Hughes. To be sure, control of New York City's public schools had changed from private to public control, but the majority of New Yorkers were Protestant and in all but a few of the city's wards, the public schools remained largely Protestant in tone and curriculum. The public schools of 1843 were much the same as those of 1841.

Yet the campaign was not a failure. Hughes had not succeeded in gaining a share of the state school fund, but there is no reason to believe he ever expected to achieve this goal. He had, however, succeeded in uniting the diverse elements of his diocese into a common cause. The school fund campaign also generated new support for parochial schools. Parish schools moved out of church basements and enrollments jumped from 5,000 students in 1840 to more than 22,000 students in 1870.

Yet this tremendous growth in parish school enrollments barely kept pace with the growth of the Catholic population as a whole. In 1870, after 30 years of sustained growth, and four years after Hughes's death, the Catholic schools were educating only a small percentage of Catholic children in New York. No matter how hard he tried, Hughes could not raise the funds necessary to provide a Catholic education for every Catholic child.

Hughes's success in bringing the public schools under public control and purging the Protestant bias from the curriculum made these institutions more appealing to Catholics than in the past. Thus John Hughes, that tireless champion of Catholic schools, should be given credit for increasing the Catholic enrollments in the public schools as well as in the parochial schools. *See also:* The Bible in the Public Schools; Catholic Schools; Common School.

Further Reading: Vincent P. Lannie, *Public Money and Parochial Education: Bishop John Hughes and the New York School Controversy* (Cleveland, OH: The Press of Case Western Reserve University, 1968); Richard Shaw, *Dagger John: The Unquiet Life and Times of Archbishop John Hughes* (New York: Paulist Press, 1977); Timothy Walch, *Parish School: American Catholic Parochial Education from Colonial Times to the Present* (Washington, DC: National Catholic Educational Association, 2003).

Timothy Walch

Humanism and the Humanist Manifestos

Historically, *humanism* has been a scholar's word, but in the culture wars of recent years it has become a fighting word. The controversy over humanism has been exacerbated by confusion, for the word can mean different things in different contexts. At least four types of humanism can be identified, but there are others as well.

Renaissance Humanism. The great humanists of the Renaissance were those scholars who recovered, translated, and taught the Greek and Latin classics, often taking from them an emphasis on civic virtue, human dignity, moral wisdom, and education. A humanistic education (the *studia humanitatis*) was an education in grammar, rhetoric, history, poetry, and moral philosophy taught by way of the classics. In time this came to be called a *classical education.*

The Humanism of the Humanities. Some scholars have claimed the term humanism for the humanities. (The words "humanism" and "humanities" both derive from the Latin *umanista,* or teacher of the classics.) When the National Endowment for the Humanities was created, it called scholars in the humanities *academic humanists.* Some scholars in the humanities have argued that a *humanistic* interpretation of persons and the world should be contrasted with a scientific or *naturalistic* interpretation of persons and the world.

Religious Humanism. Most of the great Renaissance humanists (Machiavelli would be the obvious exception) were Christians who used scholarship to deepen their understanding of the Bible and religion. They often stressed the freedom and dignity of human beings (rather than predestination and sinfulness), the power (rather than the impotence) of reason and scholarship, and the relative importance of moral action (compared with dogmatic theology). More recent *religious humanism* has come in two somewhat different varieties. The first finds its historical roots in the shift toward a more *this-worldly* orientation in Renaissance humanism; it downplays dogma and the supernatural dimension of religion, emphasizing instead human flourishing and the moral dimension of religion. The second (sometimes more conservative variety) builds on the arts and humanities, which writers, artists, and scholars have creatively used to bring together faith and reason, imagination and religion.

Secular Humanism. Secular humanism completes the shift in orientation from God and the supernatural to the human and the natural order. It emphasizes the importance of science in discrediting traditional religion, in grounding our deepest understanding of reality, and in making possible the technology necessary for ameliorating the human condition. It also draws on those (secular) liberal and libertarian ideas and ideals of the Enlightenment, including intellectual freedom, social progress, human autonomy, and the separation of church and state. Secular humanism is something more than atheism or agnosticism; it is morally committed to furthering the good of humankind.

In contemporary American culture, the idea of a secular humanism has been sharpened by the existence of a variety of *capital "H" humanist organizations,* most prominently the American Humanist Association. These organizations are relatively small, but they have achieved notoriety by way of a series of manifestos and declarations that their members have been writing, endorsing, and publishing for 70 years: The Humanist Manifesto I (from the editors of *The New Humanist,* 1933); The Humanist Manifesto II (The American Humanist Association, 1973); The Secular Humanist Declaration (The Council on Secular Humanism, 1983); and The Humanist Manifesto III (American Humanist Association, 2003). There are also declarations adopted by the International Humanist and Ethical Union—The Amsterdam Declarations of 1952 and 2002—and *The Humanist Manifesto 2000: A Call for a New Planetary Humanism* (from The International Academy of Humanism, 2000).

The manifestos range in length from 1 to 57 pages. Each consists of a statement of principles (not put forward as dogma, but as a revisable statement of broad consensus among self-identified humanists). The longer ones draw out the implications of the principles (e.g., for the economy, freedom, technology, or education) with varying degrees of specificity. They are signed or endorsed by prominent intellectuals including, in the more recent cases, a number of Nobel laureates.

While the differences among them are significant, each reflecting the concerns of its time, place, and authors, the similarities are greater: (1) While they sometimes trace the intellectual roots of humanism back to early Greek, Chinese, and Indian philosophy, they all emphasize the importance of modern science in grounding our understanding of reality, and technology in alleviating human suffering. (2) They reject traditional or dogmatic religion and supernaturalism. As the Secular Humanist Declaration puts it,

> Secular humanists may be agnostics, atheists, rationalists, or skeptics, but they find insufficient evidence for the claim that some divine purpose exists for the universe. They reject the idea that God has intervened miraculously in history or revealed himself to a chosen few, or that he can save or redeem sinners.

(3) They emphasize the social responsibility of humanists to create a better, more just, world. They ground ethics not in scripture or revelation, but in human experience, critical reason, and compassion. (4) They assert the dignity and inherent worth of all persons, and advocate democracy and broad human rights. They respect pluralism, but they do not teach moral relativism. (5) They are optimistic, affirming the possibility of moral, social, and scientific, progress. After noting the undue optimism of the first Manifesto, Manifesto II claims that

> We stand at the dawn of a new age. . . . We can control our environment, conquer poverty, markedly reduce disease, extend our life-span, significantly modify our behavior, alter the course of human evolution and cultural development, unlock vast new powers, and provide humankind with unparalleled opportunity for achieving an abundant and meaningful life.

One important difference among them is that the first Humanist Manifesto (1933) was in its own terms a religious document—albeit a very liberal one. (More than half the signers were Unitarians.) Like the later manifestos, it emphasizes the successes of modern science and the inadequacies of traditional religions. But, like John Dewey, its most prominent signer, the Manifesto distinguished between traditional religion, grounded in revelation and a supernatural God, and a religious humanism that embodies "those actions, purposes, and experiences which are humanly significant." Such a religious humanism "considers the complete realization of human personality to be the end of man's life and seeks its development and fulfillment in the here and now" rather than in any life to come.

The second Manifesto (1973) dropped this religious language, though it does say, in closing, that "These affirmations are not a final credo or dogma but an expression of a living and growing *faith*." The Secular Humanist Declaration (1983) was emphatically not a religious document; indeed, it was crafted, in part, as a response to conservative religious critics who argued that humanism was a religion (and consequently could not be taught in public schools). Manifesto III begins: "Humanism is a progressive *philosophy of life* that, without supernaturalism, affirms our ability and responsibility to lead ethical lives of personal fulfillment that aspire to the great good of humanity." (This is also the official masthead definition of humanism of the American Humanist Association.)

For many religious conservatives, the Humanist Manifestos have been symbolic of the cultural liberalism and secularism that surfaced in the 1960s. Often, the term *secular humanism* was simply a label for everything that was wrong with America, ranging from abortion and feminism to homosexuality and one-world government. There was, however, a more focused theological critique of secular humanism. As Francis Schaeffer put it in his *Christian Manifesto* (a response to the Humanist Manifestos): "*Humanism is the placing of Man at the center of all things and making him the measure of all things*" (1982, p. 23). For Tim LaHaye, we are caught up in "*a battle for the mind:* whether you will live your life guided by man's wisdom (humanism) or God's wisdom" (LaHaye, 1980, p. 9). To make man the measure of all things is symptomatic of pride, the original sin; we must submit our minds to the wisdom of God, especially as known through scripture.

Some critics talked of a *conspiracy* of secular humanists to take over America's schools. In the 1970s and 1980s, a series of controversies flared up over secular humanism in textbooks, and in 1987, Federal District Court Judge Brevard Hand ruled that 44 state-adopted textbooks in Alabama unconstitutionally promoted the *religion* of secular humanism. He argued that secular humanism constituted a broad philosophy of life, that it addressed traditional religious claims (rejecting them), and that it was taught in textbooks as a matter of faith. Hand's ruling was quickly overturned by the Eleventh Circuit Court of Appeals, and was widely criticized, but it helped give impetus to a series of studies that were highly critical of textbooks for not taking religion seriously.

The perhaps paradoxical claim that *secular* humanism constituted a *religion* was, in part a legal strategy given some force by a famous footnote in the Supreme Court's ruling in *Torcaso v. Watkins* (1961) listing secular humanism as one of the many religions of America. (Similarly, in his majority ruling in *Abington v. Schempp* [1963], Justice Tom Clark warned that public schools could not teach a *religion of secularism*.) While most scholars have rejected the claims that secular humanism is a religion and that schools teach it, the religious critique of humanism does raise important questions about the nature of religious neutrality and the extent to which schools nurture acceptance of a secular worldview, perhaps uncritically. *See also:* Dewey, John; Secularism.

Further Reading: Alan Bullock, *The Humanist Tradition in the West* (New York: Norton, 1985); Jeaneane Fowler, *Humanism: Beliefs and Practices* (Portland, OR: Sussex Academic Press, 1999); *Free Inquiry* (published by the Council for Secular Humanism); *The Humanist* (published by the American Humanist Association); Paul Kurtz, *Humanist Manifesto 2000* (Amherst, NY: Prometheus Books, 2000); Paul Kurtz, *Skepticism and Humanism: The New Paradigm* (New Brunswick, NJ: Transaction Publishers, 2001); Tim LaHaye, *The Battle for the Mind* (Old Tappan, NJ: Revell, 1980); Warren A. Nord, *Religion and American Education* (Chapel Hill: The University of North Carolina Press, 1995); Francis Schaeffer, *A Christian Manifesto* (Westchester, IL: Crossway, 1982).

Warren A. Nord

I

Intelligent Design

The debate over Intelligent Design (ID) predates Christianity and traces to the Greek and Roman philosophers. Many famous Christian philosophers and theologians have supported the design argument, including Thomas Aquinas and William Paley. Prior to Darwin, an ID paradigm thrived in the natural sciences. In the past 20 to 30 years, a small though increasing number of scientists have supported ID, as have a number of philosophers, including the noted agnostic philosopher Antony Flew.

In 1897, Oxford scholar F.C.S. Schiller wrote that, "the process of Evolution may be guided by an intelligent design." But the term "Intelligent Design" may have been coined in its modern scientific usage by the nonreligious cosmologist Fred Hoyle, who in 1982 argued that "biomaterials with their amazing measure of order must be the outcome of intelligent design" (1982, p. 28). Soon thereafter, the term was adopted by chemist Charles Thaxton and biochemist Dean H. Kenyon, and the modern ID movement was born when Thaxton, Kenyon, and other scientists convened at a 1993 conference in Pajaro Dunes, California.

According to its leading proponents, ID is a scientific theory holding that some aspects of the natural world are best explained by an intelligent cause rather than a blind, undirected mechanism like natural selection. All scientists agree that nature exhibits design. Neo-Darwinists contend that this is merely *apparent design,* the result of random mutation and unguided natural selection. Design theorists argue that design in nature is *real* and *detectable.* According to proponents, ID is a historical science using the uniformitarian principle that the present is the key to the past. Design theorists observe intelligent agents (like humans) to discover cause-and-effect relationships between intelligence and the origin of information. They then study natural objects to *infer* where intelligence is the best explanation for the origin of natural phenomena.

According to mathematician William Dembski, a defining feature of intelligent agents is their ability to generate *complex and specified information*. An event is *complex* if it is unlikely and *specified* if it conforms to some independent pattern. While

Neo-Darwinism relies upon the blind process of natural selection, ID relies upon a mechanism with foresight: *intelligent selection*. ID is therefore not simply a negative argument against Darwinian evolution, nor is it an argument from ignorance. Rather, ID uses a positive argument based upon detecting in nature the types of complexity known to come only from intelligence. Stephen Meyer thus explains that, "Our experience-based knowledge of information-flow confirms that systems with large amounts of specified complexity (especially codes and languages) invariably originate from an intelligent source from a mind or personal agent" (2004, p. 233).

A special form of specified complexity is irreducible complexity. According to biochemist Michael Behe, irreducible complexity exists in a system composed of several interacting parts that contribute to the basic function, wherein the removal of any one of the parts causes the system to effectively cease functioning. ID proponents contend that irreducible complexity challenges Darwinian evolution and represents an informational pattern that, in experience, results only from design.

Design theorists argue that various lines of scientific evidence support ID, including the language-based digital information encoded in DNA, irreducibly complex molecular machines, and the abrupt appearance of new biological information in the fossil record. ID proponents contend their approach resolves questions within systematics and genomics regarding organismal relationships and the purpose of "junk-DNA." ID proponents also detect design in the fine-tuning of the physical laws of the universe that permit the existence of life.

Despite the fact that design theorists claim to infer design using the scientific method and employing no theological presuppositions, many critics regard it as a religious viewpoint. Such charges often stem from conflating the propositions of a scientific theory with the metaphysical implications many draw from science.

Without question, many theists would regard ID as friendly towards their religious viewpoint. But if ID carries larger religious or metaphysical implications for people, this makes it no different from Neo-Darwinian theory, which is widely regarded as legitimate science. One popular evolutionary biology textbook explains that Darwinian evolution employs "undirected, purposeless variation" and the "uncaring process of natural selection," thus making "theological or spiritual explanations...superfluous" (Futuyma, 1998, p. 5). Similarly, the famous Oxford evolutionary biologist Richard Dawkins asserts that "Darwin made it possible to become an intellectually fulfilled atheist" (1986, p. 6). Clearly both ID and Neo-Darwinism have larger philosophical implications for many people. Yet both theories make their claims using only empirical data. Religious (or anti-religious) implications do not disbar either theory from being scientific.

ID aims to take a strictly scientific approach and does not attempt to address theological questions about the designer. For example, the genes encoding the irreducibly complex bacterial flagellar motor may indicate that it arose by design, but they do not determine whether the designer was natural or supernatural, nor do they identify the designer.

Critics allege that ID proponents are dishonest because they purportedly refuse to admit they believe the designer is God. Yet design proponents appear quite open about their personal views on the designer. Phillip Johnson, for example, freely admits that he believes the designer of life is the God of the Bible, but explains that this is his personal religious view and not a conclusion of ID. Thus ID's position does not stem from an attempt to be "coy," but rather demonstrates that ID aims to respect the limits of scientific inquiry.

ID is also different from creationism. Creationism is widely associated with attempts to confirm the Bible and postulate a supernatural, divine creator. Yet ID has attracted proponents from diverse religious viewpoints, ranging from agnosticism to Buddhism, Christianity, Islam, and Judaism. Such a movement is clearly not united by an attempt to prove some scriptural interpretation or a religious viewpoint.

Critics allege that the term "Intelligent Design" was invented to evade the 1987 *Edwards v. Aguillard* U.S. Supreme Court ruling that declared creationism unconstitutional. ID proponents assert that this historical account is suspect. First, "Intelligent Design" was advocated by noncreationist scientists prior to the Court's ruling. Second, the Court declared creationism a "religious viewpoint" because it postulated a "supernatural creator." Yet during the *Kitzmiller v. Dover* lawsuit, discussed below, ID proponents contended their theory has always lacked this characteristic, explaining that they preferred "Intelligent Design" terminology over creationist terminology because ID sought to scientifically investigate only the natural realm and not address theological questions about the identity or nature of the designer.

Leading ID organizations such as Discovery Institute oppose mandating ID in public schools because it politicizes this debate, which they aim to preserve as a discussion among scientists. Contrary to widespread reports, ID has never been adopted into the science standards of states such as Kansas, Ohio, or South Carolina. Rather, those states required teaching scientific criticisms of evolution without mandating the teaching of alternative views like ID.

The first attempt to mandate ID in schools occurred in October 2004, when the Township of Dover, Pennsylvania, required that teachers read a short statement to students in biology classrooms that advocated ID. Aided by the American Civil Liberties Union, 11 parents filed suit against the Dover Area School District seeking an injunction against the disclaimer, and also asking that a pro-ID textbook, *Of Pandas and People,* be banned from Dover science classrooms. After a six-week trial, district court Judge John E. Jones found that the Dover School Board members had religious motives, that ID was a religious viewpoint, and thus that it is unconstitutional to teach in public schools. *Kitzmiller v. Dover* (2005) is not binding precedent upon the parties outside of the case, and the ruling was not appealed because pro-ID Dover school board members were voted out of office soon after the trial ended.

Critics of ID praised the judge for his ruling, while proponents of ID agreed with Judge Jones's finding that the school board had religious motives, but charged, along with some anti-ID legal scholars, that Judge Jones improperly decided expansive questions about whether ID is science that were unnecessary for resolving the case. ID proponents also maintained the ruling misrepresents ID by assuming that it requires supernatural causation and wrongly asserting that ID is not supported by any peer-reviewed scientific papers, data, or research.

While the teaching of ID within science classrooms is strongly opposed by critics, some leading opponents of ID have claimed it could be discussed in religion or philosophy courses. In January 2006, a public school district in El Tejon, California, acted upon such reassurances and approved a high school elective philosophy course covering ID. The district maintained the course merely taught *about* ID, just as it is permissible for public schools to teach about any viewpoint, whether religious or otherwise. Opponents of the course contended it actively endorsed ID and sued. The case was settled before any trial, with the district being forced to cancel the course and promise to never teach "any other course" that promotes ID. It is still unclear precisely how ID may be taught in nonscience philosophy or social science courses in public schools.

The Supreme Court's test for religious establishment requires that the "primary effect" of a government policy neither "advance" nor "inhibit" religion. Critics argue ID is unconstitutional because it is an inherently religious view with a primary effect that advances religion. A long-standing legal doctrine holds that "secondary" or "incidental" effects can touch upon religion without rendering a government policy unconstitutional. ID proponents argue that because ID uses scientific methods to make its claims, any constitutional effects upon religion are secondary, not fatal primary effects. They argue that teaching ID should be treated no differently from teaching Neo-Darwinism, which has secondary effects that touch upon religion but is constitutional because its primary effect advances scientific knowledge.

The debate also raises questions about whether public school teachers have academic freedom to teach about ID. Courts have affirmed the rights of teachers to teach science, but secondary school teachers have been denied discretion to teach outside of the prescribed curriculum when administrators have reasonable concerns about constitutional violations. A teacher's academic freedom to teach ID may largely turn on whether it is a scientific or a religious viewpoint, and whether his actions are supported by administrators in the school district. *See also:* Creationism; Evolution; *Kitzmiller v. Dover Area School District;* Science and Religion.

Further Reading: John Angus Campbell and Stephen C. Meyer, eds., *Darwinism, Design, and Public Education* (East Lansing: Michigan State University Press, 2003); Richard Dawkins, *The Blind Watchmaker: Why the Evidence of Evolution Reveals a Universe Without Design* (New York: W. W. Norton, 1986); William A. Dembski, *The Design Inference: Eliminating Chance Through Small Probabilities* (Cambridge: Cambridge University Press, 1998); David K. DeWolf, John G. West, and Casey Luskin, "Intelligent Design Will Survive *Kitzmiller v. Dover,*" *Montana Law Review* 68 (Winter 2007): 7–57; David K. DeWolf, John G. West, Casey Luskin, and Jonathan Witt, *Traipsing into Evolution: Intelligent Design and the* Kitzmiller v. Dover *Decision* (Seattle: Discovery Institute Press, 2006); Douglas Futuyama, *Evolutionary Biology,* 3rd ed. (Sunderland, MA: Sinauer Associates, 1998).Fred Hoyle, *Evolution from Space* (Hillside, NJ: Enslow Publishers, 1982).*Kitzmiller v. Dover Area School District,* 400 F. Supp. 2d 707 (M.D. Pa. 2005); Stephen C. Meyer, "The Origin of Biological Information and the Higher Taxonomic Categories," *Proceedings of the Biological Society of Washington* 117 (2004): 213–239; National Academy of Sciences, *Science and Creationism: A View from the National Academy of Sciences,* 2nd ed. (Washington, DC: National Academy Press, 1999); Eugenie C. Scott and Glenn Branch, eds., *Not in Our Classrooms: Why Intelligent Design Is Wrong for Our Schools* (Boston: Beacon Press, 2006); Jay D. Wexler, "Kitzmiller and the 'Is It Science?' Question," *First Amendment Law Review* 5 (2006): 90–111.

Casey Luskin

Ireland, John

John Ireland (1838–1918), Archbishop of St. Paul from 1888 until his death in 1918, was the foremost advocate of compromise between Catholic educational values and public schools at the turn of the twentieth century. Always outspoken, Ireland alienated a conservative faction within the American hierarchy that sought to pressure Catholic parents to support parish schools. The conflict came to a head in 1891 when Ireland championed a compromise school plan in two small communities in Minnesota that encouraged Catholic children to attend public schools.

John Ireland was born in County Kilkenny, Ireland, in 1838, the son of a carpenter. As an 11-year-old, Ireland and his family emigrated to the United States and ended their journey in St. Paul, Minnesota. A bright child, young John was sent to study in France and was ordained a priest in 1861. The young priest was a passionate unionist and served a stint as a chaplain during the Civil War. After the war, Ireland was curate and rector of the cathedral in St. Paul and was made a coadjutor bishop in 1875. He became Bishop of St. Paul in 1884 and Archbishop in 1888.

Ireland's philosophy of education was but one aspect of his larger view of the relationship between the Church and American society. In fact, Ireland devoted his life to eliminating the sources of conflict between Catholics and non-Catholics and sought ways to unite the Catholic Church with American values.

To Ireland's thinking, most of the conflict between his Church and his nation had nothing to do with Church dogma or values, but was fostered by the cultural baggage of the foreign immigrants who dominated the American Church in the nineteenth century. As these immigrants became increasingly American, so also would Catholicism become an American religion. It is not surprising, therefore, that Ireland used every means available to encourage Americanization among his flock.

One means to Americanization was education and Ireland's views on education were the most liberal among Catholic Church leaders. Should the Church seek out cooperative educational ventures with the public schools or should parents be *required* to build and support parish schools? Ireland favored the former position.

As long as this issue was discussed in private, there was an uneasy peace between the liberals and the conservatives. But in 1890, at the annual meeting of the National Education Association, Ireland spoke out on the relations between "state schools and parish schools" and the truce was broken. The speech precipitated a controversy that was a hallmark of misunderstanding and bitter feelings.

His plan would use public funds to support Catholic teachers to instruct Catholic children on secular subjects in classrooms located in parish buildings. The hours from nine to three would be devoted to secular subjects; religion would be taught after the end of the school day. Ireland never claimed that these hybrid schools were substitutes for parish schools, but he did hope that the plan would ensure the religious as well as the secular instruction of children in parishes that would not or could not support parish schools. He believed that this plan offered the hope of a viable working relationship between the public and the parochial schools.

What made Ireland's ideas so controversial was the enthusiasm and support the archbishop expressed for the principles of public education. Although conservatives saw Ireland's support for public education as a plot to undermine the existing parochial school system, he saw nothing wrong with his ideas and he gave his permission to pastors in the small communities of Faribault and Stillwater, Minnesota, to sign agreements with local school boards to implement cooperative educational programs for Catholic children.

The Vatican agreed with Ireland. After months of investigation and consideration, the pope issued a statement that acknowledged the fundamental righteousness of the school legislation of the plenary councils of Baltimore, but also noted that the Faribault Plan could be "tolerated."

Conservative Catholics protested with great vigor, but the response was a disappointment to them. In May 1893, the pope wrote to Cardinal James Gibbons to tell him and the other American bishops that the Vatican saw no conflict between the Faribault Plan and the mandates of the Third Plenary Council of Baltimore.

But after more than three years of acrimony, the differences between Ireland and conservatives remained. More importantly, the conservatives felt betrayed. They feared, with some justification, that Catholic children by the thousands would drift away from parish schools.

The pope's decision to tolerate the Faribault plan was more than a vindication of Ireland or a victory for the liberals. It emphasized the harmony that existed between the Catholic Church and the American ideals of public education. It was an extraordinary achievement for Ireland and marked an end to the combative educational policy instituted by John Hughes more than 50 years earlier. *See also:* Catholic Schools; Faribault-Stillwater Plan; Gibbons, James Cardinal.

Further Reading: Marvin R. O'Connell, *John Ireland and the American Catholic Church* (St. Paul, MN: Minnesota Historical Society Press, 1988); Daniel Reilly, *The School Controversy, 1891–1893* (New York: Arno Press, 1969); Timothy Walch, *Parish School: American Catholic Parochial Education from Colonial Times to the Present* (Washington, DC: National Catholic Educational Association, 2003).

Timothy Walch

Islamic Schools

The growth of private, full-time K–12 Islamic schools in the United States is a story of two distinct groups, the Sister Clara Muhammad Schools (SCMS) and the immigrant community-based schools (ICS), which began and developed very differently but are growing more similar over time. Furthermore, both groups grew their schools out of a desire common to most private schools—to provide a holistic, identity-shaping educational experience in which the child's spiritual education reflects the religious beliefs and values of the parents.

There are between 235 and 240 full-time Islamic schools in the United States that serve between 26,000 and 35,000 students. Predominately pre-K–8 with an average of 121 students or fewer, they are located primarily in urban/suburban areas. Close to half of them are completely independent of a mosque or other entity, and 85 percent were founded less than ten years ago, with most SCMSs significantly earlier. Over two-thirds are expanding or constructing their school building (Keyworth, 2006, pp. 7–13). All teach Qur'an memorization and understanding, and many offer in-depth Arabic language instruction. They are seeking accreditation, concerned about increasing professional development, and constantly looking for ways to increase revenues. Their students are given standardized tests and participate in community service, interfaith dialogue, and typical after-school activities such as sports, Girl and Boy Scouts, and tutoring. In general, they are fairly typical of the average religious school in the United States.

The Sister Clara Muhammad Schools

The development of the SCMSs closely follows that of the Nation of Islam (NOI). Begun in Detroit in 1932 by Sister Clara Muhammad, wife of NOI leader Elijah Muhammad, the schools were initially named *University of Islam* to emphasize the universal and advanced nature of the curriculum, although they were elementary and secondary schools (Rashid and Muhammad, 1992, p. 178). Most American schools at the time were segregated and openly racist, and the University of Islam/SCMSs offered African American children a chance to form nascent identities, shielded from the stunting, contorting forces of racism. "Our children should be trained in our own schools, not dropped into the schools of the enemy where they are taught that whites have been and forever will be world rulers" (Muhammad, 1965, p. 171). These were the first, and for 30 years the only, schools in which all aspects of teaching/learning were imbued with a sense of the naturalness of the black people's worldwide and historical contributions.

Reflecting the organizational structure of their NOI "parent," these schools were fairly centralized in their curriculum, administration, and development. The 1940s, 1950s, and early 1960s saw their fledgling growth as the NOI established itself in major metropolitan areas. The schools were integral to that development, part of a centralized protocol whereby a new community's initial steps were to establish a temple [mosque] *and* a school. This was not the pattern immigrant-based schools would follow in the 1980s and 1990s.

As the University of Islam/SCMSs grew, however, so did their exposure to mainstream Islam (henceforth "Islam") and the inherent conflict that arose around two core beliefs: the oneness of God and the priority of race. The NOI believes that, "Allah (God) appeared in the person of Master W. Fard Muhammad, July, 1930, the long awaited 'Messiah' of the Christians, and the 'Mahdi' of the Muslims" (Muhammad, 1965, p. 164). Islam, on the other hand, teaches the oneness of God (no forms incarnate) and the Abrahamic line of prophets that ends with the Prophet Mohammed. Furthermore, NOI believes in the superiority of blacks over "white devils," a doctrine that is in direct opposition to the Qur'an; 49:13 (A. Z. Hammad's translation) says,

> O humankind! Indeed, We have created all of you from a single male and female. Moreover, We have made you peoples and tribes, so that you may come to know one another. And, indeed, the noblest of you, in the sight of God, is the most God-fearing of you.

These doctrinal alterations would eventually bring the University of Islam/SCMSs to a crisis.

Despite the turmoil of Malcolm X leaving the NOI for mainstream Islam, the mid-1960s marked a time of growth for the University of Islam/SCMSs. Then, in 1975, Elijah Muhammad died and left his son, W. D. Mohammed, to lead the NOI. W. D. Mohammed, however, had grown up studying the Qur'an and concluded that the NOI was espousing beliefs contradictory to Islam. Consequently, he began a stunning transition of the NOI to mainstream Islamic beliefs that impacted the SCMSs profoundly.

As W. D. Mohammed aligned foundational beliefs with Islam, restructured the University of Islam curriculum and organization, and renamed the schools in honor of his mother, Sr. Clara Muhammad, the restructuring created enormous organizational stress. Many schools grew stronger and independent, but some grew weak. Overall, the number of schools decreased from 41 schools in 1975 to 38 schools in 1992 to 23 by 2008 (Rashid and Muhammad, 1992, p. 183; Keyworth, 2008, p. 1). These remaining schools, however, are vibrant, energetic, and growing, having built independent support bases and proven to be essential community assets.

The Immigrant Community-Based Schools

Part of the stimulus for the mid-1970s cataclysmic change in the SCMSs was the increased exposure to mainstream Islam, amplified by the growing number of Muslim immigrants. These immigrants were initially intrigued by the NOI but affronted by its un-Islamic doctrines. It is unknown to what extent issues of race might have impacted that reaction. Furthermore, the NOI felt equally offended by the immigrants' unquestioning embrace of that same racist system against which the NOI was struggling. These fundamental differences created a mutual mistrust and turning away that both communities are only just now addressing.

Similar to the SCMSs, the ICSs sought to create a learning environment rich with Islam, Arabic language, and the Qur'an. But the similarities ended there, as the immigrants identified more with the dominant white society than with minorities, despite oftentimes distinctive appearances and desire for a more "moral" American milieu. The first ICSs began around the late 1970s in the New York/New Jersey area. Surprisingly, schools struggled from weak community support created by complex attitudes many immigrants held toward the West. Consequently, and unlike the NOI, immigrant communities focused first on building mosques and then schools.

Throughout the 1980s, however, a growing awareness by immigrants of the problems their children faced in public schools, coupled with an increasing financial ability (impacted by U.S. immigration policies), led to a phenomenal growth of ICSs in the 1990s. From 50 schools in 1987 to about 208 in 2008, the ICSs developed and are now governed independently (45 percent), semiautonomously (21 percent), and mosque-based (29 percent) (Keyworth, 2006, p. 12). It is important to point out that these schools are governed and financed fully by their communities and not from overseas, although many communities sought one-time donations from overseas to finance building construction.

The typical internal governance of founding an ICS is particularly interesting. Given the fact that a school is often involved with neighborhoods and school districts, the founding boards of these schools realized they needed someone who was well-educated, spoke English as a native language, and could move fluidly between the immigrant and local communities. Since very few first generation children of immigrants were old enough, the logical choice was the American-Muslim convert. Subsequently, converts—particularly women—carried out much of the founding work of ICSs in numbers far greater than their occurrence in the American-Muslim population, carving out positions of leadership and shaping the core and direction of American Islamic education.

Problematically, most immigrant communities were not generally familiar with the American cultural behaviors and expectations governing professional relationships, nor were they used to women in leadership positions. This slowed their stability and growth. Male immigrant educators suffered equally as school boards struggled to become more professional in order to retain their principals and faculty. ICSs are now more comfortable with women in leadership positions. Additionally, they are finding more effective ways to address the misperceptions in their own Muslim communities about the quality of education they offer by using savvier public relations techniques that stress their low student to teacher ratio, higher test scores, and acceptance of their graduates to prominent universities. In short, the ICSs are coming of age.

Current Issues Faced by Both SCMSs and ICSs

Today the challenges faced by both groups of schools—growth and improvement—are far more similar than different and result from an increasing demand for Islamic education. The schools are finding solutions to their challenges in interesting ways. For example, to lessen the enormous expense of a high school, some are partnering with community colleges and offering dual enrollment—students can graduate high school with two years of college already completed. Some Islamic schools are also Montessori schools. A few are taking advantage of their private status to create schools that break the public schooling mold, focusing on individualized instruction, self-directed and experiential learning, nongrade learner groupings, and progressive forms of curriculum design more in line with the American private school tradition.

Gradually the ICSs and the SCMSs are realizing that in their search for the spiritual core of their Islamic curricula there is much to learn from each other. The SCMSs have spent the better part of a century refining their efforts to build a positive Muslim identity strong enough to withstand a sometimes destructive dominant society. Muslim children, post 9-11, need to possess a strong and positive sense of self as the schools reach out to the larger community. Equally, the ICSs are skilled at presenting clear Islamic doctrine, sharply focused on core teachings. When combined, the strong identity and spiritual clarity better equip American Muslim children to contribute to and enrich American society.

Islamic schooling in the United States is a story born of necessity and nurtured on determination. There is every reason to believe the schools will continue to grow as they learn from their mistakes, come together as a nationwide community, and reap the benefits of their students' accomplishments. Islamic schools are an American success story. *See also:* Islamic Schools League of America.

Further Reading: Seema Imam, "Islamic Schools in America: The Way Ahead," *Al Jumuah Magazine* 19 (January/February 2007): 24–34; Sha'ban M. Ismail, *In-Depth Study of Full-Time Islamic Schools in North America: Results and Data Analysis* (Plainfield, IN: Islamic Society of North America, 1989); Karen Keyworth, "Sister Clara Muhammad Schools" (2008), and "Islamic Schools: Data Based Profiles" (2006), Islamic Schools League of America, at www.4 islamicschools.org; Elijah Muhammad, *Message to the Blackman* (Chicago: Muhammad's Temple No. 2, 1965); Nation of Islam, at www.noi.org; Nation of Islam Settlement No. 1, at www.seventhfam.com; Hakim M. Rashid and Zakiyyah Muhammad, "The Sister Clara Muhammad Schools: Pioneers in the Development of Islamic Education in America," *Journal of Negro Education* 61 (Spring 1992): 178–185.

Karen E. Keyworth

Islamic Schools League of America

The Islamic Schools League of America states as it vision: *The Islamic Schools League of America envisions and works towards the day when Islamic schools will be the preferred centers for learning and leadership that nurture and encourage America's youth to develop their innate creativity and inquisitive nature in the pursuance of academic excellence while anchoring their hearts and souls in a moral framework of a God-centered life.*

The idea for the Islamic Schools League of America (the League) was conceived during a conversation between Judith Amri, parent of children in an Islamic school, and Karen Keyworth, founding principal of an Islamic school. Incorporated in 1998 in Virginia, it is a 501 c (3) organization dedicated to facilitating the work of full-time K–12 Islamic schools and Muslim educators. Today, the League has an eight-member board and is making the transition from a start-up organization to an established institution.

The League began its work with two main projects: first, creating a virtual community for educators in the schools, and second, establishing and maintaining an accurate and current list of the full-time K–12 Islamic schools in the United States and Canada. Because the League was run by volunteers, these two projects would consume most of the League's limited resources for the first five years.

The virtual community began in the form of a list serve called the Islamic Educators Communication Network (IECN), which was and remains the League's primary platform for its virtual community. Beginning with 30 members in 1998, today it connects approximately 450 Islamic school educators across the United States and Canada.

The IECN was carefully crafted to provide a dynamic and safe place for Muslim educators to connect, learn, share, and grow. The list is "closed," requiring prospective members to indicate their school affiliation to be admitted. This was done for a very important reason that, in retrospect, has proven wise. In the late 1990s, most Muslim communities reflected the culture of their dominant immigrant group, which was often further influenced by a highly conservative trend. This resulted in strongly conformist religious people who were outside the field of education attempting to impose the most restrictive interpretation of Islam on the budding Muslim education community. This was stifling the growth of an independent and "homegrown" Islamic education milieu in the United States.

The League knew that to ensure the development of a grassroots Islamic education community with its own unique philosophy and authentic "voice," such stifling elements would have to be kept at arm's length while those working directly in education would be given an open forum to connect with one another, solve problems, and share ideas and resources. The result has been that over the past ten years, a vibrant and independent professional community of Muslim educators has developed. The unfettered discussions in which ideas could be fully and critically explored have facilitated the development of a Muslim education philosophy that is wholly Islamic, while uniquely American.

The second main project of establishing an accurate and current list of the full-time K–12 Islamic schools in the United States was completed when the bulk of the schools were verified in 2004. Since then, the list is vigilantly maintained by actively seeking out and adding new schools, culling out closed schools, and updating information that has changed. While this seems fairly straightforward, it took several years to complete and proved a daunting task. The League now has the most accurate and complete listing of full-time Islamic schools ever compiled, establishing that as of 2006 there were 235 full-time Islamic schools in the United States, serving approximately 32,000 students (Keyworth, 2006, p. 1). Although not anticipated initially, this one accomplishment has become an important springboard for further research critical to Islamic education in the United States.

The League serves the schools through a variety of services and projects, some of which are articulated here. The League launched its Web site www.4islamicschools.org in 2002, offering a wide range of resources such as job openings, current research, research archives, school achievements, grant information, reviewed reading lists for students, a professional periodical (*The Quarterly*), and much more. In 2006, the League partnered with National-Louis University to hold its first *Leadership Conference*, focused on school accreditation. The following year, the League partnered with Georgetown University and the Graduate School of Islamic and Social Sciences to hold *Leadership Conference 2007* that explored Islamic spiritual curricula and discussed criteria for determining what serves our children's spiritual education needs. In 2008, the League began a considerable research undertaking of a multiyear, in-depth qualitative and quantitative study of the schools.

The League continues to support Islamic education by working collaboratively with Muslim organizations, the U.S. Department of Education, universities, researchers, and other groups relevant to private education such as the Council for American Private Education (CAPE). Islamic schools in America are ideally situated to strengthen the American Muslim community's own blend of intellect, modernity, and Islam as reflective of the reality in which Muslims live in the United States. The League intends to reflect that, always keeping Islam as its spiritual and moral compass and servant leadership as its philosophy. *See also:* Islamic Schools.

Further Reading: Islamic Schools League of America, at www.4islamicschools.org; Karen Keyworth, "Islamic Schools: Data Based Profiles" (2006), at www.4islamicschools.org.

Karen E. Keyworth

J

Jefferson, Thomas

Thomas Jefferson (1743–1826), principal draftsman of the Declaration of American Independence (1776), author of the Virginia Statute for Establishing Religious Freedom (1786), and third president of the United States of America, was an advocate for religious liberty and church-state separation. His church-state views have been more scrutinized and influential on law and politics than those of any other American political figure.

Jefferson was baptized and married in the Anglican Church. He attended religious services regularly, served as an elected vestryman, and was a generous contributor to his church and other religious societies. Political foes depicted him as an "infidel" or "atheist"; he called himself a Christian. Jefferson was an adherent of natural religion. He believed, in the Enlightenment's rationalist tradition, human reason was the arbiter of religious truth and rejected key tenets of orthodox Christianity, including the Bible's divine origins, the deity of Christ, original sin, and the miraculous accounts recorded in the Bible. Nonetheless, he thought the moral teachings of Jesus Christ were "the most sublime and benevolent code of morals which has ever been offered to man."

In the wake of America's independence, Jefferson led the campaign to disestablish the Anglican Church in Virginia, which he called the "severest contests" of his public life, culminating in the enactment of the Virginia Statute for Establishing Religious Freedom in January 1786. One of the most eloquent and influential American pronouncements on religious liberty, the Virginia Statute was passed following the demise of a proposed general assessment for the support of teachers of the Christian religion.

The Statute's brief operative portion disallowed civil government from compelling religious observance and removed civil disabilities against citizens for their religious beliefs and exercises. Drawing on John Locke's *Letter Concerning Toleration,* the Statute's preamble distilled Jefferson's fundamental views on religious liberty: "Almighty God hath created the mind free" and, Jefferson believed, desired that it should remain free. He thought religion was a matter solely between a man and his God, beyond the control of the civil state. "[T]he holy author of our religion, who being lord both of body and mind," he argued, chose that religion should be propagated by reason and not by coercion. Jefferson denounced "legislators and rulers, civil as well as ecclesiastical," who have impiously "assumed dominion over the faith of others" and have "established and maintained false religions over the greatest part of the world." It is "sinful and tyrannical" to compel a man to support a religion "which he disbelieves and abhors." It is even an infringement on his freedom of choice to force him to support a "teacher of his own religious persuasion," because this deprives him of the liberty of sustaining and encouraging the pastor whose moral pattern and righteousness the citizen finds most worthy of support. He maintained that "our civil rights have no dependence on our religious opinions, any more than our opinions in physics or geometry"; and, therefore, imposing religious qualifications for civil office deprives the citizen of his "natural right" to serve in public office and tends to corrupt religion by bribery to obtain purely external conformity. Civil magistrates should not suppress the propagation of opinions, even of allegedly false tenets, because "truth is great and...has nothing to fear from the conflict" with error "unless by human interposition disarmed of her natural weapons, free argument and debate." Jefferson concluded that "it is time enough" for officers of civil government "to interfere when principles break out into overt acts against peace and good order."

In a January 1802 reply to the Danbury Baptist Association of Connecticut, President Jefferson wrote that the First Amendment had erected "a wall of separation between church and state." Jefferson said he wanted to use this letter to explain why he, as president, had refrained from issuing executive proclamations setting aside days in the public calendar for prayer and thanksgiving. Because the national government could exercise only those powers expressly granted to it by the Constitution and because no power to issue religious proclamations had been granted to it, Jefferson took the position that the national government could not issue such proclamations. Insofar as Jefferson's wall was a metaphor for the First Amendment, it imposed restrictions on the national government only. Embraced by influential jurists and commentators in the twentieth century who believe the U.S. Constitution requires a separation between church and state, the "wall of separation" metaphor has had a profound influence on American law, public policy, and discourse. In the landmark 1947 case of *Everson v. Board of Education*, the U.S. Supreme Court declared that, "In the words of Jefferson," the First Amendment has erected "a wall of separation between church and State....That wall must be kept high and impregnable. We could not approve the slightest breach."

Although a proponent of disestablishment, Jefferson occasionally adopted policies employing religious means to achieve secular objectives. In Virginia's revised code, for example, Jefferson framed legislation, along with his religious freedom bill, "Punishing Disturbers of Religious Worship and Sabbath Breakers" and authorizing the appointment of "Days of Public Fasting and Thanksgiving." This last bill required "[e]very minister of the gospel," on pain of severe fines, to "perform [a] divine service" in his church on days appointed for "public fasting and humiliation, or thanksgiving." President Jefferson's refusal to issue religious proclamations is often cited as evidence that he espoused a strict separation between church and state. Less frequently noted are his "Bill for Appointing Days of Public Fasting and Thanksgiving" and his 1779 proclamation, issued when he was Virginia's governor, designating a day for "publick and solemn thanksgiving and prayer to Almighty God." Moreover, as president, he employed rhetoric in official utterances that, in terms of religious content, was virtually indistinguishable from religious proclamations issued by his presidential predecessors and by state chief executives. He also approved an Indian treaty that appropriated federal funds to compensate a Christian missionary and erect a church.

Jefferson's understanding of the separation of powers between the national and state governments (i.e., federalism) explains some apparent inconsistencies in his church-state actions. While he opposed ecclesiastical establishments, he understood that, as a matter of federalism, the First Amendment disallowed a national establishment but left states to define their own church-state arrangements. In other words, some governmental actions disallowed by the Constitution at the national level were permissible, even if imprudent, at the state and local levels.

Education policy and religion's place in education are also important themes in Jefferson's public life and writings. He believed education was an essential function of republican government insofar as a self-governing people must be well informed. In Virginia's revised code, framed in the late 1770s, Jefferson proposed "A Bill for the More General Diffusion of Knowledge," which mandated a limited public elementary and grammar school system in Virginia. It provided for three years of primary schooling in "reading, writing, and common arithmetick" for all free children, and it provided more advanced instruction at public grammar schools for a few of the "best and most promising" pupils who could not otherwise afford further education.

He also sought to place public education on a secular foundation devoid of religious dogma and superstition. Another bill in the revised code proposed reorganizing the College of William and Mary, his alma mater, as a secular institution of higher learning, liberated from ecclesiastical control and stripped of its "school of sacred theology." In order to "give fair play to the cultivation of reason" and to avoid preferring any religious sect, his plans for the University of Virginia, which he founded in his retirement years, "proposed no professor of divinity." He also stirred controversy when, in his *Notes on the State of Virginia,* he objected to "putting the Bible and Testament into the hands of the [school] children, at an age when their judgements are not sufficiently matured for religious enquiries."

Jefferson believed that God had created the human mind free and that the mind should be left unrestrained by civil government or ecclesiastical establishments. "The legitimate powers of government," Jefferson wrote in his *Notes on Virginia,* "extend to such acts only as are injurious to others. But it does me no injury for my neighbour to say there are twenty gods, or no god. It neither picks my pocket nor breaks my leg." Truth, he believed, would prevail in the open marketplace of ideas. All religious sects must stand on their own and on an equal footing in the eyes of civil government, without government favor or aid.

See also: Everson v. Board of Education of the Township of Ewing; First Amendment and the Supreme Court; Madison, James; Separation of Church and State/Wall of Separation between Church and State.

Further Reading: Daniel L. Dreisbach, *Thomas Jefferson and the Wall of Separation Between Church and State* (New York: New York University Press, 2002); *Everson v. Board of Education,* 330 U.S. 1 (1947); Edwin S. Gaustad, *Sworn on the Altar of God: A Religious Biography of Thomas Jefferson* (Grand Rapids, MI: William B. Eerdmans, 1996); Robert M. Healey, *Jefferson on Religion in Public Education* (New Haven, CT: Yale University Press, 1962); Merrill D. Peterson and Robert C. Vaughan, eds., *The Virginia Statute for Religious Freedom: Its Evolution and Consequences in American History* (New York: Cambridge University Press, 1988); Charles B. Sanford, *The Religious Life of Thomas Jefferson* (Charlottesville: University Press of Virginia, 1984).

Daniel L. Dreisbach

Jewish Schools

Jewish day schools play a strong, positive, and expanding role in the education and socialization of Jewish children in the United States. Unlike Catholic and other larger "systems" of schooling, Jewish schools are rather separated, localized, and particular to a subgroup of Jewish religious practice, ranging from the majority that are traditional-Orthodox and Chasidic Jews schools through those related to the Conservative Jewish movement (called Solomon Schechter Schools, named for the late president of the Jewish Theological Seminary in New York), to more liberal Reform Jewish day schools (Schiff, 1968). And Jewish communities have also opened schools to serve children with special needs and immigrants as "outreach programs."

Remarkably of late, the enrollment in Jewish day schools has exceeded the 200,000-pupil mark for the first time in U.S. history—with schools doubling in number in the past 40 years, from 345 schools in 1965 to over 759 schools in 2004. And recently, as the Jewish population in the United States has shifted from the urban-metropolitan centers in the Northeast and Midwest/Great Lakes to smaller towns in the West and the South, a whole new type of full-time Jewish day schools has opened, those called "community Jewish days schools" that are inclusive of all types of Jews in their region. As one report explains, "The increase reported results mainly from the establishment of new schools, notably in the Community, Chabad, and Special education sectors" (Schick, 2005, p. 1).

Still, however, two-thirds of all Jewish day schools in the United States are located in New York and New Jersey, with the remaining schools scattered across the country in growing numbers, with most (around 70 percent) being Orthodox in some fashion. As intermarriage and assimilation are the lowest among Orthodox Jews, the number of children attending their schools has grown and remained the largest among the groups in the Jewish community.

Jewish day schools also tend to be small in size, a factor of their scattered locations, family mobility, diversity of Jewish practices, and the many types of these schools. According to Marvin Schick, "Jewish day schools are among the smallest elementary and secondary schools in the U.S., a situation that is a function of our geographic dispersal and our sectarian diversity," as 40 percent have 100 students or fewer (Schick, 2005, p. 21). Regardless of size, Jewish schools are often connected to a number of national and regional associations that represent their needs and interests.

Torah Umesorah is the largest association designed to help support the Orthodox Jewish schools; Conservative schools are part of the Solomon Schechter school movement and the United Synagogue of America; and Reform Jewish schools are affiliated with the Union of American Hebrew Congregations. The Boston-based Partnership for Excellence in Jewish Education is sponsored by JESNA (Jewish Educational Services North America) that reaches across the groups, with an annual Assembly for Jewish Day School Education that "explores and promotes linkages, collaborations, and relationships that strengthen learning at both the core of the school and its periphery. Building on concepts of learning communities, the Assembly challenges school and community leaders to look simultaneously inward and outward to build multiple connections and then mobilize sufficient institutional resources to sustain learning environments" (Jewish Education Services North America, at jesna.org).

Jewish School Growth

As shown in Table 1, by 2004 Jewish schools numbered about 759 schools out of the 29,273 U.S. private schools (not counting the million-plus homeschool families), or 2.5 percent. Total enrollment in Jewish day schools in 2002 was 198,478 children of the 5.342 million private school students (Jewish "day school" students are full-time students fulfilling compulsory education requirements, as compared to supplemental Jewish schools meeting on Sundays and after school).

Table 1, column 5, presents the total growth of Jewish day schools, indicating that they have more than doubled (from 345 to 759 schools between 1965 and 2004). The enrollment had increased at a higher rate, from 73,112 to 201,789 students, or 279 percent growth in 39 years.

Table 1 also shows the breakdown and growth of Jewish schools, which are segmented into the four major types: Orthodox, Conservative, Reform, and Community Jewish day schools.

Diversity of Schools

Table 2 presents the growing diversity of Jewish day schools in 2003–2004, which is related to a number of important Orthodox Jewish groups. The Chasidim and the

Table 1   Growth of Jewish Day Schools and Enrollment, 1965 through 2004

Schools by Year	Orthodox/ Other	Conservative	Reform	Community	Total
1965	321	19	5	–	345
1990	515	58	12	23	608
1995	520	59	19	51	649
2000	530	60	22	79	691
2004	588	57	19	95	759
School Growth: 1965 to 2004: # and (%)	+267 schools (+83%)	+38 schools (+216%)	+17 schools (+340%)	+79 schools (+344%)	+385 schools (+112%)
Students by Year	Orthodox/ Other	Conservative	Reform	Community	Total
1965	68,800	3,489	823	–	73,112
1990	99,440	11,918	3,622	12,210	129,828
1995	105,168	14,589	4,233	14,849	138,839
2000	127,067	17,563	4,485	15,211	169,751
2004	128,667	17,702	4,462	17,415	201,789
Student Growth: 1965–2004: # and (%)	+59,867 students (+87%)	+12,193 students (+349%)	+3,639 students (+442%)	+5,205 students (+235%)	+125,366 students (269%)

Chabad have created a number of new, small Jewish congregations and schools, as well as the important Yeshiva or Orthodox day school movement. The largest Jewish school sectors in descending order were Yeshiva high schools, Chasidic schools, Modern Orthodox schools, Centrist Orthodox, which are all traditional; these are followed then by the Conservative (Solomon Schechter) and the Community Jewish Day schools that accept children from a range of Jewish backgrounds.

Thus, as shown in Table 2, over 150,000 out of the 201,789 students are enrolled in Orthodox schools of the four different types, indicating the primarily traditional nature of American Jewish private schools. In particular, the largest subgroup is the Yeshivot, with 195 schools, over 54,000 students, comprising over 26 percent of Jewish schools and students.

Community Changes and Jewish Schools

Similar to other types of private schools in the United States, Jewish schools work to provide a quality general education, while also teaching Jewish history, Hebrew, Talmud-Torah, and religious rituals and celebrations. Many Jewish schools also instruct about Zionism and promote strong support of the State of Israel, as they prepare the next generation of American Jewish leaders.

Important to understand is how Jewish schools reflect changes in the U.S. Jewish community, its beliefs, practices, location, and needs. Clearly, the public schools were effective for many Jews, helping them to gain a useful education, access to further and higher/professional education, and eventually an elevated socioeconomic status. Jewish

Table 2   Proportion of Jewish Schools by Association/Type for 2003–2004

Classification 2003/2004	# of Schools by Type	% of Schools by Type	School Enroll- ment by Type	% Enrollment by Type
1. Centrist Orthodox	78	10.28%	17,570	9.06%
2. Chabad	54	7.11%	8,795	4.19%
3. Chasidic	101	13.31%	48,646	23.64%
4. Community	95	12.52%	17,515	8.50%
5. Immigrant/ Outreach	30	4.00%	8,974	2.33%
6. Modern Orthodox	87	11.46%	26,634	13.21%
7. Reform	19	2.50%	4,462	2.18%
8. Solomon Schechter	57	7.01%	17,502	8.66%
9. Special Education	43	5.67%	4,451	1.03%
10. Yeshiva	195	26.70%	54,240	26.50%
TOTAL:	759	100.00%	201,789	100.00%

education, however, has always been the mainstay of the survival of the Jewish religious practices over the centuries. Few modern leaders understood this better, perhaps, than former Israeli Prime Minister and visionary David Ben Gurion who said,

> Jewish education…means deepening the Messianic vision of redemption, which stood at the center of Jewish history, which turned the eyes of the Jewish people to the future and brought it the tidings of national redemption and the reign of justice, peace and mercy for all people. (Schiff, 1993, p. 4)

Countless factors have thus influenced this dynamic growth in Jewish day school education over the past three decades. Several are worth mentioning. Formerly, American Jews (with the exception of the most fervently Orthodox) were almost universally educated in public schools a generation ago. A more recent rise in Jewish affluence, the impact of the Holocaust on world Jewry in general, and the American Jewish psyche in particular—with the birth of the modern State of Israel and its difficult emergence on the international scene—have all led, however, to a heightened sense of cultural pride and identification, bringing many Jewish students into the Jewish private school fold since World War II.

Though the core of Jewish schools is the range of Orthodox schools, Jewish education continues to diversify and expand across the United States. While assimilation and intermarriage are still a major concern, Jewish day schools are an important link with the Jewish past, as a means to maintain religious identity, continuity, and practices. Alvin Schiff saw things clearly for the future of Jewish schools in the United States as the Jewish community works to ensure growth and improvements in Jewish education when he wrote:

> Those of us who despair about the future of Jewish education should reflect on the power of the few spiritual educators who throughout the centuries have manned the classrooms of the Jewish schools and have fanned the spark of Torah. We have no right to despair, no right to self-pity, and no right to shallowness. Jewish education deserves all the devotion and intensity of which we are capable. Like all *mitzvoth* [commandments], such effort will bring its own reward. (Schiff, 1968, p. 342)

See also: Torah Umesorah (National Society for Hebrew Day Schools).

Further Reading: Jack Cohen, "New Trends in Jewish Education," in *A History of Jewish Education in America,* ed. Judah Pilch (New York: The National Curriculum Research Institute of the American Association of Jewish Education, 1969); Bruce S. Cooper, "Jewish Schools," in *Religious Schools in America: A Selected Bibliography,* ed. Thomas C. Hunt, James C. Carper, and Charles R. Kniker (New York: Garland Publishing, 1986); Harold Himmelfarb, "The Impact of Religious Schooling: Comparing Different Types and Amounts of Jewish Education," *Sociology of Education* 50 (April 1977): 114–129; Jewish Education Services North America, at jesna.org; Doniel Zvi Kramer, *The Day Schools and Torah Umesorah: The Seeding of Traditional Judaism in America* (New York: Yeshiva University Press, 1985); Eduardo Rauch, "The Jewish Day School in America: A Critical History and Contemporary Dilemmas," in *Religious Schooling in America,* ed. James C. Carper and Thomas C. Hunt (Birmingham, AL: Religious Education Press, 1984); Alvin Schiff, *The Jewish Day School in America* (New York: Jewish Education Committee Press, 1968); Alvin Schiff, *Contemporary Jewish Education: Issachar, American Style* (Dallas, TX: Rossel Books, 1993); Marvin Schick, *A Census of Jewish Day Schools in the United States 2003–2004* (New York: Avi Chai Foundation, 2005).

Bruce S. Cooper

J.M. Dawson Institute for Church-State Studies

The J.M. Dawson Institute for Church-State Studies is an academic unit of Baylor University in Waco, Texas, the largest Baptist institution of higher education in the world. The Dawson Institute was founded in 1957, and in 1959 it began publishing the highly acclaimed *Journal of Church and State*. The institute offers graduate degrees in church-state studies (Ph.D. and M.A. in church-state studies) and religion, politics, and society (Ph.D.). It also hosts conferences, public seminars, and talks, including the annual Hugh and Beverly Wamble Lecture on Religious Liberty.

Known as the "J.M. Dawson Studies in Church and State" until 1984, it was named after the great Baptist church-state separationist and defender of religious liberty, Joseph Martin Dawson (1879–1973). An ordained Baptist minister, Dawson was co-founder of Americans United for the Separation of Church and State, for which he served as its first acting director and executive secretary (1947–1948). The first full-time executive director of the Baptist Joint Committee on Public Affairs (1946–1953), Dawson left an indelible mark on Baptist social thought, linking it for decades with a brand of church-state separationism that shaped a generation of American jurists including U.S. Supreme Court Justice Hugo Black.

Dawson opposed government funding of religious institutions, including hospitals and schools, as well as the use of public schools to teach religious doctrine. As he wrote in the inaugural issue of the *Journal of Church and State,*

> What the Constitution of the United States forbids and what the constitutions of all the states forbid. . . is the making of any law or the action of any government authority in pursuance of any law that involves the interlocking of the official functions of the state (or any of its agencies) with the official functions of any church.

In 1951, Dawson was instrumental in helping to convince President Harry S. Truman not to assign a U.S. ambassador to the Vatican. Dawson found common cause with nativists and secularists in their suspicion of the influence of Roman Catholic immigrants on American public life. Writing in *Separate Church and State Now,* he asserted: "The Catholics. . . would abolish our public school system which is our greatest single factor in national unity and would substitute their old-world, medieval parochial schools, with their alien culture." In 1957, Baylor honored its distinguished alumnus and former trustee by founding the institute that bears his name.

The Dawson Institute's founding director, and brainchild, was Paul Geren, a graduate of Baylor who had gone on to Harvard to earn a doctorate. He returned to his Texas alma mater in 1956 to serve as one of its executive vice presidents. Geren was friends with R. Matthew Dawson, the son of Joseph Martin. He and the younger Dawson were teammates as undergraduates on Baylor's debate squad. After leaving Baylor in 1959, Geren's successor as institute director was James E. Wood, Jr., a Baylor religion professor who also became the first editor of the *Journal of Church and State*. Although a passionate defender of the elder Dawson's version of church-state separation, Wood's tenure as journal editor was marked by his willingness to publish and engage dissenting views with charity and respect. Under his leadership, the institute and journal welcomed scholars from a wide variety of religious traditions from around the globe.

A prolific writer, Wood served as the institute's director and the journal's editor between 1959 and 1973 and between 1980 and 1993. Between these two stints, Wood served as director of the Baptist Joint Committee for Public Affairs in Washington, D.C. In 1973, Baptist theologian James Leo Garrett, Jr. succeeded Wood as institute director and journal editor, posts Garrett held until 1980.

When Wood retired as institute director and journal editor in 1993, Baylor named as his successor one of his most accomplished church-state M.A. graduates, Derek H. Davis, a Baylor-trained lawyer with a Ph.D. from the University of Texas, Dallas. Like Wood, Davis was a prolific writer and a staunch advocate of church-state separationism and religious liberty. Among the faculty members hired for the institute under Davis's leadership were historian Barry Hankins (1996), religious studies scholar Marc Ellis (1998), and philosopher Francis J. Beckwith (2003).

Davis remained as director and editor of the journal until leaving Baylor in 2006 when he took a dean's post at the University of Mary Hardin-Baylor in nearby Belton, Texas. Succeeding Davis as director was Christopher Marsh, a Baylor political science professor and an expert in religion in China and the former Soviet Union. The journal editorship went to Wallace Daniel, a widely respected Baylor historian and classroom teacher. *See also:* Baptist Joint Committee on Religious Liberty; Separation of Church and State/Wall of Separation between Church and State; Southern Baptists and Education.

Further Reading: Wallace L. Daniel, "The Journal and the Tradition of Religion Liberty," *Journal of Church and State* 48 (Spring 2006): 265–276; Derek H. Davis, ed., *The Separation of Church & State Defended: Selected Writings of James E. Wood, Jr.* (Waco, TX: J.M. Dawson Institute of Church-State Studies, 1995); Joseph Martin Dawson, *A Thousand Months to Remember: An Autobiography* (Waco, TX: Baylor University Press, 1964); Joseph Martin Dawson, *Separate Church and State Now* (New York: R.R. Smith, 1948); Joseph Martin Dawson, "The Meaning of Separation of Church and State in the First Amendment," *Journal of Church and State* 1 (November 1959): 37–42.

Francis J. Beckwith

K

Kitzmiller v. Dover Area School District

As reflected by litigation that began with the storied "Scopes Monkey Trial," wherein the Supreme Court of Tennessee ultimately invalidated a teacher's conviction for teaching evolution on the basis that a trial court judge improperly assessed a fine that could only have been imposed by a jury (*Scopes v. State,* 1927), controversy has long surrounded how children should be taught about the origins of humankind. *Kitzmiller v. Dover Area School District* (2005) is the latest in a long line of cases, in federal and state courts, in which proponents of the biblical perspective of the origins of humanity have sought to have their beliefs taught, or at least represented, on this contentious topic.

Following Supreme Court cases wherein the justices forbade teaching in elementary and secondary science classes that was limited to the biblical notion of evolution (*Epperson v. Arkansas,* 1968), the teaching of "evolution-science" unless accompanied by instruction on "creation-science" (*Edwards v. Aguillard,* 1987), and an array of lower court rulings on this and related topics such as where a board unsuccessfully sought to place stickers on science text books essentially indicating that it disclaimed any endorsement of evolution (*Freiler v. Tangipahoa Parish Board of Education,* 1999, 2000a, 2000b), *Kitzmiller* emerged as the newest front in the battle over how the origins of mankind should be taught to children in elementary and secondary schools.

At issue in *Kitzmiller* was a local school board policy in Pennsylvania that would have required teachers to read a statement in high school biology classes that mentioned intelligent design as an alternative to Darwin's theory of evolution. Following a lengthy and well-publicized fight over the policy, the disagreement finally made its way to court.

A federal trial court in Pennsylvania, in an often harshly worded opinion, invalidated the policy in *Kitzmiller* as unconstitutional. The court struck the policy down as violating the Establishment Clause in light of two judicially created measures to assess disputes involving religion and public education. First, relying largely on the Supreme Court's rationale in *Santa Fe Independent School District v. Doe* (2000), wherein the justices vitiated a board policy that would have allowed students to select someone to pray prior to the start of high school football games, the judge held that the policy amounted to an endorsement of religion. Second, the court ruled that the policy violated the first two prongs of the Supreme Court's tripartite *Lemon v. Kurtzman* (1971) test. In *Lemon,* the Court invalidated programs from Pennsylvania and Rhode Island that basically would have provided salary supplements to teachers who taught selected secular subjects in religiously affiliated nonpublic schools. In *Kitzmiller,* the court specified that the policy was unconstitutional because its primary purpose was to change the district's biology curriculum to advance religion and it had the primary effect of imposing a religious view of human origins into the biology courses; the Court did not review *Lemon*'s third prong, excessive entanglement, since the policy violated the first two parts of the test. In addition, the court indicated that the policy violated the freedom of worship provision in Pennsylvania's Constitution.

Turning to endorsement, the court was of the opinion that the policy was unconstitutional since it was convinced that objective observers would not only have interpreted it as motivated by a religious stance but would also have likely viewed it as an official endorsement of a religious point of view. The court was also critical of intelligent design in this part of its opinion, describing it as not being science.

As to the often-applied *Lemon* test, the court traced the history of the controversy as it played out at the district level. The court determined that proponents of the policy clearly lacked a secular legislative purpose and, in fact, acted with a religious goal, namely to introduce their faith-based perspectives into classes on evolution. The court briefly declared that the policy failed *Lemon*'s effect test because in asserting that intelligent design is not science, the judge concluded that its only real effect would have been to advance religion.

The court ended its analysis by stating that the policy violated the Commonwealth's constitution. The court reached this judgment based on its assertion that the policy would have required students to be compelled to have been exposed to religious beliefs with which they may have disagreed. *See also:* Creationism; *Edwards v. Aguillard; Epperson v. Arkansas;* Evolution; Intelligent Design.

Further Reading: *Edwards v. Aguillard,* 482 U.S. 578 (1987); *Epperson v. Arkansas,* 393 U.S. 97 (1968); *Freiler v. Tangipahoa Parish Board of Education,* 185 F.3d 337 (5th Cir. 1999), *rehearing en banc denied,* 201 F.3d 602 (5th Cir. 2000), *cert. denied,* 530 U.S. 1251 (2000); *Kitzmiller v. Dover Area School District,* 400 F. Supp.2d 707 (M.D. Pa. 2005); *Lemon v. Kurtzman,* 403 U.S. 602 (1971); *Santa Fe Independent School District v. Doe,* 530 U.S. 290 (2000); *Scopes v. State,* 289 S.W. 363 (Tenn. 1927).

Charles J. Russo

Know-Nothing Party

The Know-Nothing Party was founded by Charles Allen of New York and was started as a secret society called the Order of the Star Spangled Banner in response to the apparent growth of the political influence of Roman Catholics. Membership to this society was limited to native-born Protestants, and its activities were anti-Catholic and anti-immigrant in nature. During the party's rise to prominence in the 1850s, the country was being enveloped in an influx of immigrants, particularly Catholic immigrants, and the Know-Nothings really capitalized on the fears and resentment towards the exponential immigrant growth of the day and the rise of nativism in the Protestant population already residing in the United States. The Know-Nothing Party also emerged as a significant challenger to the Democratic Party during this period of time. The power of this party was brief, with its greatest influence spanning less than a decade, but rooted in hatred—both religious and racial.

The Know-Nothing Party achieved its name by secrecy; if nonmembers asked them about the party, the standard response was "I know nothing." The party operated largely in secret throughout 1854 and 1855, though the influence of the party on congressional and state elections was remarkable. Many members were elected who had never been in public office before; several were virtually unknown and then surprisingly upstaged long-standing favorites. During this time, the secret party found itself launched into control in several states, while having a strong minority presence in others.

In 1856, the party abandoned its platform of secrecy and campaigned as the American Party. The party hit its peak in the latter half of the 1850s by electing seven Know-Nothing governors, gaining control of eight state legislatures, and establishing a strong presence in Congress. The formalization of the Know-Nothing Party resulted in the existence of three political parties during the late 1850s: Democratic, Republican, and American. Abraham Lincoln sought to distance himself from the Know-Nothing Party in the 1850s, as he felt that its tenets were exclusive and contrary to the intent of the founders of our nation. The party chose former President Millard Fillmore for their presidential nominee in 1856, and he garnered almost 22 percent of the popular vote.

A major tenet of the Know-Nothing Party was to prohibit all Catholics and immigrants from holding public office. The party sought to increase the naturalization period for immigrants from 5 to 21 years, making it more difficult for immigrants to obtain citizenship and hold public office. Members of the party feared Catholics because they perceived Catholics as being more loyal to the pope than to the United States. More radical members of the party feared that Catholics were seeking to take over the United States, strip citizens of their liberties, and place the nation under Vatican rule.

Much of the Know-Nothings' rhetoric was anti-Catholic in nature. They asserted that Catholics were bound to serve their church before their country, and that Catholics hated the Republic (partly demonstrated by their lack of support for public schools), the symbols for American freedom such as the flag and the eagle, and the Bible. Catholics protested the infusion of the Protestant Bible into public schools, and Protestants interpreted this opposition to mean that Catholics were against the Bible as well as education.

Members of the Know-Nothing Party also frequently insulted Catholic priests, and there were several incidents of violence against Catholics during the time of the party's prominence. Even before the party came into the spotlight, its members committed such acts as targeting Irish Catholics in Massachusetts when mobs burned down a convent and killed a nun in 1834. They continually used public opinion, rhetoric, and sometimes physical force to achieve their agenda. In 1854 and 1855, Know-Nothings were involved in Election Day riots that were quite serious in nature, as members of the party were blamed for voter fraud and for isolating Catholic voters and intimidating them, keeping them away from the polls. Such harassment continued in other areas of the country. In Milwaukee, for example, it was unsafe for religious sisters to wear their garments in public. Other groups of nuns were forced to relocate their communities to different areas due to Know-Nothing harassment. In addition, Catholic efforts to establish and run their own schools met with continued harassment and violence.

The majority of members of the Know-Nothing Party came from middle- and working-class backgrounds, and they feared competition for jobs from Catholics and immigrants. Hence, the Know-Nothing Party also wished to ban Catholics from holding jobs in the private sector. This resentment was also reflected in the way that schooling was approached. For example, in Ohio, many white Protestants resented the Catholic Church for opposing taxation to finance the public schools. Catholics preferred enrolling their sons and daughters in Catholic schools, and hence felt that they should not be obligated to financially support schools that their children did not attend. The Know-Nothings hence promoted and publicized the notion that Catholics were trying to get common school funds for their own schools as well as to eradicate the Protestant Bible from public schools.

As the Know-Nothings rose to prominence in the North, they continued to legislate anti-immigrant and anti-Catholic measures. One of the actions the party took was to infuse Protestant values in the classroom, such as reading the King James Version of the Bible, and to prohibit the use of common school funds for religious schools. A "nunnery inspection" law was also passed that targeted Catholic schools, which were subject to unannounced visits by committees investigating unnamed practices and occurrences, an action that certainly constituted harassment.

With the passage of the Kansas-Nebraska Act, which repealed the Missouri Compromise of 1820 that prohibited slavery north of latitude 36-30, instead allowing people in the territories of Nebraska and Kansas to decide for themselves whether or not to allow slavery within their borders, the Know-Nothing movement gained more supporters. While the Know-Nothings were originally allied with the Whig Party, the growing debate over slavery and the Kansas-Nebraska Act helped shift the focus from, and ultimately caused the decline of, the Whig Party. While they did have impressive numbers in elective offices throughout the North especially, they were fairly unsuccessful in passing significant legislation, though they introduced such bills that called for prohibiting immigration of foreign poor and convicts, as well as tried to require registration and literacy tests for voters, again aimed at keeping immigrants away from the polls. As the 1850s came to a close, however, national attention shifted increasingly from a fear of immigrants and Catholics to the issue of slavery. The Know-Nothings' fall from power was as quick as its rise. By 1860, the Know-Nothings were no longer a strong political force, and they were absorbed into the developing Republican Party. *See also:* Anti-Catholicism in Education; Nativism.

Further Reading: Tyler Anbinder, *Nativism and Slavery: The Northern Know Nothings and the Politics of the 1850s* (New York: Oxford University Press, 1992); Ray Allen Billington, "The Know-Nothing Uproar," *American Heritage Magazine* 10 (February 1959); Ray Allen Billington, *The Protestant Crusade 1800–1860* (New York: Macmillan, 1983); James A. Burns, *The Growth and Development of the Catholic School System in the United States* (New York: Benziger Brothers, 1912); Michael F. Holt, "The Politics of Impatience: The Origins of the Know-Nothingism," *The Journal of American History* 60 (September 1973): 309–331; National Catholic Educational Association, at www.ncea.org.

Staci L. H. Ramsey

Ku Klux Klan

The Ku Klux Klan was originally founded in the 1860s primarily by veterans of the Confederate army to fight against Reconstruction in southern states. As a terrorist organization it used violence to attack African Americans and white allies who sought to vote, hold office, attend racially integrated schools, or otherwise exercise the rights that the Thirteenth, Fourteenth, and Fifteenth Amendments had given them. Among its many attacks on African Americans and whites who worked with them, the Klan organized efforts to burn racially integrated schools and beat any teacher who dared to teach in one. As Reconstruction waned and segregation became the norm across the South, the original Klan essentially disappeared in the 1870s.

In 1915, however, a new Ku Klux Klan was born out of a gathering at Stone Mountain in Georgia. While the first Klan had been specifically aimed at undermining political and economic rights for former slaves, the new Klan of the twentieth century had a broader mission. In addition to ensuring racial segregation, which was its prime mission, the Klan was also opposed to Catholics and Jews, to immigration from southern and eastern Europe or Asia, and indeed to most aspects of twentieth-century modernism. While the first Klan had been a southern institution, the new Klan was national in scope with the largest membership in Indiana. By 1924, the new Klan, with its headquarters in India-napolis, reported 4 million members across the country.

Among other Klan efforts to undermine "foreign" or "racially impure" agendas was a strong press to see that the public schools of the United States reflected what its members saw as traditional Protestant and Anglo-Saxon cultural norms. The Klan leaders wanted to use the public schools to "Americanize" immigrants and the children of families, whatever their origin, who did not share the particular definition of American culture that the Klan advocated. They did not like Catholic parochial schools and saw them as a threat to their goal of developing monolithic cultural norms. And they wanted to tap every lever of state power to ensure their vision of white America prevailed. In this, as perhaps not in other campaigns, the Klan also had some very strange allies.

In Oregon the Ku Klux Klan was the leading force, along with many Protestant churches, in a campaign to essentially outlaw Roman Catholic parochial schools. A 1922 referendum in that state mandated that beginning in 1926 every child in Oregon between the ages of 8 and 16 must attend public school. While the referendum was passed by Oregon voters, the U.S. Supreme Court overturned it in 1925 before it could take effect. Writing for the majority of the Court in *Pierce v. Society of Sisters,* Justice James C. McReynolds wrote, "the fundamental theory of liberty upon which all governments in the Union repose excludes any general power of the State to standardize its children by forcing them to accept instruction from public school teachers only." Thus, the end result of the Klan's activity in Oregon was a Supreme Court ruling that would protect the freedom of religious and private secular schools for generations.

On the national stage, the Klan joined forces with others to support the creation of a federal department of education. The campaign began during World War I when patriotic fever sweeping the nation resulted in the Espionage Act of 1917 and the Red Scare of 1919. Education was not exempt from this patriotic surge. In 1918 school administrators who were leaders in the National Education Association called for the establishment of a federal Department of Education that would oversee massive new federal aid to ensure a national program of schooling focused on "American ideals and institutions." Their goal was compulsory public schooling under the guidance of the federal government to ensure that no child was infected with "alien ideals brought to them through the medium of an alien tongue."

The alliance that pushed for this expanded federal role is an odd one. It included school superintendents meeting with the National Education Association, who believed that they represented the nation's appropriate educational leadership; Masons, who wanted to ensure that a particular set of "American values" were taught to all children; and the resurgent Ku Klux Klan committed to an America that was white, Protestant, militantly anti-black, and equally anti-Catholic. Not surprisingly, the major opposition to the creation of the department and the concomitant expansion of federal involvement and support for compulsory public schooling came from the American Catholic community, people who came to see the NEA-Masonic-KKK agenda as inimical not only to their system of parish education but the very notion of religious freedom that was, for them, at the very core of American values. In the end, the Klan and its allies were defeated again. Congress did not establish a federal department of education in the 1920s. By the late 1930s, the Klan declined again although it remained a powerful force for decades, experiencing another resurgence during the civil rights era of the 1960s. *See also:* Anti-Catholicism in Education; *Pierce v. Society of Sisters.*

Further Reading: Douglas J. Slawson, *The Department of Education Battle, 1918–1932: Public Schools, Catholic Schools, and the Social Order* (Notre Dame, IN: University of Notre Dame Press, 2005).

James W. Fraser

L

Lamb's Chapel v. Center Moriches Union Free School District

The New York legislature enacted Section 414 of the New York Education Law, which pertained to the use of public school facilities. Pertinent parts of the act stated:

> Schoolhouses and the grounds connected therewith and all property belonging to the district shall be in the custody and under the control and supervision of the trustees or board of education of the district. The trustees or board of education may adopt reasonable regulations for the use of such schoolhouses, grounds or other property, all portions thereof, when not in use for school purposes, or when the school is in use for school purposes...for such other public purposes as are herein provided.

The statute prohibited the use of school facilities for religious purposes.

The Center Moriches School District passed Rule No. 7, "The School District's Rules and Regulations for Community Use of School Facilities," this rule "authorized under Section 414, social, civic, or recreational uses...and uses by political organizations." Rule 7 in compliance with the judicial interpretation of Section 414 in *Trietley v. Board of Education of Buffalo* (1978), and accepted by the U.S. Second Circuit Court of Appeals in *Deeper Life Christian Fellowship, Inc. v. Sobol* (1991), prohibited "school premises [from being] used by any group for religious purposes."

The Lamb's Chapel, an evangelical church, twice requested permission to show a six-part film series. The film series would discuss the "influences of the media that could only be counter balanced by returning to traditional, Christian family values." The school board twice denied the application to use school facilities to show the films. The church brought suit challenging the rejected application as a "violation of the Freedom of Speech and Assembly Clause, the Free Exercise Clause and the Establishment Clause of the First Amendment, as well as the Equal Protection Clause of the Fourteenth Amendment."

A federal district court rejected the church's claims and decided for the school board. When addressing the free speech claim, it said the facilities were a "Limited Public Forum." Also since Section 414 did not allow school facilities to be used for religious worship or instruction and the films were for a religious purpose, and the lower courts had previously ruled on this issue, then the facilities were not open for showing the films. Therefore, the denial of use was viewpoint neutral and not a violation of the Free Speech Clause. A federal appellate court affirmed the district court and held "when not in use for school purposes, was neither a traditional nor a designated public forum; rather, it was a limited public forum open only for designated purposes, a classification that 'allows it to remain non-public except as to specific use'...[E]xclusions in such a forum need only be reasonable and viewpoint neutral." Denial of use did not violate this standard.

In 1993, however, a unanimous U.S. Supreme Court with Justice Byron White writing for the Court ruled the school district actions violated the Free Speech Clause. The Court noted that the school district need not allow after hours use of its property as stated in the state statute. But the school board rule provided the property could be used for "social, civic and recreational" purposes, which "opened the school district to a wide variety of communicative purposes of the property [which] were subject to the same constitutional limitations as restrictions in traditional public forums such as parks and sidewalks."

The church presented evidence that the school board allowed many groups to use the school in 1987 and 1988. These included a New Age religious group, Southern Harmonize Gospel Singers, the Salvation Army Youth Band, and the Hampton Council of Churches' Billy Taylor. Since the school board allowed school property to be used for discussing all views about family and child rearing issues except those from a religious point of view, then denying Lamb's Chapel constituted viewpoint discrimination under the Free Speech Clause.

The school board argued that it could discriminate against a particular view if it violated the Establishment Clause of the First Amendment. The Supreme Court applied the *Lemon* test (*Lemon v. Kurtzman,* 1971). Since the film series was not shown during school hours, not school-sponsored, and open to the general public, there was no realistic danger that the community would believe the activity involved a government endorsement of religion. Therefore the governmental action had a social purpose, did not have the primary effect of advancing or prohibiting religion, did not foster excessive entanglement, and would not violate the Establishment Clause. If a school opens its property to be used by a wide variety of citizens, then any particular group cannot be excluded based on its particular point of view. *See also:* First Amendment and the Supreme Court; *Good News Club v. Milford Central School.*

Further Reading: *Deeper Life Christian Fellowship Inc. v. Sobol,* 948 F. 2d 79 (CA 2, 1991); *Lamb's Chapel v. Center Moriches Union Free School District,* 508 U.S. 384 (1993); *Lemon v. Kurtzman,* 403 U.S. 602 (1971); *Trietly v. Board of Education,* 409 N.Y.S. 2d 912 (1978).

M. David Alexander

Lee v. Weisman

Lee v. Weisman (1992) stands out as the Supreme Court's first, and only, decision on the merits of graduation prayer. In light of a school board policy of inviting religious leaders to pray at graduation ceremonies, administrators in Providence, Rhode Island, asked a rabbi to offer nonsectarian prayers by following guidelines prepared by the National Conference of Christians and Jews. Even so, a student and her father initially sought, unsuccessfully, to prevent the rabbi from offering the prayers. A federal trial court in Rhode Island then permanently enjoined the board from permitting graduation prayer on the ground that doing so violated the effect prong of the tripartite test that the Supreme Court enunciated in *Lemon v. Kurtzman* (1971) by creating a symbolic union between religion and the government. The First Circuit Court of Appeals affirmed the lower court's decision.

The U.S. Supreme Court's willingness to hear *Lee* was met with great anticipation for two reasons. First, it was the first time that the Court directly addressed graduation prayer. Second, since a majority of the justices sitting in *Lee* had expressed their reservations about the *Lemon* test, there was the sense that *Lee* might result in an alternative test.

Writing for a bitterly divided 5-4 Supreme Court, Justice Anthony Kennedy's majority opinion in striking down school-sponsored graduation prayer surprised most observers by virtually ignoring *Lemon*. Kennedy found it unnecessary "to revisit the difficult...questions of the definition and full scope of the principles governing the extent of permitted accommodation by the State for the religious beliefs and practices of many of its citizens." His opinion, which was not organized around clearly identified concepts, focused on two constitutional points. More specifically, Kennedy examined the relationships between the Free Exercise and Establishment Clauses on the one hand, and the Free Speech and Establishment Clauses on the other.

Justice Kennedy's view of the relationship between the Free Exercise and Establishment Clauses is reflected in his writing that "[t]he principle that government may accommodate the free exercise of religion does not supersede the fundamental limitations imposed by the Establishment Clause." He contended that there were three key factors in this regard: coerciveness, potential for divisiveness, and the place of civic religion.

Kennedy offered two arguments to support his position that school officials violated the concept of neutrality. First, he pointed to the pervasive role that school officials played in deciding to have prayer, inviting religious leaders to pray, and offering guidelines under which the prayers were composed. Second, Kennedy believed that prayer could have been coercive since the students were truly not free to absent themselves from their graduations.

Turning to the role of civic religion, Justice Kennedy initially seemed to suggest the need for a civic religion founded in a "common ground...express[ing] the shared conviction that there is an ethic and a morality which transcend[s] human invention, the sense of community and purpose sought by all decent societies." Yet, he quickly concluded that "[t]he suggestion that government may establish an official or civic religion as a means of avoiding the establishment of a religion with a more specific creed strikes us as a contradiction that cannot be accepted."

As to the relationship between the Free Speech and Establishment Clauses, Kennedy focused on what he perceived as the different mechanisms by which these rights are protected. He probably would have been better served by using an expression such as "different emphases" since free speech "is protected by ensuring its full expression even when the government participates, for the very object of some of our most important speech is to persuade the government to adopt an idea as its own." He declared that when dealing with religious expression, the government is not supposed to be a prime participant. According to Kennedy, the government oversteps its bounds when it "disavows its own duty to guard and respect that sphere of inviolable conscience and belief which is the mark of a free people." The key factors that Kennedy considered in placing different emphases on the Free Speech and Establishment Clauses were psychology and peer pressure of social conformity, the de minimis character of prayers, and the potential loss of the benefit of attending graduation that students would have suffered had they not been present. Justices Harry Blackmun and David Souter each filed concurring opinions.

Justice Antonin Scalia's dissent disagreed with the Court in four major ways. First, he asserted that the Court went "beyond the realm where judges know what they are doing. The Court's argument that state officials have 'coerced' students to take part in the invocation and benediction ceremonies is, not to put too fine a point on it, incoherent." He indicated that the silence on the part of students did not have to be interpreted as their assent to prayer. Scalia added "that maintaining respect for the religious observances of others is a fundamental civic virtue that government (including the public schools) can and should cultivate," while challenging the Court to consider how people can come together in a pluralistic society.

Scalia next maintained that the acts of school officials in inviting clergy to pray did not amount to state endorsement. Third, he criticized Justice Kennedy's historical analyses in pointing out that unlike the time when the Establishment Clause was adopted, and civil penalties could be imposed for failing to comply with state-sanctioned religious requirements, no such penalties were at issue. Finally, Scalia distinguished *Lee* from *Engel v. Vitale* (1962) and the companion cases of *School District of Abington Township v. Schempp* and *Murray v. Curlett* (1963), earlier cases involving school prayer. Scalia explained that since attendance in class, unlike at public graduation ceremonies, is compulsory, rather than optional, and parents are excluded from the former but invited to the latter, then they were inapplicable to the dispute in *Lee*. See also: *Engel v. Vitale*; Prayer in the Public Schools.

Further Reading: *Engel v. Vitale*, 370 U.S. 421 (1962); *Lee v. Weisman*, 505 U.S. 577 (1992); *Lemon v. Kurtzman*, 403 U.S. 602 (1971); *School District of Abington Township v. Schempp* and *Murray v. Curlett*, 374 U.S. 203 (1963).

Charles J. Russo

Lemon v. Kurtzman and Earley v. DiCenso

Lemon v. Kurtzman (1971), and its companion case, *Earley v. DiCenso* (1971), is the U.S. Supreme Court's most significant case involving the Establishment Clause and education. Still, as important as *Lemon* is, having been applied in more than two dozen Supreme Court cases, and seemingly countless lower court judgments, involving both state aid to students who attend religiously affiliated nonpublic schools in K–12 settings as well as higher education and disputes over prayer and religious activities in public schools, the justices have a difficult time agreeing on *Lemon*'s meaning.

Difficulties arise when the Supreme Court applies *Lemon* in cases involving aid and religious activity in light of its failure to explain how, or why, this tripartite test has become a kind of "one-size fits all" measure but leaves lower courts and educators seeking clarity. Initially, the Court created a two-part test in *School District of Abington Township v. Schempp* and *Murray v. Curlett* (1963), striking down prayer and Bible reading in public schools. Yet, the Court later expanded its two-part purpose and effect test into the Establishment Clause standard in *Lemon,* a dispute involving state aid to religiously affiliated nonpublic schools.

The confusion generated by *Lemon* is exacerbated because as membership on the Court changes, so does its jurisprudence. For example, in *Agostini v. Felton* (1997), the Court modified *Lemon* by reviewing only its first two parts, purpose and effect, while recasting entanglement as one criterion in evaluating a law's effect. Further, in *Lee v. Weisman* (1992), the Court enunciated the psychological coercion test when addressing prayer in schools.

At issue in *Lemon* was a statute from Pennsylvania that called for the purchase of secular services along with a law from Rhode Island that provided salary supplements for teachers in nonpublic schools. The law from Pennsylvania authorized the commonwealth's superintendent of education to purchase specified secular educational services from nonpublic schools. Officials then directly reimbursed the nonpublic schools for their actual expenditures for teacher salaries, textbooks, and instructional materials. The superintendent had to approve the textbooks and materials, which were restricted to mathematics, modern foreign languages, physical science, and physical education as long as they were the same materials as were used in public schools. In Rhode Island, officials were authorized to supplement the salaries of certified teachers of secular subjects in nonpublic elementary schools by directly paying them amounts not in excess of 15 percent of their current annual salaries; their salaries could not then exceed the maximum paid to public school teachers.

During the initial round of litigation, a federal trial court in Pennsylvania dismissed the challenge to the program on the bases that some of the individuals in the suit lacked standing, or the legal ability to file suit, and that the law did not violate constitutional prohibitions regarding the establishment and free exercise of religion (*Lemon v. Kurtzman*, 1969). Conversely, a federal trial court in Rhode Island held that insofar as the program resulted in excessive entanglement with religion, it violated the Establishment Clause (*DiCenso v. Earley*, 1970).

Addressing both cases as part of a consolidated appeal, and writing on behalf of the Supreme Court, Chief Justice Warren Burger invalidated the statutes. At the heart of its analysis, he enunciated a tripartite standard destined to become known as the *Lemon* test. In creating this measure, Burger added a third prong, dealing with excessive entanglement, from *Walz v. Tax Commission of New York City* (1970), wherein the Court upheld New York State's practice of providing state property tax exemptions for church property that is used in worship services, to the two-part test it created in *Abington* (1963). Burger wrote that:

> Every analysis in this area must begin with consideration of the cumulative criteria developed by the Court over many years. Three such tests may be gleaned from our cases. First, the statute must have a secular legislative purpose; second, its principal or primary effect must be one that neither advances nor inhibits religion; finally, the statute must not foster "an excessive government entanglement with religion.

In reviewing entanglement and state aid to religiously affiliated institutions, Burger noted that three additional factors came into consideration: "we must examine the character and purposes of the institutions that are benefited, the nature of the aid that the State provides, and the resulting relationship between the government and religious authority." While the courts are generally more favorable to provide aid to religiously affiliated institutions of higher learning, they have been much more circumspect when dealing with assistance to religiously affiliated K–12 schools.

As part of his analysis, Burger reviewed the Court's prior cases on the relationship between church and state in education, concluding that total separation was unnecessary.

Burger posited that the relationship in *Lemon* was too close since the religious schools, which were an integral part of the mission of the Catholic Church, involved substantial religious activities. Catholic schools were the sole beneficiaries in Rhode Island and were virtually so in Pennsylvania.

In *Lemon,* Burger distinguished aid for teachers' salaries from secular, neutral, or nonideological services, facilities, or materials. Citing *Board of Education v. Allen* (1968), wherein the Court upheld a textbook loan program from New York, Burger ruled that teachers have a substantially different ideological character than books. In terms of potential for involving some aspect of faith or morals in secular subjects, Burger was of the view that while the content of textbooks is ascertainable, teachers' handling of subject matter is not. Burger also noted the inherent conflict when teachers who work under the direction of religious officials are faced with separating religious and secular aspects of K–12 education. Burger was concerned that the restrictions and surveillance necessary to ensure that teachers play nonideological roles give rise to the kind of entanglement that the Constitution prohibits. He contended that an ongoing history of government grants to nonpublic schools suggests that these programs were almost always accompanied by varying measures of control. According to Burger, weighing which expenditures of church-related schools were religious and which were secular created an impermissible intimate and continuing relationship between church and state. He also discussed the divisive political potential of such programs, asserting that although political debate and division generally are normal and healthy manifestations of the American government, protection against political division along religious lines was one of the principal purposes of the religion clauses of the First Amendment.

In what has developed into a kind of "catch-22" situation, programs typically passed *Lemon*'s first two prongs, only to often have had excessive entanglement serve as the basis for their being invalidated. The difficulty was exacerbated because even though the first two parts of the *Lemon* test were developed in the context of prayer cases, the Supreme Court applied it widely in disputes involving aid to nonpublic schools and their students. In light of the Court's modification of *Lemon* in *Agostini,* its future is uncertain in disputes over aid even though it is alive and well in cases over prayer and religious activity in public schools. *See also:* First Amendment and the Supreme Court; Government Aid to Religious Schools.

Further Reading: *Agostini v. Felton,* 521 U.S. 203 (1997); *Board of Education v. Allen,* 392 U.S. 236 (1968); *DiCenso v. Earley,* 316 F. Supp. 120 (D.R.I. 1970), *affirmed sub nom. Lemon v. Kurtzman,* 403 U.S. 602 (1971); *Lee v. Weisman,* 505 U.S. 577 (1992); *Lemon v. Kurtzman,* 310 F. Supp. 35 (E.D. Pa. 1969), *affirmed,* 403 U.S. 602 (1971); *School District of Abington Township v. Schempp* and *Murray v. Curlett,* 374 U.S. 203 (1963); *Walz v. Tax Commission of New York City,* 397 U.S. 664 (1970).

Charles J. Russo

Levitt v. Committee for Public Education and Religious Liberty

In this case, the Supreme Court addressed the constitutionality of a New York statute reimbursing nonpublic schools for the preparation, administration, and grading of state-mandated and teacher-prepared tests. The state-mandated tests fell into two categories: the Regents' examinations that were statewide tests of subject matter achievement; and the pupil evaluation program tests administered throughout the state in grades three, six, and nine. Nonpublic schools qualifying to participate in the reimbursement program received a lump sum per child ($27 for elementary and $45 for secondary students) with no accountability required for how the schools chose to spend the money. Qualifying schools included those that imposed religious restrictions on admissions, required attendance of pupils at religious activities, required obedience by students to the doctrines and dogmas of a particular faith, and required pupils to attend instruction in the theology or doctrine of a particular faith. Religious restrictions were an integral part of the religious mission of the church sponsoring it, had as a substantial purpose the inculcation of religious values, imposed religious restrictions on faculty appointments, and imposed religious restrictions on what or how the faculty may teach.

A three-judge federal district court in New York found the act unconstitutional under the Establishment Clause and permanently enjoined its enforcement. Direct appeal to the U.S. Supreme Court is permitted from three-judge decisions and, after granting certiorari in the case, the Court affirmed the district court decision.

The Supreme Court looked for support to *Committee for Public Education and Religious Liberty v. Nyquist* (1973), a decision handed down by the Court on the same day as *Levitt.* In *Nyquist,* the Supreme Court had invalidated another New York statute that provided direct money grants to qualifying nonpublic schools to be used for maintenance and repair of facilities and equipment with the stated purpose of ensuring the students' health, welfare, and safety. The infirmity of the statute in *Nyquist* lay in its undifferentiated treatment of the maintenance and repair of facilities devoted to the religious and secular functions of recipient sectarian schools. The Court reasoned that, since the State of New York had made no attempt to restrict payments to those expenditures related to the upkeep of facilities used exclusively for secular purposes, the statute had the primary effect of advancing religion and was, therefore, violative of the Establishment Clause.

The Supreme Court found in *Levitt* the same constitutional flaws that had existed in *Nyquist.* In the case of *Levitt,* the state statute provided for a direct money grant to sectarian schools for performance of various testing services that included a regular program of traditional internal testing designed to measure pupil achievement. Yet, despite the obviously integral role of such testing in the total teaching process, the Supreme Court opined that no attempt had been made under the statute to ensure that internally prepared tests were free of religious instruction. Although the Supreme Court refused to assume that teachers in religious schools would unconsciously or otherwise act in bad faith to use the reimbursed testing for purposes of inculcating students in the religious precepts of the sponsoring church, the Court nonetheless found the statute a violation of the Establishment Clause because, as the Court expressed it, the potential for conflict inheres in the situation. The State of New York had failed to ensure that money paid for testing was being devoted to secular functions and not being used for religious indoctrination and, thus, the Supreme Court determined that it had no choice but to find the state statute an impermissible aid to religion.

As a final broadside to the statute in this case, the Supreme Court rejected New York's position that the state should be permitted to pay for any activity mandated by state law or regulation. The essential filter for evaluating any set of facts involving the allocation of state funds to religious schools must be sufficiently fine so as to assess whether the challenged state aid has the primary purpose or effect of advancing religion or religious education or whether it leads to excessive entanglement by the state in the affairs of the religious institution. Applying this kind of filter, the Court reasoned that a state may choose to mandate minimum lighting or sanitary facilities for all school buildings, but such commands would not authorize a state to provide support for those facilities in church-sponsored schools.

Although much has changed regarding the provision of government assistance to religious schools since *Levitt,* the basic principle in *Levitt* still remains intact. Courts still distinguish between the loaning of materials and equipment to religious schools that is permissible under the Establishment Clause and the direct payment of money that is not. *See also: Committee for Public Education and Religious Liberty v. Nyquist;* Government Aid to Religious Schools; *Lemon v. Kurtzman* and *Earley v. DiCenso.*

Further Reading: *Committee for Public Education and Religious Liberty v. Nyquist,* 413 U.S. 756 (1973); *Levitt v. Committee for Public Education and Religious Liberty,* 413 U.S. 472 (1973).

Ralph D. Mawdsley

Liberty Counsel

Founded in 1989 by attorney Mat Staver as an independent public interest law firm supporting the religious and expressive rights of Christians in the Southeast, Liberty Counsel has evolved into a national leader among conservative Christian litigating firms, taking on an increasingly public role in shaping the agenda of Christian litigators in the 2000s and becoming involved in several highly publicized national disputes. Liberty Counsel is most clearly involved in religious liberties cases (in public places and public schools) as well as cases involving abortion protestation and rights. In its mission statement, it defines three primary goals: serve the needs of Christians in the public square, educate public administrators about religious freedom and public policy, and influence legal policy and precedent in ways favorable to religious tolerance in public dialogue. While litigation is its primary strategy for achieving influence, Liberty Counsel has also developed what it calls educational approaches to social and policy influence. In particular, it has worked within public schools to promote sexual abstinence through its Day of Purity program, and it has begun recruiting and training Christian lawyers through its Liberty Center for Law and Policy at Liberty University. While Staver has sought a public role for Liberty Counsel, litigation remains its primary method for achieving influence.

In the 1980s and early 1990s, Staver was among those Christian attorneys who pioneered the most significant legal strategy of the religious right's litigating wing—the free expression defense in cases raising a religious establishment claim. Throughout the 1990s, New Christian Right attorneys had tremendous success in making a free speech defense in cases involving claims by government that making space for religion and the religious would create an establishment of religion in violation of the First Amendment to the U.S. Constitution. Arguing that the free exercise of religion often involves an expression of faith that deserves protection as free speech, Staver and other attorneys have applied this logic in cases involving public expressions of faith, equal access to public property, and abortion protestation. While Staver began the Liberty Counsel with the intention of providing legal support to pro-life elements in Florida, he now counts many of the important religious issues of the day among the Liberty Counsel's primary concerns. As a result, Liberty Counsel has assumed a position of prominence among its conservative Christian litigating brethren.

During the early 1990s, the Liberty Counsel began litigating cases involving free expression of religious views in public schools while reiterating its commitment to educating administrators in a manner less adversarial than threatening litigation. By the late 1990s, this approach had changed. Early in 1999, Staver began a campaign aimed at school districts that refused equal access for Christian clubs. Around the same time, he initiated the "'Friend or Foe' Graduation Campaign" in which he promised to educate administrators, but markedly emphasized the threat of litigation.

The most prominent Liberty Counsel case in this issue area is *Adler v. Duval County School District* (2001), which involved a challenge to a school district policy allowing seniors discretion over time immediately preceding or following official graduation ceremonies. The case ended in a Staver-led victory for those trying to find a constitutionally permissible way to integrate prayer around official public school ceremonies and events after the U.S. Supreme Court's ruling in *Santa Fe v. Doe* (2000). After the Court's decision in *Santa Fe*, the Eleventh Circuit reviewed *Adler* again, deciding that the policy was constitutionally permissible because students acted as individuals and not agents of the state under the policy. The impact of *Adler*, however, is limited to the Eleventh Circuit, leading many in the New Christian Right to wish that the Supreme Court had heard this case.

A new and expanding area of concern to the Liberty Counsel's supporters is the gay rights issue. The Liberty Counsel is currently at the forefront of New Christian Right litigators in addressing gay rights issues in court. In 2004, it partnered with the American Family Association and the Thomas More Law Center to coordinate the conservative Christian response in court to gay rights policy nationally. *Largess v. Supreme Judicial Court for Massachusetts,* a case challenging an earlier decision by Massachusetts's highest court declaring the state's ban on same-sex marriage unconstitutional, serves as the clearest example of this collaboration. The case brought the Liberty Counsel considerable public attention, particularly because Staver took the unusual (and perhaps unwise) step of challenging the Massachusetts court ruling as a violation of the Republican Government Clause of the U.S. Constitution (Article IV, section 4). To date, the Liberty Counsel maintains the largest active docket of litigation in the gay rights issue area.

Staver has also identified *Madsen v. Women's Health Clinic* (1994) as a pivotal case for the Liberty Counsel. *Madsen* involved a challenge to a restraining order issued against abortion protesters. Staver won on several important points (consent provisions for personal interaction, image-observable restrictions, and restrictions on picketing around abortion clinic workers' homes were all struck down as overreaching legitimate governmental objectives), but the Supreme Court upheld the power of the state to regulate protest activity around abortion clinics.

In recent years, the Liberty Counsel has become affiliated with Liberty University School of Law. Staver serves as dean of the law school, professor of law, and director of its Center for Constitutional Litigation and Policy. In return, Liberty University has provided a pool of interns and potential employees and affiliates from which the Liberty Counsel may pull and a stable funding base. *See also:* American Family Association; Thomas More Law Center.

Further Reading: *Adler v. Duvall County School District,* 250 F. 3d 1330 (11th Cir. 2001) (cert. denied); Steven P. Brown, *Trumping Religion: The New Christian Right, the Free Speech Clause, and the Courts* (Tuscaloosa: University of Alabama Press, 2002); Fritz Detwiler, *Standing on the Premises of God: The Christian Right's Fight to Redefine Public Schools* (New York: New York University Press, 1999); Hans J. Hacker, *The Culture of Conservative Christian Litigation* (Lanham, MD:

Rowman & Littlefield Publishers, 2005); Liberty Counsel, at www.lc.org; *Santa Fe v. Doe,* 530 U.S. 290 (2000).

Hans J. Hacker

Lowell Plan

The establishment of parish schools in Massachusetts in the decades before the Civil War was difficult at best. The intense poverty of the immigrant Catholic population and the low priority given to the establishment of parish schools by the priests and bishops of the diocese combined to limit the number of parish schools in the state.

Parish pastors were well aware that Catholic parents could ill-afford to send their children to any school let alone pay for the establishment of parish schools. Catholic children were needed as wage earners to contribute to the welfare of their families. Keeping the family together was their first priority and that meant that everybody worked. Parish pastors understood the plight of their flock and asked for nothing more than the establishment and support of a church.

Yet in spite of the poor response to the call for parish schools, there was some Catholic educational activity in Massachusetts during these years. Throughout the 1830s and 1840s, the Diocese of Boston operated three Catholic schools in the state, but these institutions could provide instruction for only a few hundred of the 12,000 to 17,000 Catholic children in the diocese during those years.

The one Catholic educational venture that did achieve a measure of success was the Catholic Sunday school. By 1845, Boston Catholic Sunday schools were enrolling more than 4,000 children per year, and these schools continued to grow throughout the decade and into the 1850s. But Sunday school was a short-term measure and parish schools in Boston were virtually nonexistent in the years before the Civil War.

In this climate of inactivity there emerged in Lowell, Massachusetts, an educational experiment that was to have important implications for the history of Catholic education throughout the United States. In an effort to "consider the expediency of establishing a separate school for the benefit of the Irish population," the Lowell town meeting of 1831 appropriated $50 for the support of the local Catholic school. At the time, most Massachusetts schools were affiliated with religious denominations, and the grant to the Catholic school seemed the most logical way of providing for the education of Lowell's small but growing Irish population. The relationship worked well, and by 1835, three Catholic schools in Lowell were being supported with public funds.

The terms of the agreement between the town school committee and the parish pastors were straightforward. The committee reserved the right to examine and appoint all teachers working in parish schools; to prescribe and regulate the "textbooks, exercises and studies" used in the schools; and to examine, inspect, and supervise the school on the same basis as other town schools. The parish pastors insisted that qualified Catholics be appointed as teachers in their schools and that the textbooks contain no statements offensive to Catholics or the Catholic Church. The committee and the pastors mutually agreed that parish school buildings were to be provided and maintained by the parishes and that teachers were to be paid by the school committee.

The plan worked well throughout the 1830s and 1840s, and enrollments increased from a few hundred in 1835 to more than 3,800 a decade later. As late as 1850, Barnas Sears, secretary of the Massachusetts Board of Education, wrote that he had no schools equal in quality to the Catholic schools of Lowell.

But the "Lowell Plan," as it was later called, quickly ended in 1852 when one Catholic parish, unable to find qualified lay Catholic teachers, invited the Sisters of Notre Dame to staff the school. Catholics claimed that the school staffed by the sisters was just as worthy of support as the other Catholic schools, but the Lowell school committee objected to the nuns and this experiment in cooperation ended in acrimony and bitterness.

Even though educational cooperation ended in Lowell in 1852, the idea was too powerful and appealing to die. One small community in Massachusetts had solved the problem of public funding of parochial education and the plan worked well for almost 20 years. Other communities in other states also would try the Lowell plan with varying degrees of success in the later decades of the century. *See also:* Catholic Schools; Faribault-Stillwater Plan; Poughkeepsie Plan.

Further Reading: Jay C. Dolan, *The American Catholic Experience* (New York: Doubleday, 1985); Brian C. Mitchell, "Educating Irish Immigrants in Antebellum Lowell," *Historical Journal of Massachusetts* 11 (January 1983): 94–103; Timothy Walch, *Parish School: American Catholic Parochial Education from Colonial Times to the Present* (Washington, DC: National Catholic Educational Association, 2003).

Timothy Walch

Lutheran Schools

Sixteenth-century Protestant reformer Martin Luther wanted congregants to be more dependent on Scripture, less dependent on the institutional church. He wrote his catechism primarily for families and promoted the Lutheran school as the place where the catechism could be studied and embraced by youth. A Lutheran school has existed in the United States since 1640, but most Lutheran schools were started by German and Scandinavian immigrants in the late nineteenth and early twentieth centuries. They were established not only to advance Lutheran thought, but to preserve the heritage, language, and culture of these ethnic groups. Another significant expansion occurred after World War II.

In America today approximately 9.5 million Lutherans participate in 21 different Lutheran church bodies. The main three are the Lutheran Church–Missouri Synod, the Wisconsin Evangelical Lutheran Synod, and the largest, the Evangelical Lutheran Church in America, with 4.8 million members.

The Lutheran Church–Missouri Synod (LCMS) was formed in 1847 and is the most school-oriented, operating the largest Protestant school system in the United States. In 2007–2008, LCMS reported 1,406 early childhood centers, 976 elementary schools, and 103 high schools. The prekindergarten-through-twelfth-grade system educates 273,903 students (K–12 schools enroll approximately 140,000 students), taught by approximately 18,000 teachers. Ten Concordia colleges and two Concordia seminaries educate teachers and church workers for service in Lutheran schools and churches.

The Wisconsin Evangelical Lutheran Synod (WELS) broke fellowship with the LCMS in 1961, claiming the LCMS was too lax in its oversight of Communion, the sacrament of the Lord's Supper. A more conservative synod, only men may hold leadership positions, for example, and evolution is denied in favor of creationism. In 2007–2008, WELS reported 400 early childhood programs, 343 elementary schools in 27 mostly Midwestern states and 25 high schools with a total enrollment of 41,680 (32,113 in K–12). Martin Luther College in New Ulm, Minnesota, trains most WELS church workers and teachers.

The Evangelical Lutheran Church in America (ELCA), the result of a 1987 merger, is the somewhat most liberal of these three synods. ELCA members, for example, view the Word of God as inspired rather than inerrant, the authoritative source and norm for proclamation, faith, and life. The National Center for Education Statistics estimates that in 2005–2006 the ELCA had 111 schools with an enrollment of 17,672 students taught by 1,352 teachers. The ELCA also sponsors over 1,600 early childhood centers.

Lutheran educational philosophy embraces education of the whole child—body, mind, and spirit. Both faith development and quality academics help the child "grow in grace and knowledge," establishing Christian values and equipping the child for service. The current LCMS motto "Securing Each Child's Future" was chosen to suggest that Lutheran schools provide both a quality academic education to be a servant of God in the world and an opportunity for eternal salvation through the Gospel of Jesus Christ.

While respectful of other denominations and faiths, the Lutheran high view of Scripture, "the only rule and norm of faith and life," requires strict adherence to the Lutheran confessions, including the Lutheran catechism. With few exceptions, all students in these schools memorize the catechism and the supporting Bible verses. Of special concern is the application of the Law and the Gospel. The Law convinces humanity of its sinful condition, the Gospel convinces believers of the grace and forgiveness received in Christ. Emphasis is also placed on the common summary of Lutheran thought: Faith Alone—Grace Alone—Scripture Alone.

Each Lutheran school is autonomous. Most elementary schools are connected to a Lutheran church, to an individual congregation, or to an association, a group of churches. Most high schools are connected to a large association of Lutheran churches. The sponsoring church owns and operates the school, sets the tuition, extends a "call" to the administrator, oversees curriculum, and makes sure that LCMS doctrine is understood and embraced. Oversight of ELCA schools is generally provided by a partnership between the governing board of the school and the congregational council of the church, and between the administrator and the pastor.

Historically, the financial support for the school came from the sponsoring church(es), with families and extended families of students meeting the need. Today finances depend less on church support and more on tuition, and there seems to be a shift from church-subsidizing-school to school-subsidizing-church support.

The LCMS has its own accreditation system, offering and requiring a "Lutheran Teaching Diploma" from a Concordia college or by taking coursework online. These "synodically trained" teachers make up 60 percent of LCMS Lutheran school faculties. State certification is encouraged and frequent, but not required. Almost all WELS teachers are "synod-certified" by Martin Luther College.

Staff members are considered "called" to what is seen as ministry. A national call system allows schools to access synodically trained staff from across the country. "Commissioned and rostered" staff is considered central to the mission because they teach and practice the LCMS version of Lutheranism in the day-to-day life of the school. ELCA administrators and teachers have no synodical training requirement, only that they understand and are willing to teach ELCA theology.

Lutheran schools range from "classical" (Latin, logic, rhetoric) to "progressive," but most would be considered "traditional" and would resemble public schools in curriculum and school structure. Although the textbooks are generally secular and commercial, some topics, such as evolution in a science text, would be reviewed critically. Concordia Publishing does provide some textbooks that are specifically Lutheran, but with a LCMS slant.

In the past, the schools were for church-attending Lutherans, but today "nonbelievers" make up about 15 percent of the LCMS enrollment. They come for the quality education and they accept the Lutheran side of the educational experience. WELS schools accept nonbelievers as part of their evangelical outreach. Just over 50 percent of the ELCA students are non-Lutheran, about one-fourth are ELCA Lutheran, and the remaining are unchurched or affiliated with other denominations. ELCA also views the unchurched population as providing an opportunity to bring families into the congregations.

In all schools Lutheran doctrine is conveyed in faith training (daily devotions, weekly chapels) and religion class (study of the Bible, memorization of the catechism). There is an ongoing attempt to integrate faith in all subjects and in all aspects of the day. The local Lutheran pastor may teach the religion class at some point in the sixth, seventh, or eighth grades, and students are allowed to seek "confirmation" with the congregation, making them full members of the church and allowing them to participate in the Lord's Supper. ELCA students may take communion as soon as fifth grade, but are confirmed in eighth grade.

The future holds various challenges for the Lutheran schools. Continuity in leadership is needed, with the work force aging and with fewer young adults becoming synodically trained workers and teachers. Adequate funding is an ongoing problem. The schools want to be "community" schools, available to more than only those who can afford it, but financial constraints, especially in urban settings, make providing educational options difficult. A final challenge is keeping the Lutheran tradition vibrant and central while opening the doors to non-Lutherans and non-Christians. *See also:* Bennett Law; Council for American Private Education.

Further Reading: Walther Herman Beck, *Lutheran Elementary Schools in the United States: A History of the Development of Parochial Schools and Synodical Educational Policies and Programs* (Private publication, 1939); Evangelical Lutheran Church in America, at elca.org; Lutheran Church–Missouri Synod, at lcms.org; Lutheran Education Association, at lea.org; William C. Riestschel, *An Introduction to the Foundation of Lutheran Education* (Saint Louis: Concordia Academic Press, 2000); Wayne Elmer Schmidt, *The Lutheran Parochial School: Dates, Documents, Events, People* (River Forest, IL: Concordia Seminary Monograph Series, 2001; Wisconsin Evangelical Lutheran Synod, at wels.net.

Steven C. Vryhof